🄳 GUIDES

COLORADO

www.insightguides.com/USA

◉ Walking Eye App

YOUR FREE DESTINATION CONTENT AND EBOOK AVAILABLE THROUGH THE WALKING EYE APP

Your guide now includes a free eBook and destination content for your chosen destination, all for the same great price as before. Simply download the Walking Eye App from the App Store or Google Play to access your free eBook and destination content.

HOW THE WALKING EYE APP WORKS

Through the Walking Eye App, you can purchase a range of eBooks and destination content. However, when you buy this book, you can download the corresponding eBook and destination content for free. Just see below in the grey panels where to find your free content and then scan the QR code at the bottom of this page.

Destinations: Download your corresponding essential destination content from here, featuring recommended sights and attractions, restaurants, hotels and an A–Z of practical information, all for free. Other destinations are available for purchase.

Ships: Interested in ship reviews? Find independent reviews of river and ocean ships in this section, all available for purchase.

eBooks: You can download your free accompanying digital version of this guide here. You will also find a whole range of other eBooks, all available for purchase.

Free access to travel-related blog articles about different destinations, updated on a daily basis.

HOW THE DESTINATION CONTENT WORKS

Each destination includes a short introduction, an A–Z of practical information and recommended points of interest, split into 4 different categories:

• Highlights
• Accommodation
• Eating out
• What to do

You can view the location of every point of interest and save it by adding it to your Favourites. In the 'Around Me' section you can view all the points of interest within 5km.

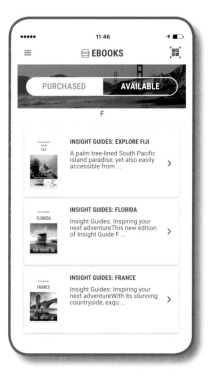

HOW THE EBOOKS WORK

The eBooks are provided in EPUB file format. Please note that you will need an eBook reader installed on your device to open the file. Many devices come with this as standard, but you may still need to install one manually from Google Play.

The eBook content is identical to the content in the printed guide.

HOW TO DOWNLOAD THE WALKING EYE APP

1. Download the Walking Eye App from the App Store or Google Play.
2. Open the app and select the scanning function from the main menu.
3. Scan the QR code on this page – you will then be asked a security question to verify ownership of the book.
4. Once this has been verified, you will see your eBook and destination content in the purchased ebook and destination sections, where you will be able to download them.

Other destination apps and eBooks are available for purchase separately or are free with the purchase of the Insight Guide book.

Contents

THE BEST OF COLORADO: TOP ATTRACTIONS

From the historic homes of Mesa Verde to the latest contemporary art in Denver, here are our top recommendations for a visit to the colorful state of Colorado.

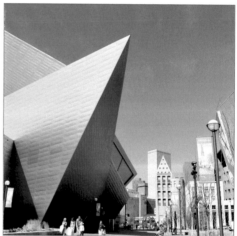

△ **Rocky Mountain National Park**. Trail Ridge Road offers soaring high country views of serrated alpine peaks, sparkling lakes, glaciers, fragile tundra meadows, charismatic mega-fauna, wildflowers, and pioneer cabins. See page 197.

▽ **Mesa Verde**. Cliff Palace is one of the most magical Ancestral Pueblo cliff dwellings at the nation's favorite archeological park, near Durango in the Four Corners region of southwestern Colorado. See page 269.

△ **Denver**. A vibrant and fast-growing city, with the largest municipal park system in the US and cultural institutions that include the pioneering Denver Zoo and the Denver Art Museum. See page 149.

△ **Grand Junction**. A mini-Napa Valley amid the carved redrock canyons of the Colorado River, this is famed for its wineries, fruit orchards, and proximity to Dinosaur and Colorado National Monuments. See page 281.

△ **Pikes Peak**. Drive, hike, or ride the Pikes Peak Cog Railroad to the top of this 14,110ft (4,301-meter) mountain which, among other things, inspired the writing of the anthem "America the Beautiful." See page 179.

◁ **Leadville**. Not only the best-preserved mining town in Colorado, with its own mining history museum, but also the highest town in the country, and possibly the most storied. See page 240.

▷ **Durango & Silverton Narrow Gauge Railroad**. Ride to Silverton and enjoy views of Mount Sneffels and the glorious Animas Valley, preferably during the fall when the aspens turn golden. See page 252.

△ **San Juan Skyway**. There are "million-dollar" views all along the narrow, winding San Juan Skyway between Durango and Montrose, but keep your eyes on the road – the dropoffs are very steep. See page 254.

◁ **San Luis Valley**. Combining traditional Hispanic culture, New Age retreats, hot springs, high peaks, America's tallest sand dunes, and overwintering sandhill cranes, the San Luis Valley surrounding Alamosa is a unique destination. See page 187.

▷ **Telluride**. The quintessential Colorado ski destination – an attractive Victorian mining town in a glorious box-canyon setting far from anywhere, offering skiing, eclectic festivals, friendly locals, and an unpretentious atmosphere. See page 258.

THE BEST OF COLORADO: EDITOR'S CHOICE

Colorado has a wealth of natural beauty, sophisticated culture, and historical significance. Here are the best spots to enjoy the Mile High State.

Comanche National Grassland.

BEST SMALL TOWNS

Ouray. The town has a well-regarded hometown museum, an ice climbing festival, and Jeep drives in the nearby mountains. See page 255.

Salida. A sporty small town with a large historic district, galleries, and local food and wine, which hosts fibARK, a major whitewater celebration. See page 180.

Creede. A remote former mining town, with an award-winning theater company and a majestic setting deep in the San Juan Mountains. See page 262.

Glenwood Springs. The popular hot springs and spa and the historic Denver and Colorado hotels are an easy drive or train ride from Denver. See page 227.

Boulder. Home to the University of Colorado, alternative healers and scientists, and the top farmers' market in Colorado, within view of Denver. See page 163.

Crested Butte. Birthplace of fat-tire biking and some of the state's quirkiest festivals, this mining town turned ski resort exudes Central Rockies charm. See page 236.

Paonia. Urban refugees, creatives, outdoorsmen, and farmers cluster in this little town in the scenic North Fork Valley near Black Canyon of the Gunnison National Park. See page 234.

BEST NATURE VIEWING

Rocky Mountain National Park. Visit during the fall rutting season to view elk bugling and bighorn sheep butting heads in a competition for mates. See page 197.

San Luis Valley. Two national wildlife refuges on the Rio Grande attract migratory elk, bison herds, and thousands of sandhill cranes in winter. See page 187.

Comanche National Grasslands. A nationally significant birding area, southeastern Colorado's prairies host unique prairie chicken mating dances at the birds' leks in May. See page 143.

San Juan Mountains. The remote San Juans may still support grizzly bears and have been the site of a successful reintroduction of lynx. See page 249.

Yampa Valley Birding. The Yampa River near Steamboat Springs is an important birding area, home to catbirds, orioles among others, and river otters and mink. See page 212.

Washboard music.

BEST CULTURAL ATTRACTIONS

Bent's Old Fort National Historic Site. Relive the days of the Santa Fe Trail at this former rendezvous for mountain men, traders, and travelers in southeastern Colorado. See page 144.
The Matchless Mine, Leadville. The ghost of Baby Doe Tabor, penniless widow of Matchless Mine millionaire Horace Tabor, haunts this old cabin in Leadville. See page 242.
Denver Art Museum, Hamilton Expansion. One of Denver's most photographed new buildings, this shiny geometric DAM expansion was designed by Polish-born architect Daniel Libeskind. See page 152.
Anasazi Heritage Center, Dolores. This state-of-the-art research center and museum holds millions of Ancestral Pueblo artifacts excavated from the Dolores River area prior to damming. See page 271.
Hovenweep National Monument, Cajone Mesa. An outlier of Mesa Verde, Hovenweep protects unusual towers and structures on Cajone Mesa, the most archeologically rich area in the country. See page 273.

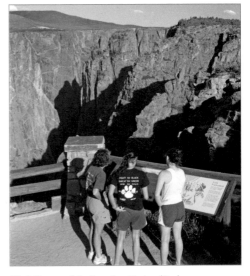

Black Canyon of the Gunnison National Park.

BEST SCENIC DRIVES

Tabegauche-Unaweep Scenic Byway. This little-traveled highway along Colorado's western edge, where mountains meet red rocks, has mining ghosts, nature preserves, and rocky canyons. See page 273.
Silver Thread Scenic Byway, Wolf Pass to Lake City. A lonesome highway connects the artsy mining town of Creede, the headwaters of the Rio Grande, and a Victorian belle, Lake City. See page 260.
San Juan Skyway, between Silverton and Ouray. Linking two popular small towns, this segment of the highway crosses Red Mountain Pass and has views that will make you feel like a million dollars. See page 254.
Lookout Mountain Park, Lariat Loop Scenic Byway. Visit Buffalo Bill's Gravesite and Museum at this popular scenic drive near Golden. See page 217.
Black Canyon of the Gunnison National Park Scenic Drive. Enjoy light on schist from overlooks above this 2,000ft (610-meter) deep, dark, narrow canyon carved by the Gunnison River. See page 236.
Alpine Loop Jeep Trail. This classic four-wheel drive leaves Ouray and heads over Engineer Pass to the ghost town Capitol City and Lake City. See page 249.

BEST OUTDOOR ACTIVITIES

Mountain biking in Colorado National Monument. A mountain-biking mecca set amid spectacularly carved red-rock canyons along the Colorado River, west of Grand Junction. See page 282.
Rafting the Yampa River through Dinosaur National Monument. The confluencing Yampa and Green rivers attract river runners through Echo Canyon, scene of an anti-damming environmental victory in the 1960s. See page 283.
Climbing the Flatirons. The distinctive reddish upended blades of this formation are a major Boulder landmark and a popular destination for climbers. See page 163.
Skiing at Steamboat Springs. This cowboy-oriented ski resort's light, frothy Champagne powder and a renovated ski village attract winter sports enthusiasts to its runs each year. See page 210.
Hiking Maroon Bells–Snowmass Wilderness. Twin peaks reflected in a mirror lake attract photographers and hikers escaping the hip scene in nearby Aspen. See page 232.

Mountain climbing safely.

San Juan National Forest in fall.

Skiing above Durango.

The bright lights of Denver, Colorado.

Mount Sneffels in the fall.

ROCKY MOUNTAIN STATE

Soaring peaks, world-class skiing, and vibrant cities lure travelers to America's alpine heartland.

A herd of elk in Rocky Mountain National Park.

"The scenery bankrupts the English language," said Theodore Roosevelt, a man rarely at a loss for words. TR was musing about the Rocky Mountains during a visit to Colorado in 1901. Indeed, no words can capture the skyward sweep of this landscape, the heady mix of humility and exaltation one feels standing atop its legendary peaks, 54 of which soar beyond 14,000ft (4,270 meters). The Rockies transcend them all.

Man has made his mark, of course. Roads blasted from bedrock curve heavenward. Railroads corkscrew up impossibly steep terrain. Dams restrain rivers. Bridges and tunnels span seemingly insurmountable distances. And is any feat of modern engineering equivalent in daring to the ancient cliff dwellings of Mesa Verde, laid up stone by stone in canyon alcoves without wheel barrows, pulleys, or levels?

In the 1800s, huge yields of gold and silver deep within the earth brought thousands of prospectors to Colorado. The mining boomtowns that sprang up are mostly atmospheric ghost towns now, their tumbledown saloons, cabins and headframes haunted by wind and tumbleweeds.

Elsewhere in Colorado, rock erosion gradually reveals the bones of Diplodocus, Stegosaurus, Camarasaurus and other dinosaurs. Colorado has produced more dinosaur fossils than any other state. It is a treasure trove of dinosaur trackways, embedded forever in solid rock.

Going for a ride in Estes Park.

And then there are the Rockies, backbone of the continent. At 80–50 million years old, their peaks, carved within the last 20,000 years during the Quaternary period by glacial ice into cirques, hanging valleys and knife-edged aretes, retain the assertive thrust of youth.

Even on the eastern plains, where grasslands roll to the horizon, the landscape dwarfs humans, as if you are no more than a cork bobbing on the waves of a vast ocean of grasses.

Colorado has many vibrant cities, attractive towns, art and culture, great restaurants, rafting, hiking, some of the world's best skiing and much else. But it is for its epic landscape that it is best known. That is the essence of Colorado – the magic it shares with every visitor.

THE CULTURAL LANDSCAPE

Hippies and yuppies, natives and newcomers – Colorado
is a mixed bag of cultures, classes, and political
viewpoints, which is what makes it so interesting.

The early 1970s, an era when Colorado's population was exploding, saw the birth of a bumper sticker fad so unusual that it was written up in *Time* and *Life* magazines. Created by Denverite Sandy Glade, the stickers bore the same distinctive green-and-white mountain silhouette as the state's license plates. The first ones were emblazoned with the single word "NATIVE," which spoke volumes. Everyone knew what they meant: "I'm not one of those newcomers who come here to jack up prices, pollute our pure Rocky Mountain springwater, take all the parking spaces, and generally "Californicate" our state – so don't blame me." Within weeks, new bumper stickers started popping up: "SEMI-NATIVE," "LOCAL," "SURVIVOR," and, yes, "TOURIST."

Since then, the native-versus-newcomer issue has become almost moot, as the state's population has more than doubled, largely due to the migration of an estimated one million Californians.

Farmer, Central Rockies.

Denver's prominent 19th-century black residents included Barney Ford, a businessman who won the vote for black males in the West, and Aunt Clara Brown, a freed Kentucky slave and laundress who took in needy African Americans.

Colorado folks are such a diverse lot that it's hard to generalize about the characteristics that make them Coloradans. Or are they Coloradoans? They can't even agree which term is correct – just ask the news editors at the *Adams State College Coloradan* and the *Fort Collins Coloradoan*. (Merriam-Webster has it both ways.)

Coloradans are urban and rural, liberal and ultraconservative, wealthy and poor. Perhaps the best way to define how Coloradans traditionally see themselves is to look at them in the context of the state's cultural landscape – that is, how they relate to the land and face the challenges of getting along with their neighbors.

Rags to riches to rags

Much about Colorado's collective self-image is reflected in its legends. Unlike other Western states, you don't find many cowboys, lawmen, gunslingers, or pioneers in Colorado's version of its own history. Although cattle ranching has been a vital part of the state's economy since the 1860s, few residents can name a single rancher, past or present. Colorado heritage is defined by tales of gold and silver prospectors, whose good and ill fortunes are a potent metaphor for many other enterprises, including tourism, land development, and the ski industry.

Some are ironic stories of losers like Bob Womack, the man who first discovered gold in the Cripple Creek District in 1891. Unable to convince others that his find was anything more than a drunken fantasy, he sold his mining claim for $300. The claim became the El Paso Mine, which produced more than $10 million worth of ore. Womack died broke.

but one unrivaled in the world for its lavish comforts. The establishment, set on a large, walled estate with lawns and bowers, tennis courts, and a swimming pool, still operates today.

Some Colorado legends are just plain bizarre. Consider the case of Alferd Packer, the Lake City guide who spent a winter snowed in with six greenhorn gold prospectors high in the San Juan mountains – and survived by eating them. He was convicted twice, not of cannibalizing his companions (which wasn't a crime) but of killing them first. He spent the rest of his life in the old Cañon City Penitentiary, where his sepa-

Cheyenne woman in ceremonial clothing.

Young Denverite.

At the other end of the spectrum was Womack's old drinking buddy Winfield Scott Stratton, a Colorado Springs carpenter who spent his summers prospecting around Cripple Creek. He returned to a claim he had twice previously explored and abandoned, after finding nothing. The third time proved to be a charm. He struck a rich gold vein that became the Independence Mine. He sold his claim for $10 million and spent the remainder of his life as a philanthropist, gifting Colorado Springs with magnificent public buildings, parks, and the finest streetcar system in the state. Upon his death, 11 years after his first gold strike, his will endowed the Myron Stratton Home in Colorado Springs. Named after his father, it was an orphanage and old folks' home,

rate cabin is now a tourist attraction. To this day, Colorado historians write papers purporting to prove his innocence. Coloradans just love Packer. At the University of Colorado, the student council voted to name a campus cafeteria after him. Trey Parker, co-creator of the raunchy television series *South Park*, wrote a stage play about Packer that was a hit in Boulder and later became a cult movie. He called it *Cannibal: The Musical*.

For love or money

The legend that best symbolizes Colorado is that of Horace Tabor and his two wives. Horace, a Leadville grocer, postmaster, and mayor, grubstaked two German prospectors $17 worth of food in exchange for a one-third interest in whatever they found. They struck silver and, five months later, declared a $10,000 dividend for each partner. Horace used his share to invest in other mines around the district, including the played-out Matchless Mine. As the story goes, the seller had "salted" it with a shotgun shell loaded with gold dust, a common fraud at the time. Digging down a few feet revealed one of the richest silver veins in Colorado history, making Horace a millionaire several times over.

Money spelled trouble for Tabor. His wife, Augusta, an austere New Englander uncomfortable with sudden wealth, continued to live frugally and rent rooms in their modest home. Horace liked the seemingly endless supply of money just fine and, at age 50, may have been experiencing a midlife crisis. He promptly fell in love with Elizabeth "Baby Doe" McCourt, a divorcee half his age. Horace and Baby Doe soon moved to Central City, where he lavished her with gifts and flowers to the tune of $1,000 a day. He persuaded a Durango judge to grant him a quick, secret – and illegal – divorce and later married Baby Doe.

Horace Tabor's bigamy became a problem when he was appointed to the seat of a deceased

Nearly a third of the cowboys in the American West were African American.

HAVE PALETTE, WILL TRAVEL

Throughout the 1800s, as Americans set their sights on expansion west, artists were there, too, recording landscapes that defied the imagination. One of the first was George Catlin, who journeyed west in the 1830s and produced 500 oil paintings that captured the nobility of American Indian cultures. Catlin's work influenced the young Charles Deas who, in the 1840s, journeyed to the Rockies and painted *Long Jakes*, a portrait of a fur trapper whose half-wild, half-civilized appearance captured the essence of the frontier.

In the 1870s, Albert Bierstadt attempted to convey in visual terms what Romantic poets like Shelley, Byron, and Wordsworth captured in verse: Nature as a religious experience, offering moral lessons for mankind. Although wildly popular, Bierstadt had his critics. "I believe this atmosphere of Bierstadt's is altogether too gorgeous," complained Mark Twain. "I am sorry the Creator hadn't made it instead of him."

In the late 1800s, a new fascination with realism emerged. In 1871, English-born Thomas Moran joined the Hayden Survey to Yellowstone. His paintings helped get the park established and paved the way for artists Charles M. Russell and Frederic Remington, who recorded a frontier way of life that is now all but gone.

US Senator from Colorado. What had been viewed in Central City as everyday recklessness – perfectly understandable to anyone who saw the homely Augusta and the beautiful Baby Doe – in Washington DC society was a scandal of monumental proportions. To gain respectability, Horace gave Augusta the lion's share of his estimated $9 million fortune in exchange for a legitimate divorce.

Ten years passed. Horace built opera houses. Baby Doe lived lavishly. Then came the silver crash of 1893, and virtually overnight they found themselves penniless. The bank foreclosed on the Matchless Mine, cutting off their only source of income. At age 66, Horace took a job shoveling slag at a Cripple Creek mine for $3 a day. To the surprise of everybody who had regarded her as a notorious gold digger, Baby Doe stood by her man. In 1898, Horace was appointed postmaster in Denver, then died the following year.

Baby Doe Tabor spent the last half of her life in Leadville, living in a converted storage shed beside the Matchless Mine and unsuccessfully looking for a way to regain ownership. She died there at age 80, destitute. Four gunny sacks she had left at the local hospital for safekeeping were found to be filled with silks, jewelry, and other treasures from her glory days. As for Augusta, she lived out her remaining years as a wealthy dowager in Pasadena, California.

The moral of the Tabors' story depends on who's telling it. What goes round comes round? Spend it while you've got it? Never give up? Take the money and run? Whatever meaning one reads into it, the tale seems strangely relevant whenever you visit one of Colorado's gold rush–era towns, whether it's now a prosperous city, a posh ski resort, or a ghostly cluster of decrepit log cabins and crumbled stone chimneys still waiting for good times that may never come again.

Immigrant heritage

As gold and silver mining developed from small one- or two-man diggings into large-scale industrial operations, immigrant laborers were hired to do the dirty work. At first, the majority were Chinese workers, who brought experience from the earlier gold rush in California (Asian Americans living in Colorado today make up just 3.1 percent of the population). Most left because of widespread persecution that culminated in the Anti-Chinese Riot of 1880. Starting as a bar brawl, the incident escalated into a mob of more than 2,000 rampaging through Denver's Chinatown, burning businesses and lynching at least one Chinese man. After that, mine and railroad jobs were filled mainly by Welsh, Cornish, and Italian workers.

A more lasting impact on Colorado's cultural landscape came with the trainloads of German-speaking immigrants from the Volga River region of Russia, who began arriving in 1880 and homesteading farms in the northeastern part of the state, growing root vegetables and winter wheat. Within two generations, many of Colorado's prominent politicians and industrialists were Rus-

The White Cloud, Head Chief of the Iowas, by George Caitlin.

sian Germans. Their greatest contribution was the introduction of sugar beet farming, one of Colorado's most important industries from 1900 to the 1960s. Most small farmers moved to the cities and towns of the Front Range during the Dust Bowl of the 1930s, but few left the region. Today, white residents reporting German ancestry make up 22 percent of the state's population.

The largest group by far are Latinos or Hispanics, commonly referred to as "Mexicans" even though their ancestors may have lived in Colorado for generations, and only three-quarters of Latinos in Colorado are actually from Mexico. As small sugar beet farms gave way to big, labor-intensive agribusiness operations, migrant labor crews were brought from

Mexico. These "contract families" were encouraged to stay in the region year-round and soon developed large *barrios* in Denver and elsewhere. Today, one in five Coloradans (and more than one in three Denver residents) is Latino. Cinco de Mayo (May 5), the annual celebration commemorating the end of French rule in Mexico, is one of Denver's biggest festivals.

The dark side of diversity

Minorities in Colorado have often been met with intolerance, bigotry and even violence. One obvious example is American Indians –

few months before the massacre. "I am fully satisfied, gentlemen, that to kill them is the only way we will ever have peace and quiet in Colorado. I say that if any of them are caught in your vicinity, the only thing to do is kill them."

Because of the massacre, Chivington was court-martialed by the Army but honored with

> According to 2014 US census figures, 37.5 percent of Coloradans have an undergraduate college degree or higher.

Chinese miners in the Edgar Experimental Mine near Idaho Springs, about 1920.

the Ute, Navajo, Cheyenne, Arapaho, Kiowa, Comanche, and other tribes that inhabited the region for countless centuries. Today, the percentage of American Indians in Colorado is a shade higher than the percentage for the United States overall (1.6 percent) but less than in any other Rocky Mountain state. Why?

On the eastern plains, the prevailing attitude toward Indians in the mid-19th century was expressed by John Chivington, the Methodist minister, political hopeful, and Colorado Militia leader who led the Sand Creek Massacre, in which some 150 unarmed Cheyenne Indians – most of them women and children – were slaughtered in 1862. "It simply is not possible for Indians to obey or even understand any treaty," Chivington said a

a parade through the streets of Denver and awarded a medal of honor by the territorial governor. Within less than 10 years, all Indians had been removed from Colorado Territory except for the Southern and Ute Mountain people, whose reservations lie along the southwestern state line. Curiously, in 1992 Coloradans elected the first American Indian to serve in the US Congress in 60 years. Republican Senator Ben Nighthorse Campbell was not a native Coloradan; like many of his constituents, he moved from California. He represented Colorado from 1993 to 2005.

By the 1920s, the Ku Klux Klan had become a powerful force in Colorado. The *Denver Post* reported that "the KKK is the largest and most cohesive, most efficiently organized political force in the state." In 1924, riding a wave of anti-immigrant (particularly anti-Mexican) sentiment, Klan leader Clarence Morley was elected governor of Colorado by a landslide. That same year, Klansmen became secretary of state and mayor of Denver, were appointed to the state Supreme Court and seven benches of the Denver District Court, and won a majority of seats in both houses of the state legislature. In the next legislative session, 1,080 Klan-sponsored bills were introduced, but almost all of them were killed in committee by Billy Adams, a Democrat who would later take Morley's place as governor. Coloradans, it seemed, quickly got fed up with the Klan's overzealous enforcement of Prohibition laws.

Molly's crusade

As with most things Coloradan, intolerance was met with a counter-movement to encourage progressive attitudes, as illustrated by another of the state's mining camp legends. Thanks to a hit Broadway musical and motion picture, most people in the US know the rags-to-riches story of Margaret "Unsinkable Molly" Brown's rise from a one-room shack in Leadville to a Denver mansion where she reigned as a leading philanthropist, and how she survived the *Titanic* disaster. What fewer people realize is that she also campaigned for an Equal Rights Amendment and ran for the US Senate three times – all before women had voting rights in most states. (In 1893, Colorado had become the second state to give women the right to vote and hold office, and the first to do so by amending the constitution in a general election in which only men could vote.) In an effort to encourage racial harmony and understanding, Molly Brown sponsored a Carnival of Nations in 1906, donating funds to representatives of 16 ethnic minorities in Colorado, including American Indians, to build "villages" in a Denver park showcasing their native culture, food, arts, and crafts. The two-week festival was an enormous success, though it has never been repeated.

In recent years, intolerance and prejudice have occasionally resurfaced. Colorado suffered national notoriety in 1992 when conservative Christian organizations sponsored a ballot measure prohibiting "special rights" for gays and lesbians. Designed to block ordinances such as those adopted in Boulder and Aspen that banned discrimination on sexual preference, the amendment passed with 53 percent of the

vote. It prompted a nationwide effort on behalf of the gay community to boycott Colorado tourism, costing the state's hospitality industry an estimated $40 million. The Colorado Supreme Court eventually ruled the amendment unconstitutional, a decision upheld by the US Supreme Court. Although feelings still run high on both sides of the gay rights issue in Colorado, the boycott had at least one positive impact. The Adolph Coors Company, whose beer had been boycotted by gays as a Colorado symbol, began giving health insurance and other benefits to same-sex partners of employees in 1994 and launched an

Peach picker in Palisade.

aggressive campaign to demonstrate its support for gay rights through advertising and donations to gay pride organizations. Coors also sponsors the Colorado Gay Ice Hockey League and funds all three teams in the league.

Meanwhile, much of the above has become moot, because Colorado's state constitutional ban on same-sex marriage was struck down in the state district court on July 9, 2014, and by the U.S. District Court for the District of Colorado on July 23, 2014. As of October 7, 2014, same-sex marriage has been legal in Colorado. In June 26, 2015, the US Supreme Court ruled in Obergefell vs. Hodges that state-level same-sex marriage bans are illegal, and it became the law of the land throughout the United States.

Changing faces

Today, more than four out of five Coloradans live in the Front Range metropolitan areas; updated US census data for the state in July 2015 indicated a 8.6 percent increase in residents from the 2010 census, to an estimated population of 5,456,574. Even there, the cultural climate is contradictory and as changeable as the weather. Colorado Springs, for example, is notorious for its conservatism. Local attitudes are shaped in part by a large military presence and by outspoken fundamentalist religious groups. Just off the interstate, not far from the US Air Force Academy, the Focus on the Family Welcome Center greets travelers with cautions about such errors as sparing the rod and spoiling the child. Even the mansion built by General William Jackson Palmer, the city's founder, is now owned and occupied by Christian evangelists.

At the other end of the Front Range Corridor, the university town of Boulder is known as a hotbed of left-wing politics and one of the West's New Age centers. Its top visitor attraction is Celestial Seasonings, an herbal tea empire, and numerous other small family-run outdoor and eco-business enterprises can

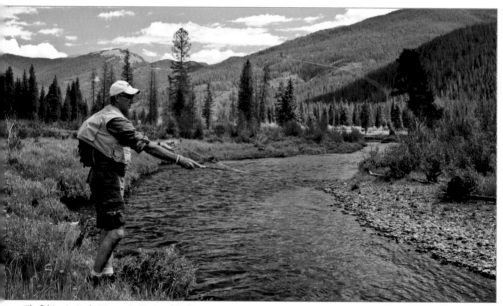

Fly-fishing in Rocky Mountain National Park.

POWER POLITICS IN THE NEW WEST

With its soaring Latino population and high-tech growth, the Front Range symbolizes the new politics of the Interior West. Once political flyover territory, the region has played a key role in securing Democratic victories in several previous elections. In 2008, Democratic candidate Barack Obama accepted his party's presidential nomination at the Democratic National Convention in Denver, and the state was a hotly contested battleground in his re-election in 2012.

The fiery 2010 midterm elections offered a case study in Colorado's flip-flop politics. Democratic candidate Michael Bennet, appointed to fill the old senate seat of Colorado-born Ken Salazar, secretary of the interior during President Obama's first term, narrowly beat Ken Buck, a Republican backed by the Tea Party, an anti-government grassroots organization with roots in the 1970s Sagebrush Rebellion. Strong support from college-educated women and Hispanics led to Bennet's win – a model successfully adopted by the 2012 Obama re-election campaign.

Bennet retained his seat in 2016, but Colorado politicians' tendency to appeal to disgruntled voters is still clear. While Colorado remained Democrat in the hotly contested 2016 presidential election, Donald Trump – eventual victor and advocate of an unmistakeably reactionary rhetoric – won a hefty 44.4% of the vote.

be found here. Downtown, on the Pearl Street Mall, you'll find a store that carries only left-wing political books and, a few blocks away, another that specializes in books for lesbians.

It's a wonder the two cities can exist in the same state. But then, generalizations don't always hold water. If you visit the Colorado Springs suburb of Manitou Springs, for instance, you'll find an artist colony regarded as the state's oldest "hippie" community. In Boulder, on the other hand, the intellectual University of Colorado atmosphere provides fertile ground not only for liberal thought but for such groups as the ultra-conservative America First Party and *Soldier of Fortune* magazine, which has sponsored clandestine training camps for Third World police officers in the nearby mountains. At a Pentecostal book-burning in Boulder, copies of such New Age tomes as Shirley MacLaine's *Out on a Limb* and Barbara Marx Hubbard's *Happy Birthday Planet Earth* were pitched into the flames before the event degenerated into a shouting match with protesters.

Environmental politics

Attitudes among urban dwellers, many of whom are transplants from the West Coast, often conflict with those of traditionally conservative old-timers. This is especially true in the realm of environmental protection. Activities such as mining, ranching, and logging have taken a back seat to the recreational use of Colorado's vast public lands.

The trend was accelerated in 1992 when voters passed a constitutional amendment known as GOCO (Great Outdoors Colorado). The law earmarks proceeds from the Colorado Lottery for "trail construction, the purchase of parks and park enhancement, open space, wildlife and river preservation, and environmental education," providing more funds for environmental causes than almost any other state. Since its inception, it has awarded more than $917 million in lottery funds for 4,700 projects in all 64 counties in Colorado.

Outdoor sports have become integral to Colorado's economy, not only promoting year-round tourism but also attracting new residents. Though they are most likely to find employment with high-tech companies along the Front Range, most new residents cite recreation as their top reason for relocating, not

jobs. Recreational opportunities range from huge events like the Bolder Boulder Marathon, in which more than 50,000 runners participate, and world-class athletic competitions such as Telluride's Extreme Ski Week and Durango's Iron Horse Bicycle Classic, to solitary expeditions into high-mountain wilderness.

Recreation has also spawned a new breed of legendary figures as colorful as any from the gold rush days. Future generations may commemorate such heroes as Friedl Pfeifer, the European ski instructor who in the late 1940s came up with the crazy idea of building Colo-

Skiing fresh powder is a real thrill.

rado's first ski slope near a down-and-out mining town named Aspen. Or Neil Murdoch, who invented and popularized the sport of mountain biking while hiding out in Crested Butte under an assumed name, dodging a federal warrant for an alleged drug offense, for 25 years (he has since disappeared).

And then there's Sandy Glade, still going strong after more than 30 years. Now her line of Colorado bumper stickers numbers more than 50. Still revealing a lot about contemporary Colorado culture, they include "MARATHONER," "MOUNTAIN BIKER," "RIVER RUNNER," "CATCH & RELEASE," "SKIER" and, perhaps most telling of all, "SAVE AN ELK – SHOOT A LAND DEVELOPER."

DECISIVE DATES

Early cultures

AD 1
The pithouse-dwelling Basketmaker people inhabit the Four Corners area.

c.1300
Drought forces Ancestral Puebloans to abandon *pueblo villages in* the Four Corners.

c.1500
Colorado is now home to the Arapaho and Cheyenne peoples in the eastern plains and the Utes in western parts of the state.

An Arapaho warrior.

Strangers from afar

1682
French explorer René-Robert La Salle claims the region east of the Rockies for France.

1739
French traders, the Mallet brothers, pass through what is now eastern Colorado en route to Santa Fe.

1765
Juan Maria de Rivera and fellow Spaniards explore the San Juan and Sangre de Cristo ranges.

Americans move in

1803
Most of what is now eastern Colorado becomes American through the Louisiana Purchase.

1806
American Lt Zebulon M. Pike and a party of 22 men explore mountains west of Pueblo and Colorado Springs.

1820
Major Stephen H. Long and an army force explore what is now Colorado.

1832
During the "mountain man" era, Bent's Fort is built by the Bents and St. Vrain Company near La Junta.

1842
Lt John C. Frémont leads the first of five exploratory missions to the Rockies.

1846
General Stephen W. Kearney leads his "Army of the West" over the Santa Fe Trail through today's southeastern Colorado to peacefully take New Mexico for the United States from Mexico. Most of what is now western Colorado becomes American two years later.

1851
The first permanent settlement in Colorado is founded at Conejos in the San Luis Valley by six Hispanic families. The Treaty of Fort Laramie assures the Cheyenne and Arapaho tribes' continued use of what was to become Colorado's eastern plains region.

Boom Times

1858
Small deposits of gold are found near the South Platte River and Cherry Creek, kicking off the region's gold rush. Denver City is founded.

1859
John Gregory's gold strike at North Clear Creek on May 6 reinvigorates local mining prospects. Some 40,000 gold-diggers flock to the area to try their luck.

1861
The US Congress establishes the Colorado Territory (pop. 25,371), so named from the belief that the source of the Colorado River was located within it.

1864
Cavalrymen slaughter about 150 Cheyenne and Arapaho men, women and children at the Sand Creek Massacre.

1867
Under the Treaty of Medicine Lodge, members of the Cheyenne and Arapaho tribes agree to move to reservations in Oklahoma. Denver becomes the territorial capital.

1871
Colorado Springs is founded by General William J. Palmer.

1875
Rich silver deposits are found near Leadville.

A newspaper article from 1879 showcases Leadville on the front page.

1876
Colorado is admitted to the Union.

1879
Indian agent Nathan C. Meeker is slain along with several others in an Ute uprising.

1881
The Ute tribes are removed onto reservations.

1888
Two cowboys are the first Anglos to see the ancient ruins of Cliff Palace at Mesa Verde

1891
One of the world's great gold strikes is made at Cripple Creek. Gold production reaches a peak of more than $20 million annually by 1900.

1893
Congress repeals the Sherman Silver Purchase Act, wreaking havoc on the silver industry.

A new century

1903–4
Miners strike for better working conditions. Militia are summoned to break strikes by the Western Federation of Miners.

1914
Twenty people, including 12 children, are killed during the Ludlow Massacre, pitting miners against state militia near Trinidad.

1915
Rocky Mountain National Park is created.

1917
"Buffalo Bill" Cody dies and is buried on Lookout Mountain, west of Denver.

1918
World War I stimulates the mining of local molybdenum (used in steel alloys); coal output reaches a new high of 12 million tons.

1931
The state's population exceeds one million.

1946
Uranium is discovered near Grand Junction.

1958
The Air Force Academy opens near Colorado Springs.

1959
The Colorado–Big Thompson system brings water to the state's populous eastern region.

1974
Huge deposits of shale oil are tapped on the Western Slope.

1982
Exxon closes oil fields in western Colorado. The 1980s bring growth in the high-tech sector.

1995
Denver International Airport opens.

2012
Colorado's estimated population reaches 5,187,582.

2013
Clashing storm systems over the Front Range cause historic flooding. Ten people die, over 1,852 homes and 203 businesses are destroyed. Damages approach $4 billion.

2014
Same-sex marriage is legally recognized in Colorado on October 7, 2014.

2015
After legalization of recreational marijuana in 2014, new businesses and sales turbo-charge Colorado's economy. Sales reach $996 million in 2015.

2016
The Denver Broncos win the NFL Super Bowl for the third time, beating the Carolina Panthers 24-10 in Super Bowl 50.

Dancing in a traditional costume.

NATIVE HERITAGE

For countless generations, the people of this land hunted and farmed and developed intricate ways of dealing with nature.

This land was their land once. The first people to move to what would later become Colorado may have arrived from Asia some 12,000 years ago, at the end of the Ice Age. Crossing into Alaska via the exposed land mass known as Beringia, they followed big game inland, down to where the Eastern Rockies meet the Great Plains.

They found a landscape of peaks and plains and cool mountain streams. The hunting was good – herds of giant bison, camel, horse, elk, deer, and antelope, clustered around lakes and marshes that also held 7ft (2-meter) long beavers and giant ground sloths. But the big prize was mammoths. Hunters pursued the huge, tusked creatures along the eastern Rockies, sleeping in cave shelters and flaking stone spear points around campfires. They butchered on site, leaving behind bones, worked stone, and chert spear points of a type known as Clovis, for the town in New Mexico where they were first identified.

A painting depicts a cooperative buffalo hunt in the Wild West.

Bison hunting

By 9000 BC, climate warming and possibly overhunting had doomed the large animals. Paleo-hunters focused instead on one creature – the giant bison. Big-game hunting required bravery and cooperation, skills that would later characterize the tribes that wandered the Plains in search of bison in the historic period. They knapped smaller spear points from obsidian obtained from high-country sites like Black Mountain near the headwaters of the Rio Grande in the San Juans. The Folsom, as they came to be called, were widespread throughout Colorado. Campsites have been found on the Wyoming border, near Fort Collins, and in the San Luis Valley. Anywhere, in fact, where there was grass and water to support large herds of bison.

A thousand years later, people of the Plano culture had refined bison hunting to a fine art, killing large numbers by herding them over cliffs. Some 200 bison were found at the Olsen Chabbuck "buffalo jump" in southeastern Colorado. Eventually, the giant bison, too, vanished, supplanted by modern bison of a much smaller size. And once again humans adapted, not only embracing the changing environment but becoming expert in the great variety of plants and animals to be found there.

Man and nature

The extensive Archaic period may well have been the most successful in human history.

Small bands wandered large, defined territories, stopping at favored campsites to hunt and harvest seasonally. It was a lifestyle that sustained the Utes of western Colorado for centuries – a perfect balance of man and nature.

Archaic people camped near springs, streams and rivers throughout Colorado, making use of rock shelters and portable hide tents known as wickiups. They hunted year-round, using snares and traps to capture small animals such as prairie dogs, rabbits and squirrels, and an atlatl, or spear-thrower, to bring down bison, deer, antelope, bighorn sheep, and elk. In summer, they

high cliffs where the sheep often traveled, perhaps hoping to attract the real thing. Shamans may also have undertaken long pilgrimages to sacred sites and painted images in red hematite on the walls: herds of bighorn sheep, flowing water and life-size, triangular figures with long thin bodies and huge, empty eyes that hovered wraithlike above dry sandy washes.

Archaic people were living in semicircular, underground homes with earthen roofs known as pithouses as early as 6,000 years ago. One 3,000-year-old pithouse was excavated east of Grand Junction. At this unusual site, arche-

An archeological excavation of a kiva.

gathered prairie turnips, wild mustard, buffalo berries, and plums on the plains, and harvested sweet, nutritious pinyon nuts from higher elevations. These wild plants were placed in woven baskets attached to a tumpline and strapped around the foreheads of women, who also carried babies this way.

A warming trend between 7,500 and 4,500 years ago may have encouraged some Archaic people to move to the Uncompahgre Plateau, where greater moisture supported more plants and animals. A number of sites, including some now immersed under Curecanti Reservoir in the Gunnison River Valley, appear to date from this time. By 2000 BC, hunters were leaving split-twig fetishes of bighorn sheep in

ologists uncovered a variety of wild ricegrass that had been cultivated to produce large seeds. By AD 100, the idea of growing food had also reached hunter-gatherers in the eastern Rockies, who were in contact with agricultural cultures in the Ohio Valley, from whom they learned home building and pottery made with a paddle and anvil.

Pueblo farmers

The tribes who lived along the Republican, Apishpa, Purgatoire, Arkansas, and South Platte rivers remained hunter-gatherers until pressure from incoming tribes and European settlers doomed their way of life in the 1800s. But the Basketmakers, the first people to settle permanently among the cool mesas (sheer-sided tablelands) and perennial streams of the canyon country of the Four Corners, eagerly embraced farming.

By the early Pueblo I period (AD 700–900), extended families throughout the Four Corners were living in hamlets of above-ground houses made of sandstone and mud adobe. Pithouses were used as underground ceremonial rooms, or kivas. Here clansmen gathered to weave cotton and discuss the most advantageous times to plant and harvest. Ritual specialists tracked the daily movements of the sun, moon, and planets across the sky. As the solstices approached, ceremonies were announced, and the priests quickly became the most important members of the village.

The Fremont

The people who lived in northwestern Colorado had much in common with their neighbors to the south. They too made pottery, grew corn, squash and, later, beans, and lived together in villages. But for them the hunter-gatherer lifestyle of their Archaic ancestors still beckoned. The Fremont are less obvious in the archeological record, perhaps because of their

> *Claims that Aztecs from Mexico used human sacrifice to subjugate Puebloans and engaged in cannibalism are supported by the discovery of coprolites (fossilized feces) containing human remains.*

fondness for remote places. They developed a hardy strain of corn that suited the highlands, fashioned plain, utilitarian pottery, and made moccasins with the dew claw of a deer for traction.

Long after the Ancestral Puebloans of the Four Corners were building large stone villages, the Fremont found comfort in pithouses – by far the most practical shelter in the cold winters and warm summers of the high desert. Their rock art, too, echoed that of early Archaic people, with depictions of large-shouldered anthropomorphs and game animals and enigmatic figures like Kokopelli, the flute player. Hundreds of Fremont pictographs dot the Douglas Creek drainage, between Grand Junction and Rangely. More can be found

throughout Dinosaur National Monument, in Echo Canyon and along the Green River near Dinosaur Quarry.

The Chaco phenomenon

By the Pueblo II period (900–1100), the Southwest was dominated by one major Pueblo group: the powerful Chaco civilization, centered on Chaco Canyon, New Mexico. Archeologists speculate that Chaco may have served as a sort of religious hub for people living in the San Juan Basin, just south of southwestern Colorado. Seasonal ceremonies at Chaco, and

A reconstructed Basketmaker pithouse serves an educational purpose.

redistribution of trade goods from as far away as the Pacific, the Mississippi River, and Mexico may have brought thousands to the remote canyon.

Satellite villages, or outliers, such as the Escalante Ruin at Anasazi Heritage Center, north of Cortez, and Chimney Rock, east of Durango, seem to have played roles in the Chaco system. Both served as pioneer Chaco communities in outlying areas, housed in typical Chaco *pueblos* (*villages*) with several kivas. The two distinctive rock formations at Chimney Rock seem to have been used by an isolated community of men living nearby. They apparently tracked the moon and cut high-country pines, which were floated down the Piedras River to Chaco for construction.

The Chaco culture crashed spectacularly in the early 1100s. Its leaders may have lost their power base during a long-running drought, leaving desperate farming families to their own devices. They fled to surrounding highlands, where resources were more plentiful, and clashed with existing residents. By the early Pueblo III period (1100–1300), the Montezuma Valley of southwestern Colorado had an estimated population of 30,000. Villages sprang up on every mesa with a stream. Lookout towers

in the late 1800s, they found more than 4,000 sites, from early pithouses and small *pueblos* to extensive fields and an unfinished, 12th-century ceremonial center on Chapin Mesa. Thousands of bowls, effigy pots, mugs, ladles, and other black-on-white pottery lay among the ruins.

Beginning in the late 1100s and 1200s, residents of Mesa Verde left their mesa-top villages and moved into homes concealed in the cliffs. Inside warm, south-facing canyon walls, next to springs, they built some 600 cliff dwellings, ranging from small villages to major ceremonial centers, such as Cliff Palace, whose unusual

Cliff Palace, which was abandoned in the late 13th century, is the largest cliff dwelling in North America, with more than 215 rooms and 23 kivas.

were built, perhaps to safeguard communities from outsiders.

These enclosed *pueblos* were hastily constructed, using large stones loosely mortared with mud, and some were now built in unusual shapes, such as the oval, circular, square and "D" shaped buildings at Hovenweep National Monument.

Mesa Verde

Just east of modern-day Cortez, Mesa Verde, an 8,517ft (2,596-meter) -high plateau with warm southern exposures and stream-carved finger canyons, had been a popular farming spot for generations. When white settlers explored it

tower kiva was probably used for astronomical observations. These cliff dwellings represented the last phase of Ancestral Pueblo life in the Four Corners. By 1300, the region was abandoned. Families moved south to New Mexico and Arizona to live along more reliable lands next to the Rio Grande and Little Colorado River. The inhabitants of 24 modern *pueblos* trace their ancestry to Mesa Verde.

At its height, Mesa Verde supported 5,000 people. By the end of the Great Drought of 1276–1300, Mesa Verde and the surrounding Montezuma Valley could no longer support the population. Without rain, fields didn't produce and wild foods disappeared. There must have been competition for what little remained. Violent episodes became more frequent.

The arrival of newcomers may have tipped the balance. Evidence suggests that nomadic Athabascans from northwest Canada, who split into the Navajo and Apache tribes in the South-

> The prehistoric Southwest culture once known as the Anasazi are now known as the Ancestral Puebloans. Anasazi, a Navajo name meaning "enemy ancestors," is unacceptable to modern Pueblo people.

west, were already in the area by the late 12th century. Utes from the Great Basin may have arrived soon after. These tribes vied for dominance in the areas abandoned by Ancestral Pueblo and Fremont farmers.

Plains culture

Just as farming transformed the lives of Pueblo people, horses revolutionized the lives of buffalo hunters on the plains. Introduced by the Spanish in the late 17th century, horses were able to draw heavily laden sleds, or *travois*, from place to place. Men on horseback joined other groups to hunt bison over larger areas. They left for long periods, leaving behind their families to gather food, tan bison skins, and make clothing at encampments of hide-covered tents, or tipis.

A man's wealth was now counted by the number of horses he owned, and his success in hunting bison and raiding other tribes for horses and slaves was vital to his status as a warrior. Warrior societies, such as the feared Cheyenne Dog Soldiers, grew up in Plains tribes, whose members performed feats of bravery during battle, such as touching their enemies (counting coup) and collecting scalps. Young men on vision quests fasted on mountain tops, seeking spiritual guidance. Most tribes practiced the Sun Dance, in which men fasted, danced, and pierced their flesh with hooks tied to a central pole – a sacrifice intended to benefit the whole tribe.

The first tribe to acquire horses in Colorado was probably the Ute, whose people were widespread throughout Colorado in the 1600s. They fought the Navajo and eventually forced them to retreat into New Mexico and Arizona.

In 1700, the Jicarilla Apaches in southeastern Colorado and Kansas were pushed into New Mexico by advancing Comanches from the north, armed with French guns. By 1775, the Comanche found themselves pushed south of the Arkansas River by Kiowa and Kiowa-Apaches. An alliance of Comanches, Kiowas, and Kiowa-Apaches dominated the southern plains and inspired fear in the Pueblos of the Rio Grande as well as European settlers.

In the early 1800s, Arapahos displaced from the Great Lakes took up bison hunting on the Plains. They wandered the eastern Rockies,

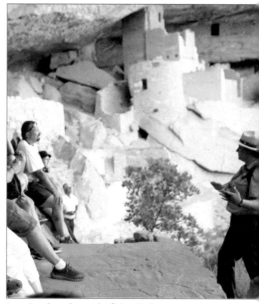

Learning about the people of Mesa Verde.

MESOAMERICAN INFLUENCES

Mexican corn culture, pottery making, and masonry construction techniques reached the Four Corners via southern traders in the early 1st century AD. From the Hohokam of southern Arizona, who practiced irrigation farming, the Basketmakers may have acquired goods from Mexico and learned to use check dams, ditches, and dry farming techniques. From the Mogollon of southern New Mexico, they learned how to make coiled clay pots and to fire them at high temperatures to make strong, airtight containers for storing and transporting grain. The refined black-on-white pottery of the Four Corners became a prized trade item.

camping seasonally in favorite spots in the Denver area and, along with Cheyenne and Sioux allies, raided Crows, Shoshones, Utes, Comanches, and others.

French and American fur trappers now appeared in Colorado. Relations between traders and Indians were generally peaceful and resulted in important alliances. Trader William Bent married a Cheyenne woman. Their eastern-educated son George would survive the bloody Sand Creek Massacre of 1864 and provide an important eyewitness account of the atrocity. Another trader married a young Arapaho woman who taught English to her brother Niwot, or Left Hand. The multilingual Niwot became a highly respected leader dedicated to peaceful coexistence during the Indian Wars. It was near Bent's Fort, in 1840, that the Southern Arapaho and Cheyenne made permanent peace with the Kiowa and Comanche, following the devastating Battle of Wolf Creek in 1837.

Manifest destiny

After Mexico ceded much of the Southwest to the United States in 1848, white-Indian

Mounted hunters pursue bison in Charles M. Russell's The Buffalo Hunt No. 39.

NEUTRAL GROUND

No trip to Bent's Fort is complete without a stroll through the *bosque* shading the banks of the Arkansas River. It is pleasant to walk through tall grass edging the steep banks, past stands of willow and box elder, listening to cottonwood leaves fluttering overhead. In the days before air conditioning, people sat under the trees to enjoy the extra breath stirred up by the shivering leaves. The wind makes a distinctive sound as it soughs through these gnarly old trees with their stout trunks, splintered branches, and runneled bark.

It's easy to imagine hundreds of tipis pitched alongside the path of the river. William Bent reported that in the spring of 1842, thousands of Native Americans from half a dozen tribes were camped up and down the Arkansas within view of the fort. Bent's Fort was neutral ground, and all animosities, tribal and personal, were suspended for as long as the tribes were camped there.

The native people engaged in horse races, powwows, religious ceremonies, and long trading sessions with the factors at the fort. Beads, blankets, kettles, knives, whiskey, and guns were bartered for beaver pelts, buffalo hides, and Ute-made deerskin clothing. Young men used this lull in their normal lives to court young women, and at night the reedy tremolo of love flutes could be heard over the barking of dogs and the whinnying of horses.

relations grew increasingly strained. Over the next decade, gold was discovered in both California and Colorado. Huge numbers of miners and settlers headed west on the Santa Fe and Oregon trails to seek their fortunes. They destroyed favorite Indian campsites with their cattle and homesteads and slaughtered buffalo by the millions, mostly for sport. Government policies instigated private ownership of what had once been communal lands, and native people were deprived of their livelihoods and forced to rely on meager handouts at government agencies. Worse still, whole bands con-

broken by settlers. Indians had no recourse but to fight back, flee, or accept what was offered.

Tragedy followed tragedy. On November 29, 1864, trigger-happy Colorado volunteers led by Colonel John Chivington took matters into their own hands and slaughtered 137 innocent women, children, and old men at Sand Creek, near the Arkansas River. Among them were chiefs Left Hand and White Antelope. The counterattacks lasted two years, until, in 1867, huge losses led Kiowa, Cheyenne, Southern Arapaho, and Comanche leaders to sign the Medicine Lodge Treaty

The Sand Creek Massacre.

tracted smallpox, measles, and other European diseases, and warriors, unable to feed their families or hunt, became addicted to alcohol.

Plains people grew increasingly desperate, and many young men turned to raiding white settlements in order to feed their starving families. The government took a hardline policy of rounding up tribes by whatever means necessary and placing them on reservations. Hunters were expected to take up farming, live with former enemies, own property, and give up their language and culture. For the nomadic tribes of Colorado, it was a disaster. As leaders such as Ouray, Black Kettle, White Antelope, and Little Raven sought to restrain their people from attacking settlements, treaties were repeatedly

confining their tribes to reservations in the Oklahoma and Kansas territories.

Many tribal members refused to go, but resistance proved futile. In November 1868, the Cheyenne leader Black Kettle, who had miraculously survived the massacre at Sand Creek, was shot down in cold blood by General George Armstrong Custer at Washita River, Oklahoma. Ten years later, the Northern Arapaho were moved to the Shoshone Reservation near the Wind River in Wyoming. The only tribe left in Colorado was the Ute, whose leaders – Ouray, Severo, and Ignacio – were left with no choice but to breach the growing divide between their people and the gold-hungry whites flooding into Colorado.

A Cheyenne man, c.1910; the Cheyenne roamed the plains of eastern Colorado until the 1860s.

BREAKING GROUND

From the 16th century onwards, Spaniards, the French, and other strangers barged right in, reconfiguring the social landscape and rewriting a whole region's history.

Colorado has plenty of spacious skies and purple mountain majesties but not a whole lot of modern history, especially as compared to a place like neighboring New Mexico. The latter was an important offshoot of New Spain, whereas Colorado was long considered remote and unpromising. Not until after the mid-19th century, when precious metals were mined and fortunes started piling up, did much development take place.

Early Spanish expeditions

The Ancestral Puebloan cliff dwellers of the Four Corners had abandoned the region long before then, moving down to the better-watered Rio Grande and Little Colorado River by 1300. Now, only nomadic Utes and Navajos roamed the former homelands of the powerful Chaco and Mesa Verde cultures. Spanish presence was minimal, too. Some 20 years after transforming Mexico into New Spain, self-financed conquistadors arrived in North America, chasing supposedly fabulous riches. They blazed El Camino Real Trail from Mexico City to Santa Fe and Taos but did nothing to endear themselves to the numerous Indian tribes who had long used the lands, and quickly returned home.

Most famous of those Spanish pioneers was Francisco Vásquez de Coronado. In 1540, Coronado and a large force crossed into Arizona, then continued northeastward into New Mexico, seeking the supposedly fabulously wealthy "Seven Cities of C'bola." Disappointed by the modest *pueblos* they found at Zuni, Pecos, and elsewhere, they returned to Mexico City two years later, empty-handed and chastened. Misled by Pecos leaders about gold in Kansas, Coronado is thought to have

Stephen H. Long, leader of an 1820 expedition.

traipsed across part of southeastern Colorado, leading the first recorded European expedition in Colorado.

Side expeditions covered a lot of ground, beheld wondrous sights, and bestowed place-names, including naming the great river laden with red sediments "the Colorado." But these gold-seekers were uninterested in starting settlements. That would come later, and only successfully in New Mexico. Colorado's fearsome nomadic Comanches and Utes would have not taken kindly to hewing wood, carrying water, or taking up farming on anyone's behalf.

Further Spanish expeditions to Colorado in the 17th century led to the discovery of various Indian settlements. Traders gradually ventured north, and by 1700 goods were being exchanged at settlements near present-day La Junta, a place on the Arkansas River close to the site where in later years Bent's Fort would become a landmark exchange place on the famous Santa Fe Trail for fur trappers, traders, and mountain men.

French colonies

Others besides Spaniards showed up, chiefly French and English colonists, followed by representatives of the newly independent United

19th-century depiction of trappers around a campfire.

States, a dynamic young republic which, as the 19th century dawned, began spreading across the continent.

Early on, Spain and France dueled for ownership of the region west of the Mississippi River now known as the Great Plains. This was a lot of land with a lot of natural resources, and it was claimed for France by the explorer La Salle in 1682. After leading a party of about 50 men downriver to the Gulf of Mexico, he grandly declared the entire territory between the Alleghenies and the Rockies to be the property of Louis XIV. Hence the name Louisiana.

A similar claim was made on Spain's behalf in 1706 by Juan de Uribarri, who frequently chased after Indian slaves fleeing their New Mexican masters. Concerned about possible French intrusion via the Mississippi River, Uribarri declared the region to be part of the Spanish realm.

Spanish authorities became obsessed with *voyageurs*. These were the trappers, often the offspring of French men and Indian women, who hunted beaver and other fur-bearing animals, conveying the pelts to market on canoe voyages. Fur was big business. Hats made of beaver fur were popular in Europe, and the trade played a major role in opening up the American West to settlement.

The turf was soon declared off-limits by Spanish overlords, quick to head off anything that smacked of trading activity. One such Spanish reaction in 1720 had disastrous results. An expedition under Pedro de Villasur, checking on reports that French settlers were infiltrating present-day eastern Colorado and Nebraska, was caught up in an ambush by Pawnee Indians at the Platte River in Nebraska. Villasur and almost his entire force were wiped out.

In the 18th century, French *voyageurs* roamed around a good part of the land that later was involved in the history-making Louisiana Purchase. The first known French explorers in the region were the Mallet brothers, Pierre and Paul, in 1739–41. Their expedition went from Canada to Santa Fe, where they spent nearly a year and wound up giving away all their goods, an action that has caused historians to suspect that what the Mallets were really interested in was sniffing out gold and silver mining deposits.

More Frenchmen came in the years ahead, traveling a route that, after Mexican independence in 1820, became the storied Santa Fe Trail. But overall their influence was minimal, and when the Seven Years' War was terminated in 1763, France was compelled to bow out of the American picture. The French ceded to Britain and Spain, respectively, territories east and west of the Mississippi River.

France did get back the western land, which included Colorado, in an 1801 agreement with Spain. But the restoration was short-lived. Two years later, the Louisiana Purchase brought an end to French designs on North America and the Lewis and Clark Expedition paved the way for American expansion westward.

Later Spanish expeditions

Colorado's awesome landscape came under scrutiny following the exploits of a couple of Franciscan friars from Santa Fe who embarked on a memorable if foolhardy journey to Monterey, California, in 1776. Padres Francisco Dominguez and Silvestre Escalante, accompanied by eight friends, set off from Santa Fe in search of a shorter route between the missions of New Mexico and California. They roamed southwest Colorado and later described in print such vividly named places as the Sangre de Cristo (Blood of Christ) Mountains and explore what eventually became known as the Gunnison River.

Charting new territory

Colorado's story takes a great leap forward with the Louisiana Purchase. That big deal added most of what is now eastern Colorado to the fledgling nation, although exactly where the boundary lay between the Spanish and American realms was left in doubt – was it the Arkansas River or was it the more southern Red River? It would take until 1850 for Colorado's physical shape to be configured once and for all.

Bent's Old Fort National Historic Site is a reconstruction of the original fort, built on the Arkansas River in 1832 as a trading center.

El Rio de Las Animas Perdidas en Purgatorio (River of Lost Souls in Purgatory).

Spain's claim to the Colorado territory was reinforced through military expeditions and other activities, including searches for precious metals. Mining was key to their economic success elsewhere in the New World, so Spanish authorities made it a priority to seek out evidence of precious metals in the greater New Mexico territory.

An early effort at prospecting was made in 1765 when a group headed by Juan Maria de Rivera came north from Santa Fe to search for gold in the San Juan and northern Sangre de Cristo mountain ranges. Although unsuccessful, they were the first known outsiders to

One of those who went forth to chart the West's topography was a young army officer named Zebulon Montgomery Pike. In 1806, he headed a 22-man expedition instructed to gather information on the source of the Arkansas and Red rivers and on Spanish settlements in New Mexico. Traveling up the Arkansas to the vicinity of present-day Pueblo, the explorers spotted in the distance a tall snow-covered mountain later named Pikes Peak. It took them two weeks to reach the mountain, and when they tried to climb to the top, Pike and his men were unsuccessful.

Arrested by a Spanish military force, the Americans were interrogated and held for a time in Santa Fe and Chihuahua, Mexico. Pike was freed in July 1807. He died five years later in the War of 1812 in Canada. Another expedition led by a US Army officer, Major Stephen H. Long, went forth in 1820, this time at the bidding of President James Monroe. The instructions were to explore the southwest boundary of the territory acquired in the Louisiana Purchase. Long's group entered Colorado via the South Platte River and explored much of the Rockies' eastern flank.

The Long expedition's botanist and historian, Dr Edwin James, became the first to successfully scale Pikes Peak, which was given the name

In 1779, an army led by Juan Bautista de Anza pursued Comanche warrior Cuerno Verde through the San Luis Valley onto the plains below Pikes Peak. Cuerno Verde and many warriors perished in a bloody battle in the Greenhorn Mountains.

COL. FREMONT
PLANTING THE AMERICAN STANDARD ON THE ROCKY MOUNTAIN

John C. Frémont planting an American flag in the Rocky Mountains in an 1856 campaign illustration.

James Peak, but hunters and trappers persisted in calling it Pikes Peak and that name stuck.

Trappers and traders

The true western pioneers were trailblazers who operated as scouts and trappers. Known as plainsmen or mountain men, these rugged individualists pushed deep into the wilderness in search of beaver and other fur-bearing animals, and becoming the stuff of frontier legend.

Their names are well-known, among them Jim Bridger, Jim Beckwourth, and Jim Baker, Tom "Broken Hand" Fitzpatrick and "Uncle Dick" Wootton, and the legendary Kit Carson, that all-purpose scout, fighter, and Indian

expert. Traversing a wide expanse, these prototypical free-traders forded streams and climbed mountains for furs and other items and in the process became intimate with the native inhabitants of the Colorado Rockies. Prices for beaver pelts soared in the 1820s and remained high until supplies diminished and the market collapsed in the late 1830s.

Carson was a familiar figure at one of the most famous of the western trading posts: Bent's Fort. The first Anglo settlement in what became Colorado, it was built in 1832 by William Bent, his three brothers, and their partner Ceran St Vrain near the present-day city of La Junta. Indians, too, traded at this early mercantile establishment, and it was here in 1840 that an enduring peace agreement was hammered out at an extraordinary meeting of Arapaho, Kiowa, Cheyenne, and Comanche chiefs.

Another busy trading post was Fort Vasquez, built for the Rocky Mountain Fur Company on the South Platte River north of what became the city of Denver. It was frequented by American trappers and hunters as well as members of Cheyenne and Arapaho tribes. In 1842, however, it was looted by Indian raiders. After the demand for beaver dried up, trading posts were generally abandoned. To protect isolated frontier settlements and trading routes, the federal government put up a string of military forts.

Kit Carson lived for many years in Colorado. Having commanded a Union force in the Civil War, he was named to head Fort Garland, in the San Luis Valley, in 1866. He died two years later at nearby Fort Lyon. Carson served as guide to a public figure whose name ranks high in western annals, the flamboyant explorer John Charles Frémont.

Natural wonders of the West

Frémont's published reports, in lively and picturesque prose, excited curiosity about the nation's vast western expanse and natural wonders. Among their avid readers were

Henry David Thoreau and the Mormon leader Brigham Young. Frémont's enthusiasm in print countered a kind of badlands view of Colorado that had taken hold in the public imagination since the days of Zebulon Pike and Stephen Long. The latter had basically written off the Colorado plains as a "Great American Desert" unfit for exploitation.

This appraisal was at odds with the grand vision of such as La Salle and the expansionist sensibility of Thomas Hart Benton, the senator from Missouri famously associated with the "Manifest Destiny" imperative – and father of the vivacious teenager with whom Frémont eloped. Jessie Benton Frémont, furthermore, turned out to be a talented writer who would greatly enhance her explorer husband's published reports and, later, his memoirs.

Thus – once he got over the shock of the elopement – was Senator Benton's purpose well served. Frémont's reportage excited interest in the edenic myth of the western landscape and its material promise. (It was the memoirs, so ably edited by Jessie Frémont, that served to fix Kit Carson's place firmly in the pantheon of American heroes.)

Sadly, Frémont's fourth expedition, in 1848, took a fearful toll in human life. Searching for a railroad route through the Rockies on Benton's behalf, he and his men became snowbound high in the La Farita Mountains of southern Colorado, and there were 11 deaths by starvation or freezing. Frémont's final expedition occurred in 1853, through the San Luis Valley and into the Gunnison River country. Earlier that year the ill-fated Captain John W. Gunnison had come by while surveying a railroad route westward through the Colorado Rockies for the US War Department, before he and all but four of his men were slain in an attack in Utah attributed to Utes but likely orchestrated by Mormons.

Colorado's first settlement

In 1851, Hispanic settlers took advantage of Mexican land grants and moved into southern Colorado. They put down roots in Conejos in the San Luis Valley and this gave rise to the first permanent town of non-Indian origin in Colorado's history. Unfortunately, such manifestations of encroachment were embittering relations with native people, and in that valley Fort Massachusetts was established to protect settlers.

In 1848, thanks to the Treaty of Guadalupe Hidalgo, Mexico gave up most of the Colorado territory that was not acquired by the United States in the Louisiana Purchase. The territory figured only slightly in the US–Mexico War itself – in 1846 General Stephen W. Kearney's army used the Santa Fe Trail, in southeastern Colorado, en route to the annexation of New Mexico.

Colorado took final shape in 1850, when the federal government bought out the last of the territorial claims on it – in this case by Texas – and entered a volatile new era marked by extraordinary cycles of boom and bust.

Kit Carson served as Frémont's guide.

THE BEAR FLAG REVOLT

Explorer John C. Frémont surveyed the West's virgin lands and natural boundaries, but he was a renegade hero. On June 13 1846, he incited a homegrown Anglo–American rebellion in Mexican-owned Sonoma, California. Known as the Bear Flag Revolt, for the flag depicting a grizzly bear flown by the republicans, the rebellion led to the rebels declaring a 26-day California Republic and installing a president. On June 23, Frémont took over in the name of the United States, unaware that the US-Mexico War was already underway. In July, the US Navy sailed to California, captured Monterey, and took command. Frémont was court-martialed.

STRIKING IT RICH

Eureka! A well-endowed territory yielded its treasures in the most boisterous chapter in Colorado history. Some got very rich indeed; many more were disappointed.

The big discovery was that there was "gold in them thar hills" and streams out west, including Colorado, with its boulder-strewn creeks and mountains. The era began famously in early 1848 when a gleaming nugget was pulled from a ditch at John Sutter's mill in California, and a decade later it was Colorado's turn – gold dust was panned from the creeks. Suddenly, what had been a so-called "Great American Desert" that fronted on an enormous mountain range now was looking like some luxuriously enticing El Dorado.

Going for gold

It was about time. Treasure-hunters had been coming up dry here ever since Coronado's expedition. But intimations of gold persisted. Traces were reported here and there, such as along the Rio Grande south of present-day Colorado, by early Spanish colonizers. Precious metal and minerals were sought in the 18th century in places like the Sangre de Cristo and San Juan mountain regions. Early in the 19th century a trapper told Zebulon Pike, the Army officer who had been sent forth to map the Louisiana Territory, of gold traces spotted in the South Platte River area.

Nuggets plucked from streams were reportedly shown to William Bent by passers-by at Bent's Fort, that prototypical rest stop on

Panning for gold near Clear Creek, c.1890.

the Santa Fe Trail. William Gilpin, who later became Colorado's first territorial governor, searched Rocky Mountain streams for it as a young man. But few people stayed for long, at least until 1851, when some New Mexicans put down roots on fertile land in the San Luis Valley and injected an Hispanic-Catholic flavor into the southern Colorado region that has resonated ever since.

Also coming by were hordes of forty-niners with pans and pickaxes and a bad case of that "California fever" sweeping the world. Making their way across the Plains, these gold-diggers either tried to skirt the obtrusive Rockies blocking their path or else seized the opportunity to poke around in the region

The 1858 discovery of gold in Cripple Creek in Colorado was especially welcome to Americans. It came on the heels of the economic panic of 1857, which brought hard times as banks and factories were forced to shut down.

while en route to the "Promised Land". One particular group came from the east in 1850, via the Santa Fe Trail to the Pikes Peak region, sifted some gold dust at a creek off the South Platte River close to today's downtown Denver, and then decided to keep pressing on to California.

The latter experience partly inspired an 1858 expedition involving William Green Russell that was considerably more successful. A native Georgian who had been in the forty-niner quest, Russell was accompanied by two brothers and some other prospectors. Setting

Miners in Ouray County, c.1920.

out from Georgia, where one of the early gold rushes had taken place in 1828–30, Russell and the others panned doggedly at a place off the South Platte called Cherry Creek before hitting "pay dirt." Before long, they were piling up bags of gold dust.

The news spread fast. Pikes Peak in what was then known as the Kansas Territory became fixed in the public imagination, a bit imperfectly, as the place where all the gold was. Fortune-seekers began flocking there, most of them from east of the Great Plains. Many of their wagons were emblazoned with banners: PIKES PEAK OR BUST. Inevitably, perhaps, a measure of disbelief set in and the euphoria dissipated as a reverse wave of luckless prospectors

headed back home, their banners now telling a different story: BUSTED, BY GOD.

Nonetheless, there were two new discoveries made in 1859, about 40 miles (64km) to the west, at a place called Clear Creek, in a canyon of the Rockies' Front Range. The excitement started all over again.

One discovery was by George A. Jackson, a Missouri trader – and cousin of Kit Carson – who in January stumbled upon a gold nugget and some gold dust near a place called Idaho Springs. The second and more substantial strike was by John H. Gregory, another native Georgian. He and his comrades dug out crumbled rock and earth while picking and shoveling along the sides of a stream on May 6, 1859. Immersed in the icy stream water, the cleansed dirt yielded a pan of gleaming gold amid much jubilation.

The place quickly boomed into Central City. For a time it rivaled Denver itself, before fading as a ghost town. Prospectors poured into the region from the Mississippi Valley, the Midwest, the East, everywhere. What became Denver grew almost overnight from the crude settlement at the juncture of the South Platte River and Cherry Creek into a major supply center. It took its name from the governor of the Kansas Territory, James W. Denver.

It was General William H. Larimer Jr, a native Pennsylvanian following on the heels of William Green Russell's expedition, who laid out "Denver City" by picking a tract on the east side of Cherry Creek and marking its center with cottonwood sticks. The date was November 22, 1858. On the other side of the creek was the rival camp of Auraria – Latin for "gold" – named after Russell's home town in gold-infused Georgia. Both camps grew rapidly.

Boom time

Within a year some $18 million in gold was extracted in the Clear Creek area. Middlemen profited by supplying the food, clothing and liquid spirits it was necessary to stock up on while roughing it in the hills, not to mention wagons, lumber, tools and much more. Denver and Auraria prospered. They merged in 1860 to become the "Queen City of the Rockies," the mile-high Denver destined for status as the leading urban center in the western expanse that stretches from Plains to Pacific.

Tent stores and log saloons sprang up along the muddy streets of raw new towns. Visitors from the East attracted by word of the so-called "camp cure" were fitted out in Denver with wagons, tents, and bedding for their sojourn into the mountains. There were exotic street scenes and types – band music, spectator sports, Native Americans, nattily garbed English sportsmen, urbane dudes from Eastern cities. Population mushroomed – Leadville's hitting a peak of 40,000 by 1880; Denver's more than tripling by 1890 to 106,000.

– "white metal" – were discovered. One early locale was Georgetown, west of Denver. It was the most important silver camp in Colorado before the fabulous discovery at Leadville in 1878.

Still more lay ahead – copper, lead, zinc, iron, bismuth, manganese, molybdenum. Like the old-time mountain men, prospectors followed icy streams into high terrain. Water was always necessary for cleaning and, more importantly, smelting, as that vital mining process was introduced. Costs grew as the focus shifted from sifting in streams to locating and extracting veins

Pioneers make camp in the foothills of the Rocky Mountains near Colorado Springs, c.1875.

Saloons, dance halls, gambling parlors, and brothels became commonplace. Prospectors who worked with single-minded diligence in less than healthful conditions came out of the hills for rest and recuperation, seeking spirits and scant lodging at inflated prices – $1 to share a bed in a makeshift room of beds at a flophouse. Gold detritus was a common currency – a pinch of gold dust between thumb and forefinger equaled 25 cents.

More gold brought more boomtowns – Golden, Gold Hill, Boulder, Fairplay, Colorado City. And when the easy-to-find surface deposits became exhausted, fortune kept smiling on prospectors. Starting in the late 1860s and into the 1870s, rich veins of silver

of ore often deeply embedded in the earth. This required the kind of capital best provided by large financial interests. Smelters were installed and railroad tracks put down in usually difficult, high-altitude terrain. Single-gauge railways of narrower dimension were introduced for shipping ore and moving supplies to high-altitude locales. It was hard, dangerous work. Avalanches were one hazard, fire another – towns of wood-frame structures hastily thrown together were subject to conflagration.

Coming of the railroads

Railroads became an important factor in conveying men and metals and opening up the territory to wider and wider development.

Although the all-important Union Pacific line was routed through Cheyenne, Wyoming, 12 miles (19km) to the north, a spur was constructed to link Colorado with that transcontinental rail corridor in 1870. This was the Denver Pacific Railroad. Two years later came completion of another important line, the Denver & Rio Grande, which connected central and southern Colorado.

In the San Juan region, the Rio Grande Southern and the Silverton Northern railroads were built under the leadership of Otto Mears, a Russian-born immigrant who had

stimulate settlement. Agricultural settlements were planted throughout the South Platte Valley, and railway extension into the territory also had the effect of mitigating the threat posed by hostile Indians.

Madams and millionaires

Immigrants came to Colorado from many points, domestic and foreign, as towns arose out of the wilderness, places such as Creede, South Park, Telluride, Silver Plume, Silverton and, most famously, Leadville. At 10,188ft (3,105 meters), fairly high up in the Rockies of

The Silverton toll road connected mining camps in the San Juan Mountains to the outside world.

come to America as a 10-year-old orphan. Mears also constructed a toll road over Poncha Pass to the Arkansas River valley and went on to erect hundreds of miles of roads, notably the "Million Dollar Highway" over Red Mountain Pass, connecting Silverton and Ouray. He became known as the "Pathfinder of the San Juans" and went on to serve in the Colorado legislature.

The railroads tended to lessen the immensity of the nation's western region in the public's imagination. In addition, they lowered travel costs as well as the time it took to traverse distances once regarded as virtually insuperable. Land became cheaper, too, as railroads publicized the availability of large tracts in order to

central Colorado, Leadville came to be called "Cloud City."

It was at the center of an area where first gold and then, in the 1870s, huge slabs of silver carbonate were discovered. Before the good times ran out, the silver yield alone was worth hundreds of millions of dollars. Such a bonanza attracted thousands of settlers. In just a few months the population shot up to 24,000, including a good number of millionaires and madams – Leadville at one point had a bordello for every 148 inhabitants.

Organizing society

Meanwhile, political jurisdictions were being carved out as early as 1858, when Miners'

Courts were set up to resolve the inevitable and often violent disputes over land, stakes and claims. A part of the Kansas Territory was carved out as Arapahoe County, followed by a short-lived entity variously known as Jefferson Territory or Jefferson State. In 1859, Congress responded to pleas that Colorado be admitted to the Union by establishing the Colorado Territory as a prelude to statehood.

Official status as a territory was proclaimed on February 28, 1861, by Abraham Lincoln, whose presidency was about to be burdened with a ferocious Civil War. Lincoln handed the reins of office to William Gilpin as Colorado's first governor. Seventeen counties were created and Colorado City was designated the capital, a distinction that soon passed to Denver and has stayed there since 1867.

On native ground

The Civil War proved to be an aggravating factor in the relationship between native and settler. That relationship was already strained with the influx of fortune-seekers that was transforming the environment. In 1860, the first enumeration of Colorado's highly fluid population counted some 34,000 people. In just two years of the 1860s, the mining rushes brought an estimated 100,000 newcomers to the Colorado plains and mountains. They overran the land, destabilized old ways of life and added insult to injury by disdaining native culture.

The preoccupation with military engagement in other theaters, compounded by the absence of miners who had returned home for army service, left isolated ranches and settlers in the Colorado Territory unprotected from attack by hostile Plains Indians. Hostility intensified in 1862 as Cheyenne and Arapaho warriors harassed settlers and prospectors, attacking wagon trains and ranches and disrupting traffic and supplies on overland corridors like the Santa Fe Trail.

An attempt was made to bring together tribal chiefs for a peace council to iron out differences. What resulted instead was the Sand Creek Massacre of 1864, one of the most notorious of the bloody incidents recorded in the annals of western history.

Sand Creek was a small stream marking the boundary of a barren patch of land that served as an Indian reservation southeast of Denver.

Encamped at the reservation in the autumn of 1864 was a band of Cheyenne people under Black Kettle, as well as Arapaho natives led by Left Hand. Both chiefs had disdained the violent acts committed by native marauders and sought the help of Fort Lyon's commander, Major Edward Wynkoop. He promised protection while terms for better relations were worked out, and gave them food and supplies.

But peace was not the goal of officials more in sync with a public mood enraged by the depredations of Native Americans, especially officials with political ambitions like Colorado's

The ill-fated silver baron Horace Tabor.

GOLD DIGGERS OF 1859

The flow of people moving west as precious metals were unearthed in California, Colorado, and elsewhere was one of America's great migrations. Horace Greeley, the sobersided editor of the *New York Tribune*, reported on Colorado's lively camp scene for his readers. While inspecting the "Kansas gold fields" in June 1859, he wrote with dismay of the "log city" of 150 dwellings at Cherry Creek (Denver) that was the scene of "more brawls, more fights, more pistol shots with criminal intent" than any place of comparable size. He found similar frenzy elsewhere in that hectic year, when fortune-seeking prospectors swamped the territory.

Territorial Governor John Evans or Colonel John M. Chivington, the "fighting parson." Chivington, a Methodist minister and Colorado hero for his resistance to Confederate incursion at Glorieta Pass in New Mexico, is said to have preached with Bible and six-shooter at hand.

Chivington launched a severe anti-Indian policy, eschewing any distinction between peaceful or hostile natives. The sympathetic Wynkoop was replaced, and Black Kettle was forced to confine his Cheyenne band to the Sand Creek strip. This was for the tribe's own safety, the chief was told. In fact, a force of about

John Chivington led an unprovoked attack on Cheyenne and Arapaho Indians at Sand Creek in 1864.

700 volunteer soldiers was on the way from Denver, under Chivington's command.

At dawn on November 29, the Third Colorado Volunteers launched a surprise attack on the Sand Creek encampment, gunfire awakening most of its inhabitants. What followed was the slaughter of some 150 people, mostly women and children. Their mutilated body parts would be waved triumphantly in Denver to raucous cheers.

Elsewhere in the nation, however, there was outrage and widespread condemnation over the wanton massacre. Chivington's expedient resignation from the Army saved him from punishment, and Governor Evans resigned as well.

The Ute solution

One final obstacle remained before fortune-seekers could exploit the land for all it was worth: the Ute Indians. They comprised several bands whose traditional native habitat was western Colorado and eastern Utah, and their turf was increasingly being overrun by miners. Skillful both as equestrians and mountain people, they hunted deer, elk, and antelope, roamed east across the Rockies to pursue buffalo on the Plains, and delighted in racing huge herds of horses across the open landscape.

Their isolation ensured a peaceful existence, until the inevitable conflict caused by a wave of prospectors at once determined and fearful of the "savages" blocking progress. Acts of horse thievery and murderous atrocity by lawless native people fed resentment in mining-suffused places like Denver, and the press helped foster a public sentiment whose undisguised message was "the Utes must go!"

A treaty was negotiated in 1863, thanks largely to the efforts of Chief Ouray, the exceptionally talented Ute leader. It promised 16 million acres (6.5 million hectares) for a vast Ute reservation in western Colorado. With the occurrence of rich new strikes, however, this was reduced when the Utes were prevailed on to sell back 4 million acres (1.6 million hectares) at a bargain price. The treaty was again undermined when strained relations between the federal Indian Bureau and the Utes turned deadly.

As agents persisted in efforts at domesticating and reining in these seminomadic people, a band of northern Utes in 1879 took

THE CIVIL WAR IN COLORADO

Colorado governor William Gilpin's staunch support of the Union during the Civil War proved costly. In 1862, he was forced out for exceeding his authority in issuing drafts on the national treasury on behalf of a military force – largely raised by himself – to represent the territory in the war. (Gilpin was replaced by John Evans, who himself would be ousted after the notorious 1864 Sand Creek Massacre.) Later, the First Regiment of Colorado helped resist Confederate advances, especially in the important engagement at Glorieta Pass near Santa Fe, New Mexico, that ended Southern designs on Western gold.

out their frustration on Indian Bureau agent Nathan C. Meeker at the White River Agency. Originally one of Greeley's editors at the *New York Tribune*, Meeker had been the guiding force behind the establishment of Union Colony, a farming cooperative northeast of Denver that established the first irrigation project in Colorado.

Meeker and six others were killed and three women taken as hostages. The marauding Utes then took on a detachment of army cavalry that had been sent to help Meeker with his domestication effort. Fourteen soldiers were killed and many wounded. Chief Ouray and Otto Mears worked out a truce, and the hostages were released, unhurt though not unmolested. Federal officials used the incident to lay aside the treaty and confine the Utes to small holdings in Utah and eventually southwestern Colorado. By the time of Chief Ouray's death in 1880, of natural causes, the days of an unbridled way of life for Colorado's native people were effectively over.

Cattle kings

The gold rush of 1859 indirectly provided the stimulus for another of Colorado's important economic enterprises: cattle raising. Cattle men took their herds north from Texas to Colorado's eastern plains, where the animals grazed before being shipped to meatpacking centers, Chicago in particular. One emerging entrepreneur was John Wesley Iliff, "cattle king of the Plains."

Iliff had some 50,000 head of cattle grazing over a wide region along the South Platte River. A thirst for western adventure had propelled this native Ohioan to the fledgling Cherry Creek gold camp in 1859, and shortly afterward he decided to invest in a small herd of cattle.

Iliff's fortune grew, as did that of another cattle baron, John Wesley Prowers. A native Missourian, Prowers went to work, while still in his teens, for William Bent, who had set up a trading center in 1832, and became a successful stock raiser and dealer who controlled 400,000 acres (162,000 hectares), opened a slaughterhouse in southern Colorado, and shipped meat to the East. Also emerging in this period was the Denver Union Stockyards, established in 1886 and quickly becoming the nation's largest sheep market.

Populations grew steadily as the 19th century wound down, reaching 413,249 by 1890 – more than twice what it had been a decade earlier and a far cry from the 1870 total of 39,864. Railroads were an important stimulus, as reflected by the terminals that went up in a wave of emerging structures and institutions. Denver got a telegraph link with the East in 1863, phones in 1878, electric lights in 1883. Colorado Seminary, forerunner of the University of Denver, was established in 1864, while Colorado State University at Fort Collins dates to 1870. Then came Colorado College at Colorado Springs in 1874. Still another new school, the University of Colorado at Boulder, held its first classes in 1877.

Ouray (center) and other Ute leaders, c.1868. Ouray led the efforts to live peacefully with the US Government.

The booming prosperity brought theaters, hotels, commercial emporiums, and public buildings. Grandly constructed opera houses went up in mining towns such as Leadville and Aspen, as well as in Denver. President Ulysses S. Grant signed the legislation which on August 1, 1876, granted Colorado admission to the Union as its 38th state. It thereupon became known as the "Silver State" and, more officially, the "Centennial State" – the nation was celebrating 100 years of independence that summer.

The first governor was John L. Routt, for whom Routt National Forest in central Colorado would be named. The state was entering its headiest period between 1876 and 1893, when suddenly everything fell apart.

The crash

Silver prices took a nose-dive in that panic year of 1893, and Colorado took it especially hard. The problem was that huge amounts of the precious metal coming out of western mines were flooding the world's markets, undermining price stability by putting the gold standard in jeopardy. This did not sit well with the power brokers in the big financial houses back East and elsewhere.

British investors were attracted to the Colorado cattle industry, which thrived in the Arkansas and South Platte river valleys. Cattle kingdoms evolved by the 1880s into large ranch companies with operations from Texas to Colorado.

heady prosperity that marked the 1880s in Colorado. Newly coined millionaires in towns like Aspen, where silver had been discovered in 1879, saw their fortunes wiped out.

The aftermath of the Meeker massacre.

For them, gold was the only measuring stick that mattered. Impassioned arguments for a policy of bi-metallism – silver and gold – by such as Henry Moore Teller, who represented Colorado in the US Senate, failed to persuade his Republican colleagues. In an attempt to rejuvenate the national economy, Congress in November 1893 repealed the Sherman Silver Purchase Act it had approved just three years earlier. That policy, which authorized the US Treasury to purchase so much silver per month, had raised the white metal's price to more than $1 an ounce.

Congress's action crippled the mining industry, worsened the state's already severe rate of unemployment, and brought an end to the

In disgust, Teller deserted his Grand Old Party for the Democrats, who made the whole money question a potent, though unsuccessful, campaign issue in 1896 under presidential contender William Jennings Bryan. "You shall not crucify mankind upon a cross of gold!" Bryan thundered in his famous speech accepting the nomination.

The only silver lining – gold, actually – was the bonanza that occurred at Cripple Creek. A mining probe at Bob Womack's cattle ranch there in 1891 unearthed a fabulous lode that would soon make the place famous as one of the world's richest gold centers. Eventually, gold production amounted to half a billion dollars.

Wild about Oscar

In one of the strangest lecture tours in literary history, celebrated wit Oscar Wilde toured America in 1882 and drew appreciative audiences in Colorado's mining towns.

A most unlikely gathering took place on April 13, 1882, in Leadville, Colorado, when the young Oscar Fingal O'Flahertie Wills Wilde, aesthete and rising star of London's smart set, could be seen putting away drink after drink with the working-class guys down in the depths of the Matchless Mine owned by Horace ("Silver King") Tabor.

The bibulous Mr Wilde emerged from his underground experience no worse for wear. The miners pronounced the Irish visitor "a perfect gentleman," while Tabor opened a new shaft in his honor – "The Oscar." Of the many memorable moments in Wilde's year-long safari through darkest America in 1882, this one surely ranked high.

Oscar Wilde's outlandish garb and wit had attracted public notice in Britain, and he and theatrical impresario Richard D'Oyly Carte were seeking to capitalize on it with an American lecture tour. Wilde arrived in New York after his maiden voyage across the Atlantic, claiming he found the ocean "disappointing" and telling the customs officer he had nothing to declare "but my genius."

Wilde jested his way cross-country, reportedly saying of the tempestuous Mississippi, "No well-behaved river ought to act that way." He reached Colorado on April 12, lecturing that night from the stage of Tabor's new opera house, then it was on to Leadville, Colorado Springs, and back to Denver again for a fourth straight night of preaching on the importance of being artful. In Leadville, he stayed next door at the Clarendon Hotel, where Tabor had installed his young paramour, Baby Doe, in an elegant suite.

Nothing to declare but my genius

A standard lecture topic was "The Practical Application of the Aesthetic Theory to Exterior and Interior House Decoration, with Observations on Dress and Personal Ornament." Gaudily attired in frilly white cravat, silk knee breeches, silk stockings, and patent-leather pumps, Wilde poked fun at American sartorial drabness by declaring the miners "the best-dressed men in America." Visiting a

Leadville saloon, he remarked favorably on a sign reading: "PLEASE DO NOT SHOOT THE PIANIST. HE IS DOING HIS BEST." Here, he said, was succinct recognition "that bad art merits the penalty of death . . . the only rational method of art criticism I have ever come across."

How much his creative flair and poetic license colored the remembrances he later put to paper is uncertain, but there were some good lines all the same. Wilde claimed that he read from the pages of the autobiography of Benvenuto Cellini, the Renaissance artisan, and was pressed by the unlettered miners as to why Cellini had not come

Oscar Wilde was a hit with Colorado miners.

along on the tour. Told that Cellini was long dead, the miners are supposed to have asked: "Who shot him?"

Wilde was the object of a prankish diversion at the start of his Colorado visit, courtesy of the muck-raking *Denver Tribune* editor Eugene Field. As interest in Wilde's impending visit mounted, Field took it upon himself to deflate some of the mystique surrounding this reputedly cultured visitor. He donned longish wig and fur-trimmed overcoat and arrived at the Denver railway station just ahead of Wilde's scheduled time of arrival.

Field was thus mistaken for Wilde and whisked off grandly through town in a carriage. By the time the real Oscar Wilde arrived, no crowd was on hand to greet him.

Cage Scene, Ajax Mine.
Flashlight by.

CHANGING FORTUNES

Beyond mines and metals lay other natural resources, and they were cultivated in a variety of ways, as a fledgling state invented itself.

Colorado has a checkered history. Plenty of ups and downs, boom and bust. Gold and silver camps flourished, then faded into ghost towns when the treasure ran dry or the bottom dropped out of the market. To survive it was necessary to adapt, which is what Coloradans did, and still do, as they seek new ways to take advantage of their plentiful resources.

In the early years of the 20th century, agriculture surpassed mining as the state's chief economic enterprise. There was abundant fertile farmland in Colorado's eastern plains region, land that would yield a bounty of wheat, corn, soybeans, and much else. What was always crucial was water, brought in by irrigation systems devised to overcome the problem of insufficient rainfall and the inconvenient fact that so much of the moisture needed was far off in the headlands of Colorado's Western Slope.

Tapping water

Irrigation schemes were undertaken, from simple diversion of water in streams and creeks to large-scale projects requiring heavy outlays of federal money and local labor. Thus did agriculture and animal husbandry flourish. Wheat was sown, fruits and vegetables grown, cattle raised, dairy goods produced. One important crop was potatoes. They burgeoned in the mid-1880s, and by 1890 more than 2,000 carloads of potatoes were being shipped by rail each year to the crowded East. Beet sugar became important, too, after a couple of pioneer Leadville merchants, Charles Boettcher and John F. Campion, got together with some others and formed the Great Western Sugar Company. A refinery was built in 1899 at Grand Junction, soon followed by another one at Fort Collins.

Dancers pose at Denver's amusement park, Elitch Gardens, c. 1930.

Sugar beets were cultivated on thousands of acres in Colorado's northeastern and east-central sections. Greeley and Fort Morgan were two other important centers.

Great Western was a bustling agribusiness by the 1920s, and Boettcher prospered as a builder and industrialist. Born in Germany in 1852, he had come to America as a teenager, later purchasing the landmark Brown Palace Hotel in Denver, among many ventures. He died in Denver in 1948 after a long life that spanned the years from Andrew Jackson to Harry Truman.

Meanwhile, the first major federal reclamation project in Colorado got under way in 1903. Its chief feature was the horseshoe-shaped

Gunnison Diversion Tunnel, which conveyed water several miles from the Gunnison River to the Uncompahgre Valley.

By 1910, Colorado had more than 46,000 farms and the state ranked first in the nation in land under irrigation – nearly 2.8 million acres (1.1 million hectares). Agriculture remained the leading economic money-maker. It was surpassed in later years by manufacturing, but recently has undergone a resurgence. Back in the early 20th century, there were some lean years for farmers after the inflationary euphoria of World War I. In the early 1920s, prices

> The Gunnison Diversion Tunnel took six years to build and cost $2.9 million. On hand for the tunnel's opening in 1909 was William Howard Taft, who was at that time the nation's chief executive.

The work went on from 1938 to 1956. Another major enterprise was the Fryingpan–Arkansas Project, authorized in 1962 and also conveying water over a long distance to the Arkansas River valley for public use.

Metals and minerals

Mining remained an important activity, even though the fervor of the early gold and silver rushes abated, and there were new gold strikes and fulsome discoveries of zinc and copper. In 1918, miners from nearby Leadville dug into deposits of molybdenum – "moly," as everybody called it. Mistaken at first for lead, it is in fact valuable as a hardening agent in the production of steel. The mine at Climax, near Leadville, accounted for a big part of the total world output of molybdenum before the decline of steel production shut it down in the 1990s.

Many other minerals and fuels were extracted, including tungsten, uranium, petroleum, and natural gas. Petroleum, the state's leading fuel resource, was found on both the eastern and western slopes. Coal was abundant, too, in both northern and southern Colorado. A record amount of it was dug up in 1918 – 12.5 million tons. Unfortunately, coal mining was at the center of increasingly strained relations between corporate overlords and earthy miners, many of the latter being foreign immigrants.

Ore processing factory, c.1905.

dropped sharply and rural areas suffered. They suffered again in the 1930s, thanks to a lengthy spell of rough weather. Extended drought and high winds, for example, caused severe soil erosion in southeastern Colorado, compounding Depression misery and creating a Dust Bowl.

The state did benefit, at least, from relief programs in the 1930s and beyond. One big undertaking was the Colorado–Big Thompson Project carried out by the US Bureau of Reclamation. Relying on a system of dams, the project diverted water from the headstreams of the Colorado River and across the Continental Divide to irrigate about 720,000 acres (291,400 hectares) of land in the state's northeastern area and supply power for the region.

In the early part of the 20th century, resentment festered over wages and workplace hazards, especially involving laborers in mine operations. For example, two mine disasters in 1910 – at Primero and Delagua – took 153 lives. Bitterness simmered, sometimes spilling over into deadly violence, as in a strike at the Cripple Creek gold field in 1903.

Massacre at Ludlow

The worst moment came in 1914, with the Ludlow Massacre. The trouble started just before dawn on April 20, the day after Easter Sunday. Before it was over, 20 people lay dead, including two women and 11 children who suffocated in a makeshift cellar beneath a tent. It was the climax of a bitter seven-month strike and one of the blackest days in Colorado history. The antagonists were coal miners evicted from company homes for striking, and John D. Rockefeller's Colorado Fuel & Iron Corporation.

National Guardsmen and security guards employed by Rockefeller and associates attacked a colony of coal miners and their families holed up in tents at Ludlow, near Trinidad, in southern Colorado. The strike by thousands of workers had begun in September 1913, following the murder of a labor

Making progress

Reform was in the air in that progressive era, and Colorado seemed a likely proving ground for its propositions. It had already, in 1893, become the second state in the nation to approve women's suffrage – the right to vote – as in 1924 it would become the second state to approve the federal child-labor amendment. In 1907, the city of Denver instituted the first Juvenile Court in America. In 1910, Colorado voters added the good-government principle of initiative and referendum to the state constitution. And the period brought other such inno-

Miners widen the Breast of Gold Standard Tunnel in Teller County, c.1900.

organizer. The tent camp was set ablaze by the attackers, who then opened fire on its panicky inhabitants, levying the deadly toll. News of the onslaught spread quickly among labor circles, and 10 days of gunfire followed. The final toll in the savage 1913–14 Colorado Coal Field Strike was 74 dead.

It was widely perceived as unbridled class warfare, which shocked newspaper readers across the country. The only saving grace, as historians see it, was that the bloodshed probably helped inspire reforms in labor-relations practice and influenced management to begin looking more benignly on collective bargaining and negotiation as a necessary means to resolving workplace issues.

vations, including workers' compensation and, for state employees, civil service status.

Physical improvements were being made, too, as the state began rolling out the welcome mat for visitors. Denver banker David H. Moffatt and associates began pressing in 1902 for a rail line traversing the Continental Divide. Twenty-five years later, it led to completion of the 6.4-mile (10.3km) Moffatt Tunnel, at an altitude of 9,094ft (2,772 meters), beneath James Peak on the Continental Divide, west of Denver. Used by the Denver & Rio Grande Railway, it put Colorado for the first time on a direct transcontinental rail route.

A toll road for motorists intent on ascending Pikes Peak was built in 1915, two years after

Colorado issued its first automobile license. The year 1915 also saw the creation of Rocky Mountain National Park as a federal preserve. In 1918, the Denver city administration set aside Overland Park as an auto campground for free use by tourists. And in 1921 the state began construction of concrete highways along its main travel corridors.

Moved by her experience atop Pikes Peak in 1893, American poet Katharine Lee Bates penned her classic anthem, "America the Beautiful."

Military influence

The military presence in Colorado went back to the frontier forts, which were charged with protecting traders, travelers, and settlers. But it was the military presence that resulted from

border where some 10,000 Japanese-Americans were interned for the duration of the war.

Camps, arsenals, ordnance centers, and aviation bases were created. In 1942, Fort Carson was established as an Army reservation on an enormous tract of land at the southern edge of

Striking miners armed for confrontation with National Guardsmen during the Ludlow Massacre.

World War II that most affected the state's development. More than 70,000 residents were inducted into the armed services, and the private sector kept busy meeting the nation's extraordinary need for metals, minerals, and manufactured goods, as well as agricultural products. But it was Colorado's emergence as a base of defense-related operations that transformed its socioeconomic profile. In 1937, the federal government opened a field school on 64,000 acres (26,000 hectares) of land near Denver for use by the Army Air Corps as a training facility for aerial photography and bombing. It became Lowry Field. Then, during the war, more bases and installations sprang up – including, unhappily, a camp on the Kansas

Colorado Springs. A dozen years later, Colorado was chosen as the site for an Air Force Academy to complement the traditional Army, Navy and Coast Guard institutions. It was based at Lowry Air Force Base in Denver, before relocating to Colorado Springs in 1958 and graduating its first class there a year later.

Colorado Springs became the base of operations as well for the North American Air Defense Command, established in 1957 and hunkering down in a cave burrowed into Cheyenne Mountain. A third of Colorado's land is federally owned. As a result, it is home to many nationally important scientific enterprises, including the National Center for Atmospheric Research at Boulder, and leading schools like the University of Colorado, the Colorado School of Mines, Colorado State University, and the University of Denver. Concerns about pollution arising out of the weapons plants and military-related manufacturing activity of the post-war period has led to major cleanup efforts to ease the fear of contamination from chemicals and other hazardous waste at places like Rocky Flats near Boulder and elsewhere, an ongoing situation.

The state at play

In the years after World War II, the state began to enjoy an enhanced reputation as a recrea-

What most famously put Colorado on the map as a vacationer's mecca, however, was its emergence as a favored location for skiing. Such activity began taking off in popularity most decidedly in the 1950s. Crude skis had been used in earlier times by pioneers and prospectors for such basic needs as laying in food and delivering mail. The year 1914 saw a ski jump built at Steamboat Springs and the start of a winter festival that has persisted ever since.

Around the same time, skiing began as a popular pursuit at Denver, Boulder, and Colorado Springs. A ski run with a jump was created

Cowboys in the San Luis Valley, 1909.

tional haven. Visitors had long been inspired by the majestic landscape. Among them were 19th-century artists like Albert Bierstadt, famous for his idealized depictions of western landscapes in paintings like *Storm in the Rocky Mountains.*

The creation of national parks such as Mesa Verde (1906) and Rocky Mountain (1915) and Dinosaur National Monument (1915) stirred public interest, and the designation of land for recreational purposes encouraged such pursuits as fishing, hunting, canoeing, camping, and mountain climbing. Colorado was attracting health-seekers, outdoors enthusiasts, and antiquarian-minded vacationers curious about the old mining camps and Gilded Age glamour evoked by historic restorationists.

on Genesee Mountain west of Denver, while in the other two towns ski clubs were formed. It was also the city of Denver that in 1938 established a ski area at Winter Park near the Moffatt Tunnel, with trains soon hauling skiers to the slopes. Colorado's first rope tow was installed in 1937 at nearby Berthoud Pass, and other communities began designating ski areas.

Two places that have become exceptionally well known in the public imagination as Colorado skiing centers are Aspen and Vail. Aspen was a roaring silver camp that made men rich in the 1880s before its luck changed. It was rejuvenated in the 1940s by the industrialist Walter P. Paepke and his wife, Elizabeth. She had taken a fancy to the shabby town high up on the

Continental Divide and induced her husband to invest in its potential. They developed it into a mountain resort that became doubly famous for winter skiing and summer cultural seminars.

A similar enterprise came into being at Vail, which was developed in the late 1950s by a master skier named Pete Seibert, and Earl Eaton, a uranium prospector. Taking note of the sport's growing popularity, they began acquiring land in the area and opened their resort in 1962. Seibert had served during World War II with the new Tenth Mountain Division based at Camp Hale high in the Rockies. Recruits were trained there for eventual ski-clad combat in the Italian Alps. The division suffered heavy losses in the war.

Tourism in Colorado has grown to huge proportions – an estimated one-tenth of the state's population is involved in the industry. Probably the most telling sign of its strength came in 1995 with the opening, after much delay, of the expansive Denver International Airport. One of the world's busiest airports, covering an area twice the size of Manhattan in New York City, it aptly represented Colorado's bullish spirit on the eve of the 21st century.

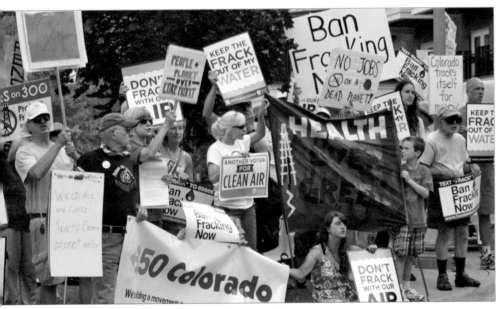

Anti-fracking demonstration, Aspen.

DISAFFECTION AND MASSACRES IN THE DENVER AREA

There's a dark side to the American Dream in the Interior West. It's easy to feel hemmed in by the cookie-cutter suburbs and dwarfed by the beautiful yet impersonal landscape. Some people flame out in spectacular ways. The Columbine High School Massacre in Littleton, on April 20, 1999, is a sobering example of what happens when parents and teachers ignore festering youth problems. Bullied by high-school jocks, and caught up in goth culture, the internet, video games, and revenge fantasies, seniors Dylan Kliebold and Eric Harris shot and killed 12 students, one teacher, and wounded 24 other students, before turning the guns on themselves. Sadly, Kliebold and Harris are not the only youngsters to have planned and executed a gun massacre in Colorado. On July 20, 2012, a mass shooting occurred inside a movie theater in Aurora, near Littleton, during a midnight screening of the film *The Dark Knight Rises*. A gunman, dressed in tactical clothing, set off tear-gas grenades and shot into the audience with multiple firearms, killing 12 people and injuring 70 others. The suspect, James Eagan Holmes, was arrested outside the cinema minutes later. In March 2013, Governor John Hickenlooper signed three separate gun-control laws: one limits ammunition, one requires background checks, and one charges gun customers for the checks. Despite challenges, these laws were upheld in court in June 2016.

Runaway growth

From the mid-1960s on, the state's most rapid growth has occurred in the crowded eastern sector that runs from Fort Collins, north of Denver, to Pueblo in southeastern Colorado, a region known as the Front Range Urban Corridor. The boom in computer-related technology intensified in the 1980s and gave rise to many high-tech businesses. As a result, the suburban landscape around the Denver Metro Area has been transformed and afflicted with such headaches as snarled highways, sprawling subdivisions of identical tract housing, and pollution. Public concern about managing infrastructure was serious enough to cause voters to decline to foot the bill when Denver was selected to host the 1976 Winter Olympics, forcing the IOC to move the event to Innsbruck, Austria.

Until the Great Recession of 2008, which saw record foreclosures in the Denver suburbs, contraction of the once-thriving jobs market, and a Colorado unemployment rate of 8 percent, young adults had been attracted to Colorado in droves. Marijuana sales have helped the economy rebound strongly since 2014, when it was legalized in Colorado, and unemployment has now plummeted to the 3.6 percent mark. Colorado is highly educated, with the second highest population of BAs in the country. The majority of new residents are California transplants, drawn by high-tech jobs, a healthy climate, and Colorado's recreational charms, bringing with them a liberal political mind-set that has rearranged the political map in Colorado. The once Republican state went Democrat in 2008 and has remained so through two election cycles, which saw Denver once again dominate the national political stage. Colorado's Democratic credentials, which have helped get gun control bills passed, as well as same-sex civil unions and recreational marijuana, derive from widespread Front Range liberalism and the influx of Latino immigrants into the Denver area. Rural parts of the state remain largely Republican, however, and still exert considerable influence. In September 2013, NRA supporters won a stunning victory in Colorado's first recall election in history, succeeding in ousting the two Democratic senators who had sponsored Colorado's gun control bills: Senate President John Morse (Colorado Springs) and Senator Angela Giron (Pueblo).

Colorado's accelerated growth is rooted in the 1950s, fueled by tourism and federal expenditures on generally defense-related enterprises. Indeed, its growth rate was four times the national average in 2010, and a state that counted 539,700 residents a century earlier is now home to 5.5 million people, most living on the Front Range. Metropolitan sprawl is a major issue. Denver's light rail has proved successful, but public transportation in the metro area is still hit or miss, and other than a few pedestrian-friendly spots such as Boulder, most Front Range residents spend hours commuting in their cars. Many choose to live in the delightful small mining towns

Suburban Erie.

in the steep foothills around Boulder, but the construction of homes in rocky, forested terrain subject to wildfires and other natural events is risky. In early September 2013, the Front Range was hit by massive flooding from a freak storm system. More than 17 inches of rain fell on Boulder and neighboring canyons to the north, such as Jamestown and Lyons, already denuded by wildfire in 2012, which were cut off for days. Ten people died, over 1,852 homes and 203 businesses were destroyed, and thousands more were damaged, and Mother Nature took charge, destroying much in her path. Damages rose to nearly $4 billion, and almost no one carried flood insurance.

Crystal River.

Red rock formations in the Garden of the Gods.

THE BACKBONE OF THE CONTINENT

The Rockies run through Colorado like a crooked spine, with more than 50 peaks soaring beyond 14,000ft (4,270 meters). The state is called America's Switzerland, but it has a character that is all its own.

I t's called the Rocky Mountain State, and mountains are its primary attraction – range after range of big, beautiful, sky-scraping peaks laid down in ancient seas, rivers, floodplains, and deserts over millennia, thrust up and tilted by volcanism, etched by glaciers, and eroded away by time.

In few other places is alpine scenery so alluring. Frigidly beautiful throughout the snowy winter, when skiers flock to the slopes. Gray and austere on the windy summits after spring melt, when nature slowly begins to wake up. Skirted in phosphorescent green meadows and brilliant wildflowers in summer, and splashed with aspen golds in fall, when warm temperatures attract hikers, campers, bikers, horseback riders, and four-wheel-drivers.

Perhaps it is because there are so many of them that Colorado's numerous mountain ranges seem so majestic. That, and the fact that 54 of the state's peaks top 14,000ft (4,270 meters), with many more clearing 12,000ft (3,660 meters). No doubt about it, this is America's Switzerland.

Varied terrain

Other than the mountains, what is less known about Colorado's geography is that it is remarkably diverse. The state is shaped like a large rectangle. To the east, the Great Plains meet the sawtooth peaks of the Front Range like an ocean lapping against the wall of a giant medieval fortress. At the southeastern end of the Rockies, between the plains and the San Juan Mountains, stretches the massive San Luis Valley, an extension of the volcanic Rio Grande Rift Valley, which lies to the south, in New Mexico.

View of the San Juan Mountains.

Most dramatic of all is the meeting of two geological provinces on the Western Slope: the Rocky Mountains and the 130,000 sq miles (340,000 sq km) of horizontal sedimentary rocks that make up the Colorado Plateau. Cracked by faults, uplifted by volcanism, and downcut by the river system for which it is named, this unique mile-high plateau of redrock mesas, buttes, and deep, shadowy canyons makes a spectacular counterpoint to the Rocky Mountains, rising to the east.

Parks and rivers

At 100,000 miles (260,000 sq km), Colorado is the eighth largest state in the Union. It is joined by Wyoming to the north, Utah to the west, Arizona to the southwest, New Mexico to the south, and Kansas to the east. The different ranges that make up the Rocky Mountains cover much of the state. Running through

Little-visited Dinosaur National Monument in northeastern Colorado preserves not only one of the country's largest caches of dinosaur fossils but also 2 billion years of geological strata, the most intact record in the National Park System.

Monument, for example, were laid down at least 1.8 billion years ago as sea sediments, which gradually hardened into horizontal sedimentary limestone strata. These Precambrian Era sedimentary rocks were later subjected to a long period of volcanism. Intense heat and pressure forced the soft sedimentary rocks to undergo a metamorphosis into hard gneisses and schists. Later intrusions of hot magma formed a core of crystalline igneous granite intrusions in these rocks. During the next 1.5 billion years, they were uplifted repeatedly, worn down into plateaus by erosion, and covered by sediments.

Sandstone formations rise above the Yampa River in Echo Park, part of the Canyons section of Dinosaur National Monument.

Rocky Mountain National Park and down through the central San Juan Mountains of the Southern Rockies is the nation's Continental Divide, where major river systems flow east or west. The Colorado River and its tributaries – the Green, Yampa, Dolores, Gunnison, and Animas rivers – flow west to the Pacific Ocean. The Arkansas and North and South Platte rivers and the Rio Grande flow east to the Atlantic.

The making of the Rockies

The towering Rockies on view today have their origins in geologic events that go back to the dawn of life on Earth. The oldest rocks in Rocky Mountain National Park and Dinosaur National

The Ancestral Rockies did not make their first appearance until the Pennsylvanian Period (325 to 280 million years ago), when a phase of mountain building, known as the Colorado Orogeny, lifted up two huge mountain islands – Frontrangia and Uncompahgria – in the midst of another inland sea. These Ancestral Rockies were much higher than the modern Rockies, with huge basins between and west of the ranges.

As the climate warmed and dried, during the Permian Period (280 to 240 million years ago), the inland sea withdrew to the west, leaving behind salt deposits several miles thick. Rainwater attacking the new mountains created streams and rivers that abraded red iron-rich sediments, carrying them from the highlands into the basins, initially mingling with the salt in colorful bands and later forming thick red-bed deposits.

One of these huge basins, the Paradox, straddled what is now the Colorado–Utah border on the edge of what's called Canyon Country. Its basement formation, the "Paradox salt formation," became so compressed by later sedimentary deposits, the salt actually became plastic and began to move away from the overburden, doming up along faults, entering joints in the rocks, and dissolving in

groundwater. As joints widened, groundwater created long fins in the sandstone that wind and ice sculpted into the arches and other famous landmarks in Colorado National Monument and Utah's Arches National Park. In Colorado, the eroded sandstone formations at Red Rocks Park, west of Denver, are far older, part of the original redbed deposits shed from the Ancestral Rockies, 300 million years ago.

Dinosaur haven

Throughout the Triassic period (240 to 200 million years ago), erosion continued to wear down the Ancestral Rockies, and the warming climate and withdrawal of the sea left behind broad floodplains and deltas. The Age of Fishes now gave way to the Age of Reptiles – huge dinosaurs such as the platey-backed Stegosaurus, the state emblem. Large and small dinosaurs sloshed about in the floodplains and marshes of northwestern Colorado, which, as the continents drifted on their red-hot sea of magma, far below the surface, was close to where West Africa is today.

Enormous conifers and cycad ferns grew in the humid conditions, becoming compressed into soft shales that would eventually yield some of the country's largest deposits of oil, gas, and coal in northwestern Colorado. During a major flood at a river crossing near the location of present-day Green River, hundreds of dinosaurs were wiped out as they tried to ford the swollen waterway. These unfortunates were buried in the river sediments where they died, gradually

NATURAL RESOURCES

Colorado is rich in gold, silver, lead, coal, oil, gas, and uranium and has long attracted miners to its lands. Early prospectors concentrated on extracting placer deposits of native gold flakes found in stream gravels and sands in the South Platte River near Denver. When these deposits played out, the prospectors sold their stakes to large mining companies with the deep pockets and latest equipment to reach lodes, or veins, of gold deep underground. Silver was discovered in the 1860s, creating overnight boom-towns in places like Silverton and Creede, followed by veins of lead and zinc, uncovered during searches for gold and silver in the San Juan Mountains.

Uranium, found in western Colorado near Paradox, is associated with the fossil-rich Chinle and Morrison formations. Following World War II, company towns like Unavan became one of the country's major producers of carnotite, which yields uranium as well as vanadium. Unavan and other uranium towns remained in business until the 1980s, when local production was no longer profitable. Small, rich deposits of oil, gas, and coal have also lured energy companies to western Colorado since the early 1900s. The Piceance Basin, north of Grand Junction, contains huge quantities of oil shale laid down in the mud of a lake 50 million years ago.

becoming entombed in the pale crumbly Morrison Formation. The skeleton of one of these dinosaur casualties – a brontosaur – was discovered in the early 1900s by Carnegie Museum paleontologist Earl Douglas (see page 285), just north of Jensen, Utah. Other museums quarried specimens for display until, in 1906, President Theodore Roosevelt set aside Dinosaur National Monument to halt the removal. The embedded bones of other dinosaurs are on display in the newly constructed Quarry Exhibit Hall, near Quarry Visitor Center at the monument.

Dinosaurs are exhibited and explained at the Museum of Nature and Science.

The modern landscape

The contemporary Rockies arose just as the Age of Dinosaurs was giving way to the Age of Mammals at the end of the Cretaceous period, 65 million years ago. In a now familiar ritual, giant blocks of ancient crystalline rock, overlaid by younger sedimentary rock, broke and were thrust upward. The origins of this major mountain building period lay to the west, off the present-day California coast, where the oceanic Pacific Plate continues to dive under the North American Plate, forcing up the Sierra Nevada and coastal mountains.

These distant seismic movements substantially changed the topography of the Interior

Carved by the Gunnison River through the Gunnison Plateau a million years ago, Black Canyon of the Gunnison National Park is deeper, narrower, steeper, and younger than the Grand Canyon, Yosemite, or Yellowstone.

West. Stretching and thinning of the earth's surface east of the Sierra Nevada created the Basin and Range topography of the Mojave Desert around Death Valley. In the Southwest, reverberating plate movements wrinkled the earth's surface into huge sedimentary uplifts known as monoclines, such as Utah's Waterpocket Fold, and in Colorado created the Rockies. Although they would be leveled once more by erosion, most of the structure of the Rockies came into being during this period of intense mountain building, known as the Laramide Orogeny. Now, where a great sea had lain 100 million years ago, the Great Plains appeared. As rivers and streams eroded materials from the highlands, it shed into this vast basin to the east. Eventually, sediments more than 13,000ft (4,000 meters) thick would cover what is now Kansas and the other Mid-western states.

The Rockies that are visible today did not appear until between 80–50 million years ago, during the Miocene-Pliocene Uplift, when faulting and regional upwarping lifted the Rocky Mountain Front Range as much as 5,000ft (1,500 meters) to its present height. In southwest Colorado, ongoing volcanism during the Oligocene Epoch, 28 million

THE GEOLOGY OF BUILDINGS

Ever wondered about the geology of buildings? David Williams has. In *Stories in Stone*, he devotes one chapter to William Brown's gas station in Lamar, Colorado. Built in the 1930s, the 15 by 35ft (4.5 by 10.5-meter) structure is made of 100 pieces of petrified wood gathered from a wash south of town and set in a castellated pattern reminiscent of a miniature castle. The *Lamar Daily News* raved: "Here is a building worthy of study… observe these marvelous trees… they stand to remind you of the ancient ages long ago, and to serve you with the modern fluid which is the vital touch of our ultra-modern motor-age."

years ago, created the San Juan Mountains, or Southern Rockies. This volcanism, which formed the major peaks of the San Juans and San Luis Valley, continues to affect western Colorado and accounts for the numerous geothermal hot springs found along faults in the western San Juans.

Lava lands

It is hot magma rising along faults at the edge of the Rocky Mountains and Colorado Plateau that has helped give the landscape of the Four Corners its distinctive appearance. In western Colorado, the ancient Uncompahgre Uplift that created the Ancestral Rockies forced up the Uncompahgre Plateau, which has been gradually exposed as the Colorado River and its tributaries cut into it. Where hot lava reached the surface within the last couple of million years, it frequently sits atop sedimentary rocks from eons of inland seas, beaches, rivers, and streams. Southwest of Grand Junction, Grand Mesa is the largest lava plateau in the world. Just to the south, the Gunnison River has carved a pathway through an enormous lava dome at Black Canyon of the Gunnison

The glacier-carved peaks of Maroon Bells.

GETTING INTO HOT WATER

Although they are found all over the state, hot springs abound in the western Rockies, where they have long been sacred to Native Americans. In southwestern Colorado, Pagosa Springs was used by Ancestral Puebloans living at nearby Chimney Rock. Later, it was called pagosa, or "big healing waters," by Southern Utes who revered the steaming pools. Utes and Arapahos laid down their arms and bathed together at Manitou Springs in northwestern Colorado. And in the western San Juan Mountains, Ouray, chief of the Northern Utes, frequently bathed in the hot springs in the town that now bears his name, in order to ease his arthritis.

Some 50 known thermal springs rise along faults in the volcanically active Rocky Mountains, ranging in temperature from 68°F (20°C) to 181°F (83°C). Rustic resorts have grown up around many of these hot spots. Some, such as clothing-optional, family-run Orvis Hot Springs, south of Ridgway, remain pleasantly low-key, while others, such as those in Steamboat Springs, Ouray, and Pagosa Springs, have been developed into popular public facilities with attached therapy rooms. Colorado's best-known hot springs are Glenwood Springs, where the 90°F (32°C) pool is two soccer fields long, the largest in the world. During the 2000 Winter Olympics, the Olympic torch was swum through the pool en route to Salt Lake City.

National Park and created an awe-inspiring, black chasm nearly a mile deep.

Where overlying sedimentary rocks were thickest, hot magma welling up along faults domed up the landscape but never reached the surface. The resulting humped formations, known as laccoliths, encircle the large basins adjacent to uplifted areas. One good place to see them is at Far View Visitor Center at Mesa Verde National Park in southwestern Colorado. Nearby Sleeping Ute Mountain and more distant Navajo Mountain have been sacred landmarks for native people for centuries. In some

The ever-shifting dunes of Great Sand Dunes National Monument at the base of the Sangre de Cristo Mountains.

instances, erosion has completely stripped away the sedimentary rocks, revealing the volcanic cores of these formations. Ship Rock, which plays a major role in the origin stories of the Navajo, is clearly visible in the 25,000 sq mile (65,000 sq km) San Juan Basin, south of the San Juan River.

The power of ice

In the Rockies, the main erosional force has been four periods of glaciation, which began during a cooling trend early in the Quaternary Period, 2 million years ago, and continued until the end of the Ice Age, 10,000 years ago. In Colorado's higher valleys, snow became compacted into rivers of ice, or glaciers, which began to flow down the narrow valleys. Telltale signs of their passage can be seen throughout the Rockies. River-cut V-shaped ravines have been widened into characteristic U-shaped valleys. Peaks have been carved into jagged pinnacles, knife-edge aretes and bowl-like depressions known as cirques that frequently fill with meltwater.

The relentless grinding of glaciers scoured the valleys, leaving behind striations, grooved and polished surfaces caused by transported rocks. Some boulders, aptly known as erratics, were marooned atop smooth granite in the high country. Other rock debris, called moraine, was carried into the lower valleys. A distinctive feature of glaciated valleys is the way moraines have been deposited. As the glaciers made their way down the valleys, debris (or till) has left behind lateral moraines. Glacial till is most visible at the bottom of valleys, where melting glaciers finally drop their largest load of eroded material as a terminal moraine. Frequently in such places, glacial meltwater has created crystal-clear lakes filled with blue-green glacial flour, made up of suspended ice particles.

Not all lakes in the high country were created by glacial moraines. The lake that gave Lake City in the San Juans its name was formed when a mud slide, the Slumgullion Earthflow, slid off the mountains and blocked the Gunnison River. Rock slides are common throughout the high country of the Rockies, where flows of massive boulders spill down steep mountainsides.

Most mobile of all are the soils that have shed from the San Juan Mountains and been carried through San Luis Valley by the Rio Grande. As the river changed course, the sandy deposits were left victim to the powerful southwesterly winds that blow through the valley. Sometimes reaching more than 40mph (64km/h), these winds scoop up the grains of sand and buffet the 14,000ft (4,270-meter) Sangre de Cristo Mountains. The sand is too heavy to funnel through the mountain passes. As the winds continue their passage out of the valley their sandy cargo is left cradled at the base of the foothills, creating sand dunes 700ft (215 meters) high, the tallest in America. The area is preserved within Great Sand Dunes National Park and Preserve.

Heritage tourism

Today, Colorado is renowned as much for its family farms and markets, and ancient cultural attractions, as for its superb skiing.

For struggling farmers, ranchers, and others in Colorado's rural areas, many of whom have worked the land for generations, ecotourism has become an important lifeline during tough times. Assisted by an innovative state heritage program, regional tourism hubs, and direct marketing on the internet, many have taken control of their own destinies, offering numerous interesting activities, from horsemanship, cattle drives, and trail maintenance to you-pick produce, egg gathering, and harvest dinners featuring local food and wine.

Southwestern Colorado is famous for its archeological heritage. At Crow Canyon Archeological Center near Cortez, you can take part in an ongoing archeological dig at a significant Pueblo site near Mesa Verde National Park. Kelly Place, a very reasonably priced bed-and-breakfast in McElmo Canyon, has 25 archeological sites on its 40-acre (16 -hectare) property and offers professionally guided tours of other archeological sites in the area. At the other end of the spectrum, Canyon of the Ancients Guest Ranch rents luxury vacation homes, and you can even pick your own produce for supper. After the Pueblo people moved on in the late 1200s, they were supplanted by the Ute Mountain Utes, whose reservation abuts Mesa Verde just south of Cortez. Regular tours to Pueblo ruins on the reservation are conducted by tribal guides. It's a unique and rugged way of viewing less well-known ruins and learning about Ute culture.

Birding and bed-and-breakfasts

Southern Colorado's San Luis Valley, southeast of Salida, is one of the most isolated areas of Colorado. It remains a tightly knit Hispanic region, in the shadow of the Spanish Peaks, where many inhabitants still speak an archaic form of Spanish and live in adobes, grow beans and grain, and ranch cattle. Its main attraction is Great Sand Dunes National Park and Preserve, which protects the tallest sand dunes in North America and is a migratory corridor for sandhill cranes and other birds. An unusual way to enjoy the valley is to stay at The Nature Conservancy–owned Zapata Ranch,

a working cattle and bison ranch adjoining the park. Visitors learn about wildlife and horsemanship and assist with the herds.

With 400 of 625 North American bird species using Comanche National Grasslands, southeast Colorado is an important birding destination. It is also a magnet for historians interested in the Santa Fe Trail. The Cimarron Cutoff branch of the trail passed directly through here, and Bent's Fort was located directly on it to take advantage of trail traffic. Picketwire Canyon, known for its unusual dinosaur tracks, and Picture Canyon, a rock art site, are both scenic and historic attractions. Canyon

Tribal artifact at the Museum of Western Colorado.

Journeys Tours can arrange hiking and driving tours and lodging in the area.

Park County, located in the central Rockies, contains the highest gold and silver mines in the country, as well as a variety of historic ranches, mining towns, and scenic railroads. An hour from Denver, it is immensely popular for driving tours amid spectacular scenery. Como, Breckenridge, Fairplay, Alma, and other communities offer a taste of mountain living. Historic bed-and-breakfasts like the Como Eating House/ South Park Hotel, built by the railroad in the old depot, have high-country character to spare, while an increasing number of historic ranches, including the 1880s Tarryall River Ranch, have been restored and now welcome visitors.

Boulder Creek flows down Boulder Canyon.

MOUNTAIN AND PRAIRIE LIFE

From alpine tundra to shortgrass prairie, Colorado's
varied terrain sustains a fascinating variety of plants
and animals in eight distinct ecosystems.

With an average elevation of 6,500ft (2,000 meters), Colorado is the highest state in the country. It's also one of the most diverse. Elevations range from 3,300ft (1,000 meters) along the Arkansas River to 14,443ft (4,402 meters) at Mount Elbert, the state's highest point. Within that 11,000ft (3,350-meter) gain are eight distinct ecosystems, supporting 900 species of wildlife from rattlesnakes, jackrabbits, and deer mice to black bear, ptarmigans and bighorn sheep. Seventy-four Colorado species are listed as state or federally endangered or threatened. These include humpback chub and other native fish affected by the damming of the Colorado River, as well as boreal toad, lynx, wolverines, river otters, and lesser and greater prairie chickens, whose numbers have shrunk due to habitat loss.

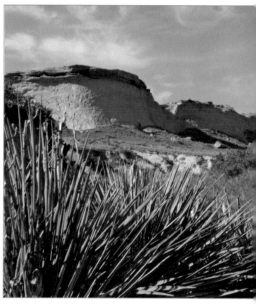

Pawnee National Grassland.

Sea of grass

Colorado is famous for awe-inspiring peaks, but nearly 40 percent of the state is grasslands. The plains are found at elevations of less than 5,500ft (1,700 meters) and roll for hundreds of miles east of the Rocky Mountains, which cast a rainshadow, limiting average annual rainfall in the region to a scant 14in (360mm). Dominating the landscape are perennials such as buffalograss, western wheatgrass, and blue grama. The native plants of the shortgrass prairie rarely exceed 2ft (60cm) in height. Their vertical blades maximize light absorption in the cooler part of the day and minimize the effects of midday radiation. Most of their biomass is contained in the root system, meaning that fire and cropping is essential for regenerating vegetation.

Grassland animals have adapted to prairie conditions. Among them are pronghorn, erroneously dubbed antelope. Pronghorn became swift runners to escape their enemy, the now-extinct North American cheetah. Family groups of pronghorn are common on the prairie.

Eastern Colorado is a historic home of another significant native species: the American bison. Millions of bison – incorrectly dubbed buffalo by the Spanish – once roamed the plains, seasonally grazing grasslands and churning the ground underfoot into a fertile mulch. Bison sustained the Plains Indians. Their entire culture centered on hunting bison, an animal that provided for much of their needs, from meat and clothing to glue, bone, and sinew.

Wildlife watchers are well rewarded at Pawnee and Comanche national grasslands, large federally managed tracts in the northeast and southeast corners of the state, respectively. Both are good for viewing badgers, foxes, mule deer, and pronghorn. Black-tailed prairie dogs are a common sight, too. These highly social creatures live in underground burrows to stay cool and avoid predators such as coyotes and red-tailed hawks, eagles, owls, and other raptors that patrol the skies.

Comanche National Grassland supports some 273 bird species, including specially adapted species such as scaled quail, pheasant, and grouse, which build nests directly on the ground. Burrowing owls have an additional

In the 1800s, free-roaming bison herds were exterminated by settlers monopolizing indigenous hunting grounds. Today, large ranches east of Denver raise them for the exploding bison meat market.

song of the canyon wren reverberates from the walls of the escarpment.

As in all dry places, water attracts life. Cottonwoods, willows, and tamarisk grow along the South Platte, Purgatoire, and Arkansas rivers

An abandoned farm on Pawnee National Grassland.

specialty: they prefer to nest in abandoned prairie dog colonies. The most famous of the grassland birds are the threatened lesser and greater prairie chickens whose frenetic mating dance in open areas called leks takes place in spring. The two units of Pawnee National Grassland, 90 miles (145km) northeast of Denver, have even more birds – 296 species at last count. Cliff-dwelling raptors such as prairie falcons and golden eagles inhabit the twin Pawnee Buttes, a geological landmark consisting of sedimentary rocks that rise above the plains, and this is one of the primary breeding grounds in the world for mountain plovers. Cliff swallows and white-throated swifts are common around the buttes, and the cascading

and their tributaries, offering shade and important nesting habitat on the otherwise treeless prairie. Small ponds and reservoirs, most intermittent in nature, lure migrant shorebirds, which pause to refuel for their long journey north in spring.

Between prairie and mountains

The canyons and foothills of the eastern Rockies and the high plateau country of western Colorado, between 5,000 and 7,000ft (1,500–2,000 meters), encompass dry shrublands, a transition zone between the mountains and the open grasslands. Directly in the shadow of high mountains, these areas are even drier than the plains, with 10in (250mm) or less of precipitation, falling mostly as snow in winter. These areas are hot in summer and frigid in winter. To survive, plants and animals have to be able to manage on little or no water for long periods.

Sandy soils are stabilized by perennial native grasses such as galleta and Indian ricegrass, whose nutritious seeds were once gathered by wandering indigenous peoples. Overgrazing has all but destroyed many native grasses, allowing woody shrubs such as sulfur-colored rabbitbrush and pungent sagebrush to take over. The montane shrublands of the Front Range are

warm rocks. Cottontails, jackrabbits, ground squirrels, and mice are the most active in the daytime. By dusk, they are safe in their burrows, avoiding crepuscular hunters like coyotes and gray foxes.

As elevation rises, dwarf forests of stunted pinyon pine and juniper trees appear. The round-topped pinyon tree bears nutritious nuts that have been valued by animals and humans for centuries. Pinyons rarely grow over 30ft (9 meters) tall and are more cold tolerant than junipers, a drought-resistant shaggy-barked shrub that is more at home in lower elevations.

Flowering cactus on the northeast plains of Colorado.

home to Gambel oak and mountain mahogany. The semidesert shrublands of the West Slope are a region of dry washes and low shrubs.

Prickly pear and other cactus are well suited to the aridity. Cactus have done away with leaves altogether and photosynthesize food from sunlight along thick, waxy pads covered in spines that keep away predators. Bright flowers attract bird and insect pollinators in spring. Animals return to eat the juicy fruits in late summer, and spread seeds through their digestive tracts. Semi-desert conditions mean plenty of reptiles and rodents make their home here. In summer, early-morning hikers may glimpse brightly hued collared lizards, horned toads, and rattlesnakes basking on

The pinyon pine-juniper woodlands zone, which now dominates much of the Colorado Plateau, supports numerous wildlife species, including noisy pinyon jays, little gray tits, and ground squirrels. In northwestern Colorado, look for herds of elk and mule deer and wild horses in the vicinity of Dinosaur National Monument, in the White River region between Rangely and Meeker.

Transition life zone

More moisture and cooler temperatures above 7,000ft (2,100 meters) allow trees to grow taller. In the transition life zone, ponderosa pine begins to appear, a tall tree with platey bark that smells of vanilla. The odd ponderosa grows among pinyon and juniper at first, then becomes the dominant tree, forming thick stands separated by natural "parks," or open meadows. Scrub oaks can often be found growing in the shade of ponderosa at lower elevations. Fast-growing, arrow-straight Douglas fir is also found in this life zone. It prefers hillsides with northern exposures where temperatures are cooler and moisture is more plentiful.

Among the birds that make their home in the ponderosa zone are bluebirds, sparrows, juncos, chickadees, and Steller's and scrub jays. Jays, a relative of the crow, flash through the

enough quantity to germinate every three to five years, during a particularly moist year.

Aspen and conifers

At higher elevations, between 8,000 and 10,000ft (2,400–3,000 meters), where precipitation averages 25in (640mm) a year, limber pine, blue spruce, and aspens appear. Limber pine, a tall straight tree often used by Utes for tipi poles, and quaking aspen, a relative of the willow, are pioneer species, meaning they are the first to take root in clearings created by fire, logging, and other disturbances. New groves of

A rufus hummingbird in bright plumage.

branches and often cause a commotion fighting over seeds. Larger mammals include mule deer and their natural predator, mountain lions, shy felines that are rarely seen. Tassel-eared squirrels and ponderosa pines have evolved an interesting symbiotic relationship. Squirrels dig around the base of ponderosas in search of fungi that grow on the roots. As they dig, they inadvertently mulch the soil and release nutrients that benefit the tree. The needles of the ponderosa are born in long bunches, which gives it an airy, umbrella shape that allows a lot of light to penetrate the forest floor. Lupine, scarlet gilia, Indian paintbrush, and other wild flowers do well here. Only trees that are over 25 years old reproduce seeds, and then only in

aspens take five to 10 years to establish themselves, and reach their maximum density in 25 to 50 years.

Once mature, an aspen forest creates enough shade to allow conifer seedlings such as Douglas fir, Engelmann spruce, and subalpine fir to take root. From then on, it's downhill for the aspens, which become crowded out by conifers and susceptible to disease, insect infestation and browsing elk and deer. For decades, spruce-fir forests dominate the scene. Eventually, they, too, fall prey to wildfire, clearing the way once again for an aspen forest to take hold on the forest margin.

One reason for the aspen's endurance is its dual reproductive strategy. In spring, flowering catkins produce small cones, which release cottony seeds that are dispersed on the wind and root in moisture-rich soils. Where moisture is abundant, this strategy works well, but dry conditions in the West necessitate a different tactic. Western aspen groves reproduce almost entirely vegetatively, sending out suckers, or ramets, from existing root systems into areas disturbed by fire, logging, or avalanches – in effect, cloning.

A mature root system can put out a million shoots per acre, which then grow 3ft (1 meter) every season, outcompeting forest species that rely on seed regeneration. Aspen clones are extraordinarily long-lived. The giant Pando clone in south-central Utah, which covers 106 acres (43 hectares) and contains more than 47,000 individual stems, may be at least 10,000 years old. So, take another look at that aspen grove. It's no accident that the trees look so alike.

Between 10,000 and 11,000ft (3,000–3,350 meters), where snowfall is heavy, tall narrow conifers with waxy needles that shrug off snow form climax forests of several-hundred-year-old Engelmann spruce and subalpine fir that cloak

Golden aspen leaves in the fall.

THE ROLE OF FIRE

Fire is essential to the health of western forests. Unfortunately, 150 years of fire suppression, poor logging practices, and drought have led to overgrowth. The problem has been particularly acute in ponderosa pine forests where young, small-diameter blackjack pines have not been selectively pruned by fire or logging. Natural forest fires in this ecosystem historically burned slowly and remained low on the forest floor, allowing pine cones to open, spill seed, and germinate. There was plenty of time for wildlife to escape. But as a thick duff of dried needles has built up, fires caused by lightning strikes or human carelessness have become deadly, racing up into the canopy during periods of hot, dry, windy conditions and obliterating every living thing in their path. The 2002 Hayman Blaze, Colorado's largest, ravaged 138,000 acres (55,800 hectares) on the southern edge of Denver and destroyed 133 homes. In 2012 and 2013 alone there were six wildfires, including 2013's 14,280-acre (5,779-hectare) Black Forest Fire, near Colorado Springs. The most destructive fire in Colorado state history, it killed two people, destroyed 511 homes, and left 28 homes partially damaged. Thinning the forests is only one solution to the problem. Home building in the so-called urban-wildland interface, an area where 30 percent of Coloradans live, also jeopardizes the ecosystem.

the mountain sides in miles of soothing velvety green. Though rarely seen, wolverines, and Canada lynx and black bears also live at this height. In the mountains near Pagosa Springs, there are tales, too, of grizzly bears, long thought extirpated from the region.

At the highest elevations, thin air, rocky soils and frigid winds are as stressful for trees as the hot, dry conditions at low elevations. This is the province of specially adapted trees, such as the bristlecone pine, which can live for thousands of years by shutting down parts of itself and bowing into the wind to

Black bear in the Rocky Mountains.

form krummholz, a German word meaning "crooked wood."

Tundra peaks

In the alpine zone, above 11,000ft (3,350 meters), life is harsh. Intense solar radiation, gusty winds, and scant oxygen are constant challenges. Even so, a surprising number of living things have adapted to the rocky soils that are buried under 40 to 60in (100–150cm) of snow each winter.

Just above the treeline, alpine meadows provide some of Colorado's most spectacular hiking areas. Places like Yankee Boy Basin in the San Juan Mountains are a riot of color come June, when snow gradually melts and livings

things race to reproduce in the abbreviated summer. Bluebells, sneezeweed, lupines, sunflowers, and Colorado's state flower, the spurred Rocky Mountain columbine, form a colorful tapestry among lush green grasses fed by snowmelt.

Picnic here after a long hike and your companions will be sleepy yellow-bellied marmots, perhaps a pine marten, pika, vole, or snowshoe hare. If you're really lucky, you may spot bighorn sheep grazing in the meadows or lounging on rocky ledges in the distance. In late fall, rutting males assert their dominance by crashing into each other's horns at speeds of up to

> The American dipper is a wren-like bird with specialized feeding habits. It plunges into raging rivers and picks insect larvae from the bottom. How such a tiny creature can withstand strong currents is a bit of a mystery.

55mph (90km/h). This is also the territory of mountain goats, whose shaggy white coats protect them from the elements, and highly specialized hooves allow them to clamber up impossibly steep terrain.

Plants at the highest elevations keep a low profile but are surprisingly numerous. Perhaps the most fascinating are the brightly colored lichens that splotch gray granite boulders throughout the alpine zone. Colorado's high mountains support 450 species of lichen. Lichen actually consists of two mutually beneficial organisms – fungi and algae – that live together and survive by making use of wind-blown particles, minerals in the rock and occasional moisture. Lichens are another important pioneer species. They secrete acids that help to break down rock into soil.

Eventually, tiny plants take root in crevices. Many, such as pink moss campion and sunny snow buttercup, look surprisingly delicate. Like the environmentally stressed plants at lower elevations, this pincushion-sized flora survives by staying low to the ground and attracting pollinators with bright colors, retaining water through woody stems, and employing a vast underground root system to collect nutrients. Like desert flora, they are easily destroyed by careless human activity. Walk lightly in the lowest and highest elevations and respect life at these outer margins.

FOUR SEASONS

Primarily a state of high mountain ranges, valleys, and rich wildlife, Colorado attracts outdoors lovers who enjoy hiking, biking, skiing, and nature at any time of year.

For many people, the winter ski season is the only season in Colorado. Former mining towns-turned-ski resorts swing into action, advertising the deepest, softest, fluffiest snow; gnarliest slopes; and best facilities for skiing and snowboarding. In the San Juans, cross-country skiers and snowshoers make their way from hut to hut; there's extreme ice jeeping in Georgetown and ice climbing in Ouray, and other oddities; while down in the San Luis Valley wetlands, sandhill cranes stop over on their migrations. Spring arrives late, often bringing the heaviest wet snowfalls. At lower elevations, warmer temperatures swell rivers and wetlands, and courtship and reproduction begin. Prairie chickens perform their odd dances in prairie leks while fawns, bighorn lambs, elk calves, and other youngsters debut. Summer is precious for its brevity and beauty in the Rockies. Travelers on the trails and scenic byways leave behind the torrid low-elevation areas around Grand Junction and Denver and head for the high country to view Rocky Mountain columbine and other stunning wildflowers in now passable mountain basins. Everything races to bloom, reproduce, and set seed before fall swoops in in September. Aspens shimmer gold across the mountain sides and bring out legions of leaf peepers on the passes, trams, scenic railroads, and ski lifts. Listen carefully and you'll hear bugling elk and head-butting bighorn sheep, heralding winter's imminent arrival.

Hiking to Flat Top Mountain and Hallett Peak in Rocky Mountain National Park can be cold at any time of year.

It is illegal to pick the Rocky Mountain columbine, Colorado state flower.

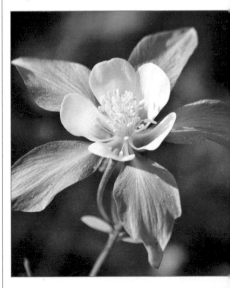

River sports, such as kayaking, are incredibly popular in the springtime, when the snow melts and rivers run at their peak.

Festive log cabin in the Rockies.

THE WINTER HOLIDAYS

Christmas in the Rockies. It's a fairy-tale setting of deep white snow, toboggans, horse-drawn sleigh rides, twinkling lights, roaring fires, cozy comforters, ear muffs, hot toddies, and caroling. Estes Park, gateway to Rocky Mountain National Park, offers a panoply of seasonal attractions, including the Catch the Glow Parade the Friday after Thanksgiving, caroling, Christmas lights, and visits with Santa. In Snowmass, Telluride, and Crested Butte, there's a torchlight parade across the mountain side on Christmas Eve. In Glenwood Springs, Hotel Colorado has a life-size gingerbread house, tree lighting, a visit with Santa, and a hotel pageant, while ski resorts like Breckenridge pull out all the stops, turning the entire town into a Victorian Christmas Village. In pretty Durango, kids all get gifts from Santa on the special Polar Express train, which runs to Silverton amid icicles and snowy mountains just like the Swiss Alps. Lights, of course, are aglow in towns throughout the state. The whole of Tenderfoot Mountain in Salida is lit up each year, while in Denver, more than a million Christmas lights adorn the Botanic Gardens.

ly male elk have antlers, which are grown each year in the ng and shed by early winter.

reme mountain biking in Telluride is a popular summer vity.

"Snowpack" in Colorado refers to the accumulation of snow over a winter season.

OUTDOOR ADVENTURE

Whatever your passion – rock climbing, backpacking, mountain biking, or whitewater rafting – Colorado offers room to roam and stunning scenery to enjoy.

In surveys of American health, Colorado routinely ranks first in fitness, last in fatness. It's not difficult to see why. Coloradans are always out running, biking, hiking, skiing, paddling, and otherwise enjoying life in the great outdoors – when they're not working out in the gym, that is. With an inviting climate and an unsurpassed wealth of mountains, rivers, and lakes to play on, Coloradans find little excuse to stay indoors.

High country scenery

There is no finer way to discover the state's magic than on foot. From easy ambles in urban parks to grueling scrambles up steep slopes to sky-high summits, Colorado offers trails for hikers at every level of conditioning and experience. High country scenery is breathtaking, and the opportunity to explore wild areas is abundant. Mountains invite exploration and encourage people to put one foot in front of the other until they reach a goal – a panoramic viewpoint, an alpine lake, a ghost town, a windswept peak.

Front Range trails are often snow-free through much of winter, but conditions are best from late spring to early fall. Wildflower season begins with avalanche lilies sprouting in the wake of melting snowfields, reaches a climax in July, and tapers off in September. Wildlife watching is best in spring and fall, at dawn, or dusk.

Trails crisscross the state. Many are near major highways or on the outskirts of cities and resort towns; others branch off from harrowing four-wheel-drive roads and lead deep into the wilderness. Trails vary in length and difficulty from handicapped-accessible paths of less than a mile to arduous treks along the crest of the

Climbing at Ouray's annual Ice Climbing Festival.

Rockies. Many ski areas operate at least one lift in summer, so visitors who want a shortcut can ride up and hike down.

Far more challenging is scaling the hundreds of peaks that rise from mountain ranges throughout the state. The degree of difficulty varies considerably from one mountain to another, but some require no special skills or equipment and can be climbed in a single day. There are oxygen-sapping heights and often violent summer storms to contend with, but most mountains have at least one hike-up route.

Hikers with little or no experience may want to set their sights on a modest goal – say, 9,250ft (2,820-meter) Crozier Peak near Estes Park. On the opposite side of the scale is a lung-searing trek to the top of one of the state's 54 "four-teeners" – mountains 14,000ft (4,270 meters) or higher – regarded with a certain reverence by avid hikers.

Be prepared

Whatever your route, thoughtful preparation is the key to a successful outing. Sunscreen, sunglasses, a broad-brimmed hat (or peaked cap and bandana protecting the neck), pants and shirts that can be rolled down for sun protection, and comfortable wool socks and hiking boots, sturdy shoes, or outdoor sandals are the minimum equipment for even a moderate hike; veteran hikers often use a single walking stick or pair of trekking poles. If you intend to reach elevations of 8,000 to 10,000ft (2,400–3,000 meters), pack a fleece jacket, waterproof shell, and a high-energy snack. Above 10,000ft (3,000 meters), you'll need cold-weather gear, including long johns, a warm hat, gloves, an emergency blanket, and extra food, even in midsummer.

A trail map is a good idea even if you intend to follow a well-marked route. In remote areas, it's essential to carry a topographical map and compass and know how to use them. GPS units

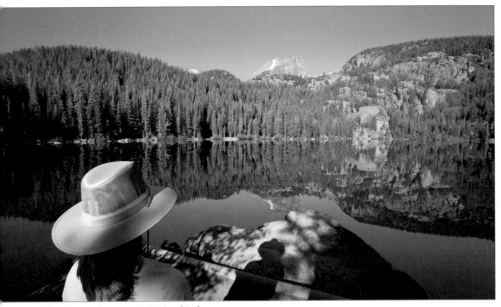

A perfect sky in Rocky Mountain National Park.

CLIMB EVERY MOUNTAIN

The term "peak bagging" refers to a successful summit ascent, and bagging "fourteeners" – mountains 14,000ft (4,270 meters) or higher – is the ultimate goal of the hardiest hikers. Although some 200,000 people a year reach the state's highest peaks, fourteeners have achieved mythic status. While some hikers are content to have done just one, others are compelled to ratchet up the challenge by, for example, climbing all 54 in Colorado, climbing them all in a year, on consecutive days, in winter, or all of the above. Every fourteener, whether it's your first or your 54th, offers a sense of being on top of the world and of having gotten there one step at a time.

Difficulty ranges widely. Some peaks, like Mount Sherman, a short drive from Denver, are a good choice for beginners. A trail leads to the summit, making for a fairly easy walk-up, though hikers unaccustomed to the elevation should take it slow. Others, like Capitol and Pyramid peaks, involve traversing knife-edge ridges, loose talus, and extremely steep slopes. These summits should be attempted only by those with excellent route-finding skills and in top physical condition.

Fourteeners can be climbed in all seasons, but the best time for casual hikers is between late June and September. Afternoon electrical storms are common in summer. Start early and get below treeline before 2pm.

are handy too, but should be used in addition to a compass, never as a substitute for one: satellite information is not the same as on-the-ground information and you may find yourself going off a cliff if you're not careful. Other basics for wilderness travel include a Swiss army knife, matches in a waterproof case, a flashlight, a whistle, a space blanket, and turned-off cell phone at the bottom of your day pack, in case you're on the trail longer than expected or need to signal for help. Most important, carry a gallon (4 liters) of water per person per day (at least a liter (2 pints) for short jaunts). Stay

Longer trips

If you like hiking, you'll love multiday excursions, which are the logical next step. A longer backpacking trip provides the opportunity to really experience the high country, to study the wild flowers, photograph the scenery, and generally steep yourself in the beauty and tranquility of the mountains.

Overnight trips are naturally more complicated to plan and require a rather daunting list of additional equipment, including a backpack, sleeping bag, mattress pad, tent, water-purifying kit, and camping stove. The design

Campgrounds in Rocky Mountain National Park.

hydrated by sipping at regular intervals, even if you don't feel thirsty, and avoid hyponatremia (an electrolyte imbalance due to low salt from sweating) by eating salty nutritious snacks like trail mix and drinking water.

Altitude sickness is another concern, especially if you're coming from sea level. Symptoms include headache, shortness of breath, fatigue, dizziness, and loss of appetite. The best preventative is to spend a couple of days adjusting to the elevation. Avoid overexertion, lay off alcohol and coffee (both are dehydrating), and drink more water than you think you need. Lastly, leave a travel plan with someone at home, so they know when and where to start looking if you don't turn up.

LIGHTNING SAFETY

Lightning isn't just a great light show; it's potentially lethal and, above treeline, there are few places to hide. If you're in the mountains when a storm moves in, descend from high, open terrain. If you can't get away from an exposed area, make yourself as small as possible, crouching down on the balls of your feet, or perching on a small rock with insulation such as a poncho or a foam pad under you, with your feet touching rock and your hands clasped around your knees. Stay clear of tall objects such as isolated trees as well as depressions, shallow caves and rock overhangs. Ground currents can be dangerous.

and quality of camping gear has never been better, though choices (and prices) can quickly become overwhelming. Unless you have an experienced friend to show you the ropes, the best advice is to start by doing a little research in books, magazines and on the internet, then go to a reputable camping-supply retailer such as REI and work with a salesperson who is willing to take the time you need to make the right decisions. Remember: comfort is key. Roughing it in the outdoors shouldn't be rough at all. The idea is to simplify your life, unload stress, and enjoy the place, people, and moment,

Always practice safe climbing techniques, and never climb alone.

not aggravate yourself with ill-fitting or poor-quality equipment that leaves you cold, hungry, achy, and miserable.

Once you're properly equipped, you can begin making the tough decisions about where to go. Colorado has 30,000 campgrounds in locations ranging from the deepest wilderness to the outskirts of cities. Choosing how and where to camp is a function of taste, budget, and availability of sites. Consider why you want to camp and how rugged you want the experience to be. In general, you'll find that the more conveniences a campground offers and the easier it is to reach, the less privacy and scenic beauty it will have.

For maximum ease, pull in to a roadside campground and use your tent, trailer, or motor home as a base for day hikes. Most drive-in campgrounds have basic sanitary facilities as well as picnic tables and grills. Private facilities may also have utility hookups (electricity, water and sewerage), showers, a laundry, a grocery, a playground, and other amenities. Electricity brings with it television, stereos, bright lights, and other "conveniences" that, in the view of many campers, spoil the point of being outdoors. Campsites at national parks, national forests, and other public lands tend to be more laid back and often feature rangers giving campfire talks or leading guided hikes.

If you want a real backcountry experience, however, you will have to leave the road behind and set out on foot to a primitive campsite or, if you're adequately prepared, camp at large in a wilderness area designated for the purpose. If that sounds like a daunting prospect, consider hiring a guide or outfitter to help you. At the most basic level, outfitters assist with trip planning, provide the necessary equipment, and perhaps shuttle your party to and from a trailhead. At the opposite extreme, many outfitters script every inch of your trip in high style – toting your gear, setting up camp, and even capping each day with dinner beneath the stars. Most of all, outfitters can share the knowledge they've acquired over years of travel. Going with an expert is a great way to learn about a place and acquire new skills – and, if you choose, sweeten the adventure with a touch of luxury.

In the end, it doesn't really matter how you experience the outdoors. The important thing is to spend time outside – to feel the sun on your face, the earth beneath your feet, the flow of a mountain stream. And to understand, as Colorado naturalist Enos Mills did, that enjoying the outdoors "will develop a love for nature, strengthen one's appreciation of the beautiful world outdoors, and put one in tune with the Infinite."

Rock climbing

Rock climbing epitomizes confident partnering in a vertical world. One climber moves up the rock; the other provides protection via the rope. Only when the lead climber is secure does the second climber begin to move. The process has been compared to chess in terms

> When nature calls, answer with a trowel. Dig a cathole at least 6in (15cm) deep for human waste and bury or carry out toilet paper. Pick a site at least 200ft (60 meters) from water sources.

of concentration and the importance of small, critical moves. The satisfaction and the self-confidence gained from rock climbing are so deep that it has become a popular component of team-building and self-esteem workshops.

Mountain Club (710 10th St, Suite 200, Golden, CO 80401; tel: 303-279-3080; www.cmc.org), which run courses covering the fundamentals of climbing technique, equipment and, above all, safety. Such classes are a great place to meet climbing companions and learn about organized field trips.

Ice climbing

For an even greater challenge, consider ice climbing, which involves scaling a cascade frozen to a steep rock wall. To gain purchase on the slippery surface, ice climbers use axes and spiky footgear called crampons. The climber

Hiker and her dog, San Juan National Forest.

The learning curve is quite precipitous for rock climbing, although even in this sport, in which technical skill and strength are paramount, the opportunities for beginners are expanding. Not too many years ago, the only practical way to learn rock climbing was to tag along with experienced climbers. Today, it's much more common for newcomers to hone their skills at climbing gyms before they actually put flesh to rock.

Beginners can learn a few basic maneuvers in just four or five hours, but there's only so much you can do without being out in the field. For that, it's best to contact an outfitter such as the Front Range Climbing Company (1370 Windmill Ave, Colorado Springs, CO, 80907; tel: 719-632-5822; www.frontrangeclimbing.com) or the Colorado

maneuvers upward in a manner similar to that of a rock climber scaling a cliff. Unlike rock climbers, however, ice climbers create their own routes by choosing where to place their tools. Despite this flexibility, ice climbing contains a constant element of insecurity because the very surface on which the climber depends can melt, shatter or break away. The changeable nature of ice also means that the same climb can vary radically from one day to another. A route's difficulty is often impossible to predict.

The premier site for ice climbing in Colorado – and perhaps the entire western United States – is the Ouray Ice Park, an area of "cultivated" ice flows in Uncompahgre Gorge. Climbing routes, including some with safety ropes and

Extreme sports

Testing one's mettle against the elements is an essential part of outdoor adventure. Numerous Colorado sporting events push human limits of strength and endurance.

For marathon runners, the **Bolder Boulder** 6-mile (10km) road race in May is a major event

A competitor in the Gold Rush Burro Race, Buena Vista.

on the calendar. With categories for professional runners, elite runners, citizen runners, walkers, and wheelchair participants, expect to see Olympic medal winners as well as grandmothers and kids. 50,765 entrants took part in 2016 – a record turnout. For scenery, it's hard to beat the **Steamboat Marathon**, **Half-Marathon**, and **10K** held in Steamboat Springs in early June. It has been listed as one of the most scenic marathons in North America and a Top 10 Destination by *Runner's World*. The route takes in green pastures and the dramatic environs of the Rocky Mountains. The **Leadville Trail 100** in August is a 100-mile (160km) run nicknamed "the race across the sky" because it takes place at elevations of 10,000ft (3,050 meters) or higher.

Events added since the first 100-miler in 1983 are a full marathon, 100- and 50-mile (160 and 80 km) mountain bike races, and a 6-mile (10km) run. Also in August, another popular road race, the **Pikes Peak Marathon** takes place in Manitou Springs. Competitors in this half-marathon follow the 13-mile (21km) Barr Trail to the summit of Pikes Peak, an elevation gain of 7,815ft (2,382 meters). A full marathon to the summit and back is run the next day.

If you don't fancy Shanks' mare, opt instead for a burro or llama. **World Championship Pack Burro Races**, a team event, are held in Fairplay in July and are surprisingly demanding. Described as the world's "highest, longest, roughest, and toughest" race, the course is 29 miles (47km) long and climbs to an elevation of 13,000ft (915 meters).

On two wheels

For mountain bikers, **Mountain's Revenge** (the 2014 revival of the former Montezuma's Revenge 24-hour race that took place until 2007), held in Montezuma County in August, is a popular outing. The race is divided into seven loops that cross the Continental Divide 10 times. Those who finish the race rack up more than 200 miles (320km) and an elevation gain of 35,000ft (10,700 meters). The world's oldest mountain bike event, **the Pearl Pass Tour,** is a two-day, 38-mile (61km) ride from Crested Butte to Aspen via 12,700ft (3,870-meter) Pearl Pass that takes place in September. For extreme cyclists, the **Iron Horse Bicycle Classic**, between Durango and Silverton, receives top billing. The 47-mile (77km) road race for ranked and non-ranked racers with 5,500ft (1,680 meters) of elevation gain over two 11,000ft (3,350-meter) passes takes place over the Memorial Day weekend and includes in-town criteriums, circuit races, road races, tours, BMX races, dual slaloms, team trail rides, and mountain bike races. The **Elephant Rock Ride** held in Castle Rock in June includes four road cycling events, from 25 to 100 miles (40–160km), plus a 26-mile (42km) off-road ride, and attracts more than 7,000 participants.

Auto races also go to the extreme in Colorado. The famous **Pikes Peak International Hill Climb** in Manitou Springs in June follows a serpentine, 12-mile (19km) gravel road to the summit of Pikes Peak, maneuvering through 156 hairpin turns with no guardrails. Vehicles include stock cars, sport cars, diesel trucks, and motorcycles.

> Even clear streams can harbor parasites that cause severe gastrointestinal illness. All water from wild sources should be boiled for at least a minute, treated with iodine, or passed through a portable filter.

bolts set in the rock, range in difficulty from easy to expert. The Ouray Ice Festival, usually held in mid-January, features gear demonstrations, competitions, and free instruction.

Riding the rivers

The possibilities for outdoor adventure become even more enticing when you consider alternative modes of transportation such as biking and rafting, which often free you from the burden of lugging a backpack and open up territory that may be unreachable on foot. If you enjoy water sports, for example, you'll get a kick out of whitewater paddling. Colorado's 13 river systems provide everything from boat-bashing rapids in early spring to gentle summer floats that can be safely done in an inner tube. The rafting season begins in May, peaks in mid-June, and typically ends in early October. Snowmelt feeds Colorado's rivers, so the biggest water and best paddling follow winters when the skiing was great.

The real beauty of rafting is that just about anybody can do it. Licensed outfitters handle all provisions and equipment. All you have to do – aside from paying the bill – is show up. More than half a million people a year put themselves in the hands of Colorado boatmen trained in whitewater navigation, first aid, and rescue. The best river guides know a great deal about history and nature, too. Trips range from calm half-day floats suitable for families with small children to multiday expeditions with camping, cookouts, and plenty of opportunities for exploring the surrounding terrain in depth.

The Arkansas River between Buena Vista and Royal Gorge is reportedly the most-rafted river in the western United States, but there are more than 10 others to choose from, including the Animas, Blue, Cache la Poudre, Colorado, Green, Gunnison, Yampa, and Rio Grande. River rafting contributed $162.6 million to state coffers in 2015, representing 508,728 commercial raft trips on 29 stretches of Colorado rivers, The government licenses all commercial raft companies, 50 of which belong to the Colorado River Outfitters

Association, a trade group that serves as a clearinghouse for information on whitewater adventures (tel: 1-800-COLORADO; www.croa.org).

For those who crave even more action, Colorado's fast-flowing rivers are best experienced in a kayak or canoe. Mobility, freedom, and the thrill of constantly testing yourself against the elements are the appeals of the sport. Kayakers talk about "playing" the water, not just navigating rapids but performing an aquatic ballet of "cartwheels," "enders," "pirouettes," and other tricky maneuvers. Unless you already have a good deal of experience under your belt, instruction is essential.

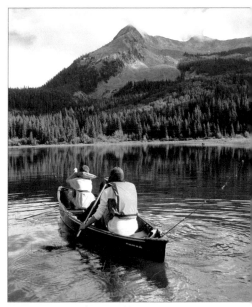

Canoeing on Lost Lake near Kebler Pass.

UP, UP, AND AWAY

For a real "Rocky Mountain high," take to the skies. Tandem hang-gliding and skydiving, where students and instructors soar together, offer the experience of free flight without training. To enjoy Colorado scenery from above, consider a sedate hot air balloon ride. Pilots use propane heaters to adjust altitude and fine-tune the flight, but the balloon essentially rides air currents. Upon landing, you are served champagne and transported back to your car. Ultralights, a sort of motorized hang-glider, are another option. Do a tandem flight with an instructor at the controls, or spend a few hours learning to fly solo.

Kayaking schools throughout the state offer clinics in basic skills such as proper paddle strokes, rolls, and water safety as well as advanced "playboating" and whitewater rescue. Most introductory courses are divided into pre-river and on-river segments. The pre-river curriculum may include pool or lake instruction.

If whitewater is for thrill-seekers, flatwater canoeing has the opposite appeal – a calm, often meditative activity as well as an efficient mode of transportation. Canoes have more room for gear than kayaks and are better suited for camping and fishing trips, especially if you're

Every Colorado resident seems to have a bike or two, and visitors often bring their own. Many resort towns have as many bike shops as T-shirt emporiums, so if you are of average size you'll have no trouble finding a rental, even if you're looking for a tandem or other specialty bike. Children's seats and trailers make cycling a family sport even if the kids aren't old enough to ride by themselves. Guided rides and overnight trips are available, too, often with van support. Special events ranging from modest bike festivals to big-time road cycling, and mountain biking competitions are held throughout the summer.

A river guide leads a family rafting trip.

traveling with kids. Basic canoeing doesn't take extraordinary skill either, just a little practice to paddle efficiently.

Pedal power

Colorado is cycling central. Local riders pedal everything from beat-up clunkers to mountain bikes and state-of-the-art touring bikes with four-figure price tags. You'll find them pedaling on thousands of miles of city streets, mountain passes, bike paths, mining roads, abandoned railroad beds, and single-tracks (trails wide enough for only one bike). The number of designated trails and suitable routes is increasing so quickly that keeping track is virtually impossible.

Recreational paths in (and sometimes between) urban areas welcome cyclists. Some are paved; others are gravel. Cycling is permitted on unpaved roads and some trails in national forests and Bureau of Land Management (BLM) regions but only on paved roads in national parks. Networks of old mining roads lead deep into the mountains and make for excellent bike routes.

Bike maps are usually available at visitor centers, ranger stations, and other tourist information facilities. Bicycle Colorado (1525 Market Street, Suite 100, Denver, CO 80202; tel: 303-417-1544; www.bicyclecolorado.org) promotes bicycling in Colorado, lobbies for improved conditions, and gives Colorado cyclists a voice.

Cycling through the Garden of the Gods.

Perfect powder at Aspen.

POWDER TO THE PEOPLE

Experts and novices alike are drawn to the
deep powder, long season, and huge vertical
drops of this high-altitude kingdom of snow.

If any place on the planet is designed for skiing, it's Colorado. And it didn't take early settlers long to discover it. It is thought that skis were first used in a mining camp along the Blue River near present-day Breckenridge during the winter of 1859–60. Father John L. Dyer, the most famous of the 50 or so stalwarts contracted to carry mail over the mountains, used skis to deliver letters and the word of God to remote mining camps.

Miners from Irwin and Crested Butte challenged each other to downhill races as early as 1886. In 1911, Norwegian ski jumper Carl Howelsen – dubbed the "Flying Norseman" during a brief stint with Barnum & Bailey's circus – thrilled crowds in Hot Sulphur Springs by soaring 79ft (24 meters) through the air. Two years later, when Denver was blanketed by one of the worst blizzards of the century, Howelsen and a handful of other skiers impressed local sportsmen by sliding down Capitol Hill. The episode inspired the formation of the Denver Rocky Mountain Ski Club, which soon became an avid promoter of the sport.

Skier at Copper Mountain.

Birth of an idea

It wasn't until the 1930s, however, that the concept of the "ski area" came into its own, thanks largely to the advent of the rope tow, which had its Colorado debut at Berthoud Pass in 1937. The first chair-lift, constructed in the fashion of a mining tram, was installed at the Pioneer Ski Area near Crested Butte in 1939. Colorado's first double chair-lift was erected nine years later at Berthoud Pass. World War II naturally put a hold on ski area development, but not on skiing. Thousands of "ski troops" were trained at Camp Hale near Leadville during the war. Afterwards, veterans of the camp's 10th Mountain Division were a prime force in creating the post-war ski boom.

The Colorado ski industry is no.1 in the nation and contributes $4.8 billion annually to Colorado tourism. Twenty-five full-fledged ski areas and resorts operate in the state and attracted 12.6 million skier visits for the 2013–14 season, a rise of 10 percent over the previous season, thanks to an early start, a late finish, drought in California, and steady snowfall. Preliminary figures for 2016 show increased skier visits of 5 percent; Colorado now accounts for 24 percent of all skier visits in the US. Choices range from low-key ski centers, where prices are moderate and the atmosphere is relaxed, to ritzy, world-class resorts, where the facilities are state-of-the-art, the clientele is chic, and the prices are stratospheric. Regardless of size, they all enjoy some of the world's finest snow conditions. Winter storms barrel down on the Rockies from the Pacific, losing moisture over the deserts of Utah, Nevada, and Arizona, before unloading tons of light, dry powder on Colorado. What Mother Nature is slow to deliver, technology provides. Snowmaking systems at most ski areas ensure an early start to the season and, coupled with expert grooming, an adequate surface throughout the winter.

Large or small, just about every ski area offers runs for skiers of all abilities, halfpipes and terrain parks for snowboarders and freeriders, rental equipment, instruction, day care, and a ski patrol trained in rescue and first aid. Major ski areas may have larger and faster chair-lifts than their smaller counterparts (and perhaps a gondola or two), but everything else is merely a matter of scale. What you'll find at the biggest and most elaborate resorts – and here we're talking about world-class destinations like Aspen, Vail, Steamboat, and Telluride – is vertical drops of 2,500 to 4,400ft (750–1,350 meters), high-capacity lifts that speed thousands of skiers up the slopes, lodgings for thousands of vacationers and a rollicking après-ski scene. The giants

Skiers with wooden skis and a single pole at Steamboat Springs, c.1916.

SOLDIERS ON SKIS

Taking a cue from the snow-savvy Finns and Scandinavians who had outmaneuvered their respective Russian and German antagonists in winter hostilities, the US military decided in mid-1941 to create its own special fighting force. General George C. Marshall gave the go-ahead to a project that would give birth to the storied 10th Mountain Division – and, indirectly, the Colorado skiing industry as we know it.

The site the Army chose as a training center was an obscure place named Pando, high up in the heart of the Colorado Rockies. Here, in a mountain valley 6 miles (10km) north of Leadville, was established Camp Hale. From it would emerge an entire division of troops trained

to ski, climb, and fight in harsh weather and on rugged turf by a cadre of mixed American and European experts.

There was plenty of frostbite and other ailments before the 10th Division was put to the test in Italy, starting in November 1944. Its warriors engaged in a series of encounters with Nazi forces in the Po Valley as they cleared a path for the US Army stretching north to the Alps. The cost was high: 992 American war deaths.

The division was eventually disbanded in October 1945. But fond memories of life in Colorado, augmented by a strong bond among comrades, brought many back. They carved out new lives in a skiing industry they did so much to energize.

among them rack up a million or more skier visits every winter and are popular summer resorts. Those closest to Denver, including Keystone, Breckenridge, Copper Mountain, Vail, and Winter Park, are jammed with both day-skiers and vacationers. Others are far enough afield to be purely destination resorts.

The Colorado ski season extends over an extraordinary eight months a year. It starts in late October or early November, when Arapahoe Basin and Loveland compete for first-to-open honors, and finishes in June or even July, though most skiers agree that prime time

Colorado Ski and Snowboard Museum and Hall of Fame in Vail chronicles the history of Rocky Mountain skiing, from postmen who trekked over mountain passes on primitive skis in the mid-1800s to 21st-century Olympic hopefuls.

is between Thanksgiving and Easter. Prices for lift tickets and lodging vary widely depending on when you go. Expect the best deals early and late in the season as well as in January. The Christmas holiday and Presidents Week (in late February) command the highest prices and biggest crowds.

The I-70 corridor

Driving west out of Denver along Interstate 70, the first major ski area west of the Eisenhower Tunnel is Keystone. Established in 1970, it burst on the scene with a network of mostly mild runs etched through the trees, a brand-new luxury hotel that stood in sharp contrast to the primitive ski lodgings of the day and, soon after, clusters of condominiums tucked into the woods. Keystone's trail system now has 135 runs on 3,148 skiable acres (1,274 hectares) spread across three mountains. It has 20 lifts and two high-speed gondolas, and is the state's only major destination to offer night skiing on a large scale. Keystone Lodge, an early bastion of ski-country luxury, has been refurbished more than once over the years and is still a fine place to stay.

Next is the exit for Breckenridge, a 19th-century gold-mining boomtown set against the soaring 10 Mile Range – a dramatic north–south chain of 10 mountains named Peak

1 through Peak 10. When it opened in 1961, with one double chair-lift and a short T-bar, Breckenridge welcomed 17,000 skiers during the first season. Today, it hosts the same number on a busy Saturday. In 1981, Breckenridge installed the world's first detachable quad chair-lift which, with a capacity of 2,800 skiers per hour, is credited with launching the sport's high-speed quad revolution. Three years later, "Breck" became Colorado's first major resort to allow snowboarding. Another lift innovation followed in 1999 with the installation of a double-loading, six-passenger chair-lift.

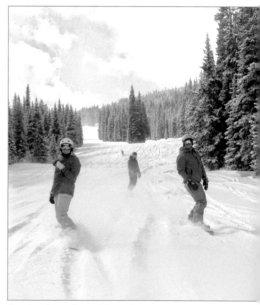

Snowboarders at Copper Mountain.

Copper Mountain, directly south of I-70, was developed 10 years after Breckenridge. Like Keystone, it was a built-from-scratch ski resort, with lodging as well as lifts. Its mountain and big backside bowl regularly win kudos for their intelligent layout, and its resort base has been totally remade in the successful formula developed by corporate giant Intrawest, which acquired it in 1997.

Mighty Vail

Farther along I-70 is Vail, America's largest ski area in terms of skiable acreage and lift capacity, and arguably its most successful resort. Vail was the brainchild of 10th Mountain Division veterans Pete Seibert, Bill "Sarge" Brown and

Bob Parker, who shared an audacious vision for a grand, European-style resort. When Vail opened in 1962 with the nucleus of an Alpine-style village, a long four-passenger gondola, two chair-lifts, and a Pomalift, it became the most talked-about ski area in the country. Skiers haven't stopped talking since – or visiting.

Vail's mammoth ski terrain stretches 7 miles (11km) from east to west, and encompasses nearly 5,300 acres (2,200 hectares), 36 lifts (14 of them high-speed quads) with a mind-boggling hourly lift capacity of 51,781, and snowriding on 193 named trails. In addition to

up-market resort, with gated entrances, monumental architecture, and some of the most pleasant cruising terrain in Colorado. The resort's legal beagles copyrighted the term "village-to-village skiing" in order to stress that its three lodging "villages" – Beaver Creek, Bachelor Gulch, and Arrowhead – are connected by trails, a fairly unusual arrangement in the United States.

Winter Park and Steamboat

If you exit I-70 at Empire and head north over Berthoud Pass, you come to Winter Park Resort,

Snowmobiling through the forests near Vail.

frontside runs cut through the trees, Vail has seven side-by-side backside bowls. Across the valley is Blue Sky Basin, added in the winter of 1999–2000. Vail Village takes in half a dozen development pods on both sides of I-70, and what is now known promotionally as the Vail Valley stretches all the way from the west side of Vail Pass to Edwards. Vail is just about as far from Denver as most people are willing to drive for a day skiing.

Beaver Creek, 10 miles (16km) to the west, was to have been developed for the 1976 Winter Olympics. Colorado refused the Games, however, giving time for the Beaver Creek plan to mature. Since it opened in 1980, Beaver Creek has grown into the state's most

popular with both vacationers and day-trippers. This is the only resort in the Rockies served by a dedicated "ski train," which departs from Union Station in Denver. Winter Park's 3,0810 skiable acres (1,247 hectares) encompass four summits, 143 runs and 26 lifts. Groswold Discovery Park is an exceptional beginner area, situated well up the mountain but isolated from faster skiers and snowboarders. The Mary Jane sector offers legendary mogul-dotted steeps, Parsenn Bowl has gobs of high-elevation powder, and the Cirque offers fly-on-the-wall pitch.

Far to the northwest, Steamboat occupies a beautiful west-facing massif near the Wyoming state line. The resort's marketing department coined the phrase "champagne powder" to describe the deep, soft snow that accumulates on broad slopes and drifts into aspen glades. Steamboat's pioneering Kids Ski Free program lures thousands of families. The traditional ranching town of Steamboat Springs is just 3 miles (5km) from the sprawling resort at the base of the mountain.

Aspen and Crested Butte

Among skiers, "Aspen" refers to four ski areas under the same ownership near the chic mountain town of the same name. Aspen Mountain, the granddaddy of them all, sprang to life in

1941 with a 10-passenger "boat" tow, comprised of an old mine hoist powered by a truck engine. A chair-lift was installed in 1946, and Aspen Mountain has set the gold standard for ski-borne excitement ever since.

Three other resorts – Aspen Highlands, Buttermilk, and Snowmass – were developed later, each with a distinct personality. Snowmass is by far the largest of the trio, with 94 trails on 3,332 skiable acres (1,348 hectares), second only to Vail; it features a wicked 4,406ft (1,343-meter) vertical drop, Colorado's biggest. A million-acre (404,685-hectare) new base village at Snowmass

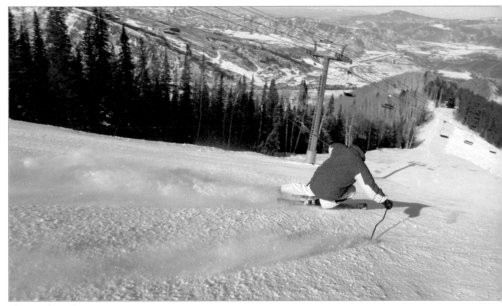

The steep slopes of Aspen.

CRISSCROSSING COLORADO

With hundreds of miles of groomed trails and virtually limitless backcountry terrain, Colorado is perfect for cross-country skiers. There are 17 Nordic centers and three guest ranches that offer groomed trails for both cross-country skiers and snowshoers and access to challenging backcountry terrain. Most have classes for skiers of all levels, as well as nature tours and guided treks. For information, contact Nordic Ski Colorado (2810 Hawthorne Avenue, Grand Junction, CO 81506; www.crosscountryskicolorado.com). Alternatively, several dude ranches trade horses for skis during the winter months, and also offer sleigh rides, sledding, and horseback riding. Most of the ranches are surrounded by thousands of acres of national forest.

For multiday journeys there's a network of 34 cabins linking 350 miles (560km) of backcountry in the Central Rockies, between Aspen, Crested Butte, Leadville, and Vail, and throughout the San Juan Mountains of the Southern Rockies. Known as hut-to-hut travel, trekking between huts requires both navigation skill and skiing ability; skiers with less experience tend to spend one or more nights in a single hut rather than travel from one to another. For further information, contact the 10th Mountain Division Hut Association, 1280 Ute Ave, Suite 21, Aspen, CO 81611; tel: 970-925-5775; www.huts.org.

has been developed by Related Westpac, complete with hotels, condos, restaurants, shops, and other visitor facilities, all with a sustainable design. It includes a children's center and mountain improvements.

Just 25 miles (40km) from Aspen as the crow flies, but an epic drive in winter, is Crested Butte. The enchanting Victorian town nestles in the valley; a separate resort area is set at the base of the lifts. The terrain is varied and quirky, wrapping part-way around a signature peak. Crested Butte offers everything from beginner slopes that are smooth as a table top to some of Colorado's gnarliest terrain, including an area dubbed Extreme Limits, described by one writer as "a staircase of huge, staggered headwalls that drop off the north side of the mountain." Though Crested Butte is relatively modest in overall size, an elevation gain of 3,062ft (933 meters) from base to summit puts it in Colorado's top 10 of vertical drop.

The San Juans

Durango Mountain Resort and Telluride are the top destinations in the snow-rich San Juan Range of southwestern Colorado. Tellu-

Hiking to the perfect spot high above Telluride.

SILVERTON MOUNTAIN

The biggest little ski area in America, Silverton Mountain is not your average resort. It opened in 2000, the antithesis of the mega-resorts that sprawl across the Rocky Mountains. This backcountry ski area is best defined by what it does not have – no conventional amenities, no novice or intermediate terrain, no trail map, no ski school, no frills. Naturally, it quickly developed a cult following among some of the best skiers and snowboarders in the land. It adjoins Silverton, a charming Victorian mining town filled with character, reached via narrow-gauge railway or the winding San Juan Skyway from Durango.

ride is the name of a gussied-up mining town as well as a nearby ski area, which encompasses a posh development called Mountain Village and an expanded terrain of 2,000 skiable acres (809 hectares) and 120 runs. Linking the old town and Mountain Village is a gondola, affording breathtaking views of the valley and surrounding peaks. Telluride's expert runs are among Colorado's most challenging, but its novice and intermediate terrain are top-notch, too.

Family-friendly Purgatory Resort is smaller and far less exclusive than Telluride, with 1,360 skiable acres (550 hectares), 88 trails, 10 lifts, five terrains, and a vertical drop that's a hair over 2,000ft (600 meters). In 2008, the resort opened its luxury $50-million Purgatory Lodge, anchor for the new Purgatory Village, followed, in 2009, by the unveiling of expanded acreage with 125 acres (50 hectares) of expert terrain. The town of Durango is about 30 minutes away.

Lesser-known resorts

In addition to the mega-resorts is an array of mid-sized ski areas, where the prices are reasonable, the atmosphere is low-key and the conditions, while not superlative, are adequate for novice and intermediate skiers.

snow falls frequently, piles up deep, and lasts late into the season. These areas are ideal for people who miss the ambience of old-time skiing, don't give a fig about fashion, and prefer snow as nature makes it. They have day lodges instead of slopeside villages, free parking instead of pay lots, and their collective 33 lifts don't include a single high-speed chair. They're decent places for beginners, but have plenty to offer intermediate and advanced skiers and snowboarders.

Loveland straddles I-70 about an hour from Denver. It has two pods: Loveland Valley for

Chair lift at Copper Mountain.

Granby Ranch, for instance, is a pleasant little ski resort north of Winter Park. It consists of an easy hill and an easier hill – a snooze if you're an experienced skier but a good choice if you're just learning or traveling with small children. Intermediate skiers and families with school-age children may prefer Sunlight Mountain Resort, near Glenwood Springs, or Powderhorn Resort, on the north side of Grand Mesa, east of Grand Junction.

Just because a ski area is small doesn't mean it's not challenging. In fact, some of Colorado's most exciting slopes are found at half a dozen sites that are short on size but long on action. Five of the six are situated on high passes along the Continental Divide, where

SKI COUNTRY, INCORPORATED

The consolidation rampant in corporate America has invaded ski country, providing capital for large-scale improvements at big resorts but homogenizing the ski experience. Vancouver-based Intrawest developed Keystone's Village at River Run and owns Steamboat Ski and Resort and Winter Park. Vail Resorts, Inc., operates lodging and all on-mountain facilities at Vail, Beaver Creek, Breckenridge, and Keystone, as well as Colorado Mountain Express and RockResorts Hotels. Aspen Skiing Company controls on-mountain facilities at Aspen Mountain, Buttermilk, Aspen Highlands, and Snowmass, and operates some Aspen lodging.

beginners and the larger Loveland Basin, which has trails woven through evergreens topped by expansive ski-anywhere terrain. Its fixed-grip quad, which unloads at 13,010ft (3,965 meters), is the world's highest four-place chair-lift.

Just over the west side of Loveland Pass is Arapahoe Basin. With a summit elevation of 13,050ft (3,980 meters), A-Basin is the country's highest lift-served ski area. A spring-skiing center, the lifts regularly operate into June, often July, and with snow-making finally installed, the season launches in October. Set in a cirque beneath the brow of the Continental

Skiers at Steamboat.

Divide, half the ski terrain is above timberline, providing vistas of treeless, craggy peaks etched in high relief against an azure sky. Steep snow-fields and relentless chutes give it a reputation as an experts-only area, but milder slopes are available, too. Beginners have free use of the Molly Hogan novice hill at the base.

Situated just east of Monarch Pass, near Salida, the Monarch Ski Area snares an average of 350in (890cm) of powder annually from the "Monarch Cloud." Nearly all the acreage is ski-able, including areas that don't appear on the trail map – uncharted powder shots through a mature forest of well-spaced pine and fir. A lodge is a couple of miles away, but there are ample accommodations in Salida.

Ski Cooper, which opened as Cooper Hill Ski Area in 1941, high on Tennessee Pass near Leadville, is the true heir to World War II's Camp Hale. This family-friendly, low-cost ski area remains a rustic outpost of casual, spirited, rarely crowded skiing. The site encompasses 39 runs on two mountain faces with a modest 1,200ft (365-meter) vertical drop. There are four lifts – two longish lifts and two short surface lifts. The front side offers easy to mid-level skiing, with slightly steeper runs on the backside.

Wolf Creek, between South Fork and Pagosa Springs, has a 465in (1,180cm) average annual snowfall, nearly 100in (250cm) more than any other ski area in Colorado save Silverton Mountain. The prodigious powder and laid-back ambience appeal to deep-snow addicts. The area comprises a long ridge that drapes down into mountain top bowls, superlative glades, and wide cruising runs. Advanced skiers and snowboarders seeking a backcountry experience can traverse to Alberta Peak, Step Bowl, and Knife Ridge, true havens of the steep and deep in southern Colorado.

Hometown advantage

The small fry in Colorado's ski scene are the modest, often municipally owned ski slopes. Many are run by volunteers and open only on weekends and school holidays for the benefit of local youngsters. These include Kendall Mountain in Silverton, Chapman Hill in Durango, and Hesperus between Durango and Mancos.

Among the largest sites in this category is Eldora Mountain Resort in Nederland, 21 miles (34km) west of Boulder, which has 680 acres (275 hectares) of cross-country and downhill skiing as well as snowboarding, and a dozen lifts. Another small ski area that casts a big shadow is Steamboat Springs' Howelsen Hill. It is the town's main winter amenity, offering night skiing, ski jumping, freestyle and race training, cross-country skiing, and ice-skating – all at a rock-bottom price. If you ski Steamboat and want to meet the locals, including a few candidates for the US Ski Team, Howelsen Hill is the place to be.

Despite their diminutive size, these local ski hills are guardians of Colorado's ski legacy, and they are just as important as the giant resorts that pull in millions of skiers and riders from around the world.

GHOST TOWNS

Visions of bygone days are evoked by former mining camps – some in ruins, others reborn as tourist havens – mementoes of those who came here seeking their fortunes.

An abandoned mill on the Crystal River, near Marble.

Here today, gone tomorrow – then, frequently, back again, in a completely different form. Colorado's many mining ghost towns are the shape-shifters of the architectural world. From potential state capital to tourism and gambling at Central City. Silver mining to celebrity skiing at Aspen, Breckenridge and Telluride. Rough mining camp to ghost town museum at Fairplay. Abandoned mountain town to vacation paradise in artsy Creede. All of these ghosts, and many more, have roared back to life, blurring the line between past and present in entirely new ways.

They are the lucky ones, the rediscovered gems of Colorado's rich and rowdy mining history. Hundreds of other mining camps and towns, with populations that once numbered in the thousands, slumber on in mountain valleys and hillsides throughout the Rockies. Today, their only inhabitants are deer and chipmunks and the occasional tourist in search of Colorado's colorful past.

Former lives

Once these towns were spectacularly alive, swarming with miners and merchants, clergymen and saloon-keepers, lawmakers and lawbreakers. Well-dressed dudes from back East brought capital for the expensive machinery required to dig deep into the earth for hidden and elusive riches. But many of the towns they created were destined to fail. When all the precious stuff was tapped out, the settlements were doomed. The bonanzas that fueled boomtowns were dramatic, the decline often catastrophic. As mineral deposits played out and miners moved on to new fields of dreams, fortunes won quickly turned to fortunes lost, and boomtown became ghost town.

Those towns built to serve surrounding mining camps never really died. Lake City, Ouray, Silverton, Telluride, Durango, and Denver were close to mines that yielded billions of tons of gold, silver, lead, and other precious metals. They grew into the largest and wealthiest towns in the state and became politically important as supply centers and seats of local and state government.

Today, they are undergoing a metamorphosis. Whole districts of Victorian mansions, company buildings, hotels, bars, and bordellos are now on the National Register of Historic Places. Many have been restored by artists, retirees, and local historical associations and turned into quirky homegrown museums, art galleries, bed-and-breakfasts, bars, and restaurants filled with mine memorabilia.

Colorado's mining boom began late, nearly a decade after the California Gold Rush, mainly due to the inaccessibility of the 14,000ft (4,270-meter) Rocky Mountains. The 1859 gold strike in Gregory Gulch attracted fortune hunters who traveled to north-central Colorado's high-altitude mining camps by whatever means they could, some hauling their worldly possessions up mountain sides in handcarts. It was the construction of toll roads and narrow-gauge railroads in the 1870s

Handcart passengers on the Cripple Creek Short Line in one of the state's richest mining districts.

that made mining economically viable, linking remote mining settlements with smelter towns like Durango. Today, these historic roads, Jeep trails, and narrow-gauge railroads have been restored and are the mainstay of a new economy – tourism – that has helped revive ghost towns throughout the Rockies.

There are more than 700 ghost towns in Colorado, by some estimates the greatest number in the West. A true ghost town has two characteristics: its population has precipitously decreased, and the initial reason for its settlement, usually a mine, no longer supports the community. Scores are no more than mysterious names on a topographical map, completely unpopulated, with dilapidated buildings, empty schools, churches, and collapsed headframes. Most, though, have a few residents who look after the buildings, conduct tours, and keep alive those forgotten places.

Frozen in time

The quintessential Colorado ghost town is a highly photogenic mining camp at the foot of breathtaking mountains, the faded timbers of its cabins and false-front buildings creaking in the wind and nearby mining tackle falling into a steep ravine filled with wild flowers. Your best bet in Colorado for this type of experience is St Elmo, 24 miles (39km) southwest of Buena Vista in the South Park mining region. Founded in the 1880s, St Elmo was typical of gold and silver boomtowns: it grew so fast that tents standing one day were replaced by hand-hewn log cabins within the week. A few months later, many cabins were supplanted by milled-lumber, false-front buildings. In the early days, if a guest arrived at a not-quite-complete hotel and asked for a private room, the hotelier drew a chalk line around one of the beds and told him that he had even given him a suite.

A supply center for nearby mines, St Elmo was a favorite Saturday night "blow off" town for miners, freighters, railroad workers, and other passers-by. When Mark Twain rode the railroad down to St. Elmo, the brakeman "had some difficulty" after the perilous journey, and Twain declined a return trip. Now the town is somnolent. Miners' cabins have become summer residences and the main activity centers on insatiable chipmunks cadging handouts from visitors. Eccentric brothers Roy and Tony Stark and their sister Annabelle owned the Comfort Home Hotel and protected the town for decades. Tony and Annabelle were among the last residents of the crumbling ghost town. Since she died in 1960, Annabelle's ghost has been seen or felt at times, still watching over the town from the hotel windows. The town is now a national historic site.

A ghost town of a different type lies not far from St. Elmo on the outskirts of the former mining camp of Fairplay, founded in 1859 by miners who found themselves shut out of diggings at Tarryall. Opened a century after the first gold strike in Colorado, South Park City is an authentic restoration of a Colorado mining town. Some 28 of its 35 buildings were brought here from all over Colorado, restored, and filled with mining-era artifacts. A schoolhouse straight out of *Little House on the Prairie* has desks, chairs, and a blackboard. A drug store is so well stocked with remedies, it looks like the movie set of *Dr Quinn, Medicine Woman*. In all, some 60,000 mining-era artifacts fill the buildings.

Nearby Cripple Creek's restoration was funded in an entirely different way: casino gambling. Slot machines and blackjack tables now fill the historic buildings in this 1890s gold-mining town, which once had a larger population than Denver. For a glimpse of what Cripple Creek once looked like, visit Victor, 6 miles (10km) to the southwest. This former gold town has rare brick-and-mortar buildings, including a two-story school, depot, church, newspaper office, and a once-elegant miners' club. Its paved streets, dug up during the Depression, were literally "paved with gold" – mine waste from local diggings. Boxing legend Jack Dempsey, who grew up in Colorado, was a mucker at the Portland Mine before becoming heavyweight champion of the world. To view more former mining towns, drive the 122-mile

Village store, St Elmo.

HAUNTED COLORADO

From ghostly beauties tempting train engineers, to dripping mine shafts echoing with the banter of men long dead, Colorado echoes with tales of unexplained phenomena. Leadville historian Roger Peterson has had several close encounters over the years.

His most powerful experience took place in Silverton, where he recorded noises in an old miners' boarding house. In the night, he was awakened by the sound of someone slamming books on a coffee table in an empty adjoining room. Playing back the tape the next day, he heard a menacing voice, sounding as if it came from inside a well, saying "Share the loot."

Cheryl Lloyd, caretaker of the Matchless Mine Museum, also tells of strange goings-on at the 1880 silver mine that made millionaires – then paupers – of Horace and Baby Doe Tabor. After Horace's death, Baby Doe occupied a shack at the worthless mine, surviving on charity from townsfolk and unrequited hope of a new silver boom. In March 1935 she was found frozen to death at the age of 81. But Lloyd says she is still very much present. Visitors send Lloyd photos taken here, showing unexplained waves, lights, and reflections in the shack. Lights flick on and off, even after bulbs are removed. And after visitors tried to sit in an empty rocking chair that already seemed occupied, Lloyd placed a sign on it: "Please don't sit on me."

(196km) Gold Belt Loop between Cripple Creek and Cañon City, which winds among the steep gulches of the south slope of Pikes Peak.

Vanished communities

St Elmo and Victor are two of Colorado's best ghost towns, but even deserted, decrepit ghosts offer much to see and photograph. Some showcase old railroad depots. Others feature mills, smelters, headframes, tramways, and other mining-related buildings and equipment. Often a boarded-up courthouse or school dominates the site. In many cases, the sole reminder that

a town ever existed is its forlorn cemetery, with weathered markers and picketless fences.

The 65-mile (105km) Alpine Loop National Back Country Byway linking Lake City, Silverton, and Ouray in the San Juan Mountains of southwestern Colorado is filled with abandoned ghost towns. Capitol City, a few miles southwest of Lake City and reachable by passenger car, briefly boomed in the 1870s, when the Galena Mining District brought untold silver wealth to the area. One entrepreneur, George Lee, was so convinced the town was set to become the state capital, he built smelters and a governor's

The Durango & Silverton Narrow Gauge Railroad.

ALL ABOARD!

Colorado's narrow-gauge railways add an element of romance to visiting ghost towns in the Rockies. The 45-mile (72km) Durango & Silverton Narrow Gauge Railway brings passengers by steam train from Durango into the heart of Silverton twice a day in summer. The 6-mile (10km) Georgetown Loop Railroad carries passengers between Georgetown and Silver Plume on an hour-long trip on a 1920s-era steam locomotive. The railway links two 1859 mining towns that boomed for 30 years, first with the discovery of gold, then large quantities of silver. Georgetown today is undergoing a renaissance as an expensive retreat, and its downtown historic district has the largest number of preserved historic

buildings in Colorado. Several of the buildings are now museums recounting the area's rich mining history. The historic railroad through Royal Gorge, the 1,053ft (321-meter) deep canyon cut by the Arkansas River, begins in Cañon City, about 35 miles (56km) from Cripple Creek. The 24-mile (38km) round-trip offers amazing views of Royal Gorge, and views of the world's highest suspension bridge. Buckskin Joe, a movie-set town with stagecoach rides, shootouts, and costumed actors, was recreated with buildings from the original mining town, northwest of Cañon City, and entertained tourists for 53 years. In 2011, it was bought by Florida billionaire Bill Koch and moved to his ranch.

mansion at the remote site. With the silver crash of 1893, the town was quickly left to the elements and has never been reoccupied.

There are people in the buildings at Animas Forks, but only for a few days each summer, when this abandoned 1870s town, located at an elevation of 11,200ft (3,415 meters) 12 miles (19km) north of Silverton, offers living history days. Costumed interpreters, including a doctor's wife, a teacher, pioneer children, and the town sheriff, serve lemonade and apple-sauce cake and chat with visitors who arrive by Jeep, mountain bike, or hiking trail.

Animas Forks was once a bustling mining community of 450 people with 30 cabins, a hotel, general store, saloon, and post office. An important mining mill and processing center, it was the San Juan County seat, where court cases were heard. One man who didn't like the outcome of his trial promised, "I'll take this to a higher court!" Responded the wry judge, "There is no higher court in Colorado."

In 1884, Animas Forks suffered a blizzard that lasted 23 days and dumped 25ft (7 meters) of snow on the town. Residents dug tunnels to get from building to building. Silverton, 2,000ft (610 meters) lower, was considered positively balmy and became a popular place to spend the winter. Laid out along the Animas River in Baker's Park in 1874, Silverton soon became the mining center of the San Juans. The arrival of the Denver & Rio Grande Railroad linked it to the new smelter town of Durango, 45 miles (72km) away, in 1882, and Otto Mears' new toll road allowed auto traffic to continue north to Ouray and Ridgway. Eventually, Silverton was incorporated and became the county seat. Among the many buildings in its authentic downtown historic district (complete with saloons, hotels, stores, and a red-light district) is a lavish courthouse next door to the county museum.

More modern ghost towns

Despite their scenic locations, authentic ghost towns are frequently homely affairs. Colorado's 20th-century mining boom netted a number of forgettable company towns dedicated to extracting copper, radium, vanadium, uranium, and oil shale to suit the energy and defense needs of an entirely different new century.

The town of Uravan on the southern end of the Unaweep–Tabeguache Scenic Byway, which follows SR 141 between Naturita and

In summer, the Alpine Loop links Silverton to communities in the central San Juans, such as Lake City, and the San Juan Skyway – connecting the western San Juans – brings thousands of drivers into the mountains annually.

Whitewater, was built in 1936 by the US Vanadium Corporation. Until the declining market forced the town to close in 1984, some 42 million lbs (20 million kg) of uranium and 220

Old houses in Animas Forks.

million lbs (100 million kg) of vanadium were extracted from carnotite rocks here. Today, the place is abandoned, and Umetco Minerals Corporation is undertaking a 15-year, $70 million reclamation project to clean up the mine site.

The fate of Parachute, just east of Grand Junction, is still in the balance. Built by Union Oil Company during the energy crisis of the 1970s to mine oil shale, the multimillion-dollar company town and processing plant was one of the largest employers in the Grand Junction area. The population has dwindled to 1,006 souls, and the town now sits beside roaring traffic along I-70, a forlorn testament to modern boom-and-bust economics in Colorado's energy-rich northwest corner.

See reconstructions of an old mining town at South Park City Museum.

RIDING THE RAILS

It took master builders to lay track over forbidding
terrain, connect Colorado with the rest of the world,
and leave a steel trail for vacationers to pursue.

Pioneers would be puzzled by our modern romance with that clanking, smoky,
iron contraption: the 19th-century steam
engine. They would see an automobile as being
so much cleaner, so much more comfortable
than a hard-backed seat on wheels. For that
matter, the diesel locomotives of today are a
great improvement – quieter, more powerful,
pulling clean air-conditioned cars on welded
tracks. You can imagine an old-timer shaking
his head, wondering why people would want
to get cinders in their hair.

On the other hand, even the toughest old
miner working his diggings in a high country
camp must have got excited seeing that column of smoke moving up the canyons of the
Colorado Rockies. With their whistles sounding, freight cars full of fancy goods from back
East, visiting relatives, and hardware for the
mines, the steam trains that huffed their way
through Colorado's mining country were a vital
link with the outside world. Back then, passengers probably leaped aboard with the same
enthusiasm as the 700,000 tourists a year who
today line up to ride one of the 10 scenic railroads that, since the 1990s, have been revived
throughout the Rockies.

The railroad vision

Although they seem quaint to us now, the 5,739
miles (9,236km) of railroad track that once
linked the far-flung communities of Colorado
were a miracle of American can-do technology
and entrepreneurial vision in the second half
of the 1800s, when most of it was laid. What
started out as a grand political move to build a
transcontinental railroad, linking East and West,
was quickly taken on as a local cause among
the movers and shakers within the states the

*Christening the Colorado Springs and Cripple Creek train
No. 2 in 1900.*

American railroad crossed. Once a cross-country
railroad became a reality, in the 1880s, businessmen like Union Pacific Railroad's Jay Gould, the
Denver & Rio Grande's General Palmer, Denver
Pacific Railroad's David Moffat, and Colorado
Central Railroad's William Loveland competed
to build branch lines that would tie remote
mining towns in Colorado to the main route,
and to markets back East. Over nearly a century,
fortunes were made and lost, as the markets for
gold, silver, coal and, in the 20th century, uranium, rose and fell and railroads changed ownership as fast as a game of Monopoly.

In 1848, remote, mountainous Colorado
seemed like the other side of the moon to the

US government in Washington DC, which had just taken ownership of the West from Mexico. From the reports of Spanish and American explorers, politicians and businessmen were keenly aware that vast mineral wealth lay under unsettled lands out there. Colorado's rugged topography presented a formidable obstacle to American settlement. It was territory known only to Utes and other native people and a few mountain men and adventurers.

One American explorer, John C. Frémont, had already made three overland trips to California, using famed scout Kit Carson to guide him

gold in California in 1848. Congress allocated $150,000 for four separate surveys and sent Captain John Gunnison to survey a potential route through the Central Rockies. Following part of Spanish friar Escalante's route, Gunnison traveled through the Gunnison River valley, staying north of the San Juan Mountains. He made it as far as Utah, where he and seven others, including well-known surveyor Richard Kern, were killed in the desert, apparently by Utes at war with Mormons during the Walker War (although this is by no means certain: anti-government feeling by Mormon militants may have played a part).

An 1894 wreck on the Florence & Cripple Creek Railroad near Anaconda.

through the Rockies. Late in 1848, a cabal of St Louis railroad promoters paid Frémont to make a fourth cross-country trip to investigate a possible transcontinental route through Colorado. After getting a late start, the expedition turned deadly in the San Juan Mountains, when Frémont and the 33 men in his party found themselves trapped by deep snows in the high country surrounding the headwaters of the Upper Rio Grande. Frémont and his men were eventually rescued, but not before 11 had died in the treacherous mountains of the Continental Divide.

It would be five years before surveyors would try again, this time as part of a major railroad survey authorized by Congress, which had fast-tracked its plans following the discovery of

Gunnison's second-in-command continued to Salt Lake City and eventually returned to Washington with a favorable report of the route. Not to be outdone, in the winter of 1854, John C. Frémont returned to Colorado, retracing Gunnison's route, proving that a year-round railroad was indeed viable.

Local railroad ambitions

A national depression, in-fighting over which towns would host the new railroad, and the Civil War delayed construction of the transcontinental railroad for a decade. But the discovery of gold in 1858, followed by a silver bonanza, finally forced the government to act. In the late 1860s, Congress chartered the Union Pacific to

Riding the train through Black Canyon of the Gunnison National Park in 1889, Rudyard Kipling noted: "There was a glory and a wonder . . . about the mad ride . . . I had to offer prayers for the safety of the train."

build a transcontinental line, and to the chagrin of the fledgling state capital of Denver, UPR chose a route through Cheyenne, Wyoming, that avoided the Rocky Mountains.

Left out in the cold, Denver businessmen hatched plans to build their own railroads north to tie in with the transcontinental line. The first to act was William Loveland, whose Colorado Central Railroad Company built track north from Golden to Cheyenne. Denver rival David Moffatt formed the Denver Pacific Railroad in 1870, linking Denver with Cheyenne. By the end of that year, 157 miles (253km) of track had been laid. The race was on.

Narrow gauge debut

Early railroads all ran on standard gauge track, but Colorado's steep mountain and canyons required a different kind of railroad. In 1870, General Palmer, former director of the Denver Pacific, founded the Denver & Rio Grande Railroad, which, from the beginning, was designed to serve the remote mining country of Colorado. An empire builder by nature, Palmer's genius was to conceive of a railroad with many feeder branches linking Colorado's far-flung mining communities. The Denver & Rio Grande operated on the 3ft (1-meter) wide narrow gauge as opposed to the standard gauge, which allowed steam trains and their cars to better negotiate narrow curving canyons in the mountains. "It doubles in, doubles out, leaving the traveller still in doubt whether the engine on the track is going, or coming back," wrote one commentator. Palmer's line was hailed as a resounding success.

Mining communities along the way, such as Animas City in southwestern Colorado, worked closely with the Denver & Rio Grande, realizing the railroad would give them an important competitive edge in business. But Palmer proved a fickle business partner. Once he had gained local support for the railroad, he drove a hard bargain with local communities that hoped to host a D&RG rail depot. When, inevitably,

local burghers balked, he would lay out his own company town nearby, complete with smelters, banks, hotels, saloons, mercantiles, and other businesses. Colorado Springs, Pueblo, Durango, Salida, and Gunnison were all Palmer towns that became important commercial centers. Once established, Palmer then created subsidiary businesses to serve the mines. One, the Colorado Coal and Iron Company, supplied coal that ran the smelters and trains. Coal mining became an important component of smelter towns like Durango, which, by the late 1800s, were wreathed in the dark smoke of coal-fired boilers.

The Durango & Silverton narrow gauge railroad.

Palmer wasn't the only one to benefit from the flurry of railroad building. By the 1880s, Denver had maneuvered itself to the center of the Union Pacific Railroad, Denver & Rio Grande, and Kansas Pacific lines, and had quickly taken over from Golden as Colorado's main supply center. In Golden, William Loveland regrouped and built a line from Golden to Denver to take advantage of its central position on the railroad. He now concentrated on building a railroad to the major producing mines of the South Slope of Pikes Peak in Clear Creek Canyon, Black Hawk, and Georgetown, and laid track to Fort Collins, due north of Golden. Other companies moved to monopolize the southern routes. In 1889, the Atchison, Topeka & Santa Fe Railroad consolidated its hold on eastern Colorado by constructing what came to be called the Banana Line (for its yellow coaches) through the San Luis Valley to Pueblo. Pueblo became a major railroad center for points south. One line, dubbed the Chili Line, was built through the agriculturally rich Rio Grande Valley of New Mexico to Española. Another went from Pueblo to the mining town of Trinidad, over Raton Pass, the gateway to the Pecos Valley, to Lamy, near Santa Fe, and continued to points south and west.

Engine 42 at the Durango Railroad Museum.

DURANGO & SILVERTON LINE

A visit to the San Juan Mountains of southwest Colorado isn't complete without a trip on the Durango & Silverton Narrow Gauge Railroad, aboard two 1920s steam trains pulling yellow parlor cars and open gondolas through the lovely Animas River canyon. The 45-mile (72km) journey takes in redrock cliffs, epic views of 14,000ft (4,270-meter) mountains in the Weminuche Wilderness, the rapids of the Animas River 400ft (120 meters) below, and the 1905 Tacoma Hydroelectric Power Plant. Trains arrive in Silverton around noon. Explore the Victorian historic district before returning by train, or take a chartered bus back to Durango.

Silver roads

The short, savvy Russian immigrant they called the "Pathfinder of the San Juans," Otto Mears, benefited twice over from the arrival of the railroad. Mears was instrumental in pressuring the Utes to sign the Brunot Treaty of 1873, which forced the majority to vacate western Colorado and move to the Uinta Basin of northeastern Utah. Within the year, he had built the San Juan Skyway from Durango to Ridgway. A few years later he sold Palmer the railroad rights-of-way for the D&RG. In just nine short months, the Durango to Silverton line through the Animas Valley had been blasted out of sheer cliffs above the Animas River, allowing Silverton to become the Silver Capital of the San Juans. By 1887, the D&RG had reached the mining town of Ouray. Two years later, it connected with Lake City in the central San Juans.

The late silver rush continued the railroad building throughout Colorado. A number of smaller spurs tied into the D&RG. The County Midland built a line to Aspen in 1890. The Silverton Railroad, linking Silverton with mineral-rich Red Mountain, was built in 1889. In 1899, the Silverton, Gladstone & Northerly Line reached Gladstone. Then in 1904, the Silverton Northern Line reached Animas Forks. In 1892, David Moffatt's Denver to Creede line through Wagon Wheel Gap took advantage of the late silver rush in the Upper Rio Grande area. That same year, Otto Mears himself built the 172-mile (277km) Rio Grande Southern Railroad, linking Durango and Ridgway with the remote mining towns of Rico, Telluride, and nearby mines. Mine profits went up 90 percent overnight.

It didn't last long. Silver prices plummeted during the Silver Panic of 1893, and many of Colorado's smaller railroads went bankrupt and were bought out by the Union Pacific and Denver & Rio Grande. The days of small-time mining were over. Corporations now used expensive new technologies to dig deeper into veins of precious metals, and to intensively cyanide-leach gold and other minerals out of previously mined areas.

With the Depression, numerous companies went bankrupt and miles of railroad track fell out of use. In the 1930s, Rio Grande Southern and Denver & Rio Grande Western converted automobiles to run on narrow-gauge railroad tracks in the western San Juans. The hybrid auto/train, fondly known as the Galloping Goose because of its odd swaying gait on the tracks, once again linked remote communities in the Dolores River valley and the Lake City to Sapinero route. Today, examples can be seen at railroad museums in Ridgway and Dolores. Short excursions in a Galloping Goose car are a highlight of the Durango & Silverton Narrow Gauge Railroad's annual Railfest in August, along with special trips to Silverton in brightly painted 19th-century wood-powered and steam-powered locomotives.

ghosts, such as beautiful women who beckoned from the side of the tracks and naughty children who skipped right onto tracks and taunted engineers. Engines themselves sometimes acted as if possessed, racing behind trains and mysteriously jumping tracks, crashing into snowbanks, and causing problems for drivers. One of Colorado's worst train wrecks occurred in August 1904, when the Missouri Pacific Express derailed in a gulch north of Pueblo, killing 96 people. Heavy rains, not ghouls, were responsible for the disaster.

Today, thanks to the commitment of numerous railroad enthusiasts, historic rail-

A 1900 "flower excursion" on the Colorado Midland Railway.

Tourism

Set in some of the most dramatic and beautiful scenery in the country, Colorado's railroads have always been popular with tourists. In the late 1800s, ordinary folks, not just miners, rode the trains as day-trippers on their days off. In the late 1880s, people from Leadville traveled to Colorado Springs, via Manitou, Ute Pass and South Park, and enjoyed a thrilling ride through a tunnel and along a huge trestle. In 1891 a cog railway was completed to the top of 14,110ft (4,301-meter) Pikes Peak.

As more people rode the rails, a lively folklore grew up around Colorado's trains. Train drivers engulfed in darkness on lonely sections of track would often report sightings of mysterious

roads are again doing a lively business, linking former mining towns all over Colorado. Train fans are spoiled for choice. For those with little time, one-hour excursions aboard historic trains are available between Cripple Creek and Victor and on the Georgetown & Silver Plume Loop, linking former mining towns in Colorado's most extensive historic mining district. Not far away, short trips of a very different type are offered up Pikes Peak aboard the historic Pikes Peak Cog Railway, and on the newly opened Cañon City–Royal Gorge scenic train ride, where you can ride in air-conditioned comfort aboard a diesel locomotive to view Colorado's deepest gorge and the country's highest trestle bridge.

HOME ON THE RANGE

For a taste of the real West, would-be cowboys
eagerly mount a horse, learn to rope or join a cattle
drive, and don't mind being called dudes.

Give us your tired, your upper middle class, your city slickers with caffeine nerves and commuter jitters, and we'll turn them into ridin' and ropin' buckaroos. That was, and still is, the promise of the dude ranch, as unique an institution as ever set up housekeeping in the American West. What other vacation spot would ask guests to help water the horses and round up the heifers – and then ask them to pay for the privilege? But so strong is the American admiration for the cowboy lifestyle that people have spent a century's worth of summers at these homes away from home on the range.

Dude ranches began as a mix of romantic escapism and economic necessity. In the late 19th century, cattle ranchers in the newly opened frontiers of Colorado, Wyoming, and the Dakotas found Eastern friends and family – and sometimes perfect strangers – arriving at their doorsteps in droves. The visitors needed a base while they hunted buffalo and explored the scenic wonders. Such was the code of hospitality that the ranchers felt obliged to board and bed these guests for free and soon found that they were being eaten out of house and home

Though they hated charging visitors, they hated going broke even more. And so, starting in the late 19th century, some ranchers accepted paying guests. Ironically, it was those guests that saved them from economic disaster. While the vagaries of the cattle business drove other ranches into bankruptcy, those with paying guests managed to hang on. The idea caught on and before long dude ranches were opening throughout the West.

Railroads and ranches

Meanwhile, the railroads had discovered that a dude-ranch vacation could lure paying

Visitors can take a horseback ride from Aspen Lodge, near Estes Park, whether they are experienced or not.

passengers on westbound trains. They promoted the ranches in their tourist brochures. Popular magazines like *Ladies' Home Journal* and the *Saturday Evening Post* published paeans to the ranch vacation. As cities in the East and Midwest grew more crowded and industrialized, Western ranch life was seen as an ideal antidote to the strains of urban living. During the golden age of dude ranching, from about 1910 to World War II, guests would head west on the train to spend entire summers learning to rope and ride. On the ranch, tired businessmen swapped boardroom pressures for bunkhouse pleasures. Children got to live the life they saw in Tom Mix or Gene Autry movies. Women, in particular, were seen to benefit. Back East they might be condemned to enduring social chitchat on the porch of a staid resort while their husbands played golf. Out on the ranch, they could ride and hike and fish, just like the men.

By World War II, dude ranches had blossomed throughout Colorado and the West. Most of the ranches offered the basics: lots of horseback riding, including lessons and guided pack trips into the back country, wholesome entertainment like rodeos, square dancing, hay rides and campfire singalongs, and great quantities of hearty food.

"dude" was not an insult but simply a description of anybody who was not a native of the Rocky Mountains. Many dudes, they maintained, could outride Westerners – and that went for women and children, too.

Westerners had to make some adjustments, too. Ranchers had to learn how to manage herds of tourists instead of herds of cattle, and ranch wives had to cook for more demanding Eastern palates. Even the horse underwent some changes. A good dude horse possessed a capable trot and gallop and, most important of all, a good disposition. Some dude ranches

Cowboys round up a herd near Yellow Creek in Rio Blanco County, 1911; a typical salary was $25 a month plus "all the horses you can ride."

Dudes vs Westerners

Naturally, there were a few bumps along the trail as Easterners got a crash course in Western ways. The very name "dude ranch" hinted at one difficulty. Was being a dude a matter of pride or shame? To many, the term carried definite connotations of Eastern effeteness, like the pair of ranch visitors described this way by a grizzled wrangler: "One wore lavender angora chaps, the other bright orange, and each sported a tremendous beaver sombrero and wore a gaudy scarf knotted jauntily about his throat."

But, fearful that the paying guests might take offense, ranch owners took pains to say that

began to breed their own horses to promote those traits.

In some ways, a dude ranch was a boon to the working cowboy: as working cattle ranches became fewer and farther between, the dude ranch provided a place where cowboys could still be paid for their skills. As one ranch manager said, "There is a real future here for a cowhand who can ride, play the guitar, and still smell nice." An able dude-ranch wrangler had to be charming to the ladies, pals with the men, and a hero to the children. The duties could be arduous indeed, as one cowboy song laments: *I'm a tough, hard-boiled old cow-hand with a weather-beaten hide,*

But herdin' cows is nuthin' to teachin' dudes to ride.
I can stand their hitoned langwidge and their hifa-
lutin' foods,
But you bet your bottom dollar I am fed up on
wranglin' dudes.

Still, despite a few burrs under the saddle, dudes and wranglers and ranchers all generally got along fine. Many families returned to the same dude ranch summer after summer, generation after generation. Teenagers who had honed their horsemanship skills as children came back to work as wranglers on summers off from college. And an experience – seeing

volleyball courts, square dancing, and even dinner theater. Yet many others stick to their roots, focusing on horseback riding, pack trips, and riding lessons.

Saddle up

Horseback riding is still the main activity at most dude ranches. But you don't have to be an expert rider – in fact, you don't have to have ever climbed into a saddle at all. A good ranch will maintain a stable of horses suited to all levels of riding ability. It will also have an ample number of wranglers capable of instructing riders from

Colorado from the back of a horse – that had once been limited to ranch owners or to the very wealthy, became accessible to millions of middle-class Americans.

That's still true today. Dude ranches may have more competition for vacation time and money than they once did; few people take more than a week or two at a time for vacations. But the dude ranch has learned to change with the times and remain competitive by catering to the needs of family vacationers.

Today's dude ranches are more plush than the ranches of yore. Some have added healthful spa cuisine to the old standards of barbecued steak, beans, and corn on the cob; others entertain guests with swimming pools, tennis and

ZAPATA RANCH

For a ranch vacation with an environmental difference, consider the 103,000-acre (41,682-hectare) Zapata Ranch adjoining Great Sand Dunes National Park and Preserve in the San Luis Valley of southern Colorado. It is owned by The Nature Conservancy and managed as a unique conservation partnership with the Phillips ranch family. Guests learn traditional and modern ranching practices and enjoy exceptional views of wildlife and the surrounding high-desert landscape. The ranch accommodates 30 guests, housed in the lodge's 1800s log ranch house, a bunkhouse, or a separate building. For more information, visit www.zranch.org.

novice to expert. Some even give advanced riders a chance to try out rodeo events.

Most ranches offer daily trail rides; many also offer longer two- or three-day horse-packing trips for guests who really want to gallop far from the madding crowd. While guests at the earliest ranches regularly herded dogies, rode fences, and performed other ranch chores, such work is harder to come by these days. But some ranches still let guests who are good riders participate in the working life of the ranch. A few, like Colorado Trails in Durango and Sylvan Dale near Estes Park, even hold cattle drives that qualified guests can join.

Freedom of choice

Although horses still reign at the dude ranch, many ranches offer other activities. The popularity of fly fishing in the West has inspired some ranches – especially those along trout streams – to offer instruction in the sport. Other outfits offer whitewater rafting, mountain biking, Jeep tours, big-game hunting, and courses in bird-watching, photography, even geology. Children's programs are also offered at many ranches.

MacGregor Ranch, near Estes Park.

CHOOSING A DUDE RANCH

Dude-ranch vacations don't come cheap. An all-expenses-paid stay at a reputable ranch in peak season costs a couple of thousand dollars a week per adult. Ask around for personal recommendations, or research online. Two good sources of information are the Dude Ranchers Association (PO Box 2307, Cody, WY 82414; tel: 307-587-2339; www.duderanch.org) and Colorado Dude and Guest Ranch Association (PO Box D, Shawnee, CO 80475; tel: 1-866-94-CDGRA; www.coloradoranch.com). Ask whether the ranch has cabins, a bunkhouse, or a lodge? Are meals included? Is there a children's program? And is accessibility an issue?

As for amenities, those can vary greatly. Some old-time ranches maintain a simple but comfortable rusticity. That may mean cozy cabins grouped along a stream and grub that tends towards the Western classics. The emphasis at these places is on an authentic ranch experience and as much outdoor activity as you can handle. Other Colorado dude ranches are more akin to resorts, with tennis courts, golf courses, and cocktails by the pool. Some of the newest ranches – places like the Home Ranch near Clark and the Kessler Canyon Ranch near Rifle – are downright luxurious, with guest suites that rival those of the finest hotels and the kind of haute cuisine you'd expect to savor in Beverly Hills.

Colorado cowboys

Ranching in Colorado produced several famous cowboys, from cowboy-archeologist Richard Wetherill to Bose Ikard, the black cowboy who inspired the character Deets in the Western classic *Lonesome Dove*.

The American cowboy has his roots in the Spanish cowboys, or *vaqueros*, who worked on ranches throughout the Southwest in the colonial era. Many cowboy terms in use today derive from Spanish words of this era: buckaroo from *vaquero*, lariat from *la reata*, and chaps from *chaparcas*. Spanish missionaries in New Mexico, Texas, and California converted indigenous farmers and taught them ranching, using hardy longhorn cattle and churro sheep from Africa. Nomadic Western Utes, Jicarilla Apaches, Navajos, and Plains Indians in and around Colorado were more interested in Spanish horses, which they quickly adopted for hunting buffalo and raiding Spanish settlements. By the early 1900s, after they had been forced to settle on reservations, many of them became expert stockmen, hiring themselves out as cowboys to the Anglo ranchers who took over their lands.

The first rancher in Colorado, Colonel John D. Henderson, established a ranch on the South Platte River in 1859 and began selling meat to mining camps, after discovering that cattle could survive on the prairie year-round. In 1866, Texan Charles Goodnight drove 2,000 head of cattle north through New Mexico on the Goodnight-Loving Trail and sold them to Denver merchant John Wesley Iliff, Colorado's first cattle baron. Iliff eventually bought 30,000 head of cattle from Goodnight and supplied not only miners but workers building the transcontinental railroad. The completion of the railroad linked ranchers with markets back east and made ranching economically viable.

By 1884, there were 58 cattle companies in Adams County alone. But they didn't last long. In 1886–7, 80 to 90 percent of ranches failed as overstocked ranges depleted grasslands and caused what came to be known as the "Big Die-Up." The days of open range were over.

Women and minorities welcome

One in three cowboys in the late 1800s was African American or Hispanic. Black cowboys like Bose Ikard, who rode for Charles Goodnight, were skilled stockmen, many of whom started their own ranches out west. "Bose surpassed any man I had in endurance and stamina," Goodnight once said. "There was a dignity, a cleanliness, and reliability about him that was wonderful . . . I have trusted him more than any man."

Nor were all cattle barons men. Cattle queen Ann Bassett ran her family's ranch in remote Browns Park in northwest Colorado in the 1880s and was a match for any man, rolling her own cigarettes and drinking whiskey straight. In 1889, Butch Cassidy courted her sister, Josie, and Ann herself was engaged to rustler

A Colorado cowpoke in his finest gear, 1911.

Matt Rush. "I've done everything they said I did and a helluva lot more," boasted Bassett.

Remote canyons were a favored hideout for cattle rustlers. Sewemup Mesa got its name for the outlaw practice of cutting off brands on rustled cattle, sewing them up with baling wire, and rebranding them with another rancher's brand.

One of Colorado's most famous cowboys gained fame for something else entirely. During a snowstorm in 1880, rancher Richard Wetherill stumbled on Cliff Palace in Mesa Verde, and a whole new career. He led excavations of Mesa Verde, Chaco Canyon, and other areas. Wetherill popularized the Navajo word Anasazi ("enemy ancestors") to describe the Ancestral Puebloans and named their predecessors the Basketmakers.

ROCKY MOUNTAIN CUISINE

From true grits to nouvelle cuisine, Colorado
has been changing its menu to satisfy budding
tastes for all kinds of savory dishes.

N ot long ago, Colorado cuisine was strictly
meat and potatoes. Steak was considered
a good meal; a big steak was considered
a great one. Fortunately, times have changed.
Thanks largely to a wave of hot new chefs in
the 1990s, an epicurean fever has taken hold
in Colorado's cities and mountain resorts.
Restaurateurs are bolder, chefs more eager to
extend their creative reach, and customers more
willing to sample cutting-edge foods.

A key element of this gastronomic shift is a
rediscovery of foods associated with the state's
history and landscape stretching all the way
back to its earliest inhabitants. What was on
the menu in old-time Colorado? Fruits and
vegetables, of course, plus game meat, fish, and
whatever else nature could serve to sustain
the native people, most of whom were superb
hunter-gatherers. Such was the case with the
nomadic Utes, who inhabited the high country
west of the Front Range, as well as the Arapaho, Cheyenne, Kiowa, and Comanche tribes
who followed the bison herds across Colorado's eastern plains.

Early days

The state's first farmers were the ancestors of
today's Pueblo people who, beginning in AD
700, built large, complex communities in the
Mesa Verde canyon country of southwestern
Colorado. Their predecessors in the area were
nomadic hunter-gatherer Archaic people in
the pre-Christian era, and the Basketmakers,
the first to stay put, build pithouse villages and
experiment with agriculture during the early
1st century AD. Wild foods and game were
abundant in this high-elevation mesa country, and Ancestral Pueblo people hunted small
game such as deer and rabbits, using bows and

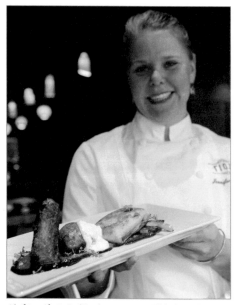

Chef Jennifer Jasinski at her restaurant Rioja in Larimer Square, Denver.

arrows. But they were primarily farmers, who
settled in and around well-watered tributary
canyons, building villages on the mesa tops and,
finally, in the 13th century, cliff dwellings in the
protective canyon walls. They dammed streams
and husbanded springs and rainwater to irrigate staple crops of corn, beans, and squash,
which they dried and kept in stone granaries
and beautifully made black-on-white pottery
containers.

By the early 1800s, Spanish settlers had fil-
tered up from New Mexico and put down
roots in the San Luis Valley, where they raised
grains, beans, and chile peppers. After them
came Anglo explorers, mountain men, and

prospectors, who hunted and traded for food at such rendezvous places as Bent's Fort in southeastern Colorado. In the late 1800s, a rudimentary food industry sprang up to nourish hungry miners struggling to wrest gold and silver from the ground. Local farms and ranches supplied the basic foods. Luxury items were shipped into the territory by rail and snapped up by the nouveau riche, who wanted to prove that there was indeed civilization on the frontier.

Although Colorado had its share of ethnic diversity among the miners and other immigrants who settled here, this particular smorgasbord of nationalities didn't make much of a dent in the culinary landscape. The diets of Coloradans tended to be blander than those in America's big coastal cities and industrialized states, where whole families from the Old World settled in dense clusters and assimilation proceeded at a slower pace. No regional style developed to produce anything distinctive like the chowders of New England, the gumbos of New Orleans, or the fiery specialties of the Southwest.

of hunting and fishing. What's been touted as "Colorado cuisine" or "Rocky Mountain cuisine" has developed into an eclectic style using ingredients that thrive in the state's high, dry climate. It's not unusual to find menus featuring ranch-raised elk and venison, Colorado lamb and local trout, artisan goat cheese and farm eggs from pasture-raised chickens, accompanied by fresh organic produce from local growers – lush peaches, corn, melon, baby squash, heirloom tomatoes, exotic mushrooms, designer asparagus, Japanese eggplant, field greens, and fresh herbs.

Hearty camp cooking is a Colorado tradition.

Home-grown flavor

What contemporary chefs are doing instead is reinterpreting the region's ranching and farming heritage as well as its long tradition

FARMERS' MARKETS

Farmers' markets are found from Denver to Ridgway and have become bona fide community attractions. Usually held once a week, they are a great way to connect with local communities, sample regional foods, learn how to cook them, and enjoy home-grown entertainment as well as delicious prepared foods. Most also sell handmade products, from wine to soap and clothing, that make usual and inexpensive gifts. The best-known farmers' market is Boulder County Farmers' Market, the largest in the state and one of the Top 25 in the nation. It takes place Wednesdays and Saturdays, May through October, next to Boulder's Central Park.

These products have graduated from oddities to staples. To raise Colorado foods up a few more notches, chefs have been busy developing distinctive salsas, marinades, glazes, infusions, vinaigrettes, spice rubs, and other such flavorful enhancements. Ingredients from the Southwest, including beans, chiles, tortillas, and tomatillos, have made their mark on Colorado kitchens but are prepared and presented with far more sophistication than typical Tex-Mex fare.

Imaginative cooks can also count on the availability of fresh, non-traditional ingredients considered vital to a rich cuisine. Fresh mozzarella, lemongrass, pancetta, miso, sesame oil, cilantro, sticky rice, and other former exotica have become commonplace as restaurants serving up French, Italian, Mediterranean, Thai, Japanese, Southwestern, and various combinations of so-called "fusion" fare pop up all over the place.

> Food & Wine magazine's Classic at Aspen is the star of culinary festivals, a three-day extravaganza featuring the most celebrated culinary talents from Colorado and beyond.

Produce at the Boulder County Farmers' Market.

UP WITH ORGANICS

Health-conscious Boulder is home to the country's first and most famous herbal tea company: Celestial Seasonings. It was started in the late 1960s by Mo Siegel and sold teas made from plants gathered in the foothills of the Rockies in folksy packaging. Now owned by Hain Foods, its factory tour is Boulder's most popular visitor attraction. Boulder is also home to White Wave organic tofu, Coleman natural beef, Redbird chicken, Earth's Best baby foods, Westbrae Natural Foods, Spectrum Oils, Rudi's organic bakery, and Great Range bison products. Organic foods and personal products are a booming business.

The trend hasn't gone unnoticed. The best of the Colorado restaurants have been singled out for diamonds from AAA, stars from Mobil, huzzahs from *Wine Spectator,* and plaudits from such trade groups as Distinguished Restaurants of America. One of the singular honors for an American chef is an invitation to cook at the James Beard House in New York. There, fussy foodies regularly gather to sample the best of the best. At last count, more than 30 Colorado chefs have cooked there and been shortlisted for annual awards. In 2013, Jennifer Jasinski of Rioja in Denver won "Best Chef in the Southwest." She was a semi-finalist for Outstanding Chef in 2016; in 2015 and 2016, Denver chefs Steven Redzikowski of Acorn, Dana Rodriguez of Work & Class, and Alex Seidel of Fruition were semi-finalists for Best Chef in the Southwest. In 2009, Hosea Rosenburg, executive chef of Jax Fish House in Boulder, won the Bravo cook-off reality show *Top Chef*.

Bread and cheese

Nowhere in the Colorado food firmament have the changes been more dramatic, and more welcome, than in the kingdom of breads. At artisan bakeries all over the state, from Paonia's chef-owned Flying Fork Café and Bakery to Rudy's Organic Bakery in Boulder, ovens produce well-crusted loaves in a variety of shapes, sizes, and

goat herd, it continues to make nine delicious, award-winning artisanal cheeses available in stores in the region and at its new cheesery in Longmont near Boulder.

Birgit S. Halbreiter and Robert Poland established the MouCo Cheese Company, a micro-cheesery in Fort Collins, in 2001. Birgit grew up in Germany and is the daughter of a master cheesemaker (her father is a consultant to the company), and the cheeses, made from local milk, follow a strong European tradition. MouCo's camembert was an instant hit, soon followed by four other cheeses: ColoRouge, Pepbert, Truffelo, and

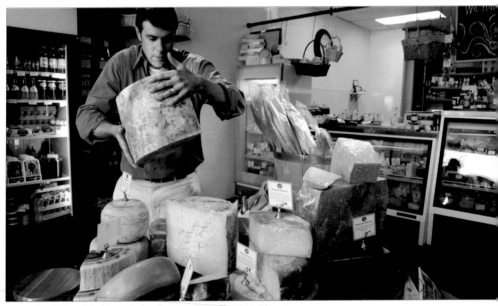

A tempting display of cheddar and other cheeses at the Truffle Cheese Shop, Denver.

colors destined for restaurant tables and serving as foundations for tasty sandwiches. Today, in addition to the homespun white, rye, and whole wheat of Colorado's traditional bread lexicon are such novelties as focaccia, boule, bâtard, and pain au levain.

Colorado has also made great strides in the field of cheesemaking. In 1989, a lapsed educator named Jim Schott bought a farm in Niwot, northwest of Boulder, added some goats and started learning the craft of cheesemaking. Schott's Haystack Mountain Goat Dairy was Colorado's first artisanal cheesery and garnered seven medals, including one gold, in the first national cheese competition it entered. Now under new management, and minus its own

Ashley. You will find these cheeses on fine restaurant menus, in cheese stores and delicatessens, in health food stores such as Natural Grocers (Vitamin Cottage), and at farmers' markets.

Cheesemaking is also making inroads on the Western Slope. In 2009, Rocking W Ranch in the Uncompahgre Valley began making farmstead cheeses using milk from the pioneer Webb family's own herd of grass-fed cows. Avalanche Cheese Company, a goat dairy located the pastoral Roaring Fork Valley near Paonia, has won awards for its superb artisanal Midnight Blue, cheddar, and chèvre (goat's) cheeses made in Basalt – all are on sale at the excellent Homestead Market, a local food cooperative in Paonia. Members of the extended James clan living on 400-acre (160-hectare) James Ranch in the Animas Valley are also dipping their toes into the cheese market. Their farmstead cheeses are made in the Dutch and Italian styles from raw milk from the family's grass-fed Jersey cows

Low in fat and high in essential fatty acids, bison meat is enjoying a revival, both for its delicious taste and health benefits. Colorado's prairies are studded with ranches raising bison meat for sale, particularly on the Front Range.

Colorado is famous for its grass-fed bison steaks.

(if you are interested, raw milk is available here by purchasing a share in the family herd). You can tour the beautiful ranch, just north of Durango, and purchase products in their store; it's a wonderful day out for the whole family.

"Field to fork"

High and dry as Colorado is, the state's short, intense growing season is well suited to cultivating a cornucopia of delicious fruits and vegetables, which comes as a delightful surprise to visitors who associate Colorado mainly with spectacular mountains and outdoor sports. In fact, Colorado is first in the nation for organic vegetable acreage in cultivation, ahead even of California. Colorado farmers plant and pick

stone fruits in the Grand Valley – sweet corn around Olathe, melons at Rocky Ford, and various vegetables and herbs – many organic – from small farms around Palisade, Paonia, and Hotchkiss (all in western Colorado); potatoes in the San Luis Valley; and organically grown tomatoes, herbs, and vegetables in what remains of agricultural areas on the Front Range.

"Fresher is better" is the new mantra and increasingly a high priority for residents and visitors concerned about their health, food safety, long-term sustainability, and supporting the people who grow our food. One of the big new trends among Colorado's top chefs, whether they work in kitchens at high-end luxury resorts or in their own small venues, is to "grow your own," cutting out the middleman to provide fresh, local, organic, and sustainably grown food that is truly "locavore." Among those experimenting with growing their own produce are two Denver chefs: Justin Cicci, chef-owner of Root Down, which has a "field to fork" menu, and Max MacKissock, ex-executive chef co-owner of two different iterations of the Squeaky Bean, a top-rated and very ambitious cafe/bakery/cocktail bar/locavore restaurant that has its own farm.

At the last count, there were some 37,054 farms in Colorado, nearly half of them small family concerns. Of those, about 864 welcome visitors for tours, farm stays, special harvest dinners, and educational programs, a business worth nearly $30 million in farm income annually; agritourism as a whole adds $2.2 billion to the state's economy. Many farms offer Community-Supported Agriculture programs (CSAs), which allow you to invest in the farm's yield for the year and receive regular boxes of produce. Some ranches also now offer herd-share programs, which under new state regulations allow people to buy a share of an animal and receive raw goats' and cows' milk products and reasonably priced grass-fed meat.

It goes without saying that one of the growth areas in Colorado is its farmers' markets. There are currently 110 such markets all around the state offering an array of fresh, Colorado-grown ingredients, from the flowers, lettuces, and herbs of spring and summer to Olathe corn, Rocky Ford melons, and Palisade peaches of late summer and the squash and apples of fall. Many growers' markets also feature local pasture-raised beef, cheese, honey, and eggs and the output of local bakeries, plus small-batch preserves, pickles, salsas, and other condiments. Come hungry on market day and enjoy breakfast pastries, sandwiches, wraps, roasted corn, salads, tamales, burritos, Asian specialties, pasta dishes, baked goods, and other eat-on-the-spot treats as well as local wines.

Local wine industry

In 1890, George A. Crawford, who had founded Grand Junction in the fertile Grand Valley of western Colorado, planted 60 acres (24 hectares) of fruit, including grapes, along Rapid Creek above Palisade. Within a decade, Colorado reported a grape harvest of 586,300 lbs (266,000kg) and wine production of 1,744 gallons (6,600 liters). This hardly made Colorado an important wine grower, but it was a good start. Nearly seven decades later, the first modern winery appeared when Gerald Ivancie opened Ivancie Cellars in the Grand River Valley. In 1990, when there were only four wineries in the state, the Colorado Wine Industry Development Board (www.coloradowine.com) was established, shifting the Colorado wine business into overdrive.

Colorado now supports 120 grape growers tending nearly 1,000 acres (405 hectares) of vineyards and more than 125 wineries and wine tasting rooms in five different growing regions – some 90 percent located in the Grand Valley. Wineries and tasting rooms are scattered around the western and central regions of the state as well as, increasingly, in the Front Range. When the climate is suitable and space allows, wineries grow all or most of their own grapes. Merlot and Chardonnay predominated during the infancy of Colorado's wine industry: these have been joined by Cabernets, Rieslings, honey wines (meads), fruit wines, port wines, and other fortified wines, as well as Champagne-style sparkling wine. The oldest and largest winery is award-winning Colorado Cellars, harvesting 450 acres (182 hectares) in the Grand Valley. It is on the site of one of the first test plots for wine-making and makes the full spectrum of wines from Colorado grapes. (For more information about Colorado wine-making, see page 276.)

Beef and bison

For a taste of what Coloradans ate in the old days, stop at The Fort, a landmark restaurant serving heritage cuisine just west of Denver. It was opened in 1963 by history buff Sam Arnold, a former reporter, radio announcer, and adman who became enamored of Bent's Fort, the fur-trading post dating from the early days

of the Santa Fe Trail. He purchased 7 acres (3 hectares) north of Morrison, where, against a backdrop of dramatic red rock formations, he built an adobe re-creation of the historic fort.

Bison dinners are served there at a rate of 50,000 a year, more than anywhere else in the country. They include such classic cuts as steak and prime rib and some you would be hard-pressed to find elsewhere, such as bison hump, barbecued ribs, center-cut shank prepared osso buco-style, or tongue, a 19th-century gourmet specialty. In addition to bison, elk, and other big game, quail and guinea fowl remain on the menu

Bottles filled with local wine from Palisade.

as a tribute to the game birds prepared in the 19th century. Chilled rattlesnake cocktail is the restaurant's most popular appetizer, and Rocky Mountain oysters are perhaps the best known. The "oysters," which have never been near any ocean, are the testicles of bison, calves, or sheep, rolled in breadcrumbs and deep-fried. The restaurant's annual "awful offal" dinner features exotic innards that people either love or loathe.

Sam Arnold died in 2006 but still remains Colorado's best-known restaurateur. He produced and hosted food shows on radio and television, wrote many magazine articles, pitched commercials, and authored such books as *Taste of the West*, *Frying Pans West* and *The Fort Cookbook: New Foods of the Old West from the Famous Denver Restaurant.*

Queen Anne Victorian House in Ouray.

Cross-country skiing through a snowy Coloradan landscape.

INTRODUCTION

A detailed guide to the entire state, with principal
sites clearly cross-referenced by number to the maps.

Grand Mesa National Forest.

Most of Colorado is in the legendary Rocky Mountains, the tallest range in the continental United States. And mountains attract dreamers eager to match themselves against the craggy peaks, rushing rivers, or parks.

Denver founder General William Larimer gambled that his new town in the foothills would emerge a thriving capital, and won the bet. Today, the Denver Metro Area monopolizes the Front Range, bringing its top attraction, Rocky Mountain National Park, ever closer to millions of urban dwellers.

In the eastern third of Colorado lie the Great Plains. Famed as a birding area, its rolling grasslands are grazed by cattle and bison herds all the way to the San Luis Valley. Here, in the shadow of the Spanish Peaks, Hispanic ranchers mingle with New Agers, and sandhill cranes overwinter near Great Sand Dunes National Park and Preserve.

The country's greatest concentration of Ancestral Pueblo Indian ruins is preserved in the Four Corners country near Durango in southwestern Colorado, at Mesa Verde National Park, and on adjoining federal and Indian lands.

Skulls decorate Glenwood Caverns Adventure Park.

Casino gambling has revived the fortunes of the Utes, and of played-out mining towns like Victor and Cripple Creek in the northern Rockies, where ritzy Aspen and Vail are now celebrity ski resorts. In contrast, ski resort towns in the Southern Rockies trade on authenticity and remoteness. Pretty Telluride and feisty Silverton, Creede, and other captivating former ghost towns are an independent bunch, attracting ranchers, artists, writers, scientists, and outdoor lovers.

The Western Slope is farm and ranch country. Below lofty Grand Mesa, set in a valley carved by the Colorado River into the dramatic red rocks at Colorado National Monument, Grand Junction thrives as a fruit-growing area. Two billion years of geology are displayed at nearby Dinosaur National Monument. The Colorado, Green, and Yampa rivers thrill river runners, but the real sparks fly in Black Canyon of the Gunnison National Park, where the Gunnison River has carved a precipitous canyon.

Colorado

THE FRONT RANGE AND EASTERN PLAINS

Colorado's largest metropolitan areas are strung along the foothills between the Rockies and Great Plains.

Leading the way to Kendall Mountain.

Flying over eastern Colorado at night, you look down and see a string of lights running north to south in a sometimes thin, sometimes clotted line. This is the sprawling Denver Metro Area, strung along the foothills of the Rocky Mountains like a snarl of Christmas lights.

Denver, home to 682,545 people, now makes up just a fraction of the busy Front Range Urban Corridor (pop. 4,757,713), which includes miles of suburbs, such as Englewood and Lakewood. Denver grew by 10 percent in the first decade of the 20th century, the vast majority of new residents from California and Hispanic in origin. The demographic shift has reinvigorated politics and the once-decaying urban core: 16th Street is a pedestrian mall, historic Larimer Square has been restored, the industrial no-man's land of LoDo has been reimagined as a hip SoHo-style neighborhood, and Denver International Airport has been built.

A local musician tunes up.

To the west is Boulder, home of the University of Colorado. Progressive and youthful, Boulder is famous for its innovative small businesses focusing on health and healing, for its spiritual centers and pedestrians-only Pearl Street Mall, and for its proximity to recreation in the surrounding wilderness and parkland.

Conservative Colorado Springs, south of Denver, sits below Pikes Peak, an equally gorgeous setting. The town's right-leaning inclinations are rooted in a large population of active and retired military personnel. Fort Carson, Peterson Air Force Base, and the US Air Force Academy are located in Colorado Springs, as are numerous conservative Christian organizations.

Fringing the Front Range are railroad towns like Pueblo, Trinidad, and Fort Collins, still focused on a traditional farming and ranching lifestyle. The vast shortgrass prairie is inhabited by rare birds and revived herds of bison – once the mainstay of Cheyenne, Arapaho, and Comanche people. Quiet and little traveled, the plains offer subtle landscapes, fascinating natural and cultural history, and a sweeping sense of space.

Wildflowers near Grand Lake.

THE EASTERN PLAINS

Complementing the alpine spectacle of peak and precipice is a wide-open expanse of rolling prairie and flatland where Colorado's history was writ large.

High plains occupy the eastern third of Colorado – a sea of grass surmounted by buttes and soaring ridges, wrinkled with creeks and shallow canyons. Cattle dot the landscape, along with the occasional antelope. Solitary ranch houses look tiny and shrunken, as if viewed through the wrong end of a telescope. Roads run at right angles, following property lines to what appears to be the edge of the earth.

A land of delicate colors and subtle contrasts, this part of Colorado contains its own allure. Mountains overwhelm, but flatlands tug seductively at the senses. Amid all this space, details tend to catch the eye: an abandoned schoolhouse standing on a lonely hill, or the spectacle of thunderstorms brooding on the skyline, or the vertical effrontery of a creaking windmill.

Beecher Island and Julesburg

If you're in a rush, I-70, I-76, and I-25 will get you across the Colorado flatlands in a hurry. These busy thoroughfares lead inexorably to the major cities that sprawl across the foothills of the Front Range. But if you've got the time and a meandering spirit, the lightly traveled roads that thread these wide-open spaces lead to interesting spots that are too often overlooked.

Take, for example, the **Beecher Island Battleground ❶**, situated near

the Kansas line about 12 miles (19km) north of US 36. One of the epic struggles between American Indians and whites in the settling of the West was fought here during nine days beginning on September 17, 1868. A party of 51 frontiersmen under the command of Major George A. Forsyth was besieged on an island in the Arikaree River by hundreds of Cheyenne, Arapaho and Lakota warriors. Again and again the Indians attacked, only to be repulsed by deadly fire from the company's lever-action rifles.

Main Attractions

Overland Trail Museum, Sterling
Koshare Indian Museum and Trading Post
Comanche National Grasslands
Bent's Old Fort National Historic Site
Picketwire Canyon Dinosaur Tracks
A.R. Mitchell Museum of Western Art

Pronghorn antelope, Pawnee National Grassland.

The Eastern Plains

0   20 miles
0   20 km

Colonel Forsyth was badly wounded; Lieutenant Frederick Beecher, second in command, was killed. For two nights running, barefoot volunteers, crawling on their hands and knees, slipped between enemy lines and made their way to Fort Wallace in northwest Kansas. The siege was lifted on September 26, when a relief column reached the site. A whitewashed obelisk marks the spot today. Every year since 1899, a reunion has been held on the premises. The grounds are open to the public year-round.

In the extreme northeast of Colorado, about 70 miles (110km) away, is the town of **Julesburg ❷** (pop. 1,227). It was founded in 1859 by a mixed-blood trader named Jules Beni at a ford of the South Platte River, where the California, Overland and Pony Express trails converged. From the beginning the post had an unsavory reputation. Beni fought openly with his boss, Jack Slade, until Slade could stand no more and killed him. Legend has it that Slade celebrated the victory by slicing off Beni's ears, tacking

one to a fence post and fashioning the other into a watch fob. In 1865, Indians enraged by the Sand Creek Massacre (see page 47) torched the fledgling town. Later, in the 1870s, it was a favorite stopover of railroad workers who patronized the bars and bordellos, earning it a reputation as "the Wickedest City in the West."

The nearby **Fort Sedgwick Depot Museum** (114 E. 1st Street, Julesburg; tel: 970-474-2061; late-May–early-Sept Mon–Sat 9am–5pm, Sun 11am–5pm), housed in a former Union Pacific station, displays railroad equipment, pioneer tools and Pony Express memorabilia as well as artifacts from Fort Sedgwick, which was established in 1864 to protect wagon teams and travelers.

Buttes and battles

You'll find an even greater variety of pioneer artifacts at the **Overland Trail Museum** (110 Overland Trail, Sterling; tel: 970-522-3895, Apr–Oct Tues–Sat 9am–5pm, Nov–Mar Tue–Sat 10am–4pm; free) about 55 miles (90km) away in the trim little town of **Sterling ❸**. The grounds include

A vintage billboard brings the past to life at Centennial Village.

Generals Merritt, Sheridan, Crook, Forsyth, and Custer around a table.

SAND CREEK

On November 29, 1864, 700 US volunteer soldiers led by Col. Chivington attacked 500 Cheyennes and Arapahos led by Chief Black Kettle, encamped along the banks of Sand Creek in southeastern Colorado. Seven hours later, the troops had killed and mutilated the bodies of at least 150 people, mostly children and the elderly. The atrocities committed were decried by the public and resulted in three federal investigations. About 12,500 acres (5,000 hectares) in Kiowa County, Colorado, are now set aside as Sand Creek Massacre National Historic Site (see page 47), symbolizing the struggle of American Indians to keep their ancestral lands. The park has a ranger station, exhibits and a trail leading to the massacre site. It is open weekdays year round, 9am–4pm, and on weekends by appointment.

The mountain goat was introduced to Colorado in the 1940s to expand hunting opportunities. It was declared native to the state in 1993.

Plains Indians pinned down a party of frontiersmen and soldiers at the 1868 Battle of Beecher Island.

a replica of an Old West fort as well as a schoolhouse, church, country store, and barn. Exhibits range from antique farm equipment and a stagecoach to wedding dresses, sun bonnets, and household items.

About 35 miles (56km) away, in the prairie southeast of Sterling, is the **Summit Springs Battlefield ❹**, site of a clash between Cheyenne Indians and US soldiers in 1869. Cheyenne dog soldiers raiding deep into Kansas in the spring of that year killed several settlers and captured two women. The Fifth Cavalry under Major General Eugene A. Carr, 250 strong with 50 Pawnee Scouts, including Buffalo Bill Cody, rode off in pursuit.

On Sunday morning, July 11, scouts discovered a Cheyenne camp along White Butte Creek, which flows out of Summit Springs. First to see the army was a 15-year-old boy, who swung onto his horse and raced for the village to sound the alarm. The troopers charged, but their horses were exhausted, enabling many Cheyennes to escape. One of the captive women was killed, as was Tall Bull, the

Cheyenne chief. The soldiers burned the native lodges, along with possessions and supplies. There are two monuments at the site, one describing the battle, the other commemorating the Cheyennes who died there.

Farther west, about 40 miles (65km) outside Sterling, the **Pawnee Buttes ❺** (off CR 110) tower in lonely splendor over **Pawnee National Grassland** (660 O Street, Greeley; tel: 970-346-5000; www.fs.fed.us.r2/arnf). It takes a bit of navigating to reach the buttes, but it's worth it. The squat sandstone formations rise side by side to a height of 250ft (76 meters). Archeologists trace human occupation of the region to 12,000 years ago, the end of the last Ice Age. A 1½-mile (2.5km) hiking trail leads over eroded arroyos (dry gulches) to the foot of the west butte. As well as numerous bird species, a variety of mammals, including pronghorn antelope, mule deer, prairie dogs, badgers and coyotes, are found in the area.

For a glimpse of prairie life from the 1860s to the 1920s, stop at **Centennial Village Museum** in **Greeley** (1475 A Street; tel: 970-350-9220; May–Sep

i–Sat 10am–5pm, Sun noon–5pm).
ving history demonstrations bring
e past alive at a collection of more
an 35 buildings on the 8-acre (3 hec-
re) property, including a blacksmith
op, church, and schoolhouse.

rontier life

ll roads lead to **Limon** ❻ (pop.
857), nexus of the regional highway
stem. Originally a railroad town,
w an agricultural hub, Limon
hymes with "Simon") was devastated
1990 by a tornado that caused $20
illion of damage. About 70 miles
10km) east via I-70, **Burlington** ❼
op. 4,003) features the **Old Town
useum** (420 S. 14th Street; tel: 719-
6-7382; Mon–Sat 9am–5pm, Sun
on–5pm), a facsimile of an early
th-century high-plains community,
mplete with a blacksmith shop and
saloon that in our more temperate
e sells mostly lemonade. Burling-
n is also home to the **Kit Carson
ounty Carousel** (815 N. 15th Street;
l: 719-346-7666; www.kitcarsoncoun-
arousel.com; late May to early Sep-
mber daily 11am–6pm), a fully

restored 1905 merry-go-round built
by the Philadelphia Toboggan Company and now designated a National
Historic Landmark. A small museum
is open the same hours.

From Limon, Route 71 makes a bee-
line from the South Platte watershed,
over a barely detectable hump known
as the Palmer Divide, into the Arkansas River valley. In the 1870s and 1880s,
Hispanic settlers from Santa Fe and
Taos introduced a system of *acequias*
(irrigation ditches) in the fertile bot-
tomlands along the Arkansas River
and began growing the excellent agricultural produce for which the region
is famous. **La Junta** ❽, the major
town in this cluster of agricultural
communities, is home to the **Koshare
Museum and Trading Post** (115 W.
18th Street; tel: 719-384-4411; www.
kosharehistory.org; Mon, Wed, Fri, Sat,
Sun 10am–5pm), on the Otero Junior
College Campus, which contains one
of the largest collections of American
Indian artifacts in the region.

South of La Junta lies the **Timpas
Unit of Comanche National Grassland** (1420 E. 3rd Street, La Junta;

*The entrance to
Pawnee National
Grassland.*

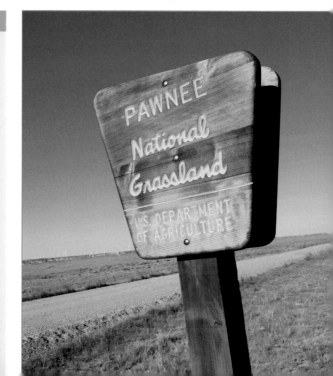

PRAIRIE BIRD TOUR

Pawnee National Grassland attracts
some 250 bird species, including grassland birds, migrant waterfowl, and
shorebirds, and is popular with birding
enthusiasts from all over the world. On
the 36-mile (58km) self-guided auto
tour of Pawnee Buttes, which begins in
Briggsdale, you can enjoy the "larking"
(singing courtship flight) of lark bun-
tings, horned larks, meadowlarks, and
longspurs from late May through June.
Prairie birds include mountain plovers,
chestnut-collared and McCown's longspurs, burrowing owls, and long-billed
curlews. The box elder/willow riparian
area at Crow Valley Campground
attracts a variety of eastern and mountain birds from April through June and
late August through October. Murphy
Reservoir offers good shorebird and
waterfowl viewing.

tel: 719-384-2181). With more than 400,000 acres (160,000 hectares) of range land, the area abounds with wildlife, including 275 species of birds, 40 species of reptiles, and mammals such as mountain lion, black bear, pronghorn, coyote, fox, and bobcat.

Traders of the plains

The crown jewel of the eastern plains is **Bent's Old Fort National Historic Site** (35110 Highway 194; tel: 719-383-5010; www.nps.gov/beol; daily June–Aug 8am–5:30pm, Sept–May 9am–4pm), just east of La Junta. The fort was built in the 1830s by three St Louis fur traders – brothers Charles and William Bent and Ceran St Vrain – and became a major stop on the Mountain Route of the Santa Fe Trail. William Bent was married to a Cheyenne woman, and so effective were his peacekeeping skills that each year thousands of Indians from all over the plains gathered in the *bosque* along the Arkansas River to parly and trade.

The Mexican War brought soldiers into the region and upset the delicate balance. A cholera epidemic broke out, the bison herds dwindled, an both settlers and natives cut down t cottonwood groves along the riv In 1849, with the world crowding i William Bent set fire to the fort ar moved downstream to Big Timbe near present-day Lamar.

The reconstructed fort is now living history museum run by t National Park Service, depicti frontier life during the heyday of t Santa Fe Trail. Guided tours in su mer are often led by costumed inte preters. Annual events include t three-day **Santa Fe Trail Encam ment**, a re-enactment featurin mountain men, dragoons, explore merchants, and Indians.

For a detour, follow US 50 east Las Animas, then 2 miles (3km) sou on Route 101 to the ghost town **Boggsville** ❿. Founded in 1862 Thomas O. Boggs (William Ben son-in-law), the town served as a tra ing center and county seat until t construction of the railroad farth north in 1873. Legendary scout k Carson moved here in 1868. Exhib chronicling Boggsville history, fro

Bent's Old Fort National Historic Site.

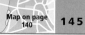

Carson's days through World War II, are on display at the **John W. Rawlings Heritage Center** (560 Bent Avenue, Las Animas; tel: 719-456-6066; www.bentcountyheritage.org; Mon–Fri 12:30–4:30pm).

Big Timbers

To the east, a dense growth of trees known as the Big Timbers once stretched along the Arkansas River for 45 miles (72km). Composed mainly of cottonwoods, the *bosque* provided refuge for Indians and settlers from the harsh winters of the southern plains. William Bent built his new fort in 1853 about 6 miles (10km) west of present-day **Lamar** ⓫ in the heart of the Big Timbers country. Despite social upheavals, many Indians remained loyal to Bent, and in the spring and fall they pitched their lodges nearby. Bent later sold the fort to the US government.

Big Timbers Museum (7515 W. US 50, Lamar; tel: 719-336-2472; www.bigtimbersmuseum.org; summer Tue–Sat 10am–5pm, winter 1–4pm) is one of those small-town, grab-bag repositories that feature a little bit of everything – guns, wedding gowns, spinning wheels, dolls, quilts, surgical instruments, farm tools, battle flags, and more. A display of newspapers and photos recounts the 1928 murder of prominent father and son bankers by the notorious Fleagle Gang, sparking one of Colorado's greatest manhunts.

US 287-385 drops south from Lamar, toward the **Carrizo Unit of Comanche National Grassland** ⓬ (27204 US 287-385, Springfield; tel: 719-523-6591; www.coloradodirectory.com/nationalparks/comanche.html). Here the east fork of Carrizo Creek flows through a small canyon of the same name, shaded by juniper and cottonwood trees. An impressive array of prehistoric Indian petroglyphs – images of mountain goats, elk, and deer – is etched on the canyon walls. **Picture Canyon**, south of Springfield, is also filled with fine examples of rock art, several of astronomical significance. For directions to the petroglyph sites, inquire at the ranger station in Springfield.

TIP

If you visit Comanche National Grassland in spring, you might see the courtship ritual of the lesser prairie chicken. Male chickens arrive on the leks (elevated dancing grounds) to establish their territory. To attract females, the males dip their heads, bob their wings, hackle their feathers, and stomp their feet, all the while emitting a gobbling sound from the reddish air sacs on their necks.

Snowy fields near Lamar.

Lavish Bloom Mansion in Trinidad.

Trinidad: a history

It's a long and lonely ride west on US 160 from Springfield to **Trinidad** ⓭ at the foot of the Sangre de Cristo Mountains. The Spanish Peaks rise in the distance, spangled by the late afternoon sun. Mesa de Maya – dark, hulking, heaped with volcanic cinders – looms on the left. From this vantage, little seems to have changed since the 1870s, when cattle baron Charles Goodnight led his herds on a secret trail over the mesa in search of pastures lusher than those in Texas or New Mexico.

Back then, eastern Colorado was poised on the cusp of momentous change. The 1862 Homestead Act, which famously offered newcomers 40 acres (16 hectares) and a mule, attracted swarms of settlers, who sallied forth from the green hills of the Midwest hoping to find the same sort of arable land west of the 100th meridian. The days of land barons comfortably ensconced on Spanish land grants were quickly coming to an end. The beckoning spaces of eastern Colorado were on the verge of being snapped up by hordes of land hungry immigrants.

Trinidad (pop. 8,465) lies at the junction of US 160 and I-25, at the foot of Raton Pass, near where the Purgatoire River debouches onto the plains from its headwaters in the Culebra Range. Prior to 1860, Trinidad was little more than a way station on the mountain branch of the Santa Fe Trail that wound slowly up to the summit of Raton Pass and the dividing line between the territories of Colorado and New Mexico.

In the early 1860s, *comancheros* (traders) from Taos and Santa Fe began hauling supplies north over the pass to the boisterous town of Denver, where gold had been discovered. Impressed with the productivity of the soil along the Purgatoire River, 12 families from the town of Mora, in northern New Mexico, settled there in 1862. Officially incorporated in 1876 (the year Colorado became a state), Trinidad underwent a remarkable transformation in a few short decades from a rustic adobe village to a brick and iron city graced with stately Victorian houses.

By the turn of the century Trinidad was a polyglot community of many nationalities, drawn from all over the world by the coal seams that glistened in the foothills like dark ribbons. Labor unrest between owners and miners festered for years, culminating in the brutal Ludlow Massacre of 1914. The massacre site, located about 10 miles (16km) north of Trinidad (via I-25, Exit 27) is commemorated by an impressive statue erected by the United Mine Workers of America.

Trinidad today

Trinidad today is one of the unspoiled gems of the American West. Handsome structures such as the **Trinidad Opera House**, the **Columbia Hotel** and **Temple Aaron** (one of Colorado's oldest synagogues) line the brick streets of the Corazon de Trinidad Historic District. The town has attracted more than its share of idealists and desperadoes. Mother Jones once walked these streets, clamoring for workers' rights. It's the place where train robber Black Jack Ketchum ordered a doctor to cut off his arm without an anesthetic because he didn't want anyone to take advantage of him while he was unconscious. Legendary labor organizer Louis Tikas was buried here after dying at the hands of the Colorado State Militia during the Ludlow débâcle. It's said that his funeral cortege stretched more than a mile, and that all you could hear in the cold gray air was the muffled clump of marching feet and the ruffle of black bunting.

Two historic residences are lovingly preserved onsite by **Trinidad History Museum** (312 E. Main Street; tel: 719-846-7217; Wed–Sun 10am–4pm; tours every 30 minutes in summer). **Baca House** is a Territorial-style adobe dwelling built in 1870 and purchased in 1873 by rancher Felipe Baca for 7,000 of wool. Period furnishings reflect a mixture of traditional Hispanic and Victorian styles. The 1882 **Bloom Mansion** is constructed in comparatively lavish Second Empire

style, with ornate furnishings reflecting high Victorian fashion and the availability, via railroad, of imported goods. **Santa Fe Trail Museum**, housed in an adobe outbuilding, chronicles the homestead period with old wagons, cowboy gear and other artifacts. The Barglow Building, built in 1906 as a medical office and family apartment, displays four Doric columns and a Greek pediment porch. Today the building houses the Davenport Gallery, a book and gift shop, ticket office, education center and the Colorado Byways and Tourist Information Center. The **Baca-Bloom Heritage Gardens** are planted with heirloom varieties similar to those tended by Hispanic and Anglo settlers. The **Louden-Henritze Archaeology Museum** (Trinidad Junior College, 600 Prospect Street; tel: 719-846-5508; www.trinidadstate.edu/museum; Mon–Thu 10am–3pm; free) specializes in the prehistory of the region, with exhibits of fossils, geologic samples, and Indian artifacts. A free trolley carries visitors around the historic downtown.

A lone church beckons to the faithful of the high plains.

A church in historic Trinidad.

DENVER

There's much to experience in this sprawling Western metropolis, which fortune spawned from a ragged mining camp along the banks of a lowly creek.

Writing to his wife in Kansas, General William H. Larimer, the self-proclaimed founder of Denver, blustered that "Everyone will soon be flocking to Denver for the most picturesque country in the world, with fine air, good water, and everything to make a man happy and live to a good old age."

A natural-born finagler, Larimer had actually claim-jumped a little settlement established in 1858 by a party of Georgia prospectors who found a few flakes of gold in Cherry Creek. Hoping to curry political favor, he named the fledgling town after territorial governor James Denver, unaware that the governor had already resigned. Realizing that the place needed links to the civilized world, he bribed a stagecoach company to establish its headquarters there. Faced with competitors from three nearby settlements, each vying for recognition as the territorial capital, he bought them off with a barrel of whiskey.

Like the gold fields that spawned it, Denver was a gamble. It lacked most of the basic requirements of a city, such as a navigable waterway, and was isolated by hundreds of miles of dry, treeless prairie. Its own gold deposits proved paltry, and when a huge strike was reported at Central City, the town was nearly deserted. A catastrophic fire in 1863, a flash flood in 1864, and Indian hostilities in the late 1860s

nearly wiped it out. It seemed Denver's fate was sealed when the Union Pacific bypassed Colorado in favor of a transcontinental route through Cheyenne, Wyoming. Larimer, failing to become the mayor of Denver or the governor of Colorado, abandoned the place.

Rail hub

But Denverites were not so easily defeated. They raised funds and donated labor to build their own railroad, the Denver Pacific, which in 1870 was linked to the Cheyenne line. Not long

Bronco Buster sculpture, Civic Center Park.

Denver

500 yds
500 m

Black American West Museum

BENEDICT FOUNTAIN PARK

St Andrew's Episcopal Church

LAWSON PARK

Molly Brown House Museum 9

St Paul's Lutheran Church

Cathedral of the Immaculate Conception

Brown Palace Hotel 11

Central Presbyterian Church

Trinity United Methodist Church

One Corporate Center

State Capitol 1

Colorado Veterans' Monument

Holy Ghost Church

US Custom House

Federal Bldg & Courthouse

First Interstate North

Lincoln Center

Amoco Bldg

World Trade Center

WAR MEMORIAL PARK

State Judicial Building

State Office Bldg

Wells Fargo

Denver Post Tower

History Colorado Center 8

1999 Broadway

1801 California

18th/California

LOWER DOWNTOWN (LoDo)

Sakura Square

Main Post Office

Denver Bus Terminal

Denver Place

Denver Place Plaza

US West

18th/Stout

16th/California

16th/Stout

Dominion Plaza

Masonic Bldg

Denver Dry Bldg

Denver Pavilions

Pioneer Monument 2

Brown Palace Hotel 11

Republic Plaza Tower

Club Bldg 13

Paramount Theatre 10

16th St Mall

Greek Theater

Bronco Buster 7

Denver Art Museum 5

Byers-Evans House 6

Denver Public Library 3

Clyfford Still Museum

CIVIC CENTER PARK

Camera Obscura

City & County Bldg

Firefighters Museum 12

US Mint 4

Indigos

Native American Trading Company

Denver Conv. & Visitor Bureau

Theatre District/Convention Ctr

Colorado Convention Center

Coors Field 19

AT&T

17th St Plaza

SKYLINE PARK

Independence Plaza

US Bank Tower

D&F Tower

Shops at Tabor Center

Federal Reserve Bank

Tabor Center 14

Ice House

Wynkoop Brewing Company

Union Station (Amtrak) 17

Oxford Hotel

RTD Market St Bus Station

Barclay Towers

Writer Square 15

Larimer Square 16

University of Colorado at Denver

Denver Tramway Building

Helen Bonfils Theater Complex

Auditorium Performing Arts Complex

Boettcher Concert Hall

Temple Buell Theatre

Denver Performing Arts Complex

Curtigan Exhibition Hall

Tattered Cover Book Store

Museum of Contemporary Art Denver 18

Punt the Creek

PE/Event in Denver

Emmanuel Gallery

Science Library & Media Center

King Center

St Cajetan's Center

North Classroom

Athletic Fields

Tivoli Student Union

Plaza

Golda Meir House

St Elizabeth's Church

Metropolitan State College

St Francis Center

Central Classroom

South Classroom

Community College of Denver

9TH ST PARK

Care Center

Coors Field at Auraria

COMMONS PARK

REI

CONFLUENCE PARK 20

FISHBACK PARK

CENTENNIAL PARK

Pepsi Center Elitch Gardens

Elitch Gardens Theme and Water Park 22

Downtown Aquarium

Children's Museum of Denver 21

Pepsi Center

AURARIA

Visitor Parking

Parking & Transportation Center

Child Development Center

Campus Police & Security Office

Administration

Facilities Management Street

Bectory Office

Rectory Office

Printing and Distribution Center

West Auraria

Sports Authority Field at Mile High

New Life in Christ Church

Riverside Baptist Church

JEFFERSON PARK

PLATTE RIVER GREENWAY

GATES CRESCENT PARK

LINCOLN PARK

Sports Authority Field at Mile High

Auraria Invesco Field

University of Colorado

Denver Performing Arts Complex

Skyland

Denver Zoo

CITY PARK 24

Denver Museum of Nature & Science 23

City Park

Congress Park

Cheesman Park

Denver Botanic Gardens 25

CHEESMAN PARK

Cherry Creek North

Tattered Cover Book Store

State Capitol

Capitol Hill

Golden Triangle

Country Club

after, the Kansas Pacific reached town, and Denver became the hub of a rail network that stretched in all directions. The railroad brought gold, minerals, and coal to the town's smelters, agricultural products from the plains, and immigrants from Europe. In 1878, Leadville mines yielded the richest silver strikes in the nation's history, and Denver once again was at the crossroads of a prospecting frenzy. By 1900, 100 trains a day steamed in and out of Union Station.

Other hardships befell the fledgling city, as the cycle of boom and bust alternately yielded riches and ruins. Through it all, Denver kept its nose to the grindstone, diversifying into light manufacturing, military facilities, aviation, energy and, in recent years, high-tech industries. In 2015, Denver's estimated population was 682,545, making it the fastest-growing major city in the nation. Ironically, many people are relocating here from California in a kind of reverse migration.

Mile-high sightseeing

Start your tour of Denver at one of the city's most photographed spots – the 18th step of the **Colorado State Capitol ❶** (203 E. Colfax Avenue; tel: 303-866-2604; Mon–Fri 7.30am–5pm; free tours every 45 minutes), where a plaque informs visitors that they are standing one mile above sea level. Patterned after the US Capitol, the Colorado State Capitol is built in the shape of a Greek cross, with Corinthian columns, a central rotunda, and other neoclassical features. Construction of the 18-story structure began in 1886 and took 22 years and nearly $3 million to complete. All the stone used in the building – granite, sandstone, marble – was quarried from locations around the state. The crowning glory is the dome, wrapped in gold leaf donated by Colorado miners in 1908.

The interior is equally impressive, with stained-glass portraits of Colorado pioneers, and murals chronicling key moments in state history. The rose onyx wainscoting is from Beulah, Colorado, and is the world's entire supply of this rare stone. Four full-time employees are responsible for polishing the ornamental brass railings around the rotunda. From

The interior of the state capitol, the construction of which consumed the entire known supply of Colorado rose onyx, a rare red marble from the small town of Beulah.

The dome of the capitol in Denver is covered in real gold leaf.

WE WERE HERE, TOO

The **Black American West Museum** (3091 California Street; tel: 720-242-7428; www.blackamericanwestmuseum. org; Tue–Sat 10am–5pm) was founded by Paul W. Stewart, who as a child had been told that there were no black cowboys. In fact, nearly a third of cowboys in the American West were black, and when Stewart grew up he met one who had led cattle drives at the turn of the 20th century. To set the record straight, Stewart set about compiling this eye-opening collection of artifacts, oral histories, and documents that tell the story of black Western heroes such as Nat Love (alias Deadwood Dick), mountain main James Bekwourth, as well as other African-American pioneers who became miners, ranchers, military heroes, and millionaires.

Denver Art Museum has an extensive collection, but is known primarily for its American Indian art.

Denver Public Library.

the third floor, you can climb 93 steps to the dome's observation deck for a panoramic view of the city.

Descend the front steps of the Capitol, pass the red sandstone Colorado Veterans Monument, and cross Civic Center Park. To the far right, the **Pioneer Monument ❷** commemorates the end of the Smoky Hill Trail, a stage road connecting Denver with the Missouri River. The fountain, which depicts a pioneer mother, a miner, and a trapper, sparked some controversy when it was erected in 1911; a figure of an American Indian that originally topped the piece was replaced with a statue of frontiersman Kit Carson.

On the south end of the park is the lifelike *Bronco Buster* (1920), a statue by Alexander Proctor. The cowboy Proctor used as a model was arrested for horse rustling after posing for the artist. Nearby, the open-air **Greek Theater ❸** (1919) is used for a variety of performances and public gatherings; it is adorned with murals by Alan True, whose work is also found in the Capitol. Bracketing the park on the west side is the grand semicircular **City and**

County Building, a government building completed in 1932.

Behind the City and County Building is the **United States Mint ❹** (320 W. Colfax Avenue; tel: 303-405-4761; www.usmint.gov/minttours; Mon–Thurs 8am–3.30pm; free tours by reservation only). One of only two mints in the United States, it churns out $6 million daily in small change, a total of 52 million coins, about 40 percent pennies.

About three blocks away, just south of Civic Center Park, is the **Denver Art Museum ❺** (100 W. 14th Avenue; tel: 720-865-5000; www.denverartmuseum.org; Tue–Sun 10am–5pm, until 8pm on Friday). The original North Building was designed by Gio Ponti in 1971.

The spectacular Frederic C. Hamilton Building, a recent extension, has doubled the size of the museum, creating much-needed space for more than 40,000 works of pre-Columbian, Spanish Colonial, Asian, and modern American and European art. The collection of Western and Native American art is incomparable, with objects representing tribes throughout North America and works by such Western masters as

George Catlin, Frederic Remington, Charles Russell, and Alfred Jacob Miller. Designed by celebrated Polish-born architect, Daniel Libeskind, the building is covered in 9,000 titanium panels that reflect the Colorado sunshine and recall the peaks of the Rocky Mountains and the geometric rock crystals found in the foothills near Denver.

Another landmark art museum building sits nearby. It houses the 2,000-piece private personal collection of works by famed American Abstract Expressionist artist Clyfford Still, which was bequeathed to the city of Denver by his widow in 2004. The $7 million **Clyfford Still Museum** (1250 Bannock St; tel: 720-354-4880; Tues–Sun 10am–5pm, until 8pm Fri) which opened in November 2011, consists of a 28,500-sq-ft (2647 sq meter), two-story, poured-concrete building, with a cantilevered lobby leading to open-plan galleries displaying works by Still made between the 1920s and 1979.

Behind the Denver Art Museum is the historic **Byers-Evans House Museum** ➏ (1310 Bannock Street; tel: 303-620-4933; Tue–Sun 10am–4pm; half-hour guided tours), built in 1883 by *Rocky Mountain News* founder William Byers and later purchased by businessman William Gray Evans. A 30-minute guided tour is preceded by a film detailing the history of these prominent families. Visitor numbers are limited, so arrive early if you haven't booked in advance. The former carriage house contains the **Denver History Museum**, which chronicles the development of the city from the gold rush to World War II.

Across the courtyard from the museum is the **Denver Public Library** ➐ (10 W. 14th Avenue; tel: 720-865-1111; www.denverlibrary.org), housed in a distinctive contemporary building designed by architect Michael Graves and Denver firm Klipp Colussy Jenks DuBois. This is the largest library between Chicago and Los Angeles and contains the highly regarded Western History Collection of rare books, maps, and photos. A Western gallery is on the sixth floor; changing exhibitions are on the eighth.

The newly built **History Colorado Center** ➑ (1200 Broadway; tel: 303-447-8679; www.historycoloradocenter.org;

TIP

US Mint tours are by reservation only, but standby tickets due to no-shows and returns are sometimes available on a first-come, first-served basis on the day of the tour. Check at the information booth on Cherokee Street at 7.30am.

The Hamilton wing of Denver Art Museum, designed by Daniel Libeskind.

Mon–Sat 10am–5pm, Sun noon to 5pm) opened in late 2011, replacing the old Colorado History Museum. State-of-the-art, hands-on exhibits range from Ancient Puebloan artifacts and Plains Indian art to mining equipment and memorabilia belonging to ill-fated silver king Horace Tabor.

It's a six-block walk through the Capitol Hill neighborhood to the **Molly Brown House Museum** ❾ (1340 Pennsylvania Street; tel: 303-832-4092; www.mollybrown.org; Tue–Sat 10am–5pm, Sun noon–5pm), former home of the celebrated Margaret Brown, survivor of the *Titanic* disaster and subject of the popular musical and film *The Unsinkable Molly Brown*. A costumed guide recounts Margaret's rags-to-riches story as you tour the 1889 Queen Anne–style residence. Never fully accepted by high society, Margaret was self-educated, spoke five languages, and was an avid campaigner for women's and children's rights. Ironically, she was never known as Molly during her lifetime. Meredith Willson, the musical's composer and lyricist, bestowed the name upon her

because he thought it would be easier to sing.

16th Street Mall

In the early 1980s, a mile-long stretch of 16th Street between Broadway and Market Street was bulldozed to make way for the **16th Street Mall** ❿. This popular thoroughfare – pedestrian-only except for free shuttle buses – launched the revitalization of downtown Denver. Today, the Mall, which was designed by famed architect I.M. Pei, is one of the liveliest urban spaces in the state. In summer, its shady central boulevard comes alive with bubbling fountains and some 50,000 flowers, and folks lounge on benches and at outdoor cafés or play chess under the trees.

Starting near the top of the Mall, at 16th Street and Tremont Place, is the glitzy **Denver Pavilions**, a two-block-square, open-air complex of shops, restaurants, and movie theaters linked by the "Great Wall," a neon-lit, upper-story marquee that straddles Glenarm Place with its signature DENVER sign.

A block from the Mall is the landmark **Brown Palace Hotel & Spa** ⓫ (tel: 303-297-3111; www.brownpalace. com), which stands on a triangular lot at 17th and Tremont. The hotel was built by Henry Cordes Brown, a carpenter-turned-entrepreneur who settled in Denver in the 1860s. Brown donated land for the Capitol, then made a fortune selling off his property on Capitol Hill. But he reserved the three-sided pasture where he grazed his cow to build a grand hotel. Designed in Italian Renaissance style by Frank E. Edbrooke, architect of the State Capitol and much else, the hotel was completed in 1892 at a cost of $1.6 million after four years of construction. It was worth every penny. The Palace rivaled the splendor of the finest eastern hotels, impressing guests and residents alike with its red granite and sandstone facade, soaring eight-story atrium, golden onyx pillars, and stained-glass ceiling. Luminaries such as Theodore Roosevelt, Dwight

The "unsinkable" Molly Brown.

Eisenhower, and Harry Truman were frequent guests. Even if you can't stay here, don't pass up an opportunity to see the lobby, join a historical tour (Wed and Sat at 3pm), or enjoy the sumptuous afternoon tea.

If time permits, consider another detour on Tremont Place for a self-guided tour of the **Denver Firefighters Museum** ⑫ (1326 Tremont Place; tel: 303-892-1436; www.denverfirefighters museum.org; Mon–Sat 10am–4pm). The museum is set in a historic firehouse and displays an array of steam pumpers, fire trucks, and other equipment dating back to the 1860s. Children can try on firefighting equipment and slide down a pole.

The **Masonic Building** (1889), also by Frank Edbrooke, stands at Welton Street. Gutted by fire in 1985, its stone facade was rescued by erecting a new steel skeleton within. Next door, the **Kittredge Building** (1891) houses the **Paramount Theatre** ⑬ (1621 Glenarm Place; tel: 303-623-0106; www.paramountdenver.com), Denver's only surviving movie palace, which opened in 1930. It's worth catching a

performance, if only to view the Art Deco interior.

Two blocks farther on, a detour to the left leads to the **Denver Performing Arts Complex** ⑭ (1400 Curtis Street; tel: 720-865-4220; www.artscomplex.com). Encompassing four city blocks and eight theaters, it is the world's largest center of its kind under one roof – an impressive glass arch 80ft (24 meters) high and two blocks long. Drama, musicals, cabaret, opera, ballet, and concerts are staged here.

At Arapahoe Street the view opens onto distant mountains. On the right is one of the city's oldest landmarks, the **Daniels and Fisher**, or **D&F, Tower** ⑮ (1601 Arapahoe St tel: 303-293-0075). Colorado's first "skyscraper" is 330ft (100 meters) tall – 375ft (114 meters) to the top of the flagpole – and was the highest building west of the Mississippi when it was completed in 1909. Modeled after the campanile in St Mark's Square in Venice, the tower has its original clockworks, thought to be the largest of their kind in the country. The weights are wound by hand several times a

TIP

The small but highly regarded **Museo de las Americas** (861 Santa Fe Drive; tel: 303-571-4401; www.museo.org; Tue–Sat noon–5pm) south of downtown is dedicated to Latino culture, ranging from Pre-Columbian civilizations to contemporary works.

Larimer Square.

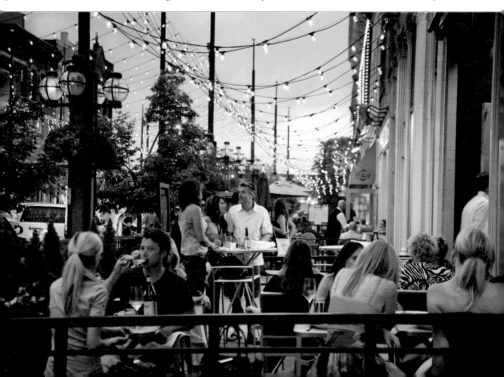

week. The lobby displaying the mechanism is open to the public, and the five floors are home to loft residences and often used for parties, weddings, and corporate events.

Rest in **Skyline Park**, a leafy plaza rescued from neglect by an ambitious redevelopment plan in 2003. On the next block is the glass-walled **Tabor Center**, a lively shopping mall with more than 50 retailers and restaurants, wandering entertainers, and a visitor information booth. Opposite is **Writers Square**, a complex of shops, offices, and apartments built around a central plaza.

Cut through Writers Square to **Larimer Square 16**, a block of restored Victorian-era buildings on Larimer Street between 14th and 15th streets housing restaurants and shops. The Granite Building at 1228 15th Street stands on the site where General William H. Larimer built his log cabin, using coffin lids for doors. Western legends like Bat Masterson and Buffalo Bill Cody also had Larimer Street addresses at one time or another during their Western sojourns.

The grand atrium of the Brown Palace Hotel, designed by architect Frank Edbrooke and completed in 1892.

On the north side is the square's trendiest hangout, **The Market at Larimer Square**, where you can soak in the scene over coffee, pastries, sandwiches, or ice cream. Some of Denver's best restaurants can be found here including award-winning Rioja, a top destination for foodies. Horse-drawn carriages depart from the Square for rides along the 16th Street Mall.

LoDo

Anchoring the restored Lower Downtown (or LoDo) on Wynkoop Street is **Union Station 17**, built in 1881 and still serving as a railroad terminal. Amtrak runs two cross-country lines through Union Station as well as the weekend Ski Train to Winter Park. Modern restaurants have been added to the wings, but the central waiting room is still a vision from an Edward Hopper painting, with tall-backed wooden benches, overhead reading lights and arched windows.

Next to the station, the 1903 **Ice House**, a former cold storage plant for the Littleton Creamery, is said to

THE LODO DISTRICT

The restoration of Larimer Square in the 1970s started a revitalization movement that culminated some 25 years later with the resurrection of a blighted warehouse district known as Lower Downtown, or LoDo. Encompassing about 25 square blocks from Larimer Street to Union Station, and Cherry Creek to 20th Street, LoDo contains a remarkable concentration of early 20th-century industrial buildings. During its heyday, LoDo was a bustling commercial district full of sprawling warehouses and showrooms that were the forerunners of modern department stores.

Denver was a major rail center, and the warehouses were packed with goods for distribution throughout the West. By the early 1990s, however, LoDo had been all but abandoned – a haven for drug dealers and the homeless that was strictly off-limits after dark. All that changed in 1995 with the opening of the 50,000-seat Coors Field baseball stadium at Blake and 20th streets. Suddenly thousands of people were trooping through LoDo, and their custom sparked the regeneration of the neighborhood. Within five years, LoDo went from having no taxpaying residents to about 5,000, a number that has grown steadily ever since. Dozens of bars, restaurants, and brewpubs, as well as some 30 galleries, keep the place buzzing year-round, though summer evenings – when the young and beautiful go clubbing – tend to be the liveliest.

have stored furs and corpses as well as dairy products. The spooky basement level lends credibility to the tale, but otherwise the building sports a smart lobby, a restaurant, and a deli. Across the street, the **Wynkoop Brewing Company**, Colorado's first brewpub and a LoDo pioneer, occupies the beautiful turn-of-the-20th-century J.S. Brown Mercantile. Around the corner, at 17th and Wazee streets, is yet another Frank Edbrooke creation, the **Oxford Hotel**, built in 1891 and embodying all the grand aspirations of Colorado's silver boom.

The **Museum of Contemporary Art Denver** ⑱ (1485 Delgany Street; tel: 303-298-7554; www.mcadenver. org; Tue–Wed noon–7pm, Thurs noon–9pm, Fri noon–10pm, Sat–Sun 10am–5pm) houses works by modern masters such as British artist Damien Hirst. The building itself is a work of art, a sustainable structure on a former brownfield site that has won gold LEED designation for its sustainable construction. It was designed in 2006 by Tanzania-born David Adjaye, one of Britain's leading architects, and

contains five galleries, a store, a café, and a lecture hall.

On the north side of LoDo is **Coors Field** ⑲, home of the Colorado Rockies. Opened to much acclaim in the mid-1990s, the $215 million stadium was designed in the spirit of the classic ballparks of the 1940s and 1950s. The **Sandlot Brewing Company**, owned by the corporate giant that sponsors the park, provides appreciative fans with specialty beers.

A three-block walk from the stadium is the small Japanese enclave of **Sakura Square** (19th and Larimer streets). During World War II, when people of Japanese descent faced hostility in the United States, Governor Ralph Carr welcomed them to Colorado. A bronze bust honors his memory. The **Pacific Mercantile Company**, which sells Asian foods and gifts, opened here in 1942. Otherwise, there's not a great deal of interest for tourists.

South Platte Valley

Due west of LoDo, where Cherry Creek flows into the South Platte

Some rides were relocated from their home at the original Elitch Gardens in northwest Denver to the current site in the Platte River Valley.

The Tattered Cover Bookstore.

TATTERED COVERS

Denver's Tattered Cover Bookstore is one of the West's great independent bookstores. The historic LoDo store (1628 16th Street; tel: 303-436-1070; Mon–Fri 6:30am–9pm, Sat 9am–9pm, Sun 10am–6pm) occupies two cavernous floors of the former Morey Mercantile building. The Colfax Avenue Store (2526 East Colfax Street; tel: 303-322-7727; Mon–Sat 9am–9pm, Sun 10am–6pm) is located in the Lowenstein Theater and contains some 150,000 titles, an extensive news stand and reading nooks with comfy chairs. There is a third branch in Aspen Grove (7301 S. Santa Fe Drive, Littleton; tel: 303-470-7047; Mon–Sat 9am–9pm, Sun 10am–6pm), and branches in Union Station and Denver International Airport. All three have cafes. Call for author reading schedules and other information.

The Museum of Nature and Science has more than 1 million artifacts, ranging from Egyptian mummies to dinosaurs.

Dinosaur exhibit at the Museum of Nature and Science's Prehistoric Journey.

River, is **Confluence Park ㉑**. Kayakers can often be seen testing the rapids above the confluence, and kayaks can be rented on nearby Platte Street. For decades this stretch of the South Platte was an industrial wasteland – polluted, cluttered with trash, and prone to flooding. A reclamation project launched in the 1970s has worked a marvelous transformation, and today the river front is a popular public space, with some 12 miles (19km) of biking trails, picnic areas, and even wetlands where native species like beaver thrive.

The **Children's Museum of Denver ㉑** (2121 Children's Museum Drive; tel: 303-433-7444; www.mychildsmuseum.org; Mon, Tues, Thurs, Fri 9am – 4pm, Wed 9am7:30pm, Sat–Sun 10am–5pm) has interactive exhibits that encourage kids to play the role of storyteller, artist, scientist, and more. An outdoor challenge center gives children an opportunity to try skating, snowboarding, and skiing in safety. Outside the museum is a stop for the **Platte Valley Trolley**, an open-air streetcar reminiscent of

those operated by the Denver Tramway Company in the early 20th century. It follows a scenic route along the South Platte on railroad tracks dating to the 1890s.

Across the river is **Elitch Gardens Theme and Water Park ㉒** (2000 Elitch Circle, I-25 and Speer Boulevard; tel: 303-595-4386; www.elitchgardens.com; open daily April–Oct, June–Aug 10am–7pm, until 10pm on weekends, hours vary in Apr, May, Sept, and Oct). The park was originally located in northwest Denver, where in 1890 John and Mary Elitch started a "pleasure garden" in an orchard. Moved to a much larger site on the South Platte in 1995, it currently has four steel and wooden roller coasters and eight other thrill rides, including the highest free-fall drop swing in Colorado and a white water rafting ride, a 300ft (90-meter) observation tower, a 100ft (30-meter-high) Ferris wheel, and a 10-acre (4-hectare) water park.

The large soda-can-shaped building near Elitch Gardens is the **Pepsi Center**, a top concert venue and home of the Colorado Avalanche hockey team. **Invesco Field**, where the Denver Broncos play soccer, is on the opposite side of the river, off I-25.

City Park

With more than 6,200 acres (2,509 hectares) of traditional parks and parkways, including 2,500 acres (1,012 hectares) of urban natural land, more than 300 acres (121 hectares) of parks, designated river and trails, and an additional 14,000 acres (5,666 hectares) of spectacular mountain parks, Denver has one of the largest municipal park systems in the United States. One of the oldest is **City Park**, created in 1881 when 314 acres (127 hectares) of sagebrush were transformed into a sanctuary of green lawns and rose gardens. **Denver Zoo ㉓** (2300 Steele Street; tel: 720-337-1400; www.denverzoo.org; daily 10am–5pm, extended summer hours) was founded here a few years later. Its first exhibit was an orphaned black bear named Billy Bryan, who was tethered to a tree. Bear Mountain, built in 1918, was the first naturalistic habitat – an enclosure without bars – an idea that wouldn't catch on at other zoos for another 50 years. Today, the zoo is home to about 3,500 animals representing more than 650 species. Among the zoo's highlights are the Primate Panorama, a habitat for some 29 primate species, ranging from pygmy marmosets (which weigh as much as an airmail letter) to 600lb (270kg) lowland gorillas; Tropical Discovery, a simulated rain forest; and a pack of Arctic wolves.

On the east side of the park is the **Denver Museum of Nature and Science** ㉔ (2001 Colorado Boulevard; tel: 303-370-6000; www.dmns. org; daily 9am–5pm; charge), the fifth largest natural history museum in the United States. Exhibits cover familiar territory – mummies, meteorites, totem poles, tepees, wildlife dioramas, and much else. Where the museum really excels is in the field of paleontology. Prehistoric Journey, an exhibit on the third floor, chronicles 3½ billion years of life on earth. The highlight is a collection of dinosaur fossils, including an 80ft (24-meter) long Diplodocus and an Allosaurus and Stegosaurus engaged in battle. In the next room is a diorama of a nightmarish creature known as a Dinohyus, nicknamed the "terminator pig," stalking its prey about 20 million years ago. The museum is also home to the **Gates Planetarium**, which features daily star shows, and the Phipps **IMAX** 3D Theater.

Denver Botanic Gardens

Denver Botanic Gardens ㉕ (1007 York Street; tel: 720-865-3501; www. botanicgardens.org; daily 9am–5pm, summer until 9pm) is one of the top botanical gardens in the country. It encompasses 24 acres (10 hectares) planted with over 16,000 examples of more than 250 plant species at its York Street gardens and two satellite locations: Chatfield, a picturesque nature preserve along the banks of Deer Creek, and Mount Goliath, which showcases alpine tundra. The Boettcher Memorial Tropical Conservatory is housed in the only major tropical conservatory in the Rockies. For the best view, ascend to the overhead platforms on an elevator disguised as a banyan tree. Plants from all over the world are featured in 30 outdoor gardens, including a Japanese garden with a teahouse and the Monet Garden, with flowers and water lilies inspired by the canvases of French Impressionist painter Claude Monet. Colorado native plants take pride of place in gardens of rare wildflowers, alpine species, medicinal plants used by American Indians, and heirloom varieties brought to Colorado by Anglo pioneers. Special events are held throughout the year, including summer garden strolls and a concert series. WiFi is available throughout the botanic gardens, so you can work online and enjoy the outdoors.

Denver Botanic Gardens.

FESTIVALS

Colorado is famous for the sheer number of its festivals. Almost every community has a festival during the year – some of which fall on the odd side of the spectrum.

When you have a spectacular setting like the Colorado Rockies, you like to show it off to its full advantage. Some communities in Colorado, though, have hit on some unique festivals to attract visitors. Manitou Springs has not one, but two, weird festivals, in addition to its popular Wine Festival: the Great Fruitcake Toss in early January, celebrating the famous American dislike of Grandma's Christmas fruitcake, and the Emma Crawford Coffin Races in October, a blackly humorous race up Pikes Peak commemorating the 1890 death of Emma Crawford, her burial on Red Mountain, and the subsequent refusal of her remains to stay buried there. Just as macabre is Frozen Dead Guy Days in Nederland, near Boulder, in March, which culminates in an excursion to a wooden shed to view the remains of an elderly Norwegian man whose remains were unable to be repatriated and instead were frozen here forever. Mike the Headless Chicken Festival in Fruita in May is equally strange, celebrating a chicken that managed to live after its head was cut off. Compared with these fests, fibARK, the biggest whitewater convocation in the country, on the Arkansas River in downtown historic Salida in early September, is fun in the sun, as is Rolling River Raft Race, in Pueblo in July. And the International Rhubarb Festival on the Fourth of July celebrating Silverton's only crop. Positively mainstream.

The annual Emma Crawford Coffin Race in Manitou Spr[...] is run in honor of Emma Crawford, who was buried on Re[...] Mountain following her death from tuberculosis in 1890. Legend has it that her coffin was later dislodged by heavy r[...] and came sliding down the mountain.

Vinotok is Crested Butte's celebration of the changing of th[...] seasons, from summer to fall to winter.

The Green Man battles the Grump in Crested Butte's fall festival of Vinotok.

The chainless bike race is one of the highlights of Fat Tire Bike Week in Crested Butte.

FUN IN THE MOUNTAINS

Tucked away in a gorgeous box canyon in the Western San Juans, Telluride is decidedly off the beaten track. Until a few years ago, it was mainly popular as a destination ski resort in winter but welcomed fewer visitors during the summer. Until, that is, local tourism boosters hit upon the brilliant idea of turning the small town into a summer festival destination. Today, throughout the summer and at other times of year, there is always something going on in Telluride, from its Blues and Brews Festival, Bluegrass Festival, International Film Festival, and Mountainfilm Festival to more obscure offerings such as the Telluride Mushroom Festival and the tongue-in-cheek Nothing Festival, a weekend when everyone stays home for a change (tagline: "Thank you for not participating"). Telluride is not unique in the community fun stakes. The tiny ski resort town of Crested Butte also has quite a roster of home town festivals, including Flauschink, an off-the-wall, end-of-ski-season celebration in March; Fat Tire Bike Week in June; the Rubber Duckie fundraiser in July; and Vinitok, celebrating the change in season in late September.

RK, the whitewater festival in Salida, has been attracting ...ers since 1949. It is America's oldest kayak festival.

...ffin races at Frozen Dead Guy Days are a spectacle unto ...elves. The event also features a polar plunge.

The chainless bike race in Crested Butte, where some contestants lose more than their chains.

BOULDER AND ENVIRONS

The mind-set is strictly forward-looking in this quintessential college town set amid the scenic splendors of the Rocky Mountain foothills.

The city of **Boulder** ❶ is sometimes referred to as "twenty-five square miles surrounded by reality." Though only 30 miles (48km) from downtown Denver, this city of 105,101 people is a world apart. Both unapologetically New Age yet fast-paced and intellectual (the average age of the population is 29), Boulder is a place where past, present, and future co-exist quite happily, with former hippies now running some of the city's most successful health products businesses, alternative health and meditation schools, science think-tanks, and outdoor companies. Boulderites are liberal in outlook, with a penchant for political correctness. Residents share a fanatical commitment to fitness and a strong interest in educational, spiritual, alternative health, environmental, and social issues.

The city has been focused on education ever since the University of Colorado was established here in 1876, the year Colorado achieved statehood. One-third of the city's population is now connected to UC Boulder, famed for its science programs, and the city hosts several major science research centers, including the National Center for Atmospheric Research, the Space Science Institute, and the Rocky Mountain Institute.

Furniture store in downtown Boulder.

Boulder Mountain Parks

Etched into the national consciousness along with other such "progressive" towns as Austin (Texas), Berkeley (California), and Madison (Wisconsin), Boulder arguably has the most scenic location. The tilted rock slabs known as the **Flatirons** and a procession of nearby peaks form a splendid western backdrop that captures the light and lifts the spirit. These formations comprise the heart of **Boulder Mountain Parks** (tel: 303-678-6200; www.bouldercolorado.gov), part of the

Main Attractions

Boulder Mountain Parks and The Flatirons
Boulder Creek
Colorado Chautauqua
Pearl Street Mall
Boulder County Farmers' Market
University of Colorado Campus Museums

Pearl Street Mall in Boulder is the perfect place to go shopping for an unusual or handmade item.

city's approximately 45,000 acres (18,211 hectares) of open space and parks. Open space in general, and the mountain parks in particular, are more than a buffer against suburban sprawl. They are laced with hiking, biking, and equestrian trails that form a 300-mile (480km) urban trail system.

Urban park

The 7-mile (11km) stretch of **Boulder Creek Path** that hugs the contours of the creek east–west across the city is typically crowded with cyclists, in-line skaters, runners, walkers, and parents pushing baby carriages. Majestic cottonwoods shade the creek banks, and benches, kids' fishing and fish-spotting areas, historic markers, and sculptures are diversions along the way. Kayakers navigate Boulder Creek's rapids just upstream from the mouth of **Boulder Canyon**, while tubing is a cool way to enjoy the creek between pretty **Eben Fine Park** (at the west end of Arapahoe Avenue) and **Central Park** (Broadway between Walnut and Canyon). The Boulder Creek

Festival takes place here every Memorial Day weekend.

Credit for these amenities goes to the foresight of city officials. They purchased thousands of acres of open land as early as 1967 and adopted stringent zoning and growth control in the 1970s. Boulder's policy has been to reuse existing buildings and fill in empty lots, rather than endlessly sprawl outward, with a few carefully thought-out subdivisions on the edge of town. What Boulder has done for decades other cities are now, often belatedly, envying and emulating.

An enlightened colony

Boulder lies in a broad open valley with the Flatirons and foothills to the west, Davidson Mesa to the south and a gentle, nameless ridge to the north. From this high perch, it seems like a small settlement tucked among the trees, especially in summer when they are fully leafed out. On a clear day in any season, the eye is drawn above the trees and rooftops to the majestic mountain backdrop, culminating in 14,255ft (4,325-meter

Longs Peak, the highest along the Front Range, just 40 miles (64km) northwest of Boulder.

When the Southern Arapaho tribe wintered here, the valley was high prairie virtually devoid of trees. On October 17, 1858, the first Anglo settlers established a rough camp below Red Rocks at the mouth of **Boulder Canyon**. A plaque at **Settlers Park** commemorates their arrival. Just four months later, the Boulder City Town Company was organized, with A.A. Brookfield as president and 56 shareholders. They platted 4,444 parcels of land priced at $1,000 each. Encompassed by Kansas Territory until February 28, 1861, when Congress created the Territory of Colorado, Boulder City became a supply town for prospectors seeking gold and silver in the mountains to the west. Residents, longing for respectability, opened the territory's first school in 1860, created a stable town government in 1871, and cheered the arrival of the railroad in 1873.

By 1900, such residential neighborhoods as Goss Grove, Whittier, and Mapleton Hill had taken shape around the downtown commercial core. Now designated as historic districts, they have the patina of old Boulder, albeit far leafier than the city's founders could have envisioned. **Historic Boulder** (1123 Spruce Street; tel: 303-444-5192; www.historicboulder.org; Mon–Fri 9am–5pm) sponsors guided tours of the neighborhoods (charge) and sells inexpensive pamphlets for self-guided walking tours.

In 1898, Boulder was chosen by Texas educators and local citizens as a location for the Chautauqua movement, a summer colony devoted to educational enrichment, spiritual enlightenment, and physical health. The **Colorado Chautauqua ❷** (tel: 303-442-3282; www.chautauqua.com) was founded on a hillside southwest of town, where the wooden auditorium, the dining Hall, and tent cabins were erected. Quaint wood-frame cabins long ago replaced the tents as popular vacation rentals; the auditorium is now home of the summer **Colorado Music Festival**

Street performer in Boulder.

Naropa University offers classes in Eastern spiritualism.

Art Deco court house, Boulder.

(tel: 303-665-0599; www.comusic.org), while the Chautauqua **Dining Hall** (tel: 303-440-3776 for reservations) is a fine, year-round restaurant. The expansive lawn is popular with picnickers and Frisbee-throwers. Trailheads for three of the best trails in the Boulder Mountain Parks are on the perimeter. Hiking information is available at the Ranger Cottage in **Chautauqua Park** (Baseline and Grant; tel: 303-441-3440; www.bouldercolorado.gov; May–Sept Mon–Fri 9am–4pm, Sat–Sun 8am–6pm (Oct until 5pm on weekends), Nov–Apr 9am–4pm daily; park event hours vary). The cottage stocks maps; ranger-guided hikes depart from here.

Around "The Mall"

In 1977, four blocks in downtown Boulder between 11th and 15th streets were set aside as a pedestrian mall. The town's commercial district, and much of its public life, centers around the **Pearl Street Mall ❸**, one of the country's first (and still one of the most successful) pedestrian-only zones. Gradually,

most traditional stores and services moved elsewhere, replaced by trendy boutiques, art galleries, craft shops, restaurants, and nightclubs. Beautifully landscaped, it is the perfect place for strolling, shopping, dining, or sitting at a sidewalk café and watching the world go by. With warm, sunny days common even in winter, outdoor tables at south-facing establishments are popular throughout the year.

"The Mall" attracts jugglers and buskers, but it's also the setting for many special events, including the **Bolder Boulder 10K** marathon in May; **Bands on the Bricks** concerts, June through August; the **Downtown Open Arts Fest** in late July; and **Switch on the Holidays**, the Friday after Thanksgiving. (Tel: 303-449-3774; www.boulderdowntown.com)

Just a block from the Mall is the 1909 **Hotel Boulderado** (2115 13th Street; tel: 303-442-4344; www.boulderado.com), which has a gorgeous *fin-de-siècle* lobby topped by a soaring stained-glass ceiling. Around the corner, **Boulder Theater** (2034

14th Street; tel: 303-786-7030; www.bouldertheater.com), an Art Deco landmark, hosts concerts, dance, films, and the weekly broadcast of National Public Radio's *e-Town*. Nearby, the landmark **Boulder Dushanbe Tea House** (1770 13th Street; tel: 303-442-4993; www.boulderteahouse.com) is an exotic polychrome tile structure from Dushanbe, Tajikistan, one of Boulder's six sister cities.

Just south of the teahouse, **Boulder Museum of Contemporary Art** (1750 13th Street; tel: 303-443-2122; www.bmoca.org; Tue–Fri, Sun 11am–5pm, Wed until 8pm, Sat 9am–5pm; charge) features impressive shows by visiting artists and a diverse series of lectures and workshops. **Boulder County Farmers' Market** (tel: 303-910-2236; www.boulderfarmers.org; Apr and Nov Sat 8am–2pm, May–Oct Sat 8am–2pm, Wed 4–8pm), one of the nation's top farmer's markets, occupies 13th Street between Canyon Boulevard and Arapahoe Avenue, and is well worth a visit. Entrance to the Boulder Creek Path is steps away, at 13th and Arapahoe.

Centers of culture and learning

In 1874, Boulder donated 45 acres (18 hectares) to the **University of Colorado ❹** for the purpose of establishing an institution of higher learning on the wild frontier. **Old Main**, built in 1877 for classrooms, offices, and the president's living quarters, now houses **CU Heritage Center** (tel: 303-492-6329; www.cuheritage.org; Mon–Sat 10am–4pm, free), a museum devoted to the university's history and traditions. One room honors CU's 15 alumni astronauts, including Kalpana Chawla, who perished in the Columbia explosion.

University of Colorado Museum of Natural History (Henderson Building, 15th and Broadway; tel: 303-492-6892; www.cumuseum.edu; Mon–Fri 9am–5pm, Sat 9am–4pm, Sun 10am–4pm) houses more than 4 million artifacts in the fields of paleontology, zoology, and anthropology, including exhibits of Ancestral Puebloan art, dinosaur fossils, and specimens of native species. The Discovery Corner is a hands-on section designed

The campus of the University of Colorado at Boulder has all been designed in the same architectural style.

Busker, downtown Boulder.

Dushanbe Tea House.

especially for children. Three galleries offer changing exhibitions.

Fiske Planetarium (2414 Regent Drive; tel: 303-492-5002; www.fiske. colorado.edu; call for show times) is the largest facility of its kind between Chicago and Los Angeles. It presents star shows, workshops, and labs, as well as laser shows set to pop music. Amateur astronomers can gaze at the heavens through 16-, 18- and 24-in telescopes at **Sommers-Bausch Observatory** (Regent Drive and Kittridge Loop; tel: 303-492-6732; www.sbo.colorado. edu; public viewing Fri night when school is in session). Weekly stargazing sessions focus on such themes as black holes, extraterrestrial life, and planetary exploration.

The southern fringe

Begin exploring the outskirts of town by driving south on Broadway to Baseline Road, then west up steep, tortuous Flagstaff Road into 7,400-acre (2,995-hectare) **Boulder Mountain Park ❺**. Pullouts along the way offer panoramic views of Boulder, the Front Range, and the Continental Divide.

Boulder Mountain Park.

Hiking trails cross the road at various points, and at the summit of **Flagstaff Mountain** are picnic tables, an amphitheater built in the 1930s by the Civilian Conservation Corps, and a rustic cabin with nature exhibits.

Return the way you came, turning south on Broadway to Table Mesa Drive for a winding uphill ride to the **National Center for Atmospheric Research ❻** (1850 Table Mesa Drive; tel: 303-497-1000; www.ncar. ucar.edu; Mon–Fri 8am–5pm, Sat–Sun and holidays 9am–4pm; free guided tour weekdays at noon). Designed by architect I.M. Pei and set dramatically at the base of the Flatirons, the facility's sandstone walls and rectangular masses recall the ancient cliff dwellings of Mesa Verde. A series of interactive exhibits explores weather and the science of climatology.

About 8 miles (13km) south of Boulder, in the hamlet of **Eldorado Springs ❼**, the area's best outdoor swimming pool is operated by water-bottling company **Eldorado Artesian Springs** (tel: 303-604-3000 ext, 3093; www.eldoradosprings.com; daily

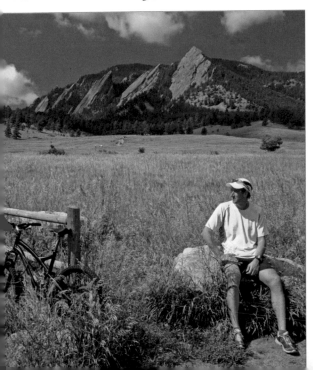

CELESTIAL SEASONINGS

Celestial Seasonings (4600 Sleepytime Drive; tel: 303-581-1266; www.celestial seasonings.com; Mon–Sat 10am–4pm, Sun 11am–3pm; tea shop: Mon–Sat 9am–6pm, Sun 10am–5pm; Celestial Café: Mon–Fri 7am–2pm), is the country's largest producer of herbal teas and Boulder's top visitor attraction. Enjoy sampling their range and learn how the teas are grown, dried, blended, and packaged on free tours (an astounding 8 million teabags are produced every 24 hours.) A visit to the aromatic Mint Room – one of the tour highlights – is an olfactory tour de force. A gallery displays the original paintings for the folksy tea packaging. Red Zinger, Grandma's Tummy Mint, and other popular teas are sold at a discount in the tea shop.

June–Aug 10am–6pm; charge). The pool is all that remains of the ritzy Eldorado Springs Resort, which opened in 1905. It hosted such luminaries as boxer Jack Dempsey and Dwight and Mamie Eisenhower, as well as actor W.C. Fields, the well-known tippler, who famously declared "I never drink water because of the disgusting things fish do in it"; he reluctantly tried a sip of spring water. **Eldorado Canyon State Park** (tel: 303-494-3943; http://cpw.state.co.us/placestogo/parks/EldoradoCanyon is Boulder's premier rock-climbing area, with 500 routes, picnic sites, and 12 miles (19km) of hiking trails. During the resort's heyday, daredevil Ivy Baldwin entertained guests by walking a tight-rope across the canyon. He made the trip 86 times – the first in 1906, the last, at age 82, in 1948.

orth of town

On the north side of town, just off the Diagonal Highway (CO 119), is **Celestial Seasonings**, the country's top herbal teas producer (see page 168), and nearby **Leanin' Tree Museum** of **Western Art** ❽ (6055 Longbow Drive; tel: 303-729-3412; www.leanintreemuseum.com; museum and gift shop Mon–Fri 8am–6pm, Sat 9am–5pm, Sun 10am–5pm free tours Mon-Fri 10am–2pm), which features the private collection of Ed Trumble, founder of a greeting card company specializing in Western themes. Scores of paintings and bronze sculptures – nearly all created after 1950 – are jammed into a handful of galleries.

Northeast of Boulder, in the town of **Longmont** ❾, is **Longmont Museum & Cultural Center** (400 Quail Road; tel: 303-651-8374; www.longmontcolorado.gov/museum; Mon–Sat 9am–5pm, Sun 1–5pm; free but charge for special exhibitions), a striking contemporary structure inspired by the region's agricultural heritage. Two galleries display permanent exhibits, including "Front Range Rising," the museum's signature exhibit about area history. Traveling shows are presented in the other two galleries.

Rugged west

The region's hardscrabble mining era reveals itself as you travel into

Celestial Seasonings tea shop.

Inner tubing down the creeks and rivers of Colorado is a popular way to spend a hot summer's day.

Biking in Boulder Canyon.

the mountains west of Boulder via Boulder Canyon Drive (CO 119). Eight miles (13km) up the twisting, rock-rimmed road is **Boulder Falls**, a 70ft (21-meter) cascade that's been called, with considerable hyperbole, "the Yosemite of Boulder." Eight miles (13km) farther on, **Boulder Canyon** opens into a wide valley occupied by Barker Reservoir, a good place to fish for trout, and the town of **Nederland** ⑩, a former mining camp known today for its hippie-ish, New Age ambience, funky shops and eateries, and four summer festivals: Frozen Dead Guy Days in March (see page 170), the High Peaks Art Festival in June, Old Timers and Miners' Days in July, and NedFest in August. Information on all events is available by calling 303-258-3936.

Seasonal visitors may enjoy **Nederland Mining Museum** (W 2nd Street; tel: 303-258-0567; June–Oct Fri–Sun 10am–4pm; free), a collection of artifacts and hands-on exhibits that highlight life in a 19th-century mining camp.

From Nederland, head north about 12 miles (19km) on CO 72 (also known as the Peak-to-Peak Highway) to **Ward** ⑪, a former silver mining town now best known as a high-country outdoors retreat. Eight miles (13km) west of town, on Brainard Lake Road is **Brainard Lake National Recreation Area**, popular for summer hiking, winter cross-country skiing and snowshoeing, and jaw-dropping views of the Indian Peaks in any season (see page 171).

The only downward route out of Ward is **Lefthand Canyon Drive**. About 7 miles (11km) along, turn right onto Lick Skillet Road, a steep dirt track that twists into the **Gold Hill** mining district. In the quaint village of **Gold Hill** (10 miles/17km northwest of Boulder) are log cabins, mining artifacts, and the **Gold Hill Inn** (tel: 303-443-6461; www.goldhillinn.com), built as a hotel in 1872 and now an atmospheric seasonal gourmet restaurant (May–Dec). From the crossroads, take Sunshine Canyon Road directly to Boulder's fancy Mapleton Hill neighborhood. The route is downhill all the way.

FROZEN DEAD GUY DAYS

Nederland is famous for what may be the oddest home town festival anywhere. Frozen Dead Guy Days is held annually over an early March weekend to commemorate the 1989 death (and future reanimation) of Bredo Morstoel, an elderly Norwegian gentleman whose body resides in the world's only "do-it-yourself cryogenic facility" – a garden shed packed with dry ice. The scheme was hatched by Bredo's grandson, Trygve Bauge, who was deported back to Norway before he was able to find his grandfather more suitable lodging. The event features a coffin race, Grandpa lookalike contest, a frozen salmon toss, an evening dance known as Grandpa's Blue Ball, a midnight visit to the shed, and a pancake breakfast. For more information, tel: 303-506-1048 or log on to www.frozendeadguydays.com.

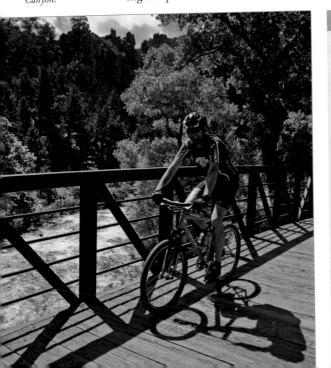

Indian Peaks Wilderness

Rising from Boulder's backyard, the Indian Peaks soar to 13,000ft (3,960 meters) and rank as a Colorado backcountry favorite.

Forty-three designated wilderness areas, accessible only on foot, form protected islands of scenic beauty within Colorado's vast sea of publicly owned lands. The 73,391-acre (29,700-hectare) Indian Peaks Wilderness, straddling the Continental Divide, isn't the state's largest wilderness area, but it is the most accessible.

Of the more than 70 mountains in Indian Peaks Wilderness, seven soar to 13,000ft (4,000 meters) or higher, 23 to at least 12,000ft (3,660 meters), and 32 to 11,000ft (3,350 meters). Indian Peaks' northern anchor is 14,255ft (4,345-meter) Longs Peak, just outside the wilderness boundary, in Rocky Mountain National Park. At the southern end looms massive James Peak. Between them are such commanding summits as round-topped Mount Audubon, the twin summits of Arapaho Peak, pointy Mount Toll, and Apache Peak, a giant bracketed by three enormous ridges.

Giving the peaks the names of Indian tribes was the idea of botany teacher Ellsworth Bethel in the spring of 1914. Of the 11 he named, the US Board on Geographic Names kept six. The Indian Peaks were included in Enos Mills' (see page 202) original proposed boundaries for Rocky Mountain National Park but were removed from the proposal to avoid conflicts with mining interests and local development.

National forest land serves as the gateway to the wilderness. Fourteen trailheads provide access even to the most remote and seldom visited areas. More than 100,000 people enter the wilderness each year: judging by the number of cars parked at popular trailheads, you might wonder how such a heavily used area could possibly be called a wilderness. The answer lies in the hidden peaks, high lakes, and surprisingly secluded valleys deep within Indian Peaks, far from the trappings of civilization.

A day trip to Brainard Lake from Boulder

Among the easiest places to get a flavor of the region is Brainard Lake National Recreation Area, just beyond Indian Peaks' eastern boundary. A paved road circling the lake leads to picnic sites and a campground. Reaching nearby Long Lake within the wilderness area requires only a gentle, half-mile hike, though the trailhead elevation of 10,500ft (3,200 meters) makes it a lung-buster for those who aren't yet acclimated to the elevation. In midsummer, open meadows and streambanks are ablaze with wildflowers, and in fall, stands of aspen glow gold against the clear blue sky.

Splayed above Brainard Lake is one of Colorado's most enticing panoramas. This craggy landscape, formed by a vast geological uplift and carved by glaciers whose remnants cling to the highest summits, is stunning to look and a real draw for hikers, climbers, and photographers. Fans of backcountry skiing and snowboarding ascend year-round snowfields packed into vast glacier-carved cirques, and anglers head to more than 50 frigid, cobalt lakes.

Roads closed by heavy snowfall effectively expand Indian Peaks' boundaries and serve as a backcountry getaway for Nordic skiers and snowshoers. The first heavy snow usually arrives in October, and a sufficient cross-country skiing base is soon deposited. Permits are required for overnight campers June to September. Contact Boulder Ranger District (tel: 303-541-2500) for information.

Fly fishing is a popular activity.

COLORADO SPRINGS AND ENVIRONS

Growth is a constant here, practically from the moment a one-time general laid the foundation for a city in the shadow of Pikes Peak.

Colorado Springs ❶ owes much of its flair to William J. Palmer, railroad baron and Civil War general. In 1871, Palmer bought 10,000 acres (4,000 hectares) in the Pikes Peak foothills, where he laid out a spacious, progressive city with plenty of schools, parks, and churches. He discouraged heavy industry as well as bars and gambling houses. So successful were his strictures that Colorado Springs remained "dry" until the repeal of the 18th Amendment in 1933.

Nearby Manitou Springs, with its clamorous bawdy houses, attracted a rougher clientele. Thirsty miners, down from the diggings around Victor and Cripple Creek, much preferred the raucous joints where they could drown their woes in a flood of rotgut and soothe their aching limbs in the bubbling springs that trickled from the mountain sides. Meanwhile, General Palmer's straitlaced community in the foothills to the east enjoyed some of the purest air in the nation, and it wasn't long before the railroads were transporting hordes of people out to Colorado from back East to take the waters and breathe the salutary air.

Mining wealth

The city's economic fortunes were intimately tied to the health of the nearby mining communities, the most prominent of which was Cripple Creek, set high in the mountains behind Pikes Peak. Many of the miners who struck it rich built lavish homes in Colorado Springs and established a solid social base still evident in the mansions around the Broadmoor Hotel and the sturdy domiciles in the old residential districts downtown. From 1900 to 1910, Colorado Springs had the highest per-capita income of any comparable town in the country.

Main Attractions

Colorado Springs
Manitou Springs
Pikes Peak Cog Railway
Florissant Fossil Beds
   National Monument
Royal Gorge
Cripple Creek

The bridge over the Royal Gorge sits 955ft (291 meters) above the Arkansas River below.

World War II stimulated growth, particularly in the military sector. Fort Carson was built south of town in 1942; the US Air Force Academy opened in 1954; and NORAD, a vast air defense command center within Cheyenne Mountain, became operational in 1966. Growth in recent years has been a mixed blessing. While the downtown core around Acacia Park has been preserved, suburban sprawl has resulted in a familiar glut of strip malls and tract housing.

Downtown and beyond

Start your visit in the downtown area. The **Colorado Springs Pioneers Museum** ❷ (215 S. Tejon Street; tel: 719-385-5990; www.cspm. org; Tue–Sat 10am–5pm; free), housed in the former county courthouse, showcases a first-rate sampling of historic artifacts from the Pikes Peak area, including guns, mining equipment and household items as well as a restored 1903 courtroom. The **McAllister House Museum** (423 N. Cascade Avenue;

tel: 719-635-7925; www.mcalliste house.org; tours May–Aug Tue–Sa 10am–3pm, Sept–Dec and Feb–Ap Thur–Sat 10am–3pm), built in 187 by civic leader Henry McAllister, i one of Colorado Springs' histori landmarks. Original furnishings giv visitors a glimpse of life in a well-to do 19th-century household.

A few blocks away, **Colorad Springs Fine Arts Center** ❸ (30 W Dale Street; tel: 719-634-5583; www csfineartscenter.org; Tue–Sun 10am 5pm) features a wide array of 19th century, modern and postmoder artworks housed in a distinctiv 1930s Pueblo Deco building, includ ing works by New Mexico artist Peter Hurd and Georgia O'Keeffe and Edward Hopper. Of specia interest to aficionados of Western ar is the Charles Russell Room, with collection of sketches and letters b the "cowboy artist."

East of Downtown, the **US Olym pic Training Center** ❹ (1750 E Boulder Street; tel:719-866-4618; www teamusa.org; Mon–Sat 9am–5pm free) occupies a 35-acre (15-hectare

Colorado Springs and Environs

0   20 miles
0   20 km

complex, including the headquarters of the US Olympic Committee, and receives 140,000 visitors a year. Visitors watch the athletes work out in a wide range of sports, including fencing, gymnastics, volleyball, and swimming. Hourly 45-minute tours begin with an inspirational film on Olympic history. Those who prefer winter sports may be intrigued by the **World Figure Skating Hall of Fame and Museum** ❺ (20 First Street; tel: 719-635-5200; www.worldskatingmuseum.org; Tue–Fri 10am–4pm) in the southwest corner of town, which commemorates the history of ice skating and celebrates such well-known skaters as Sonja Henie and Peggy Fleming.

Cheyenne Mountain

Cheyenne Mountain Zoo ❻ (4250 Cheyenne Mountain Zoo Road; tel: 719-633-9925; www.cmzoo.org; daily 9am–5pm), situated high on the slopes of Cheyenne Mountain, overlooking the city. Giraffes and elephants have long been the zoo's mainstays and are showcased in the naturalistic African Rift Valley exhibit, part of a $50 million renovation that also includes the Mountain Sky Ride chair-lift. The zoo is home to about 500 animals in all, including a variety of rare and endangered species such as snow leopards, orangutans, lowland gorillas, and Amur tigers.

Admission to the zoo includes entry to the **Will Rogers Shrine of the Sun** (tel: 719-578-5367; daily 9am–4pm), a slim granite tower clinging to a steep slope. It was built in 1937 in honor of the folksy entertainer, who died in a plane crash in 1935. The remote, aerie-like location offers stupendous views of Colorado Springs.

Equally stunning is **Seven Falls** ❼ (2850 S. Cheyenne Canyon Road; www.sevenfalls.com; daily May–Oct 9am–8pm, reduced hours rest of the year), set at the end of a narrow redrock canyon at the foot of Cheyenne Mountain. Seven ribbony cataracts spill 181ft (55 meters) down the face of a billion-year-old rock mass into a clear pool of plump, basking trout. If you are reasonably fit, climb the 200-plus steps to the

The Will Rogers Memorial offers beautiful views of the Colorado Springs area.

The Pioneers Museum chronicles the region's colorful past.

VAN BRIGGLE POTTERY

Van Briggle Art Pottery (1024 S. Tejon Street; tel: 719-633-7729; www.vanbriggle.com; Mon–Sat 9am–5pm, Sun 1–4pm; free), the oldest continuously operated pottery in the United States, was founded in 1899 by Artus Van Briggle, a brilliant American artist of Dutch descent who trained in Paris and Italy and worked with the famed Rookwood Pottery in Ohio. Van Briggle developed a sensuous pottery style influenced by natural forms and glazed with a beautiful satin matte colored with natural earth minerals. His health failing due to tuberculosis, he took a train out to Colorado Springs and continued making his unique pottery before succumbing to the disease. Tour the pottery to watch ceramicists produce Art Nouveau-inspired designs, then shop in an enormous showroom.

observation platform. Otherwise, take the elevator. American Indian dances are performed several times a day at the base of the falls.

Top guns

The biggest attraction in Colorado Springs is the **US Air Force Academy** 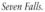 (2304 Cadet Drive; tel: 719-333-2025; www.usafa.af.mil/information/visitors; visitor center daily 9am–5pm; free, all visitors must enter via the North Gate), exit 156B off I-25, about 14 miles (23km) north of downtown. Founded in 1954, the academy is situated on 18,000 acres (7,000 hectares) of preserved land in the foothills of the Rocky Mountains. Most of the campus is off-limits to civilians, but visitors can take a self-guided tour starting at the Visitor Center, which features exhibits and films on the academy's history. The highlight is the Cadet Chapel, a daring contemporary structure whose 17 aluminum spires evoke both the heavenly aspirations of the faithful and the sleek soaring figures of jets in flight. If you time your visit

Seven Falls.

right, you may see cadets drilling o the parade ground or parachutin over the Thunderbird Airmanshi Overlook.

Near the North Gate, the **Wester Museum of Mining & Industry** (225 Northgate Boulevard; tel: 719 488-0880; www.wmmi.org; Mon–Sa 9am–4pm, guided tours 10am an 1pm) brings the history of Colorad mining to life with exhibits of mor than 3,000 artifacts, including a re created assay office, a wide array o machinery and equipment, a simu lated mining tunnel, and tableau illustrating life in a 19th-centur mining camp. Visitors can try pan ning for gold, too.

Another mainstay of Western lor is celebrated at the **Pro Rodeo Hal of Fame & American Cowbo Museum** (101 Pro Rodeo Drive tel: 719-528-4764; www.prorodeoha offame.com; Wed–Sun 9am–5pm south on I-25 at Exit 147. Exhibit chronicle the evolution of the cow boy, from hired hand to Hollywoo icon; rodeo stars are honored in th Hall of Champions.

Rock garden

For another taste of the Old West, head south on I-25 then west on US 24 to the **Ghost Town Museum** (400 S. 21st Street; tel: 719-634-0696; www. ghosttownmuseum.com; June–Aug Mon–Sat 9–6pm, Sun 10am–6pm, Sept–May 10am–5pm daily), a collection of vintage buildings relocated from various parts of the state and reassembled in an indoor hall.

Just across US 24 is **Old Colorado City** (2431 W. Colorado Avenue; 719-577-4112; www.shopoldcoloradocity.com), a former mining camp founded in 1859 and notorious for its saloons and brothels. It was later annexed by the city of Colorado Springs and designated a National Historic Landmark District, and is best known today for its galleries and boutiques.

Farther west on US 24 is the turnoff for **Garden of the Gods** ⓾ (1805 N. 30th Street; tel: 719-634-6666; www. gardenofgods.com; visitor center daily summer 8am–7pm, winter 9am–5pm; free), a 1,300-acre (500-hectare) park renowned for its dramatic sandstone formations. Between 60 and 30 million years ago, the mountain building episode (Laramide Orogeny) that pushed up the Rocky Mountains through the earth's crust tilted horizontal slabs of sedimentary rock into bold, vertical angles. Today, these "blades," as they're called, catch and reflect the colorful hues of morning and evening light. For hundreds of years, the site was an important Indian gathering place. It's said that old people, knowing their time had come, would position themselves on the high shelves and ledges so they could draw their last breath as the first rays of dawn warmed their faces. Today, a series of loop roads and trails enables motorists, hikers, joggers, and walkers to explore just about every corner of the park. It's a popular spot among rock climbers, too, and they are often seen scaling the walls. The visitor center presents exhibits on the area's human and natural history, and naturalists are usually on hand for free nature tours and brief lectures.

At the east entrance to the park is **Rock Ledge Ranch Historic Site** (30th Street; tel: 719-578-6777; www. rockledgeranch.com; June–Aug Wed–Sun 10am–5pm), an assembly of late 19th- and early 20th-century buildings staffed in summer by interpreters in period costume who work the ranch in traditional fashion. The ranch hosts numerous cultural events throughout the year, including pioneer handicrafts, traditional music festivals, and an intertribal powwow.

Manitou Springs

Just west of Garden of the Gods is **Manitou Springs** ⓫, a pretty little town (pop. 5,051) known for its effervescent mineral springs, elaborate Victorian architecture, and abundant art galleries and interesting shops. Among the most notable buildings in town is **Miramont Castle** (9 Capitol Hill Avenue; tel: 719-685-1011; www. miramontcastle.org; late May–early Sept daily 9am–5pm, early Sept–late May Tue–Sun 10am–4pm; tours every half hour; tearoom May–Sept 11am–3pm), an 1895 stone mansion constructed

Steel, aluminum and glass define the soaring interior of the Air Force Academy Chapel.

Pikes Peak Cog Railway.

The Garden of the Gods.

in an eccentric combination of styles by a wealthy French priest who had come to Manitou Springs in search of a cure for his tuberculosis. It now serves as a museum, with 30 rooms filled with exhibits of period furnishings, antique toys, and an elaborate toy train collection. The popular Queen's Parlor Tearoom serves lunch and Victorian-era afternoon or high tea by reservation in summer.

Cave of the Winds 🄑 (Cave of the Winds Road, off US 24; tel: 719-685-5444; www.caveofthewinds.com; daily late May–early Sept 9am–9pm, early Sept–late May 10am–5pm; charge) has been a top tourist attraction for more than a century. A 45-minute guided Discovery Tour leads visitors through passages "decorated" with bizarre limestone formations – stalagmites and stalactites, icicle-like soda straws, smooth flowstone, and myriad delicate crystals. Other options include a Lantern Tour, in which visitors equipped only with a hand-held lantern see the cave much as 19th-century tourists did; and the green Eco-Venture Tour, where the lights in the cave are turned off after 5pm and flashlights only are used.

The Ancestral Pueblo ruins at **Manitou Cliff Dwellings** (US 24; tel: 719-685-5242; www.cliffdwellings museum.com; daily May–Sept 9am–6pm, Oct–Nov, Mar–Apr 9am–5pm, Dec–Feb 10am–4pm; charge) are real though they were relocated from a site in southwestern Colorado and are out of place on the Front Range. Skip this one if you plan to visit Mesa Verde National Park or other Ancestral Pueblo sites. Indian dances are held daily in summer.

America's mountain

Towering above Manitou Springs is 14,110ft (4,301-meter) **Pikes Peak**, not the highest mountain in Colorado but surely the most famous. Named after explorer Zebulon Pike, who never actually reached the summit, and associated with the gold fever that swept the Central Rockies in the late 1800s ("Pikes Peak or bust!," declared thousands of hopeful prospectors), the mountain's most enduring role has been that of a tourist attraction.

espite Pike's proclamation that the ountain would never be climbed, in e 1870s, tourists routinely scaled the ak. In 1891, a cog railway reached e summit, followed in 1916 by an to road.

The **Pikes Peak Cog Railway** 15 Ruxton Avenue; tel: 719-685-401; www.cograilway.com; May–Dec partures 8am–4pm, Jan – early ar 9:20am and 1:20pm) departs om Manitou Springs for a breath-king 9-mile (14km) ascent to the mmit. The tracks follow a cascad-g creek through Englemann Can-n before climbing precipitously he grade reaches 25 percent in me spots) above timber line into pine tundra, a boulder-strewn panse where bighorn sheep are ten seen grazing on thin mosses, asses, and wildflowers. A round-ip takes about three hours and minutes, including a 30-minute opover at the summit house. Be re to bring warm clothes. Frigid inds and violent electrical storms, ten accompanied by hail or snow, e common even in summer.

About 5 miles (8km) northwest of Manitou Springs, at the little town of Cascade, is the entrance to the famous **Pikes Peak Highway** (tel: 719-385-7325; www.pikespeak. us.com; daily, weather permitting, summer 7:30am–6pm, September 7:30am–5pm, Oct–May 9am–3pm; toll charge), a 19-mile (31km) auto route to the summit. This is decid-edly not a drive for the faint of heart. The curves are sharp, the slope is precipitous, there are no guard rails and only the first 7 miles (11km) are paved. However, the views from the peak are truly spectacular. On a clear day, you can see west to the Conti-nental Divide, east across the plains to Kansas and Nebraska, and south to New Mexico. It's the same view that inspired poet Katharine Lee Bates, after visiting in 1893, to write the lyrics of the popular anthem *America the Beautiful*.

Blast from the past

Continuing west, US 24 soars up through **Ute Pass** (9,165ft/2,794 meters) toward the hamlet of

Exploring Cave of the Winds.

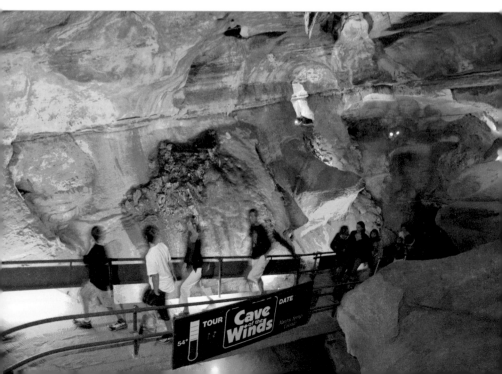

Florissant and the turn-off for **Florissant Fossil Beds National Monument** (15807 Teller County 1; tel: 719-748-3253; www.nps.gov/flfo; daily June 1–early Sept 8am–6pm, fall and spring 9am–5pm, winter 8am–4.30pm). Set aside in 1969, the park is dedicated to the preservation of fossil deposits and petrified redwood from the Oligocene Period. About 35 million years ago, volcanic eruptions blanketed what was then a lush and humid forest with lava and ash, preserving an invaluable fossil record of ancient plants and insects. Brief orientation talks and a 60-minute Petrified Forest tour are offered daily.

At **Wilkerson Pass** (9,507ft/2,898 meters), US 24 seems to sail off into thin air as magnificent vistas of **South Park** open up below. Bison and other wildlife followed the same route through Ute Pass to this vast high-elevation meadow on the backside of Pikes Peak. Paleo-Indians armed with stone-tipped spears tracked the game, as did their successors – Ute, Comanche, Arapaho – mounted on Spanish horses. Later came white men clad in furs and buckskin searching for beaver.

The town of **Buena Vista (BUNE Vista)** ⑮, founded by silver miners in 1879, sits in shady repose at the western edge of South Park. The town is aptly named – residents enjoy some of the finest views in the state. West of town stands a dense cluster of "fourteeners" known as the **Collegiate Peaks** – Mount Yale (14,194ft/4,326 meters), Mount Princeton (14,197ft/4,327 meters), Mount Harvard (14,420ft/4,395 meters), Mount Oxford (14,153ft/4,314 meters), and Mount Columbia (14,075ft/4,290 meters). At the foot of this majestic range lies the valley of the Arkansas River, which rises farther north near Leadville. Depending on the quantity of the spring melt-off, the north Arkansas River in the Buena Vista area runs hard and fast through toothy rapids, giving whitewater enthusiasts an exhilarating ride.

At **Salida (sal-EYE-da)** ⑯ the river turns east toward Royal Gorge and the town of Pueblo, where it debouches onto the Great Plains and

Petrified trees at Florissant Fossil Beds National Monument.

s transformed from a frothy mountain stream to a placid rill. Salida was founded in 1880 as a railroad town and, like Buena Vista, had a reputation for the rowdiness of its bars and bordellos, a quality that is noticeably absent from the sedate historic district today. The river is as rambunctious as ever, though, and there are plenty of experienced outfitters in this increasingly hip little town who can make the necessary arrangements for a whitewater trip. The **Arkansas Headwaters Recreation Area** stretches 48 miles (77km) along the river on either side of Salida and has put-ins, hiking trails, campsites, and picnic areas.

Southeast of Salida, CO 69 angles through the Wet Mountains Valley to the town of **Westcliffe** ⑰, founded in 1885 by Englishman Dr J.W. Bell, and regarded by some Coloradans as one of the state's few remaining unspoiled locations. It's not difficult to see why. Situated between the Wet Mountains and the mighty Sangre de Cristos, the town sits in a broad valley generously watered by snowmelt and filled with lush meadows and pastures.

Across the great abyss

About 48 miles (77km) east of Salida is **Royal Gorge Bridge and Park** ⑱ (off US 50; tel: 719-275-7507; www.royalgorgebridge.com; daily late May–early Sept – 10am–7pm), a deep and narrow fissure carved through the mountains by the Arkansas River. For those with nerves of steel, an aerial tram glides across the abyss on a slender cable. Only slightly less exhilarating is walking across what was until 2004 the world's highest suspension bridge (1,053ft/321 meters), peeking between the wooden slats, and feeling the 1929 structure sway beneath your feet. For a closer view of the canyon, consider a ride on the incline railway, which plummets more than 1,500ft (460 meters) at a 45-degree angle to the river's edge.

Note: About 90 percent of the park adjoining Royal Gorge was destroyed by the Royal Gorge Fire on June 11, 2013, including 48 buildings and attractions and nearly 3,000 acres

The Museum of Prisons in Cañon City is appropriately placed, as there are nine state and four federal penitentiaries in town.

Once a boisterous railroad town, Salida is known today as a gateway to the Arkansas River.

(1,214 hectares) in the Royal Gorge area. The park partially reopened in 2014 with a grand opening. It now includes a new visitor center, tram and zip line, incline railway, mini-train, and a large children's play area on the Southside side of the Bridge. The Skycoaster, a gargantuan sling-like contraption that swings riders over the gorge at the end of a tether, did not suffer any fire damage.

Just before reaching **Cañon City** ⑲, look for **Skyline Drive**, a 3-mile (5km) scenic route that leads motorists up an 800ft (240-meter) high ridge before depositing them in a leafy residential neighborhood. The road was built in 1906 with convict labor – fitting for a town that describes itself as the "prison capital of Colorado." There are 13 correctional facilities in the area.

Housed in a former women's prison, the **Museum of Colorado Prisons** (201 N. Street; tel: 719-269-3015; www.prisonmuseum.org; daily late May–early Sept 10am–5pm, early Sept–late May 8.30am–6pm) chronicles life behind bars since territorial

The Incline Railway at Royal Gorge was constructed in 1931.

days, with an often grisly collectio of artifacts. Included are pictures Alferd Packer, who served 17 yea for murder and cannibalism; Anto Wood, the youngest inmate in th state's history who, at the age of 1 was sentenced to 25 years for mu dering a neighbor in a dispute ov a watch; a gas chamber last used 1967; and the "Old Grey Mare," a flo ging post used to temper the spirits rebellious inmates.

You'll find Indian artifacts, vintag firearms, mining equipment, ar other Old West artifacts at the **Roy Gorge Regional Museum and Hi tory Center** (612 Royal Gorge Boul vard; tel: 719-269-9036; www.rgmhc.o Wed–Sat 10am–4pm). An authenti cally furnished 1860 log cabin and stone Victorian-era house are also the grounds. The history museu now houses the fossil exhibits th were formerly in the town's **Dinosa Depot Museum**. The Garden Pa Paleontology Society will contin to hold permits to work and colle fossils in the Garden Park Fossil Ar north of town.

POLICING THE SKIES

Deep inside a Colorado mountain is a small army of men and women on perpetual guard against an attack on North America. The place is the Cheyenne Mountain Air Force Station, about 6 miles (10km) outside the city of Colorado Springs and tucked securely below almost 2,000ft (610 meters) of granite. It is like a small city in itself.

At the heart of the 15-building complex is the North American Aerospace Defense (norad) command center. Here, eagle-eyed military personnel keep tabs on just about anything that moves in the skies above the US and Canada, including shuttles launched into outer space.

The actual address is 1 NORAD Road, and the joke is that armed guards won't let anybody in but the local pizza deliveryman. The base does, in fact, have its own eatery and much else – chapel, barbershop, gym, softball field, medical clinic, and more. Built to absorb a 30-megaton nuclear attack, the bunker was opened in 1966.

With the end of the Cold War, norad's focus narrowed to such relatively minor concerns as stemming drug traffic. But the worry over international terrorism fueled by the events of September 11, 2001, has brought renewed reliance on its defensive value. On a lighter note, NORAD's popular NORAD Tracks Santa website (www.noradsanta.org), which tracks Santa as he delivers gifts across the world on Christmas Eve, attracts more than 20 million web visitors.

Located in the Santa Fe Depot is the boarding station for the **Royal Gorge Route Railroad** (401 Water Street; tel: 19-276-4000; www.royalgorgeroute.com), a two-hour, 24-mile (38km) fine-dining and scenic train traveling through the Royal Gorge on tracks laid by the Denver & Rio Grande Railroad more than 120 years ago.

Gold strikes and jackpots

A few miles east of Cañon City, Phantom Canyon Road turns north off CO 50 and snakes for about 30 mostly unpaved miles (48km) through the **Gold Belt BLM Recreation Area** to the old mining town of Victor ⑳. During its heyday in the 1890s, Victor was home to 18,000 people, though costly strikes in the early 1900s reduced the number by half. Attempts by the miners to unionize were met with hostility by the owners, who called out the dreaded Colorado State Militia in September 1903. Rioting erupted in the aftermath of a bloody mine accident in 1904, resulting in the deaths of several miners.

Fewer than 400 people live in Victor today. It's a quiet, rather forlorn town, notable primarily for the **Victor-Lowell Thomas Museum** (3rd St at Victor Avenue; tel: 719-689-5509; www.victorcolorado.com/museum; late May–early Sept Wed–Sun 9:30am–5:30pm), dedicated to the life and career of the journalist and radio broadcaster who grew up here and cut his teeth professionally at the *Victor Record*.

The scene is livelier at nearby **Cripple Creek** ㉑, a busted-out gold town that was given a second lease on life when gambling was legalized in 1991. Most of the original buildings were gutted for casinos; vacant land was paved for parking lots. For an overview, check out **Cripple Creek Heritage and Information Center** (9283 S. CO 67; tel: 719-689-3315; www.visitcripplecreek.com; daily Apr–Oct 9am–5pm, Nov–Mar 10am–4.30pm, free), which has state-of-the-art exhibits that are family-friendly. Then mosey over to **Cripple Creek Jail Museum** (136 W. Bennett Avenue; tel: 719-689-6556; daily; free) housed in a restored red-brick museum that served as the

Onlookers watch from a distance as an 1899 blaze consumes downtown Victor.

Teller County jail for 90 years. Among the infamous occupants was Robert "Kid" Curry, a member of the Wild Bunch. Two museums offer a glimpse of Cripple Creek's glory days: **Cripple Creek District Museum** (5th and Bennett; tel: 719-689-9540; daily late May–early Sept 10am–5pm, early Sept–late May Sat–Sun 10am–4pm) and the surprisingly elegant **Old Homestead House Museum** (353 Myers Avenue; tel: 719-689-9090; June–Oct daily 11am–5pm); which occupies a former brothel.

Just outside town, visitors can take an elevator 1,000ft (300 meters) underground for a look at the **Molly Kathleen Mine** (CO 67; tel: 719-689-2466; www.goldminestour.com; daily May–Sept 9am–5pm, Mar–Apr and Oct 10am–4pm; call for reservations). The **Cripple Creek & Victor Narrow Gauge Railroad** (520 E Carr Avenue; tel: 719-689-2640; www.cripplecreekrailroad.com; May–Oct daily 10am–5pm) makes a narrated, 45-minute run through the gold-mining district, where more than 600 tons of the precious stuff was extracted from the earth.

Pueblo

Thirty-five miles (56km) sout of Colorado Springs via I-25 lie **Pueblo** ㉒, one of Colorado's mo underrated cities. Geography playe a pivotal role in its developme – the town sits on the plains at th confluence of Fountain Creek an the Arkansas River but lies clos enough to the mountains to hav benefitted from trapping and mi ing. Native people found the area productive place to hunt. Spaniar traipsed through in the 18th centur looking for gold. Comanche, Kiow and Arapaho warriors terrorized th region in the latter part of the 18t century, until they were crushed b a Spanish military force led by Jua Bautista de Anza at the foot of nearl Greenhorn Mountain in 1786.

In 1842, famed trapper Jim Bec wourth built a trading post whe Fountain Creek flows into the Arka sas. Over the next decade, Puebl attracted a mix of Mormon settle Indian agents, trappers, and traders. disaster occurred at Christmas 185 when drunken pioneers allowed

Slot machines crowd a Cripple Creek casino.

party of Utes inside the stockade; the Indians massacred all but one man and three children.

The post languished for over a decade. Settlers came and went, but few tried to make a life there. Turmoil on the frontier during the 1860s drove more people to the settlement, and Pueblo was officially incorporated as a township in 1870. The Denver & Rio Grande Railroad arrived two years later, followed in 1876 by the Atchison, Topeka & Santa Fe. Coal smelters were built over the next few decades, and steel mills came shortly after.

The **Historic Arkansas Riverwalk** – with its bike paths, pedestrian walkways and landscaped gardens – sits at the heart of downtown. A farmers' market takes place here every Thursday afternoon 4–8pm. Other attractions include **El Pueblo History Museum** (301 N Union Avenue; tel: 719-583-0453; www.historycolorado.org/museums/el-pueblo-history-museum; Mon–Sat 10am–4pm, until 8pm Thurs, Sun noon–4pm), built on the site of the 1842 trading post, which displays Indian artifacts and

equipment from the iron and steel industry.

The **Sangre de Cristo Arts and Conference Center** (210 N. Santa Fe; tel: 719-295-7200; www.sdc-arts.org; Mon–Sat 11am–5pm) is the cultural hub of South Colorado. The three-building complex includes six galleries, a 500-seat theater, and a hands-on children's museum. The **Pueblo Weisbrod Aircraft Museum** (31001 Magnuson Avenue; tel: 719-948-9219; www.pwam.org; Mon–Sat 10am–4pm, Sun 1pm–4pm; charge), housed inside and outside two hangars at the airport east of town, has a fine collection of World War II aircraft and early jets. During the war, the airport served as an air base to train B-24 Liberator crews – a slice of history preserved at the **International B-24 Memorial Museum**, a small museum within Pueblo Weisbrod Aircraft Museum. Pueblo is also the site of the **Colorado State Fair** (1001 Beulah Avenue; tel: 719-561-8484; www.coloradostatefair.com; Mon–Wed noon–11pm, Thurs–Sun 10am–11pm), which is held at the end of August.

Cripple Creek and Victor Narrow Gauge Railroad.

Great Sand Dunes National Park & Preserve.

SAN LUIS VALLEY

Between two mountain ranges lies the San Luis Valley region, known best for its deeply rooted Hispanic heritage and one of Colorado's most unusual geological phenomena.

Main Attractions

Crestone
Great Sand Dunes National Park and Preserve
Luther Bean Museum, Adams State University
Cumbres & Toltec Scenic Railroad, Antonito
San Luis Museum and Cultural Center
Highway of Legends, Cuchara Pass

America's Tibet, it's been called. And it's easy to see why. The San Juan and Sangre de Cristo Mountains rise in snowcapped majesty on the flanks of the San Luis Valley, a remote, sparsely populated basin in south-central Colorado. It's a place of startling contrasts. The valley encompasses Colorado's only true desert but sits atop an aquifer brimming with water. It is situated in a depression between two mountain ranges but rises in places to nearly 8,000ft (2,400 meters). Agriculture is the primary industry, but annual precipitation rarely exceeds 8in (20cm). It's the site of North America's tallest sand dunes but is 600 miles (950km) from the nearest sea.

Early inhabitants

Utes roamed the region centuries ago, when it was occupied mostly by wetlands. Later came Plains Indians – Arapaho, Kiowa, Comanche, Jicarilla, Apache – riding mounts descended from Spanish herds. The Spanish were the first Europeans to venture into the area. Diego de Vargas led a foray north from Santa Fe in 1694 and dubbed the region Sierra de las Grullas – Mountains of the Cranes. Though the Spanish never actively settled the valley, they guarded it jealously as a buffer against foreign incursion. The first Anglo American on the scene was explorer

Zebulon Pike after whom Pikes Peak is named, who stumbled out of the Sangre de Cristos with 10 hungry men in 1807, built a stockade in a cottonwood grove on the Rio Grande, and was promptly arrested by the Spanish as a trespasser.

Anglo mountain men like Jim Bridger and Tom "Broken Hand" Fitzpatrick quickly arrived, scouring the Sangre de Cristos for beaver. They were followed in 1820 by entrepreneurs like William Becknell, who pioneered the Santa Fe Trail connecting Franklin, Missouri with Santa Fe. Spanish-speaking

The San Luis Valley is said to be a center of UFO activity.

people from New Mexico established Colorado's first permanent settlement in 1851, shortly after Mexico ceded the territory under the 1848 Treaty of Guadalupe Hidalgo. The US Army built Fort Massachusetts in 1852 to protect the village from Indian raids.

New Age center

The most scenic way to approach the valley is from the north. US 285 climbs over **Poncha Pass** to CO 17, which arrows into the heart of the valley. At the hamlet of **Moffat,** County Road T veers due east to the town of **Crestone** ❶, nestled in the foothills of the Sangre de Cristos. The discovery of gold lured hordes of prospectors to the mountains, and in 1880 Crestone was born. Ten years later, when the Denver &

Rio Grande built a spur into town, the population swelled to 2,000. More gold was discovered in 1896, but the mines soon played out and within a decade the population dwindled to 100.

Real estate developers breathed new life into the place in the 1970s, with a scheme to subdivide a nearby ranch. As a tax write-off, they donated parcels of land to religious groups such as the Sri Aurobindi Center, the Naropa Institute, and the Carmelite Sisters. The development failed, but the town became a New Age phenomenon, and a variety of spiritual gatherings offered year-round.

Great Sand Dunes National Park and Preserve

From CO 17, turn east on Six Mile Lane toward **Great Sand Dunes National**

Park and Preserve ❷ (11999 Hwy 150; tel: 719-378-6395; www.nps.gov/grsa; daily 24 hrs, visitor center summer 8.30am–6.30pm, winter 9am–4.30pm). A geological oddity, the dunes encompass 39 sq miles (101 sq km) of breathtaking sand formations that contrast with the snowcapped mountains behind them and the desert valley at their base. They are a remarkable sight – mounds of gleaming yellow sand heaped on one another in rows sculpted by wind. Medano Creek slides out from the mountains in a long ripply wash, edging the dunes along their eastern rim for a mile or two, before bubbling out of sight.

A few hardy plants and animals manage to eke out an existence in this harsh place. Plants include blowout grass, Indian ricegrass, and prairie sunflowers. Animals are even scarcer. Kangaroo rats – nocturnal creatures that extract moisture from seeds – live here, as do several species of insects found nowhere else on earth. Peripheral animals – mule deer, elk, bobcat, coyote – skirt the edges of the dunes, leaving occasional tracks.

Around Alamosa

Southwest of the park is **Alamosa ❸** (pop. 9,531), the biggest town in the San Luis Valley. Founded in 1878, when the Denver & Rio Grande chose the site for the terminus of its "chile line" to New Mexico, the town retains a certain workaday homeliness. As of 2015, a record 3,701 undergraduates now attend **Adams State University**, built in 1923 and home of the **Luther Bean Museum** (208 Edgemont Boulevard; tel: 719-587-7151; www.adams.edu/lutherbean; summer Mon–Fri 1:30–:30pm, extended hours during session; free), featuring a beautiful 1930s interior and works by Hispanic, Indian, and cowboy artists.

To the east of town, **Alamosa National Wildlife Refuge ❹** (9383 El Rancho Lane; tel: 719-589-4021, http://fws.gov/refuge/alamosa) encompasses 11,169 acres (4,520 hectares) of wetlands in the floodplain of the Rio Grande. Meadows, oxbows, and riparian corridors sustain songbirds, water birds, and raptors as well as deer, beaver, and coyote. In the spring and fall, some 20,000 sandhill cranes migrate through, along with a few rare

According to a recent study, Great Sand Dunes National Park & Preserve is the quietest of all parks in the lower 48 states.

Medano Creek meanders near Great Sand Dunes, attracting wildlife.

GREAT SAND DUNES

The dunes in Great Sand Dunes National Park and Preserve were created by winds blowing northeast across the San Luis Valley. The winds carried the residue of glacial till deposited by the meandering Rio Grande. Whenever the river changed course, exposed sediments were swept across the valley to the Sangre de Cristos. Seeking a way over the barrier, the wind surged up through low mountain passes, transporting lighter particles but leaving heavier sand crystals at the foot of the mountains. Sand near the base of the formations has a relatively high moisture content, as a result of snow and rain and is responsible for the remarkable stability of the dunes. By contrast, surface sand, chapped by wind and sun, is constantly molded into new and delicate patterns.

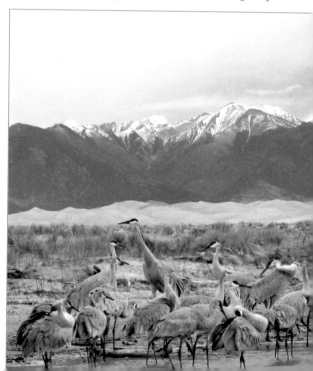

whooping cranes. A 2-mile (3km) trail begins at the visitor center.

About 20 miles (32km) south of Alamosa via US 285 is the hamlet of **Manassa** ❺, birthplace of Jack "Manassa Mauler" Dempsey (1895–1983), the heavyweight boxing champion who started his career fighting in mining camp saloons. The **Jack Dempsey Museum** (412 Main Street; tel: 719-843-5207, http://museumtrail. org/jackdempseymuseum.asp; May–Sept Tue–Sat 10am–5pm; free) is housed in a log cabin on the main drag and displays photographs of young Jack and other memorabilia.

Tiny **Antonito,** situated farther south on US 285, is the terminus of the **Cumbres & Toltec Scenic Railroad** ❻ (tel: 888-CUMBRES; www. cumbrestoltec.com; May–Oct Sat–Thu), a 64-mile (103km) narrow-gauge line winds through the San Juan Mountains via Cumbres Pass to Chama, New Mexico. The line is a remnant of the Denver & Rio Grande's San Juan Extension, constructed in 1880 to serve the mining camps of southwestern Colorado. Now the vintage

locomotives haul tourists, most of whom opt for a six-hour, one-way train ride with a return by motorcoach. The train stops so that passengers can eat lunch at the ghost town of **Osier**.

Colorado's Hispanic heart

East of Manassa, CO 142 passes through the scrub desert of the San Luis Hills, one of the few elevated areas in this mostly flat valley. **San Luis** ❼ (pop. 620), founded in 1851 by Hispanic immigrants from New Mexico, is the oldest town in Colorado. To protect themselves from hostile Indians, the settlers built an adobe *pueblo* around an easily defended plaza. Each family was allotted a narrow strip of land anchored at a stream and trailing back through meadows and woodlands, giving them access to water, grass, and timber. Unlike Anglos elsewhere in the valley, who viewed water as a commodity belonging to whoever claimed it first, Hispanics utilized a traditional method of communal distribution. Colorado's first water collective, the San Luis People's Ditch, established in the 1850s, still parcels out irrigation allocations via a network of *acequias,* or irrigation ditches.

Of particular interest in town is the **San Luis Museum and Cultural Center** (401 Church Place; tel: 719-672-0999, http://museumtrail.org/sanluis museum.asp; daily summer 10am–4pm, winter 9am–4pm), built by the Works Progress Administration in the 1930s. It features murals and *santos* (sacred Spanish Colonial artworks depicting saints such as *retablos* (religious paintings on wood), *bultos* (carved figures) and a replica of a *morada*, or chapel used as a meeting place by the secretive Penitente sect. Across CO 159, a looping path leads to the top of La Mesa de la Piedad y de la Misericordia (Hill of Piety and Mercy) to the **Stations of the Cross Shrine** by celebrated local sculptor Huberto Maestas. The trail of 15 figures culminate at a lovely chapel with twin towers

A statue at the Jack Dempsey Museum.

nd a distinctive cupola. Miniatures maquettes) of the figures are in the atican collection.

Sixteen miles (26km) north on CO 59, near the junction with US 160, is **ort Garland** ❽. Named for Brigaier General John Garland, the fort as built in 1858 after an earlier post as abandoned. The 100-man garrin served a dual purpose: to protect ttlers from Ute raids and provide a cial and trading center in an othwise desolate location. Kit Carson ommanded the fort in 1866–7, his last ilitary post. **Fort Garland Museum nd Cultural center** (29477 CO 159; l: 719-379-3137; www.museumtrail.org/ rtgarlandmuseum.asp; Apr–Oct daily am–5pm, Nov–Dec 31 Wed–Sat am–4pm, closed Jan–April 1, open by ppointment) displays a wide range of dian, Mexican, and Anglo artifacts as ell as a sampling of Hispanic folk art.

panish peaks

the east, US 160 loops out of the n Luis Valley to the summit of **orth La Veta Pass** (9,413ft/2,869 eters), before coasting down to the rdant folds of the **Cuchara Valley** the foot of the **Spanish Peaks**. On clear day they can be seen on the ains from the parapet of Bent's Old ort, 80 miles (130km) away.

Follow CO 12 around the base the peaks to a village named **La eta** ❾, "The Vein," for the blades volcanic rock that radiate from e mountains. The town's historic nterpiece is **Fort Francisco**, the st structure in the Cuchara Valley, ilt in the 1860s by Colonel John ancisco and Judge Henry Daigre. n the grounds stands a cottonwood anted by Colonel Francisco in 1878, hich served not only as a shade tree it as an impromptu gallows for 17 leged bandits. **Francisco Fort Museum** (306 Main; tel: 719-742-5501; www. nciscofort.org; May–Sept Tues–Sat am–4pm) displays artifacts from e period. Run by the Huerfano

Historical Society, the museum also offers educational programs.

CO 12, known as the **Highway of Legends**, winds to the summit of **Cuchara Pass** (9,941ft/3,030 meters), where meadows are filled with columbines and the surrounding mountains are blanketed with groves of aspen, fir, spruce, and pine. Several lakes along the road have good fishing.

The road dips south into the leafy Purgatoire River watershed and the town of **Stonewall** ❿, named for the granite wall visible from the highway. A hideaway for fishing enthusiasts, Stonewall was established in the late 1860s by Juan Gutierrez, nephew of Gabriel Gutierrez, one of the founding fathers of nearby Trinidad.

CO 12 turns east at Stonewall and follows the Purgatoire River to the town of **Segundo,** with a gleaming white church named in honor of Ignatius. Ten miles (16km) farther on is **Cokedale** (pop. 119), a once bustling coal mining center founded in 1906 by the American Refining and Smelting Company. It is now a sleepy national historic district.

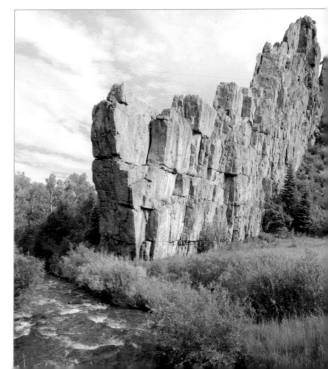

An outcrop of the Spanish Peaks.

Marron Lake.

ROCKY MOUNTAINS

World-class skiing, Old West towns, and
backcountry adventure await travelers in
the mountainous heart of Colorado.

The historic Strater Hotel in Durango.

"I looked at the Alps, but they are nothing compared to the majestic grandeur of our wonderful Rockies," wrote painter Thomas Moran in 1911. Moran was among the first artists to see the Rocky Mountains while traveling to Yellowstone with the 1871 Hayden Survey. Both he and Albert Bierstadt, whose painting of Longs Peak for the Earl of Dunraven helped promote the Rocky Mountains as a national park, were forever changed after viewing the Rockies.

What could be more stirring than to glimpse the iconic Rockies, the backbone of America, for the first time, massed against the western horizon, backlit by a blood-red sunset? For Americans in the mid-1800s, the mountains represented the American Dream: a place to create a new life, and maybe even strike it rich.

Hundreds of mining towns boomed overnight and busted just as quickly. Rocky Mountain National Park was set aside in 1915, just in time to attract Americans no longer able to travel to war-torn Europe. In the late 20th century, chunks of the remote San Juan Mountains were set aside as wilderness, luring mountain lovers to the little-known southern Rockies.

Glenwood Caverns Adventure Park.

Interstate 70 in northern Colorado, Interstate 50 in central Colorado, and US 160 in southern Colorado opened the whole state to tourism. The busy I-70 corridor between Denver and Glenwood Springs offers rapid access to natural attractions like Rocky Mountain National Park and St Mary's Glacier, and connects Denver foothill communities like Golden and Evergreen with Georgetown, Vail, Aspen, and other famous former mining towns that have risen from the dead as ritzy ski resorts and tourist towns, as well as with the redrock canyon country on the Utah border.

Easier access to Durango, via US 160, skirting the southern edge of the San Luis Valley and San Juans, has been a boon for the region. But mountain communities, such as Silverton, still slumber peacefully in the off season. That, for many visitors, is their main attraction.

En route to Flat Top Mountain,
Rocky Mountain National Park.

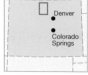

ROCKY MOUNTAIN NATIONAL PARK

Straddling the Continental Divide, the park contains sky-scraping peaks, 150 lakes, rushing mountain streams, alpine tundra, pristine forests, and an amazing array of wildlife.

hen Pope John Paul II journeyed to Denver in 1993, he asked to see **Rocky Mountain National Park ❶**. The pontiff's hiking outfit was a bit unusual – His Holiness wore a white cassock, gold pallium, and sneakers with matching gold shoelaces but the visit confirmed what lovers of the park already knew: Rocky Mountain is truly a religious experience. Like John Paul, millions of pilgrims have thrilled to this sea of mountains since the park was created in 1915. Many peaks soar over 12,000ft (3,660 meters). "There are higher peaks elsewhere," author Freeman Tilden wrote in 1951. "But for a sheer sense of towering density, of closely packed mountaintops, I know of nothing like this."

By the time Zebulon Pike set eyes on the Rockies in 1807, indigenous people had been venturing into the high country for at least 7,000 years. Mounted hunters of the Ute, Arapaho, Cheyenne, and Shoshone tribes tracked deer and buffalo in the foothills and bighorn sheep on the alpine slopes. Late in the 19th century, a flood of trappers, miners, and ranchers tried to tap the mountains' natural wealth. Mining camps such as Lulu City sprang up overnight and disappeared just as quickly.

Among the pioneers was a different breed, too – people like Enos Mills, (see page 202) who mined peace and rejuvenation from the mountains and made a living sharing them with others. Hailed as the "John Muir of the Rockies," Mills hatched the idea for the park and spent years rallying support and lobbying Congress, which finally gave its consent in 1915.

Estes Park and Trail Ridge Road

If you're coming from the east, start your trip in **Estes Park ❹**, a lively resort town adjacent to the park, with a bounty of restaurants, galleries, gift

Main Attractions

Estes Park
Trail Ridge Road
Beaver Meadows Visitor Center
Alpine Visitor Center
Old Fall River Road
Longs Peak

Estes Park.

Rocky Mountain National Park

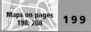

shops, and lodging. The pioneers who settled this region are the focus of the **Estes Park Museum** (200 4th Street; tel: 970-586-6256; www.visitestes park.com/listings/estes-park-museum/515/; May–Oct Mon–Sat 10am–5pm, Sun 1–5pm, Nov–Apr Fri–Sat 10am–5pm, Sun 1–5pm; free) and the **MacGregor Ranch Museum** (180 MacGregor Lane, off US 34; tel: 970-586-3749; www. macgregorranch.org; June–Aug Tue–Sat 10am–4pm), an 1896 homestead and working ranch where visitors get a glimpse of life on the frontier in the late 19th century. **Estes Park Aerial Tramway** (420 E. Riverside Drive; tel: 970-586-3675; www.estestram.com; daily May–Sept 9am–6pm) whisks passengers to the summit of Prospect Mountain for panoramic views of Longs Peak, the Continental Divide, and Estes Park.

Enter the national park via US 36 for a tour of **Trail Ridge Road**, the park's main thoroughfare, arguably the most scenic drive in North America. Open seasonally from mid-May until the first heavy snowstorms blanket the interior in October, it features more than a dozen spectacular overlooks

and exposes visitors to a large expanse of alpine tundra, one of the rarest ecosystems in the lower 48 states. Note: the main eastern access to Rocky Mountain National Park experienced a number of road closures and damages to bridges and trails as a result of severe flooding along the Front Range in September 2013. Major thoroughfares into the park have now reopened, but some backcountry trails, footbridges, and other areas have been destroyed and await repair. For current conditions, inquire at the visitor center.

Starting at **Beaver Meadows Visitor Center ❸**, US 36 climbs gently through foothills scattered with ponderosa pine and sagebrush. At **Deer Ridge Junction**, Trail Ridge Road veers left and makes an abrupt ascent along **Hidden Valley Creek**, dammed in several places by beavers which usually emerge from their lodges in the early evening. The creek is also home to rare greenback cutthroat trout; a roadside exhibit provides information on them.

Just beyond, the overlook at **Many Parks Curve ❸** perches over deep valleys cut by Pleistocene glaciers more

The ballroom of the historic Stanley Hotel is supposedly haunted.

THE STANLEY HOTEL

The 138-room Stanley Hotel in Estes Park is one of America's most recognizable historic *grand dames*. It was built in 1909 by F. O. Stanley, inventor of the Stanley Steamer automobile, who moved to Estes Park in 1907 after being diagnosed with tuberculosis. Stanley constructed his European-style luxury hotel from timbers salvaged from the Bear Lake Burn and created an access road from Lyons, over which he brought his guests. The hotel has a reputation for being one of the most haunted hotels in America and served as the inspiration for Stephen King's novel *The Shining*. An onsite museum chronicles the careers of Stanley and his twin brother F. E. and the history of the hotel. For more information, tel: 970-577-4000 or visit www.stanleyhotel.com.

Poppies grow well in the dry soil of Colorado.

A prospector in the Estes Park area in 1922.

than 13,000 years ago. (Several small glaciers remain in Rocky Mountain, most straddling the eastern edge of the Continental Divide in the park's central area.) Overhead, a red-tailed hawk or golden eagle may be scanning the land below, looking for an opportunity to snatch a small rodent or even a marmot sunning itself on a rock.

Trail Ridge Road passes through stands of fir and Engelmann spruce that are common in the subalpine zone and then, beyond the stunning overlook at **Forest Canyon**, enters alpine tundra. One of the highest overland routes on the continent, Trail Ridge Road stays above the tree line for 11 miles (18km), cresting at 12,183ft (3,713 meters) near **Lava Cliffs**.

Alpine tundra

A treeless, windblown realm, alpine tundra exists only in the highest reaches of the Rockies. For a closer look, walk the self-guiding **Tundra Communities Trail ❷** near **Rock Cut**. As you walk the trail, look closely for camouflaged ptarmigan, a member of the grouse family whose plumage changes from snowy white in winter to mottled brown in summer. You may also spy a water pipit foraging for insects, tiny pikas, or pudgy yellow-bellied marmots scampering across a talus slope, or perhaps bighorn sheep, elk, or mule deer grazing warily in a distant meadow.

Only the hardiest plants can survive in these arctic-like conditions. Stunted by wind and cold, gnarled whitebark pine hugs the ground; although no larger than bushes, some are as much as 200 or 300 years old. Silver-dollar-sized patches of lichen (actually an alga and fungus that grow symbiotically) can be centuries old as well. A bouquet of wild flowers – including lupines, yellow snow buttercups, shooting stars, daisies, and blue Colorado columbines – send a blush through the meadows in late June and often last until the first snowfall of autumn. For more information about alpine tundra ecology, stop at the **Alpine Visitor Center ❸**, which is just a short drive from the Tundra Communities Trail.

Trail Ridge Road dips about 1,000ft (300 meters) in 4 miles (6km) and then, at **Milner Pass ❻**, crosses the

Continental Divide. Known as the backbone of America," the Divide has profound effect on climate. Trapped behind mountain peaks, clouds blowing in from the Pacific Ocean dump rain and snow on the western slope, in turn supplying the headwaters of the Colorado River. Half as much moisture falls east of the Divide, and incessant, drying winds tend to rob the land of what little water it receives. Naturally, there's a difference in vegetation and wildlife as well. The lush riparian environment of the western side sustains moose, river otter, Colorado River trout, and a profusion of conifers. The more arid, eastern landscape is home to Abert's squirrel, endangered greenback cutthroat trout, ponderosa pine, prickly pear, and wood lily.

From Milner Pass, the road zigzags several dizzying miles and then heads south toward the **Colorado River Trailhead G**, where you can start a moderate 2-mile (3km) hike to the tumbled-down cabin of Joe Shipler, a miner who tried his luck here in the 1870s. About 2 miles (3km) farther north, a few old shacks are all that remain of **Lulu City H**, where hundreds of prospectors, hearing stories of gold and silver strikes, came to make their fortunes in the early 1880s. The trail follows the North Fork of the Colorado River, which here is hardly more than a trickle. Believe it or not, this is the beginning of one of the mightiest rivers in the West – the same rushing waters that flow through the Grand Canyon several hundred miles away.

About 2 miles (3km) farther south, a short trail leads to the **Never Summer Ranch I**, a dude ranch founded in the 1920s and now operated as a "living-history" exhibit, complete with guides in period costume. The final stretch of Trail Ridge Road descends into Kawuneeche Valley to the **Kawuneeche Visitor Center J**. Coniferous forests grow thick here, and the Colorado River is fringed with aspens and willows that explode with glorious colors in the fall. Moose and elk are a common sight and bird-watching opportunities, especially for neotropical songbirds such as warblers, thrushes, and finches, are excellent.

Just south of the park is **Grand Lake,** Colorado's largest natural lake and the highest yacht anchorage in the United States. Grand Lake drains into two large reservoirs, **Shadow Mountain Lake** and **Lake Granby**, making the area a haven for boaters, hikers, and snowmobilers looking for a low-key, rustic getaway.

Horseshoe Park

There's plenty to see and do beyond Trail Ridge Road. If time allows, plan a side trip to **Horseshoe Park K**, a popular area for wildlife-watching northeast of Estes Park. From the visitor center, take US 36 into the park, then turn right at the junction with US 34 to **Sheep Lakes**, where naturally occurring mineral licks attract bands of bighorn sheep. The **Old Fall River Road**, a one-way unpaved lane open only in summer, starts at **Endovalley** and makes a 9-mile (14km) climb, much of it above tree line, to

Female moose near Lake Granby.

The Colorado chipmunk can be identified by the dark and light stripes along its side and back. They like to eat nuts and berries.

Stopping to enjoy the view.

the **Alpine Visitor Center**. This road was severely damaged by flooding in 2013, and although it was repaired and reopened in July 2015, trail access to the alluvial fan area was destroyed.

Bighorn sheep are frequently seen in this area. About 200 bighorns graze on the lush meadows and rocky slopes around Horseshoe Park. During the winter breeding season, males vie for dominance, using their massive corkscrew horns in dramatic head-butting contests. The report can be heard echoing through the mountains. Elk are frequently spotted here, too, never far from the forest edge.

Another option is to explore **Moraine Park ①** and **Bear Lake Road,** which leads into one of the most picturesque and heavily used regions of the park. The area is laced with interconnecting trails, and it's possible to spend a day or more hiking from one mountain lake to another and experiencing a variety of different life zones. Hikers can spend the morning wandering among tree-ringed glens and turquoise lakes, and then make a push towards the Continental Divide, where

glaciers send meltwater cascading down the eastern slope. Get your bearings at the **Moraine Park Museum**, where exhibits and a short interpretive trail explain the area's cultural and natural history, and then strike out on any number of possible tours.

A short drive to the **Cub Lake Trailhead** enables you to explore Moraine Park or to make the gentle 4-mile (6km) climb to **Cub Lake**, **Fern Falls** and **Fern Lake**; an extension trail makes a steep connection to the stark shoreline of **Odessa Lake**. Farther south, a free summer shuttle bus runs from Glacier Basin to the end of Bear Lake Road.

An easy nature trail around **Sprague Lake ⓜ** makes a pleasant stroll through a storybook mountain setting. Farther down, a steep 4-mile (6km) round-trip takes hikers up to and around the forested shore of **Bierstadt Lake**. You'll find tougher hikes at **Glacier Gorge Junction ⓝ**, which has branches that go to the foot of **Andrews Glacier** and **Taylor Glacier** via **Loch Vale** as well as a 5-mile (8km) scramble through **Glacier Gorge** to frigid **Black Lake**, well above tree line

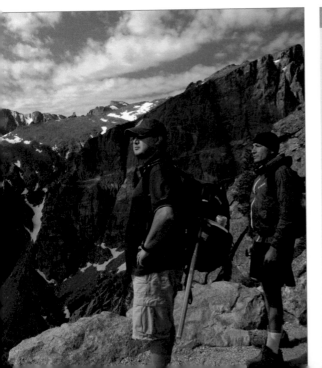

NATURE BOY

Kansas-born Enos Mills was a sickly boy who came to live with relatives on their ranch in Estes Park and became enthralled by the great outdoors, climbing 14,256ft (4,345-meter) Longs Peak at the age of 15. Over the years, Mills worked as a snow observer and a forestry specialist and wrote several books about his experiences in the Rockies. Mills' mentor was naturalist John Muir. The two met during Mills' 1898 trip to San Francisco and remained friends until Muir's death in 1914.

Mills promoted Muir's message of conservation and was largely responsible for convincing Congress to set aside Rocky Mountain National Park in 1915. His cabin is now a small museum, south of Estes Park. Tel: 970-586-4706 for hours and directions.

The most traveled and possibly most beautiful route is from **Bear Lake O** to **Dream Lake P**, which is cupped in a high-country basin with the snow-dusted summits of **Flattop Mountain** and **Hallett Peak** rising grandly from behind.

Longs Peak and Wild Basin

Farther south, an ascent of **Longs Peak Q** is a challenge even to the most ambitious and physically fit hikers. At 14,255ft (4,345 meters), Longs Peak towers over the eastern side of the park; its flat summit and nearby **Chasm Lake** are considered by many to be the most magical destination in the park. And although technical equipment isn't necessary to make the climb, it's a big mistake to underestimate just how arduous the 16-mile (26km), 12-to-15-hour round-trip hike can be.

Hikers should be prepared for high winds, biting cold, and a fair amount of hand-and-foot scrambling. It is essential to start your hike well before daybreak to avoid the dangerous afternoon lightning storms; many hikers stay at nearby **Longs Peak Campground** the night before. Greenhorns can inquire about climbing lessons and guide services for Longs Peak at the Colorado Mountain School in Estes Park.

Finally, if you really want to escape the crowds, try the **Wild Basin R** region, off CO 7 just south of Longs Peak. Cut off from the rest of the park by a crescent of mountains, this isolated pocket of lakes and waterfalls is still recovering from a 1978 forest fire and the 2013 flooding. In the early days, a park official tried promoting Rocky Mountain by dressing a woman, dubbed Eve, in animal skins and letting her wander around Wild Basin, much to the delight of reporters looking for a tantalizing story.

Hikers can spend a leisurely afternoon on the moderate, 3-mile (5km) trail leading to **Calypso Cascades** and **Ouzel Falls**, named after the tiny river-faring bird that naturalist John Muir found so enchanting. The trail branches a bit farther on, following a string of lakes into the highlands. Note: following the 2013 floods, the Ouzel Falls bridge has been replaced and is open, but the spur trail to Ouzel Lake is damaged.

The view of Longs Peak in Rocky Mountain National Park.

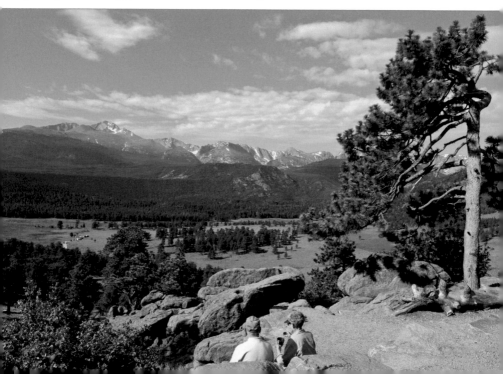

PEAK BAGGERS

Climbers flock to the Rockies to scale the state's 54 peaks that are over 14,000ft (4,270 meters), and wilderness stewardship programs attempt to clean up after them.

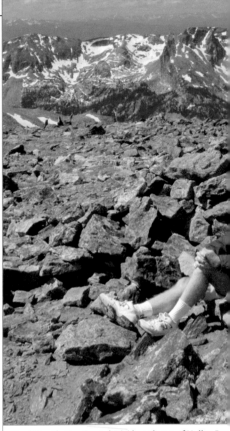

The Colorado Rockies have 54 peaks over 14,000ft (4,270 meters), or "fourteeners," as they are known by climbers. Among the most storied peaks are Longs Peak and Pikes Peak at either end of the Front Range, where the Rockies meet the Plains. Pikes Peak, looming over Colorado Springs, is accessible to climbers from the 13-mile (21km) trail above the highway and Pikes Peak Cog Railroad Depot, the highest railroad in the world. The Maroon Bells–Snowmass Wilderness in the Elk range is close to Aspen and a popular destination for high country lovers who enjoy its mirror lakes and wild flowers in summer. The Sangre de Cristo range creates a sheer, toothy skyline above the San Luis Valley. The range includes Colorado's fourth highest peak, 14,345ft (4,372 meter) Mount Blanca, sacred to the Navajo. Poncha Pass, a favorite fall color drive, separates the Sangres from the Collegiate Peaks in the Sawatch range. Of the 15 fourteeners, one peak, Mount Elbert, is the highest in the state at 14,433ft (4,399 meters), and several are named for Ivy League colleges such as Harvard and Yale, hence their nickname. The San Juan Mountains, headwaters of the Rio Grande, are increasingly popular as a ski, hiking, and four-wheeling destination. Yankee Boy Basin near Ouray is the main trailhead for Mount Snefells Wilderness, also popular with the Jeep crowd.

Climbers should always take appropriate precautions before attempting a new climb.

Straddling the Continental Divide at the top of Hallett Peak in Rocky Mountain National Park. The peak can also be reached by hiking the Flattop Mountain Trail.

Evening comes early when the sun sets behind the mountain

...ing requires the appropriate equipment, including boots, poles, ...gear, and a means of contacting help in case of emergency.

...s Peak at sunrise. The pink tinge of the rocks comes not from ...sun, but rather from a large amount of potassium feldspar.

Rocky Mountain Field Institute volunteers.

THE MIGHTY FOURTEENERS

Every year, nearly 500,000 people visit the 54 fourteeners in Colorado. Concerned about increased visitors and impacts on fragile wilderness, in 1994 five outdoor organizations – Colorado Mountain Club, Outward Bound West, Volunteers for Outdoor Colorado, Rocky Mountain Field Institute, and Leave No Trace Center for Outdoor Ethics – joined with the US Forest Service to protect and preserve the state's fourteeners through active stewardship and public education. Using an all-volunteer staff, the Colorado Fourteeners Initiative (CFI) has completed impact studies on all 54 fourteeners, identified the 35 most impacted peaks. Today, CFI is the nation's leading high-altitude trail-building, terrain-restoration, and visitor-education organization. It has built 29 sustainably located, designed, and constructed summit routes on 26 peaks, with its work garnering honors and awards from Congress, the US Forest Service, the National Forest Foundation, and other organizations. If you're interested in getting involved, volunteers are needed to carry out weekend field projects, become peak stewards and assist in other ways, including collecting wildflower seeds to revegetate trampled areas. For information, contact www.14ers.org.

Trail maintenance is a big part of wilderness stewardship, an area where many Coloradans volunteer their time.

STEAMBOAT SPRINGS

Skiing is a way of life in this Northern Rockies town celebrated for its "champagne powder", Olympic athletes, and Wild West atmosphere.

S teamboat Springs has a scenic setting on the Yampa River in the heart of Colorado's Northern Rockies. It's a cowboy-flavored ski town, which owes its down-to-earth Western feel to its ranching history and proximity to the Wyoming border. The mountains here seem gentler than those to the east and south, rising in swells from broad valleys and cloaked in forests, meadows and alpine lakes. Nomadic Utes once summered in the valley of the Yampa River, which flows in relative tranquility through town before careening toward its confluence with the Green River. French fur trappers were the first Europeans to explore the area, and it was a party of such *coureurs de bois* who mistook the burbling of a hot spring for the sound of a steamboat, apparently giving the area its name.

Pioneer settlement

In 1875, American homesteader James H. Crawford staked a claim here, and soon a handful of pioneers formed the nucleus of a community they called Steamboat Springs. By the mid-1880s, the town had a newspaper, post office, general store, and hotel, although travel and communication were regularly bogged down by heavy snow. Townspeople, cowboys, and mail carriers struggled through the long, hard winters, sometimes using primitive skis or snowshoes to get around. The mail

came up from Wolcott, 60 rugged miles (96km) to the south – by wagon when the passes were clear, or by skis when the snow was too deep for horses. It was late 1908 before the railroad reached town, and no effort was made to keep primitive auto roads open year-round.

Through it all, the early settlers grazed livestock in lush meadows during the short, pleasant summers. They practically lived on horseback, at ease with the landscape, the animals, and the big sky overhead. Cowboys worked hard and played hard, and skis

Main Attractions

Old Town – Steamboat Springs
Yampa River Botanic Park
Old Town Hot Springs
Fish Creek Falls
Steamboat Ski Area
Yampa River Preserve

Steamboat Ski Area.

There are more than a dozen natural hot springs in and around Steamboat Springs.

were used for winter recreation as well as for strictly utilitarian purposes. The *Steamboat Pilot*, the local newspaper, reported that the Hot Time Festival of 1898 featured an orchestral performance, a literary event, a dance, foot races, and bronco riding. Rodeo was a summer tradition by the early 1900s, and it continues to this day during **Cowboy Roundup Days**, the centerpiece of the town's Fourth of July celebration for more than a century.

Historic heart

Get your bearings in **Steamboat Springs ❷** by first stopping for an orientation and brochures at the **Visitor Center** (125 Anglers Drive; tel: 970-879-0880; www.steamboat-chamber.com; late May–early Sept Mon–Sat 8am–6pm, Sun 10am–4pm, Sept–May Mon–Fri 8am–5pm, Sat 10am–3pm). **Old Town**, a tidy 27-block grid between Third and Eleventh Streets looks much as it did before the ski boom. **Routt County Courthouse** (522 Lincoln; tel: 970-870-6586), for example, stands stolidly at the corner of 6th and Lincoln, its cream brick facade trimmed in

sandstone and terracotta. The interio – hardly altered since its 1923 com pletion – houses a small collection o artifacts and historic photographs. Th neighborhood's modest commerci buildings are mostly two or three sto ries, many sporting elaborate trim an cornices. Most are now occupied b fancy boutiques, galleries and restau rants, though quite a few still have weathered charm.

Western outfitter **F.M. Light & Sons** (830 Lincoln Avenue; tel: 97(879-1822; www.fmlight.com), owne by the same family for four genera tions, is the town's oldest store, sel ing cowboy hats, boots, saddles, an other gear since 1905. Just down th street, **Lyon's Corner Drug and Sod Fountain** (840 Lincoln Avenue; te 970-879-1114; www.lyonsofsteamboa com) is housed in a 1908 brick offic building that has served as a pharmac since 1920. Walk past the souvenirs t the old-fashioned soda fountain i the rear and you will feel as if you'v stepped back in time.

Another way to turn back the clock to visit the **Tread of Pioneers Museun**

(800 Oak Street; 970-879-2214; www. treadofpioneers.org; Tue–Sat 11am–5pm), a repository of rustic furnishings, Indian artifacts, ranching gear, and other objects related to frontier life. Set in a 1908 Queen Anne–style house, the museum features exhibits of vintage skis (including those used by early mailmen), a collection of historic firearms, Ute Indian basketry, a stagecoach used in the 1890s to transport passengers from Wolcott, and a snowcat that operated between Steamboat and Hahn's Peak in the 1940s. Pick up a copy of the self-guided historic walking tour, which starts at the museum, then continue to the Beaux-Arts railroad depot that houses **Steamboat Springs Arts Council** (1001 13th Street; tel: 970-879-9008; www.steamboatspringsarts.org; Tue–Sat 11am–5pm; free). Pick up an *Art in Public Places* walking tour map, and combine the itinerary with the historic tour.

Around town

Even local hardbodies training for the popular **Steamboat Marathon, Half-Marathon, and 10K** in June use the gentle 4-mile (6km) **Yampa River Core Trail** for a quick run. It's equally popular for evening walks, family bike rides, and simply enjoying the sound of rushing water and perhaps stopping to identify wildflowers that grow along the bank. The trail connects with the west side of 6-acre (2.4-hectare) **Yampa River Botanic Park** (1000 Pamela Lane; tel: 970-846-5172; www.yampariverbotanicpark.org; open May–Oct, daily dawn–dusk; free). The park is laid out in 36 themed gardens, including the Garden for All Seasons, splashed with colorful blossoms from spring to late summer.

Also on the south end of downtown is **Old Town Hot Springs** (136 Lincoln Avenue; tel: 970-879-1828; www.oldtownhotsprings.org; Mon–Fri 5.30am–10pm, Sat 7am–9pm, Sun 8am–9pm), a multi-use complex of eight hot spring pools, plus fitness facilities for both residents and visitors. Open year-round, with areas set aside for water slides, lap

swimming, and peaceful soaking, it is a family favorite.

Take a short drive east on 3rd Street and follow the signs 4 miles (6km) to **Fish Creek Falls** (Fish Creek Falls Road; tel: 970-879-1870; www.fs.fed.us/r2; open year round, dawn to dusk; free), a thundering 283ft (86-meter) cascade and the town's most-visited attraction. A flat, paved walkway leads to an overlook; a quarter-mile (500 meters) dirt trail snakes gently down to the base, then leads 6 miles (10km) through aspen groves, alpine meadows, and steep switchbacks to Long Lake near the Continental Divide. A word of advice about visiting the falls: beat the crowd by arriving early in the morning or just before dusk, when alpenglow illuminates the scene.

In summer, when the sun goes down, Steamboat Springs' cultural scene heats up. **The Strings in the Mountains Music Festival** (tel: 970-879-5056; www.stringsmusicfestival.com), established in 1988 to foster an appreciation for fine music, presents live chamber music, jazz, folk, country, and world music at the Strings Music

The annual Cowboy Downhill race.

Fish Creek Falls.

Hot air balloonists prepare to take to the skies outside Steamboat Springs.

Pavilion in 7-acre (3-hectare) Strings Festival Park, at the entrance to the ski mountain, as well as a series of popular free noontime concerts at Yampa River Botanic Park. Also in the area is **Perry Mansfield** (40755 CR 36; tel: 970-879-7125; www.perry-mansfield.org), the oldest performing arts school and camp in the nation. Theater and dance performances are staged on the rustic 76-acre (31-hectare) property north of town, from late June to early August, and include student productions as well as workshops for professionals developing new work.

Winter sports

Steamboat's nickname, Ski Town USA, isn't an idle boast. With 2,965 acres (1,200 hectares) of skiable terrain, 165 trails, and 16 lifts on five mountains, **Steamboat Ski Area** ❸ (2605 Mount Werner Circle, tel: 970-879-6111 info, 877-783-2628 reservations; www.steamboat.com; daily Nov–Apr), about 2 miles (3km) southeast of downtown Steamboat Springs, is one of the largest and most balanced ski resorts in the nation. The mountain range snares

Winter Carnival.

an annual average of 335in (850cm) of snow so light and fluffy it inspired the marketing department to coin the phrase "champagne powder." Since 2007, facilities at the ski area have received a face-lift to the tune of nearly $30 million. The resort village now includes improved walkways, lodging, restaurants, ski shops, and other businesses. An outstanding childcare facility and children's ski school occupy prime space in the mountain village, and the beginner slopes, with dedicated lifts, are just steps away.

The main port of entry from the base complex is the eight-passenger Silver Bullet gondola, which leaves from the pedestrian promenade and climbs 2,200ft (670 meters) to a plateau called Thunderhead, where non-skiers can hang out and take in the view, eat at one of several restaurants in the rambling day lodge, or join a free naturalist-led snowshoe tour. From Thunderhead, skiers and snowboarders drop down to Burgess Creek, then ride higher up on the Storm Peak chair-lifts or glide down to Priest Creek for the Sunshine Peak fts. Wide trails of various pitches appeal to skiers and snowboarders of all abilities, while skiing through the Steamboat's widely spaced aspen trees delights powder hounds. Steamboat's upper mountain terrain has the resort's fluffiest powder as well as some of its prettiest scenery and is a real mecca for tree-skiing aficionados. Continuing beyond Storm Peak, skiers and riders reach a parcel of intermediate and advanced terrain called Morningside Park. Tucked in behind Sunshine Peak is Pioneer Ridge, a snow-kissed bowl laced with a handful of medium-to-steep trails and still more glades.

Snowboarders gravitate to the four terrain parks: L'il Rodeo, Sunbeam, Rabbit Ears, and Mavericks. At 14 acres (5.7-hectares), Mavericks the largest and most advanced, boasts nearly a dozen terrain features, including Mavericks Superpipe, a 650ft (200-meter)-long halfpipe with 15ft (4.5-meter) walls, reputedly the longest in North America.

Steamboat, 160 miles (260km) from Denver, is too far away to be inundated with day-trippers, so it remains largely a multiday destination. The resort pioneered subsidized flights from major US cities, as well as a landmark Kids Ski Free program. Families enjoy free lodging, lift tickets, and rentals for children 12 and under, and even discounts on multiday lift passes for teens. Summer activities include mountain biking, hiking, and picnicking. Steamboat Gondola ascends Mount Werner for gorgeous views of Yampa Valley (tel: 970-871-5252; late June–early Sept daily 10am–4pm).

Overshadowed by Steamboat is **Howelsen Hill** ❹ (tel: 970-879-8499 for snow conditions), a smaller and older ski hill that in any other location would be the main attraction. Municipally owned and noted for ski jumps and groomed cross-country trails, Howelsen has been the training ground for generations of Steamboat's competitive skiers. Residents and visitors alike enjoy its short and demanding ski runs, night skiing, year-round ice skating, and reasonable prices. In summer, Howelsen offers an alpine slide (a sled-like contraption that

Elk graze in the high country.

Nestled amid the mountains is Steamboat Springs.

THE FLYING NORSEMAN

Planning a leap down Howelsen Hill? Remember to give credit to the man who made it – and Steamboat Springs – a skiing landmark. That would be Carl Howelsen, who came to America in 1905 after winning fame as a young skier in Norway. On this side of the Atlantic he thrilled crowds at summer outings with his ski-jump prowess on artificial turf and was billed as "The Flying Norseman" with the Barnum & Bailey circus. But he was born for the great outdoors and thus gravitated to Colorado.

In 1912, at Hot Sulphur Springs, he organized a winter carnival. His own 79ft (24-meter) leap was thrilling enough to give rise to an annual tournament, and he stirred similar enthusiasm at Steamboat Springs, where he built a rudimentary jump and taught the locals to ski.

Thanks to Howelsen an enduring tradition was begun in 1914 – the Steamboat Springs Winter Carnival. For openers, Howelsen stunned the crowd with a prodigious leap of nearly 110ft (34 meters). Contests in the early years included ski jumping, cross-country skiing, and an event that required contestants to climb the 0.25-mile (0.5km) hill and slide back down.

A hill fashioned in 1915 was named for him. Howelsen returned to Norway in 1922, and died in 1955. He was among the first inductees into the Colorado Ski Hall of Fame.

speeds down a windy track), hiking trails, and professional rodeo action at Romick Arena at the base of the slopes.

Backcountry adventures

For those who prefer warm weather, summer sports abound. The rafting season on the Yampa River – the last undammed river in the Colorado Basin – runs from about mid-May to early July, though spring runoff tends to produce the wildest rides in the first week of June. Outfitters in the area offer float trips ranging from a few hours of gentle tubing to a full-blown wilderness adventure taking in some of the most spectacular canyons in the West.

Steamboat is also a convenient starting point for backcountry journeys into **Medicine Bow–Routt National Forests** (tel: 970-879-1870), encompassing more than 2.2 million acres (890,300 hectares) of stunning alpine terrain laced with hiking trails and Jeep roads. Two areas are especially popular. **Rabbit Ears Pass ❺**, a broad "saddle" in the mountains about 12 miles (19km) from town via US 40, accommodates motorized recreation

The gondola at Steamboat will whisk you to the top of the mountain.

(snowmobiles in winter, ATVs in summer) at the East Summit, while non-motorized users (Nordic skiers and snowshoers in winter, hikers and mountain bikers in summer) concentrate on the West Summit.

Farther afield, a drive north through the **Elk River Valley** (via CO 129) is an excursion into the rural past. New subdivisions quickly give way to ranchland. Just past the tiny hamlet of **Clark ❻**, about 18 miles (29km) north of Steamboat, you'll find **Seedhouse Road**, which offers access to numerous trails. To the north, nestled at the base of soaring Hahn's Peak, man-made **Pearl Lake and Steamboat Lake state parks** (tel: 970-879-3922; www.parks.co.state.us parks) offer fishing, boating, and other water sports.

For those who really like to rough it, three wilderness areas – **Mount Zirkel**, **Flat Tops,** and **Sarvis Creek** totaling more than 440,000 roadless acres (178,000 hectares) – are nearby. The only hitch: motorized vehicles and bicycles are not permitted. The only way in is by foot or on horseback.

BIRDING ON THE YAMPA RIVER

The Yampa River is significant for supporting a rare riparian forest type dominated by narrowleaf cottonwood, box elder, and red-osier dogwood, and is home to a huge array of wildlife. It has been designated an Important Birding Area by the Audubon Society and supports numerous bird species, including bald eagles, bobolinks, Cooper's hawks, great horned owls, red-tailed hawks, sandhill cranes, warblers, and woodpeckers. Two Nature Conservancy preserves in the Yampa Valley offer a close-up look at this important habitat. The 6,000-acre (2,428-hectare) Yampa River Preserve, 17 miles (27km) west of Steamboat Springs, is home to river otters, beaver, mink, and catbirds, and has a pleasant 2-mile (3km) trail through its Morgan Bottoms area. Carpenter Ranch, 20 miles (32km) west of Steamboat Springs, was pioneered in 1903 by J.B. Dawson, then leased beginning in 1925, and later owned by Farrington "Ferry" Carpenter. Ferry was a Harvard Law graduate and one of the area's most prominent citizens, serving as nearby Hayden's first attorney and as the first director of the federal Grazing Division, now the Bureau of Land Management. TNC operates the property as a working ranch, research, and education center. It has listed ranch buildings, riparian areas, and the historic ranch house. Yampa River Preserve is open year round; Carpenter Ranch is open May–Sept Thu–Sat 9am–noon. For information, tel: 970-276-4626; www.nature.org.

An old barn in Steamboat Springs.

I-70 AND THE HIGH ROCKIES

A unique alpine freeway leads motorists over bridges and through tunnels, into a world of ski slopes, soaring peaks, and gold rush history.

Sad but true, Colorado has no cruise ships. For many Denverites, the next best thing is a weekend trip on a segment of Amtrak's California Zephyr route that goes 200 miles (320km) west to Glenwood Springs (especially during the fall colors season, when seats are booked months in advance).

The only problem with such a trip is that travelers can't get off for detours into the surrounding Rocky Mountain high country. The solution, of course, is to drive. Admittedly, Interstate 70 is a fast, busy freeway. This guarantees that drivers will arrive at the hot springs with jangled nerves, but the rewards are great. Just about every exit along the way leads to a spectacularly scenic side trip. Glistening lakes and aspen forests, idyllic creekside parks and historic ghost towns – and even a ghost city or two – await adventurous motorists along this cross-section of Colorado's alpine heartland. For winter travelers, this is also the way to some of America's most famous ski resorts.

Buffalo Bill and beer

Near the western edge of the Denver metro area, **Golden 1** (I-70 exit 259) got its start as the gateway to the mountains during Colorado's 1859 gold rush and, two years later, became the territory's first capital. It

is home to the 1874 **Colorado School of Mines**, where points of interest include the **Geology Museum** (1600 Maple Street; tel: 303-273-3823; www.mines.edu/Geology_Museum; Mon–Sat 9am–4pm, Sun 1–4pm; free), presenting gem and fossil specimens as well as walk-through replicas of a cave and an old-fashioned gold mine. Also on campus, the **National Earthquake Information Center** (1711 Illinois Street; tel: 303-273-8420; www.earthquake.usgs.gov/contactus/golden/neic.php; free guided tours, by reservation only,

Main Attractions

Golden
Mount Evans Scenic Byway
Georgetown
Breckenridge
Vail
Glenwood Springs

Washington Avenue, Golden.

*Barrels of beer at the
Coors Brewery,
Golden.*

Mon and Thu) includes a chance to view seismographs that track tremors around the world.

Another unique Golden attraction, **Mother Cabrini Shrine** (20189 Cabrini Boulevard; tel: 303-526-0758; www.mothercabrinishrine.org; daily summer 7am–7pm, off-season 7am–6pm; free), offers a soul-soothing respite from the hectic traffic of I-70. The shrine commemorates St. Frances (Francesca) Xavier Cabrini, the Italian nun who came to America in 1889, founded an orphanage in Denver, and established this stonework complex in the forest as a summer camp for children. Her larger-than-life marble statue gazes out over Denver from the top of a 373-step "Stairway of Prayer." The main chapel at the site features magnificent stained-glass windows that depict key events in the saint's life, including a solo journey across the Andes and a miraculous healing.

Aficionados of vintage trains shouldn't miss the **Colorado Railroad Museum** (17155 W. 44th Avenue; tel: 303-279-4591; www.colorado railroadmuseum.org; daily 9am–5pm).

The 15-acre (6-hectare) site has dozens of locomotives and cars, tracks, switches, and a museum housed in an 1880s-style depot.

Golden is best known for a more mundane attraction – the **Coors Brewery** ❷ (13th and Ford streets; tel: 303-277-2337; www.millercoors.com/brewerytours/golden-brewery-tour.aspx; special summer tours June–Aug Mon–Sat 10am–4pm, Sun noon–4pm, rest of the year Thu–Mon 10am–4pm, Sun noon–4pm; free). Founded by Adolph Coors, a young German immigrant, in 1873, it's the world's largest single-site beer plant. From the public parking area at 13th and Ford streets, a shuttle bus takes visitors on a short guided tour of town en route to the plant, where they witness every phase of the beer-making process from blending specially grown barley malt, hops and Rocky Mountain spring water in huge copper kettles to canning the end result. (The aluminum beverage can, visitors learn, was invented by a member of the Coors family.) The high point, so to speak, is a final stop at the sampling room.

Visitors are well advised not to do too much beer sampling before driving up **Lookout Mountain** to **Buffalo Bill Museum and Grave** ❸ (Lookout Mountain Road; tel: 303-526-0744; www.buffalobill.org; May–Oct daily 9am–5pm, Nov–Apr Tue–Sun 9am–5pm). The paved road climbs 2,000ft (730 meters) in just 4.6 miles (7.7km), rounding dozens of curves, including seven tight switchbacks. Showman and dime-novel hero William F. "Buffalo Bill" Cody is said to have selected the mountain top as his gravesite for its panoramic vista overlooking the Great Plains. The long-fringed, beaded white buckskin outfit Cody wore in his Wild West show is on exhibit at the adjacent museum, along with several of his firearms and other memorabilia, and an exhibit about his changing attitude toward American Indians.

Buffalo Bill probably foresaw that his gravesite would become one of Colorado's top tourist sights. The scenic route up the mountain had been completed three years before he passed away in 1917, and near the summit, the now-defunct Lookout Mountain Resort was being promoted as "Denver's greatest future attraction." **Genesee Park** (tel: 720-865-0891, http://denvergov.org/parks/MountainParks/Genesee Park), the largest and oldest park in the extensive 46-unit Denver Mountain Parks system, was also established around the same time to provide habitat for the city's small buffalo herd, the only one outside Yellowstone Park at that time, to save the American bison from the threat of extinction. Now flanked by subdivisions and bisected by I-70, the park still contains about 25 bison; a "buffalo only" tunnel lets them graze in pastures on either side of the interstate.

A passel of parks

Originally named Lariat Road, the road up Lookout Mountain is now one segment of the 40-mile (64km) **Lariat Loop Scenic Byway**, which leads motorists to three dozen more Denver Mountain Parks and Jefferson County Open Space Parks, covering a combined area of 40,000 acres

TIP

The numbered exits along I-70 indicate the distance from Colorado's western boundary. When taking the interstate through the Rockies, you can tell how far you are from downtown Denver by subtracting the exit number from 274.

Buffalo Bill Cody, a consummate showman, in an 1888 portrait.

(16,000 hectares). To follow Lariat Loop, continue on Lookout Mountain Road as it winds down the south side of the mountain. Head west on Mount Vernon Canyon Road (US 40), the old highway that parallels I-70, to the historic El Rancho restaurant and lodge, and turn south there onto four-lane Evergreen Parkway (CO 74).

Large developments of identical condominiums and townhouses fill the mountainsides for much of the way to **Evergreen** ❹, formerly an isolated ranching community until easy interstate access transformed it into an upscale Denver-area bedroom community. Vestiges of the town's past survive in the historic district, as the original town's main (and only) street is known. Visitors can hike through the shady ponderosa forests of **Dedisse Park**, wander wildflower-strewn **Elk Meadows**, or stroll around the shoreline of **Evergreen Lake**.

The real showplace of historic Evergreen is **Hiwan Homestead Museum** (4208 S. Timbervale Drive;

tel: 720-497-7650; year round Tue–Sun noon–4pm; free), on the east end of town. The 17-room log mansion started as a barn in the 1890s and was expanded one room at a time over 25 years as the mountain retreat of Dr Josepha Williams, one of Colorado's first woman physicians, who operated a tuberculosis sanatorium in Denver. The furnishings are handmade and rather plain; the decor is enhanced by Dr Williams's collection of museum-quality Navajo rugs, Pueblo pottery, and other American Indian artifacts, along with vintage photographs. Visitors may encounter children baking cookies in the old-fashioned kitchen – a traditional school field trip. Other vintage homes line Upper Bear Creek Canyon Road for several miles west of Evergreen Lake.

Red Rocks Park and dino tracks

Mountain parks appear one after another along the next segment of the Lariat Loop, following CO 74 as it narrows and winds east down Bear Creek Canyon from Evergreen to

Interstate 70.

CHAIN STATION

Morrison. The colorfully named **Lair 'the Bear Park** and a host of others, including **O'Fallon Park**, **Little Park**, **Corwina Park,** and **Mount Falcon Park,** were acquired by Denver or Jefferson County and now form an almost unbroken strip along the silvery, gently rippling creek. Side roads cross stone bridges to give picnickers, hikers, and anglers access to hidden side canyons.

To the north of the highway, just before reaching **Morrison**, is **Red Rocks Park ⑤** (18300 W. Alameda Parkway; tel: 720-865-2494; www.red rocksonline.com), site of a 10,000-seat amphitheater built into sandstone outcroppings. The Beatles, Jimi Hendrix, Waylon Jennings, and countless other big-name acts have performed here. A sunrise service is held on Easter morning. Farther north, near the intersection of CO 26 and 470, is **Dinosaur Ridge**, where a slab of sandstone is crisscrossed with dinosaur tracks laid down 100 million years ago at the edge of an inland sea. From Dinosaur Ridge, it's a short hop on CO 26 back to I-70.

Striking it rich... maybe

Central City ⑥ is all about the past, or at least it used to be. No other town in the Colorado Rockies has had such a roller-coaster history as this one, situated a few miles north of I-70 via either CO 119 or the new Central City Parkway. Founded in 1859 as the epicenter of the gold rush, it was promoted by newspaper publisher Horace Greeley as "the richest square mile on earth." Within a few years, as placer gold prospecting gave way to large-scale industrial mining that employed droves of Welsh, Cornish, and Chinese laborers, it became Colorado Territory's largest city, with a population of 30,000 – but only in the summer. Cut off from the outside world by snow, it dropped to 1,500 residents during the winter months.

Central City outlived most gold boomtowns, and its mines kept operating for decades, as the giant, colorful slag heaps attest. By 1900, though, its population had shrunk to a few dozen souls. The multistory brick and stone buildings along Central City's downtown streets endured, as did many of the Italianate mansions on

Mountain biking is a popular summer activity at many winter ski resorts.

This type of sunflower is an arnica mollis, commonly known as a hairy arnica, and can be found growing in the wild throughout Colorado.

INVENTOR OF THE WILD WEST

In 1872, at the ripe old age of 26, William "Buffalo Bill" Cody, already well known as a Pony Express rider, Army scout, Indian fighter, and bison hunter, moved to Chicago to star in a stage play, *The Scouts of the Prairie*. The next season he produced his own play, which later evolved into Buffalo Bill's Wild West, a circus-like spectacular featuring hundreds of horseback riders, real-life Indians, and herds of cattle, elk, and bison.

The Wild West show toured the United States for nearly 40 years and played to enthusiastic crowds across Europe (including a performance for Queen Victoria's Golden Jubilee in Britain in 1887). Among its numerous stars were trick shooter Annie Oakley, "King of the Cowboys" Buck Taylor and, briefly, Sitting Bull. In 1890, the US Army called on Cody to return to the Western plains to help quell the "ghost dancer" uprising, but nearly two decades on the road had altered his attitude toward native people. He arrived in South Dakota with a group of Indians from his show and advocated on behalf of the Lakota Sioux, negotiating peace between the tribe and the army.

William Cody died of kidney failure on January 10, 1917 and lay in state at the Colorado capitol in Denver. He is buried on Lookout Mountain, overlooking the town of Golden.

Fly fishermen will find an abundance of trout and other game fish in the icy streams of the Central Rockies.

Red Rocks Amphitheater.

the overlooking hillsides. The city was resurrected as a high-class tourist town in 1932, when the Central City Opera House reopened. It soon became the state's most popular ghost town, and the once-abandoned buildings were transformed into curio shops. But by the 1980s, Central City's popularity had faded as a new generation of tourists headed for other revived mining towns deeper in the mountains instead. One by one, its stores and restaurants closed their doors for good.

In a last-ditch effort to rescue Central City and neighboring Black Hawk from decay, the Colorado state legislature legalized limited-stakes casino gambling in the three ghost towns in 1991. The results varied greatly between the towns. **Black Hawk**, with plenty of open space and relatively few historic buildings to preserve, has been transformed into a mini-Las Vegas, a strip of huge casino resorts and parking structures with few evident vestiges of the gold rush days. In Central City, casinos displaced virtually every other business in town. Even the **Teller House** (120 Eureka Street)

was turned into a casino/restaurant when the gambling boom hit. Th elegant hotel was where silver baron Horace Tabor kept his mistress, Bab Doe; a second-story walkway used t connect it with Tabor's upstairs offic in the opera house.

Central City Opera House (12 Eureka Street; box office tel: 303-29 6700; www.centralcityopera.org), the se ond oldest in the country, built in 187 and restored in 1932 after falling int disrepair, remains Central City's mos thriving enterprise. It puts on two op ras every summer as part of its popula music festival in an event as antic pated as the Santa Fe Opera seaso Tickets go on sale months in advance

At the upper end of Central Cit most streets turn into unpaved fores roads leading to picturesque old gho towns such as **Nevadaville** and **Ape** The most dramatic of them, **Count Road 279**, starts at the upper end c Spring Street. After passing **Russel Gulch**, an old mine camp now repo ulated as a cluster of vacation cabin and artists' studios, motorists come t a hand-lettered sign that reads "OI

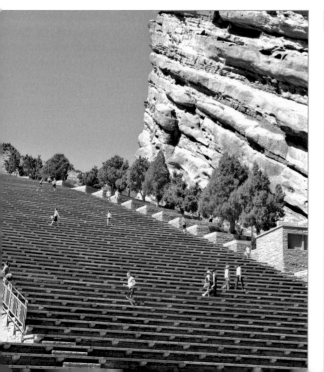

HIDEE GOLD MINE

Central City isn't particularly child friendly, but one place the whole family is likely to enjoy is Hidee Mine, just outside Central City off Central City Parkway, one of the few mines in the area still operational. Owner Ed Lewandowski leads 1.5-hour-long tours into the gold mine, a well-ventilated shaft where visitors can chip away at the mine's vein for souvenirs of gold ore. Lewandowski, a former miner and an expert geologist, still works the vein – since 1859, mines in this area have produced $1 billion in gold and silver. Dress warmly, as temperatures underground are cool, and don't wear open-toed shoes. One-hour tours are offered daily 10am – 4pm; charge. For more information and reservations, tel: 720-548-0343; www.hideegoldmine.com.

MY GAWD ROAD." The reason for the nickname soon becomes obvious as the road plunges down 8 miles (13km) of steep, edgy switchbacks, ending at Idaho Springs. Though well maintained, the route is not for the faint-hearted – or anyone driving a motor home.

The highest highway

Located between I-70 exits 241 and 239, **Idaho Springs ⑦** has preserved its gold rush heritage without the aid of legalized gambling. Mining has never entirely ceased there; though the gold played out before the end of the 19th century, rich deposits of uranium and valuable alloy metals such as tungsten and molybdenum were discovered in the surrounding rock. Today, several of the old mines offer tours. Premier among them is the **Argo Mine, Mill, and Museum** (2317 Riverside Drive; tel: 303-567-2421; www.historicargotours.com; May–Sept daily 10am–4pm), where visitors can also see the end of the remarkable tunnel that ran through solid rock all the way from Central City, providing ventilation, drainage, and gold ore transportation for numerous mines along the way. Note: due to insurance requirements, you must wear closed-toed shoes to go on the tour. Others that are open to the public include the working **Phoenix Gold Mine** (Trail Creek Road; tel: 303-567-0422; www.phoenixmine.com; daily 10am–6pm), operated by the oldest continuous gold mining family in Colorado, and the Colorado School of Mines' **Edgar Experimental Mine** (365 8th Avenue; tel: 303-567-2911; www.mines.edu/edgarmine; tours by advance reservation at varied times), where new mining techniques and equipment are tested.

Idaho Springs is the starting point for one of the area's most popular scenic drives, the **Mount Evans Scenic Byway ⑧** (tel: 303-567-3000; www.mountevans.com; vehicle access to final 5 miles/8km Memorial Day–Labor Day only, first 10 miles/16km until

Oct only; charge). Billed as the highest paved automobile road in North America, the "highway" up the 14,240ft (4,340-meter) peak was built by the City of Denver beginning in 1917; the Pikes Peak Highway had been completed the year before, and Denver's mayor feared losing his city's tourist trade to Colorado Springs. From Idaho Springs, paved CO 103 climbs for 13 miles (21km) to **Echo Lake**, a quintessential alpine lake with a picnic area and a walking trail around the wooded shoreline. CO 5 turns off at the lake and runs above timber line for 14 miles (23km) to a parking lot 0.25mile (0.5km) from the summit, where visitors get a panoramic view that takes in Pikes Peak, Longs Peak, and Rocky Mountain National Park. Descending to Echo Lake, motorists can return to Idaho Springs by the same route or continue on CO 103 along a ridgeline with magnificent views to Squaw Pass and then down to the Evergreen Parkway near I-70 exit 252.

A secret spot tucked away 9 miles (14km) from exit 238 of I-70, **St. Mary's Glacier ⑨** (7599 Fall River

Beware of the sun in Colorado. At higher elevations, it can be stronger than you think.

Central City.

Galleries, gift shops, and restaurants occupy Georgetown's historic main street.

The Georgetown Loop Railroad prepares for departure.

Road, Idaho Springs; tel: 303-567-4449; www.stmarysglacier.com) is the southernmost true glacier in North America. The glacier itself is not visible from the road but can be reached by a 1.5-mile (2.4km) trail that leads to St. Mary's Lake, filled with ice water that melts from the glacier in summer and irrigates a river of lush greenery on its way to the lakeshore. Nearby, the forlorn old **St. Mary's Lodge**, once a popular resort, waits for someone to come along and restore and reopen it, and a schoolhouse and other historic buildings remain in the old mining town of **Alice**, now sparsely repopulated with a hodgepodge of mobile homes, log vacation cabins, and larger custom-built summer homes.

Georgetown

The big sightseeing attraction at **Georgetown ⑩** (I-70 exit 228), the **Georgetown Loop Railroad** (1111 Rose Street; tel: 888-456-6777; www.georgetownlooprr.com; May–Sept daily, Oct daily 10am–2.15pm, extended hours on weekends and special trains) offers the only narrow-gauge steam

train excursion that can be taken easily as a day-trip from Denver. Though with only 4.5 miles (7km) of track, the round-trip to **Silver Plume** takes just 80 minutes, it's one of the most thrilling excursions in the state, climaxing with a trestle that doubles back on itself 90ft (33 meters) above the floor of Devil's Gate Canyon. The trip includes an optional tour of the historic **Lebanon Gold Mine**, accessible only by train.

Georgetown's historic district features ornate Victorian-era storefronts, many of which now house galleries and cafés. The highlight is the **Hotel de Paris Museum** (6th and Taos streets; tel: 303-569-2311; May–Sep Mon–Sat 10am–5pm, Sun noon–4pm, Oct–December weekends only, closed Jan–May), which once ranked among the most elegant hostelries in the West. Of particular interest are the ornate former restaurant and the two "salesman's rooms" – extra-large guest rooms designed for traveling salesmen to display their wares, featuring desks that converted into beds at night as well as diamond dust mirrors, fireplaces, and fine art.

HISTORIC GEORGETOWN

Lovers of vintage architecture and decor will appreciate Georgetown's historic preservation program, which started in 1971 with the restoration of the Hamill House, built in 1879 by William Hamill, a successful English silver mine owner, politician, and banker. Challenging the notion that only the homes of the wealthy merit preservation, the five-part program has added other properties that now form the 200-building Georgetown–Silver Plume National Historic Landmark District. The Bowman-White House was owned by a professional man and mine owner; the Kneisel House belonged to a merchant; the Tucker-Rutherford Cottage was a miner's home; and the Johnson Cabin was an early prospector's log cabin. For more information, tel: 303-569-2840 or visit www.historicgeorgetown.org.

Spectacular scenery compensates for potholed pavement, washouts and rocky unpaved stretches on the Guanella Pass Road (Forest Road 81), which winds up the steep mountain slope at the south end of town. Leveling off above 11,000ft (4,000 meters), the road takes motorists past alpine lakes, trailheads and recreation areas among the Douglas firs and aspen, finally rising above timber line for an eye-popping close-up view of the west side of Mount Evans. After about an hour's drive, it descends gently into South Park, joining US 285 about 28 miles (45km) east of Fairplay.

South Park is an expanse of high-altitude grasslands where herds of cattle graze and hay grows for shipment to other ranches throughout the state, flanked on all sides by 14,000ft (4,300-meter) peaks. The sole tourist attraction is South Park City ⓫ (100 4th Street, Fairplay; tel: 719-836-9387; www.southparkcity.org; daily May 15–Memorial Day 9am–5pm, June–Sept 9am–7pm, Sept–Oct 10am–5pm), open seasonally in the little mining town of Fairplay. The open-air museum is made up of 35 gold rush–era wooden structures – some in their original sites, others moved from abandoned mine camps nearby. They include an assay office, a mercantile store, a newspaper building, a pharmacy and, of course, a saloon, all fully furnished with 19th-century artifacts to give visitors a sense of what other Colorado ghost towns must have been like in their prime.

Eisenhower Memorial Tunnel

Before 1973, the Colorado Rockies posed a major obstacle that made winter travelers, from early-day pioneers to 20th-century long-haul truckers, seek easier east–west routes through Wyoming or New Mexico. It was not unusual for snow to close the route that is now I-70 for days at a time. The opening of the Eisenhower Memorial Tunnel ⓬ changed all that. Though the 1.7-mile (2.7km) tunnel under the Continental Divide trimmed only about 9 miles (14km) from the old route over Loveland Pass, it made the four-lane interstate highway possible and thus reduced the driving time between Denver and Vail from four hours to 90 minutes.

Even for Coloradans, whose ancestors had been digging underground for more than a century, the tunnel (or "bore" in mining lingo) was a monumental undertaking, requiring $108 million and more than 1,100 laborers working in three shifts round the clock for five years. It carried traffic in both directions until 1979, when the parallel eastbound Johnson Memorial Tunnel (named not for the ex-president, as one might think, but for the former Colorado governor and senator who had promoted the project) was completed. Though technically only the westbound tunnel is named for President Dwight D. Eisenhower, Coloradans refer to both bores as the Eisenhower Tunnel.

A mountain goat grazes on spring blooms.

Loveland Pass and Breckenridge

If you enjoy mountain driving, check out what the tunnel bypassed by taking US 6 over **Loveland Pass** , a steep route that traverses rocky alpine tundra at an elevation of nearly 12,000ft (4,370 meters). The pass was named after William A.H. Loveland, the Golden railroad magnate who planned the first railroad over the Continental Divide to Leadville in 1878. (Loveland planned to build a tunnel where the Eisenhower Memorial Tunnel is today, but before completion Union Pacific bought out his railroad and rerouted it over the pass which now bears his name). At the top of the pass, a hiking trail leads up nearby Mount Sniktau ("Sniktau" was the pen name used by a popular *Rocky Mountain News* columnist in the 1870s) for a dramatic view of I-70 and the tunnel entrance, from high above. The highway also passes the Arapahoe Basin and Keystone ski areas before descending to rejoin I-70 at Dillon (exit 205).

In theory at least, the resort town of **Dillon** ⓮ has a past dating to 1883, when it got its start as a stagecoach stop. In reality, however, the original town was flooded in the 1960s by the construction of **Lake Dillon**, a large flood control reservoir at the confluence of the Blue and Snake rivers, and a new town with the same name was built along the north shore. Today the centerpiece of the bustling resort community is **Dillon Marina** (tel: 970-468-5100), which rents craft ranging from kayaks to sailboats, as well as party barges, for those who wish to explore the lake's 25-mile (40km) shoreline.

A few remnants of the area's history can still be found in **Frisco** ⓯, on the lake's south shore at I-70 exit 203, where a cluster of 19th-century log homes, a chapel, and a jail, along with an old schoolhouse that now serves as the town's museum, have been restored in **Frisco Historic Park and Museum** (120 Main; 970-668-3428). The reigning queen of the Lake Dillon area, though, is Breckenridge, a world class ski resort 10 miles (16km) from Frisco on CO 6.

Established during the 1859 gold rush, **Breckenridge** ⓰ never yielded

International Snow Sculpture Competition, Breckenridge.

The Gold Belt Tunnel near Silver Plume, about 1920.

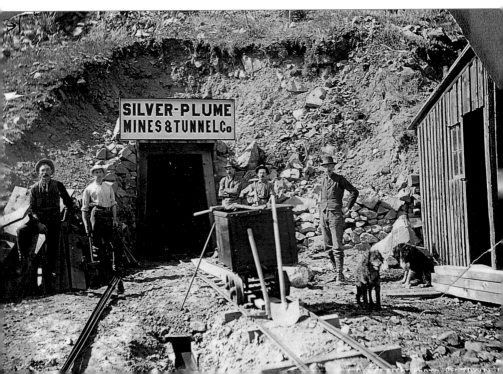

re deposits large enough to warrant the kind of industrial-scale mining seen in Central City or Idaho Springs, but enough small strikes were made to attract a steady flow of small-time prospectors. Its reputation was assured when the largest gold nugget ever found in North America was unearthed there. Abandoned in the early 20th century, the town was revived in the 1960s as the nearest large ski resort to both Denver and Colorado Springs. Since most of Colorado's first generation of instructors and other ski slope personnel immigrated from older resorts in the Austrian, Bavarian and Swiss Alps, Breckenridge soon developed a unique character that persists to this day, blending Old West architecture and Old World sensibilities.

In winter, Breckenridge's 2,908 acres (1177 hectares) of ski slopes sprawl across three mountains known simply as Peak 8, Peak 9, and Peak 10. In summer, too, outdoor recreation dominates. Among the public recreational facilities are a year-round ice rink, a skateboard path, a mountain bike trail system, and riding stables. A chair-lift takes fun-seekers up to the **Peak 8 Fun Park**, a sporty playground that offers an alpine slide, a rock climbing wall, bungee jumping, miniature golf, and a large maze as well as hiking and biking trails. Even so, Breckenridge can still feel like a ghost town in summer, and travelers who eat dinner in one of its numerous good restaurants are likely to find that the staff outnumber the patrons.

Grand-scale skiing

Breckenridge ski resort, along with the smaller slopes at Keystone, Arapahoe Basin, Arrowhead, and Beaver Creek, is now owned by Vail Resorts, Inc., the world's largest ski resort operator. **Vail** ⓱ itself, the company's original resort, is Colorado's largest ski area – and the largest single-mountain ski complex in North America. Located 27 miles (44km) west of Lake Dillon at I-70 exit 176, the slopes span 5,289 acres (2,140 hectares) of skiable terrain served by 31 chair-lifts, including two gondolas; together, in peak ski season, they carry up to 61,000 skiers per hour up the mountain.

When the roads are full of snow and ice, you have to be creative in finding ways to commute: skis, sleds and sometimes even snowshoes.

Dillon Reservoir does more than supply water; it's the perfect place to sail for an afternoon.

RECREATIONAL TRAIL

Glenwood Canyon Recreational Trail was created when I-70 replaced the former highway. The paved route rises only 400ft (146 meters) from the west end of the canyon at Glenwood Springs to the east end at Dotsero. Although most cyclists and rollerbladers start from the Glenwood Springs end of the trail, where rental bikes and other gear are available, four interstate exits provide access to trailheads along the route. The most popular trail goes to Hanging Lake, a fern-draped, aquamarine-hued pool perched high on the wall of a side canyon. Although the hike is only 1¼ miles (2km) long, it is quite steep, climbing nearly 1,000ft (365 meters), but there are pleasant resting points along the way, and the view from the top makes the effort worthwhile.

Vail's sheer size makes up for its lack of Old West heritage. The town did not exist before the beginning of Colorado's downhill skiing boom in 1962. That was when three old army buddies, who had discovered Vail's now-legendary Back Bowls while training with the 10th Mountain Division during World War II, obtained funding to develop the ski area in what up to then had been a sparsely populated ranching valley. With no historic buildings to preserve, they were free to invent their own architectural style. The result was **Vail Village**, a Disneyesque version of a Tyrolean town designed to look its best when the roofs and streets are covered with snow. In summer, shade trees along the Eagle River make for pleasant walking along paved paths between clusters of art galleries, restaurants, and chic sportswear shops. Though Vail does have first-rate summer recreational facilities, including golf courses, tennis courts, mountain bike trails, and hiking access to the vast Eagles Nest and Holy Cross wilderness areas, the economic mainstay outside of ski season is conferences; its hotels offer prestigious venues for everything from legal and medic[al] association meetings to symposiums o[n] international trade relations.

For travelers who are just passin[g] through, two points of interest, bot[h] just off I-70 exit 176, make for uniqu[e] sightseeing stops. The **Colorado Ski &** **Snowboard Museum Hall of Fam[e]** (231 S. Frontage Road; tel: 970-47[6]-1876; www.skimuseum.net; May–Sept dai[ly] 10am–6pm; donation) displays 19t[h]-century wooden skis used to carry ma[il] to snowbound mine camps, and trace[s] the growth of Colorado's ski resorts. A[t] the **Betty Ford Alpine Gardens** (530 [S.] Frontage Road; tel: 970-476-0103; ww[w.] bettyfordalpinegardens.org; daily dawn t[o] dusk; free), idyllic walking trails mean[-] der among six themed gardens fille[d] with flowers and herbs from the Rock[y] Mountains and other alpine range[s] around the world, including the Peru[-] vian Andes and the Himalayas of Nepa[l.]

Glenwood Canyon

From the resort towns of the Vail Va[l-] ley, I-70 follows the Eagle River down [a] long, gentle grade through open mead[-] ows and forested hills to its confluenc[e]

Breckenridge.

with the Colorado River headwaters at the tiny town of Dotsero and the upper end of **Glenwood Canyon** ⓲. The 19-mile (31km) route through the canyon was the last segment of I-70 to be converted into a four-lane divided highway. In earlier times, road builders might have simply hacked away at the cliff face to widen the roadbed, but by the early 1990s, when the $500 million project began, Colorado had enacted some of the nation's toughest environmental protection laws. Not only were the contractors prohibited from defacing the rock walls, but for every single piece of flora disturbed during construction they faced penalties ranging from $35 for a raspberry bush to $22,000 for a Douglas fir. The eastbound and westbound lanes were stacked one atop the other on pillars 80ft (24 meters) above the canyon floor, and a tunnel nearly a mile long was hollowed out of the cliff to conceal the roadway from hikers.

After a long hike, or even a long drive on the freeway, there's nothing better than to sink into the bathwater-temperature mineral water of **Glenwood Hot Springs** (401 N. River Road; tel: 970-945-6571; www.hotspringspool.com; June–Sept daily 7.30am–10pm, Oct–May 9am–10pm), the world's largest geothermal pool. Notables from President Theodore Roosevelt to gunslinger Doc Holliday came here to "take the waters." With the waning popularity of hot springs health spas in the early 20th century, Glenwood Springs' grand hotels fell into disrepair, and for years the town's economy depended on its main agricultural crop – strawberries.

Sky-high room rates in Aspen, 45 minutes' drive away, have boosted the popularity of **Glenwood Springs** ⓳ as an affordable alternative, and the completion of the Glenwood Canyon Recreation Trail has assured this century-old resort town's status as one of Colorado's hottest "new" destinations. Opened in 1893, **Hotel Colorado** (526 Pine Street, tel: 970-945-6511; www.hotelcolorado.com) has been restored to its former grandeur, and the equally historic **Hotel Denver** (402 7th Street; tel: 800-826-8820; www.thehoteldenver.com) has been renovated in lavish Art Deco style. And, of course, there's always the train!

Taking to the waters at Glenwood Hot Springs.

Vail Village is modeled on European ski resorts.

Freestyle skiing in Aspen.

ASPEN AND THE CENTRAL ROCKIES

Once a scruffy mining camp, Aspen is now a chic mountain resort patronized by the Beautiful People. Welcome to the "Beverly Hills of the Rockies."

Although **Aspen** ❶ and Crested Butte are only 25 miles (41km) apart, the terrain in between is impassable to cars, requiring a drive of more than 200 miles (320km). This chapter combines two possible highway routes between the towns into a 450-mile (725km) loop tour. En route lie the deepest canyon, the highest mountain, and the largest lake in Colorado. You will also discover a 19th-century miners' utopia, the place where the marble for the Lincoln Memorial was quarried, some of the state's best-preserved ghost towns, and a historic hot springs resort.

As the central hub of the Rockies, the loop tour can be divided into segments that connect many other scenic routes, most notably Interstate 70 (see page 215), the San Juan Skyway (see page 254) and the San Luis Valley (see page 187). Whichever destinations you pick, your trip will take you through the heart of the Rockies.

The richest town in the Rockies

"This place is getting to be like Aspen," locals say in revived Victorian towns throughout the Rockies whenever a new bed-and-breakfast, café, or art gallery opens – and they don't mean it in a good way. Yet, secretly, many small-towners would love to see their communities become "the next Aspen" – if only they could still afford to live there. Aspen is the prototype for every other former ghost-town-turned-tourist-resort.

In the silver boom of the 1880s, Aspen grew into a town of 12,000 people. Then, following the silver crash of 1893, it faded away until its population numbered just 350 and its brick buildings stood empty or collapsed. Gingerbread mansions with smashed windows could be bought up for a few hundred dollars in back taxes, if anybody had wanted to own them. Aspen

Main Attractions
Aspen
Paonia & West Elks Scenic Loop
Black Canyon of the Gunnison National Park
Crested Butte
Salida
Leadville

Heading to the slopes, Aspen.

survived only because it was the seat of Pitkin County, which otherwise consisted entirely of national forest land.

Then, after World War II, something happened in Aspen that nobody could have predicted: Friedl Pfeifer, an Austrian ski instructor, announced plans to build Colorado's first ski resort. The idea was, of course, absurd. Few Americans skied and, before I-70 was built, Aspen itself was in one of the most remote places imaginable. Yet Pfeifer, with financial backing from Chicago cardboard box tycoon Walter Paepke, succeeded in building his ski slope, and in 1950 it was selected as the site of the World Alpine Ski Championships. In 1960, the first televised Winter Olympics introduced many Americans to the sport, and within five years the number of skiers in the US grew by a phenomenal 850 percent. Aspen experienced a boom unrivaled even in the old mining days.

Summer fun

Pfeifer and Paepke also anticipated a problem that has confronted every

other ski resort town since: what to do during the eight months of the year when there's no snow. In 1950, the town garnered national attention with the Goethe Bicentennial Convocation, an alpine festival of philosophy and music, with Albert Schweitzer as keynote speaker – the only time he ever left Africa. Also featured were some of the nation's leading classical musicians, including pianist Arthur Rubinstein and the Minneapolis Symphony Orchestra. Though the Goethe connection was dropped the next year, the festival inspired the Aspen Institute, the Aspen Music Festival, and the Aspen Design Summit, all of which continue to this day. Other prestigious summer celebrations have been added, including two jazz festivals and one of the largest dance festivals in the United States.

Visitors today approach Aspen via CO 82 south from Glenwood Springs. The four-lane freeway up the **Roaring Fork Valley** runs between hillsides stacked high with multimillion-dollar homes and past the busy airport, its tarmac lined

Hotel Jerome.

Skiing down Ajax Mountain, Aspen.

ASPEN AMBIENCE

Aspen is not really about sightseeing; it's about ambience. After Twentieth Century Fox acquired the Aspen Skiing Company in 1978 (it's now owned by the Crown family of Chicago), the town became Colorado's answer to California's Beverly Hills – a very expensive place where tourists are tolerated but outnumbered by the rich, famous, and absolutely fabulous. You can shop for a painting that costs more than an automobile or take in a ballet. Go to a nightclub where it's hard to get in, then have sushi delivered to your suite at midnight. Learn to climb rock cliffs, ride whitewater in a kayak, or paraglide, but keep your eyes open for the beautiful people. Word has it that billionaires have purchased so many homes in Aspen that there are none left for mere millionaires.

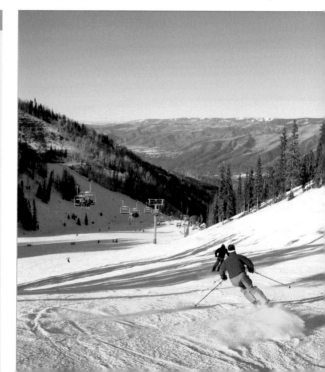

with Lear jets. Arriving at last in the compact, lavishly refurbished historic district, the place to start sightseeing is the **Wheeler/Stallard Museum** Ⓐ (620 W. Bleeker Street; tel: 970-925-3721; www.aspenhistory.org/tours-sites/wheeler-stallard-museum/; year round Tue–Sat 1–5pm, June 14–Sept 10:30am–4:30pm), a magnificent Victorian mansion in Queen Anne style built in 1888 by the founder of Macy's department store in New York. Period furnishings and historical photographs recall Aspen's history from the 1880s to the present day.

The museum is the starting point for guided and self-guided tours of the historic district. A highlight is beautifully restored **Wheeler Opera House** Ⓑ (320 E. Hyman Avenue; tel: 970-920-5770; www.wheeleroperahouse.com; Tues–Sat noon–6pm,; free guided tours), which offers a full schedule of performance events during the evening, and houses the town's visitor information center. Other historic district sights include the **Pitkin County Courthouse** Ⓒ (506 E. Main Street; tel: 970-925-7635), with its

solid silver dome, and the elegant old **Hotel Jerome** Ⓓ (330 E. Main Street tel: 855-331-7213; www.hoteljerome aubergeresorts.com).

Aspen can feel very heady. To reconnect with your quieter natural self head to one of the most scenic spot in the Rockies, photo-perfect **Maroon Lake**. The lake is located 10 miles (17km) south of Aspen at the end of Maroon Creek Road and mirrors the majestic **Maroon Bells**, twin 14,000ft (4,265-meter) peaks whose sheer angular rock faces are stained red by iron oxide. A gentle trail leads around the lakeshore and past beaver ponds and hikers can continue as far as Crater Lake at the base of the mountains

Other trails lead deep into the **Maroon Bells–Snowmass Wilderness** ❷. The only way to reach Maroon Lake is by taking one of the year-round Castle Ridge/Maroon shuttle buses, which leave every 20 minutes from the newly remodeled **Rubey Park Transit Center** in downtown Aspen (450 E. Durant Street; tel 970-925-8484; www.rfta.com; daily 8am-5pm) for Aspen Highlands Ski Area

Aspen

0 ___ 500 yds
0 ___ 500 m

from there, you can pick up a Maroon Bells tour bus.

Another vantage on Aspen's past awaits visitors to **Ashcroft** ❸, 12 miles (20km) south of town, on Castle Creek Road. Only nine empty buildings remain at the site, a ghostly remnant of a town that in its heyday was larger than Aspen. Friedl Pfeifer originally planned to build his ski area at Ashcroft, which might have changed its fate.

Redstone, coal, and marble

Thirty miles (48km) north of Aspen on CO 82, CO 133 branches off to the left at Carbondale for the start of the 205-mile (330km) **West Elk Loop Scenic and Historic Byway**, a lasso-shaped backroute around the spectacular West Elk Mountains and the lush North Fork Valley.

The road meanders 17 miles (27km) southwest along the peaceful two-lane highway to **Redstone** ❹, a hideaway town. It got its start in the 1880s as a company town for a coal mine owned by industrial visionary John Cleveland Osgood. Believing that a better living

environment would make laborers more productive, Osgood built 84 Swiss-style chalets for his married mine workers and a rambling inn for the bachelors—among the first homes in Colorado to have electricity and indoor plumbing.

Osgood's own grandiose 42-room sandstone mansion, **Cleveholm Manor** (58 Redstone Boulevard; tel: 970-963-3463, tours Fri–Mon 1.30pm; charge), otherwise known as Redstone Castle, is at the end of the town's main street. Eventually, Osgood lost his mining interests in a hostile takeover. The coal mine was closed down, the miners moved away, and Osgood and his new wife went into seclusion in their mansion in the otherwise abandoned village. Today, the town is still about the same size as it was in Osgood's time and is inhabited mainly by artists and craftspeople who sell their creations in Aspen, Denver, or elsewhere. The bachelor miners' lodge has been converted into the **Redstone Inn** (82 Redstone Boulevard; tel: 970-963-2526; www.redstoneinn.thegilmore collection.com), a bed-and-breakfast.

FACT

The small farm town of Paonia was named after the Latin word for peony in 1882 by its founder Samuel Wade, who brought peony root stock with him to Colorado. Peonies still grow in the town park.

A few cabins are all that remain of Independence, a former gold-mining camp outside Aspen, founded in 1879 and abandoned in 1899.

Five miles (8km) up CO 133, a narrow paved road turns to the left and goes to the former ghost town of **Marble ❺**. The town was founded as a marble quarry and mill, which produced blocks of snow-white stone used for massive public sculptures, including the Tomb of the Unknown Soldier and the Lincoln Memorial. At the **Old Mill Site**, huge slabs and blocks of marble lie haphazardly scattered from before the mill closed down in 1942. The small **Marble Museum** (412 W. Main Street; tel: 970-963-9815; www.marblehistory.org; May–Sept Thu–Sun 11am–4pm, Oct–Apr Sat–Sun; free), exhibits vintage photographs and memorabilia in the town's first high school, built in 1910.

Farm country

The artsy farm town of **Paonia** on the North Fork of the Gunnison River is the gateway to **Delta County**, one of the richest farming areas in Colorado. The area was once a broad floodplain where, during the spring run-off, walls of water gushed through

Chief Ouray was chief of the Uncompahgre Ute tribe. He is pictured here with his wife Chipeta.

the Black Canyon of the Gunnison inundating the valley and enriching the soil. The flooding halted with the completion of Blue Mesa Reservoir on the river above the canyon. The North Fork Valley communities are gaining in popularity with outdoors lovers and creative people escaping the city to enjoy the idyllic pastoral setting at the base of the West Elk Mountains. The scenic byway continues through the valley, passing organic farms (each with its own farmstand selling cherries, peaches and other produce); grass-fed cattle ranches; an artisan goat dairy; 11 wineries (many part of the West Elks Wine Trail food-and-wine event, held in August); and organic local foods cafes and bed-and-breakfasts.

CO 133 meets CO 92 at the crossroads hamlet of **Hotchkiss**. From here, West Elks Loop continues south on CO 92, passing through historic **Crawford** and its distinctive Needle Rock formation, a spectacular drive south to US 50, following the east side of Black Canyon of the Gunnison National Park.

If you turn right at Hotchkiss and drive 20 miles (32km) west on US 50, you reach homely **Delta** ❻, located at the confluence of the Uncompahgre and Gunnison rivers. **Fort Uncompahgre Interpretive Center** (440 Palmer Street; tel: 970-874-8349; www.incompahgre.org; June–Oct Tues–Sat 9am–4pm; charge) was once a rather disheveled 1990 replica of a trading post established in 1828 by fur trader Antoine Robidoux that became the first permanent settlement here. After renewed interest in the site, in 2015, it was reenvisioned and reopened as a living history museum. Self-guided tours take you through a Trapper's Cabin, Horno, Cocina, Trade Room, Powder Magazine, Blacksmith's Forge, and other pioneer exhibits manned by costumed interpreters offering demonstrations of frontier life. Entrance is through a visitor center/ bookstore, where you will find an information desk.

Montrose, 21 miles (34km) south of Delta on US 50, anchors the north end of the popular San Juan Skyway Scenic Byway. It is the nearest city to both Ouray and Telluride and the western gateway to the South Rim of Black Canyon of the Gunnison National Park.

The top attraction in Montrose is the **Ute Indian Museum** ❼ (17253 Chipeta Road; tel: 970-249-3098; Tue–Sat 9am–4:30pm), known for its Ute artifacts and as a focal point of tribal celebrations on the West Slope. The museum sits on 8.65 acres (3.5 hectares) of land homesteaded by Ute Chief Ouray.

Chief Ouray was an impressive American Indian spokesman who led diplomatic missions to Washington, DC, and negotiated a government treaty that reserved the entire southwestern region of Colorado Territory for the Utes in 1873. He guided his people through the transition from nomadic hunting and trading to agriculture, becoming an excellent farmer himself. Visitors can view a poster-size photo of the signed treaty and learn how, eight years later, when gold was discovered in the San Juan Mountains, the federal government broke the treaty and relocated the Northern Ute

An overlook at Black Canyon of the Gunnison National Park.

Ralph Lauren store in Aspen.

Black Canyon of the Gunnison is so named due to the extreme steepness of the canyon walls. It is difficult for light to penetrate to the bottom, and the rock walls often appear black in the daytime.

tribe to a reservation in Utah. Adjoining the museum is **Chief Ouray Memorial Park**. Ouray's beloved wife Chipeta is buried here; she is said to have started the colorful columbine gardens that still fringe the park's broad lawn.

Edge of the abyss

Fifteen miles (24km) east of Montrose on US 50 is the turn-off for the South Rim of **Black Canyon of the Gunnison National Park** ❽ (tel: 970-641-2337; www.nps.gov/blca; year-round). The South Rim has a modest visitor center, a 7-mile (11km) long scenic drive that leads to 12 overlooks, picnic areas, two year-round campgrounds (water May–Oct only), and a moderate rim trail suitable for all the family. There are no food outlets, lodging, or other services in the park.

The canyon itself couldn't be more dramatic. It is more than twice as deep as it is wide, with dark-hued, vertical walls of 1.7-billion-year-old granite and schist dropping an average 2,000ft (610 meters) from the rim to the river below and narrowing to as little as

40ft (12 meters) wide at river leve Adventurous visitors can obtain fre wilderness permits from the visito center to make the strenuous hike t the bottom or do a whitewater raftin trip through it.

Upriver, virtually all of the car yon was flooded to make the thre reservoirs in **Curecanti Nationa Recreation Area** (tel: 970-641-2337 www.nps.gov/cure). **Crystal Reservoi** and **Morrow Point Reservoir**, bot long, slender lakes that seem mor like big, lazy rivers, are out of sigh of the main highway, have no boa ramps, and are only open to kayak inflatables, and other hand-carrie boats. You can't miss **Blue Mesa Re ervoir**, just west of Gunnison: US 5 follows its shoreline and crosses ove it on a long bridge. Colorado's lar est lake, it attracts boaters, water-sk ers, and windsurfers from all over th state. Its cold depths provide habit. for kokanee salmon and giant mac inaw trout. Camping, hiking, an information are available at Blu Mesa Point.

Mountain bike heaven

Nearby **Gunnison** ❾ is home t **Western State Colorado Universit** With a student body of 2,400 and total population of only 5,973, on would expect this college town to b livelier than it is. The economy focus on outfitting fishermen, hunters, an horseback riders for expeditions in **Gunnison National Forest**, a 1.7-mi lion-acre (690,000-hectare) expanse evergreen woodlands and towerin granite peaks that reaches north to th Maroon Bells. Long, rocky forest roa follow creeks up into the mountai and provide access to pack trails f the West Elk, Raggeds, and Maroo Bells–Snowmass wildernesses.

The paved route into the nation forest, CO 135, begins as Main Stre and winds north along the Gunr son River headwaters for 28 mil (46km) to **Crested Butte** ❿, a fo mer ghost town turned ski reso

The town's location, surrounded by four 12,000ft-elevation (3,655-meter) peaks, makes for magnificent views at any time of year, and the mid-summer wildflower displays on the mountain slopes are among the best in the Rockies. Unlike most other historic ski towns, the ski runs, chair-lifts, lodges, and a 252-room resort hotel at Crested Butte Ski Resort (www.skicb.com) are located 2.5 miles (4km) away in the modern village of **Mount Crested Butte**. Built in 1881 as a coal-mining town for the railroad that ran through Gunnison, historic Crested Butte was declared a National Historic District at the same time ski area development began, so no new construction is allowed in town. Refurbished and carefully pre-served, it's a town of eccentric little bed-and-breakfasts, bars, gourmet res-taurants, and art galleries in old min-ers' cabins and saloons.

Even more than for its skiing, Crested Butte is famed for mountain biking. Colorado's most popular sum-mer sport was invented here in the early 1970s by Neil Murdoch, a young hippie who adapted an old newspaper bike for riding on Jeep roads and trails. He organized the first "fat tire" bike races over the mountains between Crested Butte and Aspen and pro-moted them into Fat Tire Bike Week, the largest mountain bike event in America, which takes place each year in June. Then in 1999 federal officers showed up in Crested Butte with a warrant charging that Murdoch was a fugitive living under a false identity, wanted for failure to appear in court on a drug charge 25 years before. Mur-doch, then in his fifties and a pillar of the community, eluded the officers and disappeared. His whereabouts are still unknown.

There are more than 50 designated mountain bike trails in and around Crested Butte. Bikes are for rent all over town in the same shops that rent skis in the winter; guided bike tours are also available.

Up the river

Back on the main highway, US 50 continues east for 61 miles (100km), climbing above timber line to cross

Mountain biking on the plateau near Fruita.

the Continental Divide over 11,312ft (3,353-meter) **Monarch Pass**, with its small ski resort and its summertime aerial tram (tel: 719-530-5000; www.skimonarch.com; May–Sept daily 8.30am–5.30pm), before intersecting US 285 at the crossroads village of **Poncha Springs**. Drivers following the West Elks loop route back to Aspen will turn north here, but first, why not take a break and stroll around Salida, 5 miles (8km) farther east on US 50?

According to the *Colorado Historic Preservation Review*, **Salida** ⑪ (est. pop. 5,467) has "the finest collection of historically significant buildings in the state." The main street leads through a classic residential area with tidy lawns on its way downtown, where metal plaques identify 78 historic buildings, many of them beautifully restored and now serving as art galleries and excellent small restaurants and cafés serving local foods. Salida is increasingly becoming a hot art destination and affordable retirement town, but, like its neighbor **Buena Vista**, it's best known as a jumping-off point for all kinds of outdoor activities, from mountain biking and climbing the nearby mountains to camping, hiking, and fishing.

In a category all by itself is the superb whitewater rafting and kayaking on the **Arkansas River Headwaters Recreation Area** (307 W Sackett Avenue; tel: 719-539-7289; daily 8am–5pm). During the **FIBArk Whitewater Festival** in June, 10,000 people come to town to take part in the oldest, longest whitewater race in the world. The 150-mile (240km) long stretch of the Arkansas River that runs from above Buena Vista to Cañon City, below Salida, is the most heavily run whitewater river in the country. Depending on the year, 250,000 people or so run it in the two-month whitewater season. The rafting industry is worth $55 million to the local economy.

Returning to Poncha Springs and heading north on US 285, it's 16 miles (26km) to the tiny village of **Nathrop**, the starting point for whitewater rafting trips through **Brown Canyon**, the only segment of the

Monarch Pass in fall.

upper Arkansas River that does not run alongside a highway. In fact, the steep-walled canyon is only accessible by backroad at one point in its entire 10-mile (16km) length.

Directly across the highway from Nathrop, a road climbs to **Mount Princeton Hot Springs ⑫** (15870 CR 162; tel: 719-395-2447; www.mtprinceton.com; year-round). The original spa resort dates to 1879, when a three-story hotel was built on the site by the wealthy owners of a nearby mine. The hotel's fortunes waxed and waned over the years, and in 1950, it was disassembled for lumber and shipped to Texas to build a housing subdivision. The current resort was built in 1960. It has been completely renovated by new owners and now includes not only the lodge but new cabins by the river. The lap pool, soaking pool, and spa are open to the public and have a grand view of 14,197ft (4,327-meter) **Mount Princeton**.

Although the pavement ends at the hot springs, the road continues for 15 miles (25km) around the south face of Mount Princeton to **St. Elmo ⑬**,

one of the best-preserved ghost towns in the state. Established in 1878, the old mining camp grew into a town of 2,000 people before its mineral wealth ran out and it was abandoned. As of the 2010 census, it had a population of eight. More than two dozen weathered wooden buildings are still standing, including a saloon, the old county courthouse and jail, the church, and an unusual two-story outhouse, as well as a General Store (tel: 719-395-2117; www.st-elmo.org; open daily May–Oct 9am–5pm). Mount Princeton is part of a mountain range known as the **Collegiate Peaks**. Motorists driving north on US 285 will also pass **Mount Yale**, **Mount Columbia**, **Mount Harvard,** and **Mount Oxford**, all over 14,000ft (4,270 meters) tall. Mount Harvard and Mount Yale were named in 1869 by a professor who escorted a group of Ivy League geology students to Colorado and climbed the 9 peaks. The others were named by members of the Colorado Mountain Club after their alma maters.

At the foot of the range is **Buena Vista**, an unremarkable town of 2,736

Tabor Opera House Museum.

ICE PALACE

In 1876, following the silver bust three years earlier, boosters in Leadville decided to recruit unemployed miners to build the world's largest ice palace. Five thousand tons of ice blocks were hoisted onto a timber framework, then sprayed with boiling water to seal them together, creating an ice palace covering 5 acres (2 hectares) and reaching 90ft (27 meters) tall, with twin towers and an enormous arched doorway. Inside, glittering in the glow of electric lights, were a restaurant, an ice rink, a dance pavilion, a carousel, a casino, and toboggan runs. Admission was 50¢ and, although sold out regularly, the ice palace was a financial disaster and was never repeated. A model of the palace is on display in the Leadville Heritage Museum.

Fourth of July parade, Leadville.

Leadville Ice Palace in 1876.

that is the main commercial center for **South Park**, a bowl of grasslands and hills that stretches between the Collegiates and the west face of Pikes Peak. The large facility on the southern outskirts of town is the Colorado State Reformatory, Buena Vista's largest employer.

Twenty-two miles (35km) north of Buena Vista at **Twin Lakes**, a cluster of lodges and cabins near the shores of two reservoirs, CO 82 turns off and climbs over the Continental Divide for the return trip to Aspen. Before taking it, though, sightseers will want to detour another 15 miles (24km) north to Leadville, a famous mining town as different from Aspen as can be.

Leadville

At an elevation of 10,152ft (3,094 meters), **Leadville** ⓮ claims the distinction of being the highest town in the United States. It got a fitful start during the "Pikes Peak or Bust!" gold rush of 1859, but it was not until major deposits of gold and silver were discovered there 20 years later that its

population exploded from 1,200 to 45,000 almost overnight, making it one of the largest cities in the state. Though it deflated just as quickly when silver prices collapsed in 1893, large-scale mining continued at the nearby Climax Molybdenum Mine until 1980. Today, a large percentage of the town's 2,580 residents ride the daily workers' shuttle to hotel jobs in Vail, 37 miles (60km) away on the other side of the Continental Divide.

Leadville has its share of scenic beauty, as walkers, bikers, and joggers can see for themselves along the paved 12.5-mile (20km) **Mineral Belt Trail**, which loops around the outskirts of town. There's camping and a full range of water sports (but no marina) at nearby **Turquoise Lake**, a large reservoir with a wooded shoreline. But Leadville's main attraction is its history. This is the town where some of Colorado's most famous historical figures struck it rich — figures like Horace Tabor and his two wives, Augusta and Baby Doe, and J.J. Brown and his "unsinkable" wife Molly (see page 154).

The best introduction to the town's colorful past is the **Leadville Heritage Museum** (102 E. 9th Street; tel: 719-486-1878; www.leadvilleheritagemuseum.com; May–Aug 10am–5pm, by appointment rest of the year). In addition to memorabilia from the gold and silver days, the museum features an exhibit about the US Army's 10th Mountain Division, whose soldiers on skis trained in the surrounding mountains before and during World War II. The founders of the ski resorts at both Aspen and Vail first came to the region as part of the division and returned after the war.

Another peek at local history awaits just up the street in the **Healy House** (912 Harrison Avenue; tel: 719-486-0487; May–Oct daily 10am–4.30pm), a gingerbread mansion built for a mining engineer. Guides in Victorian-era costumes show visitors through the period-furnished rooms. Behind the Healy House, and included on the same ticket, is **Dexter Cabin**, built of logs by a prospector who later became one of the district's first millionaires

and converted it into a gentlemen's poker club.

The **National Mining Hall of Fame and Museum** (120 W. 9th Street; tel: 719-486-1229; www.mininghalloffame.org; daily May–Oct 9am–5pm), dubbed "the Smithsonian of the Rockies," traces the history of hard-rock mining from the gold rush days to the present. Mining equipment, models, ore samples, and fluorescent minerals are on display, along with exhibits about pioneer miners and prospectors.

Although Horace Tabor, Leadville's famed silver tycoon, is not remembered for his philanthropy as other mining millionaires like Molly Brown and Winfield Scott Stratton are, he did make public contributions in the form of opera houses in several of the region's larger towns. In his home town of Leadville, it was the **Tabor Opera House** (308 Harrison Avenue; tel: 719-486-8409; www.taboroperahouse.net; May–Sept Mon–Sat 10am–5pm, tours most days noon–6pm). When it was built in 1879, it was said to be the finest theater between St. Louis and San Francisco, and the opera house today remains a symbol of a bygone era. In 2015, it was sold to the city of Leadville, which aims to restore the dilapidated theater with help from donations and grants. In 2016, the opera house was listed as one of Colorado's Most Endangered Places, a Colorado Preservation, Inc. program to raise awareness about Colorado's most endangered landmarks and fund restoration. In the meantime, the theater hosts a full roster of summer concerts on the stage where Oscar Wilde, John Phillip Sousa, and the Metropolitan Opera Company appeared – and Harry Houdini disappeared. (The trap door he used still works.)

Leadville's must-see attraction, the **Matchless Mine Cabin** (E. 7th Street; tel: 719-486-3900; daily 9am–4.45pm), may not be much to look at, but it fairly crackles with history. This was the site where grocer and town mayor Horace Tabor made the rich silver strike that made him one of the wealthiest men in Colorado – until the crash in silver prices following the repeal of the Sherman Silver Act in 1893 left him a pauper. He was working in a Denver post office when he passed away. Legend has it that his dying words to his second wife, Baby Doe, were "Hold onto the Matchless as it will pay millions again." Although in fact the Matchless had already been foreclosed by creditors.

Visitors who are intrigued by Baby Doe's story can see her depicted in a one-woman show performed on summer evenings at the Healy House.

Independence Pass

Returning south to Twin Lakes, motorists who turn onto CO 82 (closed in winter) find themselves headed directly toward a wall of peaks that appears impassable. The road scales the near-vertical granite face by switchbacks to 12,095ft (3,686 meter) **Independence Pass** Ⓖ, the highest mountain pass in the United States that can be reached by paved road. At the summit, a trail leads across alpine tundra strewn in summer with thousands of tiny wildflowers, to an overlook from which on a clear day you can see at least 18 "fourteeners" – peaks that stand more than 14,000ft (4,270 meters) above sea level.

At the center of this breathtaking panorama, toward the southwest, you can pick out the easily recognizable shapes of the Maroon Bells at the heart of the wilderness that lies between Aspen and Crested Butte. On the other side of the highway stands the summit of **Mount Elbert**, at 14,433ft (4,400 meters), the highest mountain in Colorado. The fact that it doesn't look all that big emphasizes how high the pass summit is. From here, CO 82 makes a somewhat more gradual descent into Aspen, completing this grand tour of the central Colorado Rockies.

Baby Doe Tabor.

View from Independence Pass.

Durango and Silverton Narrow
Gauge Railroad.

WESTERN COLORADO

Breathtaking canyons, Indian ruins, dinosaur
bones, and a scrappy frontier spirit lure
travelers to the Western Slope.

Palisade winery.

The Western Slope is where the Rocky Mountains give way to the redrock Canyon Country of the Colorado Plateau, a 130,000-sq-mile (337,000 sq-km) region uplifted by faults and carved by rivers into a maze of valleys, canyons, and weathered mesas. Distances are great but settlements are small. Here, farmers, ranchers, and miners have shaped a way of life that is quiet, down-home friendly, and close to the land.

The earliest settlers were prehistoric Ancestral Puebl-oans in southwestern Colorado and, in the northwest cor-ner, Fremont Indians, who combined elements of Pueblo culture with a nomadic hunter-gatherer way of life. Their successors were nomadic Utes, whose descendants today occupy the Ute Mountain Ute Reservation near Cortez, and reservations in Utah.

After explorer John Wesley Powell made his famous survey of the Colorado and Green rivers in 1869 and 1871, the Western Slope began to attract Anglo settlers. Set along the Colorado River in the shadow of verdant Grand Mesa, Grand Junction is renowned for its fruit and is now an important wine-making region and mecca for lovers of the outdoors. To the west, the spectacularly eroded landscape of Colorado National Monument hosts avid mountain bikers and scenic drivers, while the carved canyons of the Colorado River lure river runners for trips

Mesa Verde National Park.

all the way to Moab, Utah. You can visit dinosaur trackways in Fruita, then continue north through the oil-rich Piceance Basin to Dinosaur National Monument, famed for the bones at its Dinosaur Quarry.

The southwest corner holds Western Colorado's internationally famed cultural attractions: the beautifully preserved mesa-top *pueb-los* and cliff dwellings built by people of the Ancestral Pueblo culture in the 13th century and preserved at Mesa Verde National Park and nearby Hovenweep and Canyon of the Ancients National Monument. Durango, with its charming narrow gauge-railway, college, and out-standing nearby natural and cultural history, offers easy access to the parks and, via the winding San Juan Skyway, revived mining towns like Ouray, Silverton, and Telluride.

SAN JUAN MOUNTAINS

Abandoned mines, historic railways, white-knuckle roads, and a vast mountain wilderness testify to tough frontier life in the Southern Rockies.

In the 1870s, the silver mining camp of Galena City, 9 miles (15km) west of Lake City, seemed to investor George Lee to be destined for great things. It was close to the biggest silver mining claims in the Galena Mining District. It would soon be linked to the other important mining towns of Ouray and Silverton by a road over the high passes of the western San Juans. And if transportation king Otto Mears, the Russian immigrant known as the "Pathfinder of the San Juans," had anything to do with it, a branch of the railroad wasn't far behind.

Like Mears, Lee not only wanted to be wealthy, he wanted to be powerful. He dreamed of becoming governor of Colorado and turning Galena City into his own personal fiefdom. He had the name of the mining camp changed to Capitol City in anticipation of its being crowned state capital, and brought in bricks from Pueblo to build a grand governor's mansion, complete with a formal ballroom and a small theater with an orchestra pit. Lee's dream seemed within reach in 1877, when big silver strikes brought prosperity to the smelters at Capitol City and the population grew to 400.

By 1893, though, the bottom had dropped out of the silver market and, with the boom-and-bust mentality of the times, miners quickly moved

on to gold mining in other parts of Colorado. Capitol City went the way of thousands of mining towns in the San Juans, which have vanished in the mountain mists. Today, it's a ghost town, with only the remnants of the old post office and Lee's brick smelter visible amid the aspens and evergreens beside Henson Creek.

Alpine Loop Jeep Trail

Capitol City is one of 11 town sites established between 1875 and 1885 on a 65-mile (105km) long backcountry

Main Attractions

Alpine Loop Jeep Trail
Durango & Silverton Narrow
  Gauge Railroad
San Juan Skyway Scenic
  Byway
Telluride
Silver Thread Scenic Byway

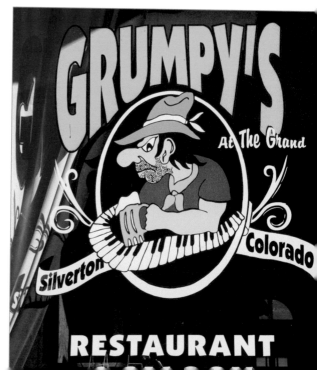

Grumpy's Restaurant and Saloon, Silverton.

FACT

The San Juans attract extreme sports enthusiasts. Mountain bikers compete in the Iron Horse Classic, racing the narrow gauge train from Durango to Silverton, or undertake the "Death Ride" – the whole San Juan Skyway in one day!

byway through the western San Juans known as the **Alpine Loop Jeep Trail**. The rugged route (most of it requires a high-clearance, four-wheel-drive vehicle with a powerful engine) crosses 12,800ft (3,900-meter) **Engineer Pass** and 12,620ft (3,846-meter) **Cinnamon Pass**, offering glimpses of silent ghost towns, glaciated 14,000ft (4,270-meter) peaks, and glorious **American Basin**, where you can frolic knee deep in Rocky Mountain columbines, the state flower.

The loop links three towns. On the eastern end, in the central San Juans, is pretty little Lake City, at the northern end of the Silver Thread Scenic Byway. At the western end are Ouray and Silverton, two former Victorian mining towns on the 236-mile (380km) San Juan Skyway Scenic Byway. All thre towns are typical of the New Wes where hundreds of former minin towns have sprung back to life und the care of new residents looking for sense of community and history awa from mainstream America.

Getting around

The San Juan Mountains are in th Southern Rockies and occupy abou one- third of what is called the Wes ern Slope. The huge province stretch from the headwaters of the Ri Grande and the Continental Divide i the north to the New Mexico–Colo rado state line in the south, and fro the San Luis Valley in the east to th Utah–Colorado line in the west. Th San Juans have more thirteeners an fourteeners than anywhere else in the Rockies, and within their boundaries are dozens of lesser ranges: the Needles and Grenadiers, the La Platas and La Garitas, and the Wilson Peaks and West Elks.

The vast majority of the landscape is public land managed by the National Park Service, the Bureau of Land Management, and the US Forest Service. The Rio Grande, Uncompahgre, Gunnison, and San Juan national forests encompass more than 2 million acres (4.1 million hectares) of the land mass. Easy access to public lands has made the San Juans a magnet for outdoor lovers. Horseback riding is popular throughout the southwestern corner, where almost every home has a corral and views of a mountain trail. The Rio Grande, San Juan, Gunnison, and Dolores rivers, along with numerous high country creeks and lakes, are renowned among fly fishermen for trout and other game fish. River runners choose from baby rapids on the Animas River and Class IV whitewater in boulder-strewn Black Canyon of the Gunnison National Park.

There's no more beautiful place than the San Juans in summer, when high mountain basins explode in eye-popping wildflower color beneath sharp granite peaks. Hikers have thousands of square miles to explore, on trails that range from easy day hikes close to tiny mountain towns, to week-long backpacking trips in the Weminuche, Lizard Head, and other wilderness areas.

For a real San Juan experience, it's hard to beat a backpacking trip combined with a ride on the historic Durango & Silverton Narrow Gauge Railroad through the Animas River Canyon. By special arrangement, you can ride the train from Durango to the edge of the Weminuche Wilderness, then disembark and backpack directly into the mountains, as hundreds of passengers cheer you on your way. Now, that's a send-off!

Crossroads town

Located at the junction of US 550 and US 160, **Durango** ❶ (pop. 17,557) has a physically dramatic setting in the 6,500ft (2,000-meter) high desert, where the Southern Rockies and the Colorado Plateau meet. High red mesas and distant mountains enclose the town on three sides. Durango itself sits in a broad river valley created by the Animas River. The Rio de las Animas Perdidas (River of Lost Souls), named by Spanish explorers in the late 1600s, rises to the north in the San Juans near Silverton and has carved a deep canyon through the mountains. South of Durango, it parallels US 160 for a while, then heads south next to US 550 on its way to its confluence with the San Juan River.

Durango is the only sizeable town in southwest Colorado. It was founded by the railroad in 1880 and operated as a supply center and smelter town. After mining declined, many of the town's elegant Victorian brick and wood buildings were abandoned and Durango fell on hard times. Things changed in the 1950s, when **Fort**

After years of decline, Durango's rail lines are busy again.

Abandoned cabin, Animas Forks, near Silverton.

Guests at Durango's Strater Hotel have included Will Rogers and author Louis L'Amour, who wrote several Western novels while living there.

Lewis College relocated from Hesperus to Durango. It was just the shot in the arm this conservative company town needed, infusing Durango with a youthful energy and expanded vision that has brought the streets alive and ensured a healthy mix of businesses and cultural activities much of the year.

Many of the students who attend Fort Lewis College stay on as residents. Some have helped restore the numerous historic redbrick buildings, "painted ladies," and "gingerbread" mansions, turning them into businesses, private residences, and unique inns. One bed-and-breakfast, the 8,000-sq-ft (740 sq meter), turreted **Gable House** (805 E. Fifth Avenue; tel: 970-247-4982; www.durangobedandbreakfast.com), served as the town's hospital from 1913 to 1962.

A self-guided walking tour booklet describing many historic homes can be picked up at the **Animas Museum** (3065 W. 2nd Avenue; tel: 970-259-2402; www.animasmuseum.org; May–Oct Mon–Sat 10am–5pm, Nov–Apr Tue–Sat 10am–4pm; charge), which occupies the old schoolhouse, or the

Durango Area Tourism Office (802 Main Avenue; tel: 970-247-3500; www.durango.org).

Return of the railroad

Tourism is the other cornerstone of Durango's economy. After World War II, growing numbers of people began visiting nearby Mesa Verde National Park, the oldest and most popular archeological park in the country. Improved highways have helped connect this remote area with the rest of the Southwest and have boosted the population. The icing on the cake was the revival of the Durango & Silverton Narrow Gauge Railroad in 1991. The echo of the steam train whistle and puffy clouds of locomotive smoke and cinders rising above the valley gives Durango a romantic charm rooted in an authentic past.

The **Durango & Silverton Narrow Gauge Railroad** ❷ (479 Main Avenue; tel: 888-872-4607; www.durangotrain.com; charge) operates May to October, with limited excursions in winter and during the holidays. Two trains leave early in the morning from the depot for a

3.5-hour ride through Animas Canyon, which, for a while, parallels US 550, then heads into the mountains, clinging to the side of the Animas River canyon, sometimes 400ft (120 meters) above the river. The steam train makes scheduled stops at the private resort of Tall Timber, Needleton, and Elk Park (where you can get off and hike into the wilderness, by special arrangement), arriving in Silverton around noon. At 2.45pm, the train returns to Durango, but many people elect to ride a chartered bus home, shaving an hour off the return time.

You can banter with your neighbors and the train conductor if you ride the tightly packed, open-air gondolas, which are interspersed between parlor cars, throughout the train. If you opt for a gondola, wear dark clothing that won't be ruined by flying cinders. And don't forget a jacket. Summer in the mountains means afternoon thunderstorms and chilly temperatures. Come prepared.

Silver (by the) ton

Like Durango, the 1874 mining town of **Silverton** ❸ (pop. 637), established in an area called Baker's Park, has benefited from the train and the town's location on the San Juan Skyway. The whole of Silverton is a designated National Historic District, and there's plenty to see and do in the couple of hours you will spend here. Handlebars Saloon, with its parade of stuffed game animals on the walls, buffalo burgers, and spit-and-sawdust atmosphere, is typical of many businesses in the historic Downtown, where residents spring into action to serve as many hungry customers in as short a time as possible each day.

Take time to stroll Blair Street, the old redlight district, and imagine what Silverton was like in its wilder days. Ex-miners lead tours of **Mayflower Gold Mill National Historic Site** (tel: 970-387-0294; May–Oct; www.sanjuanhistoricalsociety.org), 2 miles (3km) east of town on SR 110.

You can also tour **Old Hundred Gold Mine** (721 CR 4A; tel: 970-387-5444; www.minetour.com; daily May–Oct 10am–4pm), 3 miles (5km) beyond the Mayflower Gold Mill, where an electric train will take you to the heart of Galena Mountain on a narrated one-hour tour through the mine's various shafts and tunnels. Both mines offer gold panning in a stream as part of the tour. Many people find at least a small flake, which can be placed in a vial and taken home.

The 1902 County Jail Museum (Greene Street; tel: 970-387-5838; www.sanjuancountyhistoricsociety.org; May–Oct 10am–5pm), run by the San Juan County Historical Society and located in the four-story, 1902 sheriff's home next to the courthouse, at the north end of town, commemorates Silverton's more law-abiding past. The home doubled as the county jail, and you can still see cells and hammocks used by prisoners and view a variety of memorabilia, from Derringer guns to old toll road tickets. Admission includes entry to the adjoining **Mining Heritage Center,** a recreation of

A cocktail waitress at the famous Diamond Belle Saloon at the Hotel Strater in Durango.

A signpost in Silverton, a Victorian-era mining town.

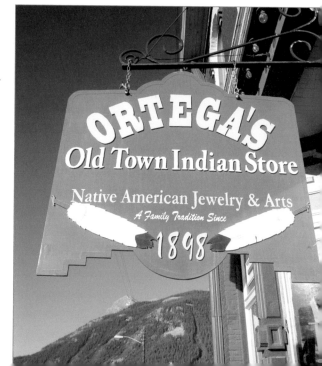

The Durango &
Silverton Narrow
Gauge Railroad.

the experience of hard-rock mining, complete with clammy tunnel and mining exhibits.

Silverton's small size and isolation attract residents with an independent, creative streak. Ex-miners, artists, writers, psychologists, hikers, extreme snowboarders, ecologists, and even snow scientists (this is prime avalanche country) rub elbows here in this quintessential mountain town far from the madding crowd.

This laid-back style is also a feature of Silverton's unadorned approach to outdoor activities. **Silverton Mountain Ski Area** (tel: 970-387-5706; www.silvertonmountain.com) and the inexpensive, family-oriented **Kendall Mountain Recreation Area** offer downhill and extreme skiing and snowboarding in one of the most natural settings in southwestern Colorado. In addition, miles of groomed trails beckon cross-country skiers, snowshoers, snowmobilers, and sledders. In summer, hiking and mountain biking are just a chairlift ride away on Silverton Mountain. Jeeping is also popular on the Alpine

Loop Jeep Trail and other mining routes. Get help planning a trip into the mountains or purchase maps and books at the US Forest Service's Silverton Field Station (1468 Greene Street; tel: 970-387-5530; May–Sept, Thu–Tues 9.30am–3.30 pm).

San Juan Skyway Scenic Byway

The descent to Silverton is dramatic. The Grenadier Mountains rise in the east as the road switchbacks down 10,910ft (3,325-meter) **Molas Pass** ❹ into the Silverton valley, then climbs out again in a series of sharp twists and turns through the mountains. This section of the San Juan Skyway has been called one of the most awe-inspiring scenic drives in the world, with good reason. The modern road follows the original single-track toll road built by Otto Mears in 1884, using a route taken for centuries by Ute Indians. Not much has changed since. You will need to keep your eyes tightly on the road and pull off to admire the scenery; there are a number of steep dropoffs here. Those who suffer from vertigo may want to consider a different route.

The section between Silverton and Ouray is dubbed the **Million Dollar Highway**. It may have received its name because it cost a million dollars to build. Others say it's because gold ore was used in the roadbed. But more likely, it's because, as you climb the highest point, **Red Mountain Pass** (11,018ft/3,358 meters), the views make you feel like a million bucks, even if you don't have a penny.

Until the mines in the **Red Mountain Mining District** closed, there was much wealth to be had here. More than a hundred mines yielded 4 million ounces of gold, 21 million ounces of silver, and 12 million tons of lead, zinc and copper. Thomas Walsh, an Irish immigrant who struck it rich when he bought the Camp Bird Gold Mine in Ouray in 1896, was even able to buy his daughter Evalyn the Hope Diamond, the world's largest.

In the 1980s, the 17-sq-mile (44 sq km) Red Mountain area became one of the first Superfund Cleanup sites in the country. It has undergone extensive reclamation by mining giant Idarado, and the Yankee Girl Mine headframe is now safe. Some 10,500 acres (4,250 hectares) will eventually be acquired through the congressional Land and Conservation Fund and added to the adjacent San Juan and Uncompahgre National forests and Ouray County Parks for public recreation (www.ocs-fortlewis.edu/redmountainproject.com). Stop at the wayside exhibit at the pull-out just south of Ouray to learn more and for views of mine shafts and the Treasury Tunnel Trestle, the eastern end of the tunnel linking the Idarado mine with the **Pandora Mine**, 2 miles (3km) from Telluride.

In 2012, the population of Silverton was 637.

Alpine town

Ouray 5 (pop. 1,013), named after the famous Ute chief, is often called the "Switzerland of America," and it's easy to see why. This charming little town, founded in 1875, is walled in on all sides by mountains that go straight up in the most extraordinary fashion, leading to the Mount Snefells Wilderness in the west and the Weminuche Wilderness in the east. US 550 goes

The downtown of former mining town Silverton is a National Historic Landmark District.

SILVERTON RHUBARB

The growing season lasts barely a couple of months at high-elevation Silverton, but one wild crop actually grows quite prolifically here without any help from gardeners – rhubarb, which can be found sprouting in gardens all over town in late June. Actually a vegetable not a fruit (only the stalk is edible; the leaves and root of the plant are toxic), rhubarb requires heavy sweetening before it can be the starring attraction in homemade pies, cobblers, crisps, and crumbles.

If you are a rhubarb fan, don't miss Silverton's famed International Rhubarb Festival over the Fourth of July weekend, where local chefs and enthusiasts compete to put rhubarb in as many dishes (and other products) as possible. Rhubarb beer, anyone?

right through Ouray, where, since the 1970s, people have been buying modest miners' shacks and mining mansions and restoring both the infrastructure and a strong sense of community. After years of being boarded up, the 1886 **Beaumont Hotel** (505 Main Street; tel: 970-325-7000; www.beaumonthotel.com) reopened in 2003, following a painstaking $7 million private restoration. Its restaurant has gourmet dining, and you will often find regional authors reading in the **Buckskin Booksellers store** (tel: 970-325-4044; www.buckskinbooksellers.com) in the same building, which specializes in Western literature.

Ouray County Museum (420 6th Avenue; tel: 970-325-4576; www.ouraycountyhistoricalsociety.org; May 16–Sept 30 Mon–Sat 10am–4:30pm, Sun noon–4:30pm, call for off-season hours) has been called by the Smithsonian Institution "The Best Little Museum in the West." Indeed. Mining museums are ubiquitous throughout the San Juans, but Ouray County Museum, housed in the 1887 brick hospital, is a cut above the rest and is

quite fun to visit. Each of the rooms of the old hospital offers a window to the past, recreating the Soda Fountain and General Store; Dr Spangler's Office; the Patients' Hospital Room: the Operating Suite; the Transportation Room; the Victorian Child's Playroom; and the Ute Indian room, displaying arrowheads and an old stuffed brown bear named Nemo. Ouray County Historical Society also sponsors workshops and private walking tours of Ouray.

Water seems to be everywhere in Ouray. Don't miss the waterfall in **Box Canyon Falls Park** (3rd Avenue; tel: 970-325-4464; 8am–dusk), snugged into a canyon 20ft (6 meters) wide and 285ft (87 meters) high. This lovely misting fall is visited by rare black swifts in summer and is used by ice climbers in winter. The faulting that pushed up the San Juans some 25 million years ago has led to many hot springs in the Ouray area. Bathing in the million-gallon public hot springs pool on the north of town is your cheapest bet and a magical way of soothing away the kinks from the road.

Cowboy camp, about 1890; ranching is still a way of life in the San Juans.

Around Ridgway

eeping is big news in Ouray. Several utfitters offer tours of the nearby mountains, or you can rent a Jeep Wrangler with humungous tires and ead out alone. The western entrance o Alpine Loop Jeep Trail, just south f town, starts off very rough and gets ougher on its ascent to Engineer Pass nd Lake City. Even more popular are ankee Boy Basin and Imogene Pass, est of town, which take you through he Mount Snefells Wilderness to Teluride. Imogene Pass is the most direct oute to Telluride from Ouray but cerainly not the fastest. For that, you'll eed to continue on US 550 to **Ridgay** ➏ and turn left onto US 145.

Historic **Orvis Hot Springs** (tel: 70-626-5324; www.orvishotsprings.com; aily 9am–10pm), located in a beaufully landscaped, rustic setting on S 550, a few miles south of Ridgway, ffers the rare opportunity to bathe *au aturel* in seven bathing-suit-optional ools that range from 97°F to 105°F 6–41°C). There's a homey feeling t this surprisingly affordable familyun establishment, with a kitchen, two rst-come, first-served private tubs, r Bronner's peppermint soap in he bathroom, beautifully renovated uest rooms, and campsites. A bonus: vernight guests can access the pools 4 hours.

If the open high country around uiet, unpretentious Ridgway looks miliar, that's because it provided he backdrop for the 1969 Westrn movie *True Grit*, starring John Jayne. The *True Grit* paddy wagon now on display at **Ridgway Raiload Museum** (150 Racecourse oad; tel: 970-626-5181; www.ridgway ilroadmuseum.org; June 1–Sept 30 aily 9am–5pm, spring and fall daily 0am–3pm; free), which tells the ory of how Ridgway was founded y railway pioneer Otto Mears. The pic story of how Mears brought the ilroad to western Colorado is told rough indoor and outdoor exhibits the old railroad depot.

Mears also helped negotiate the 1873 Brunot Peace Treaty with Ute Chief Ouray, which banished most Utes to the Uinta Ute Reservation in northeastern Utah, leaving a small number at the Ute Mountain Ute Reservation, near Cortez, and the Southern Ute Reservation, headquartered at Ignacio, south of US 160. The forced Ute exodus opened the way for mining in 1874, but you can still feel the American Indian presence throughout the San Juans in the colorful place names, in the spring Bear Dance held at Ignacio, the Council Tree Powwow site at Delta, and the impressive Ute Indian Museum, just south of Montrose.

Ridgway is a tight community, with a seasonal farmers' market in downtown's Hartwell Park on Friday mornings (www.farmersmarketridgway.com) and down-home restaurants serving barbecue and Western fare. It's popular with celebrities who like its setting in an open mountain basin, the proximity to Durango and Telluride, and relative anonymity. Gulf War general Norman Schwartzkopf owned a home

WHERE

You're never far from a designated wilderness area in the San Juans. One of the largest in the country – the 490,000-acre Weminuche Wilderness – is easily accessed from the towns of Ouray, Pagosa Springs, Lake City, and Creede.

Ouray, high in the San Juan Mountains.

With a year-round population of only 2,319, Telluride retains a friendly, small-town atmosphere.

here, and designer Ralph Lauren has an enormous ranch west of town. Ridgway also has another celebrity connection: its **Billings Artworks** (609 Clinton Street; tel: 970-626-3860; www.billingsartworks.com), run by Buffalo Bill lookalike John Billings and his son, is the gallery/foundry for the Grammy Awards.

Telluride

There's little anonymity in **Telluride** ❼, but that's fine with folks there. Situated on the San Miguel River, in a dramatic box canyon in the mountains, the mining town began life as a mining camp in 1876. Most say it was named for its Tellurium, the non-metallic matrix that sometimes bears both gold and silver, although a few suggest the name was a play on the expression "to Hell you ride," an apt description of its early days.

With the arrival of the Rio Grande Southern Railroad, Telluride grew into a respectable and prosperous town with a formal hotel, the **Sheridan**, and an adjoining opera house that once presented Sarah Bernhardt,

Lillian Gish, and William Jennings Bryan. Far from other communities, Telluride's prosperity made it vulnerable. In 1889, Butch Cassidy and his gang of outlaws carried out their first robbery at the San Miguel Valley Bank.

Telluride was rediscovered in the 1970s, when a ski resort opened here. Today, there's no getting away from the hip quotient in Telluride. Expensive homes, condo developments, fancy restaurants, day spas, cyber cafés, and an inordinate amount of real estate offices and glossy home-grown lifestyle magazines are much in evidence, and Tom Cruise, Oprah Winfrey, and Sylvester Stallone are among the movie stars with homes here.

But, remarkably, Telluride has not sold out. That's largely due to the original homeowners in the 1970s – many of them lawyers – who purchased old buildings in the historic downtown and immediately enacted tough preservation laws to prevent the runaway growth that has ruined another popular ski resort town: Aspen. Telluride proves that

WHEN BUTCH MET SUNDANCE

It's thought that they met at a horse race in the Cortez area. Harry Longabaugh had an eye for the ponies, having spent time on a cousin's ranch. Robert Leroy Parker, a wayward Mormon rancher's son from Utah, had a brother who worked nearby. By 1888, Parker, known to all as George "Butch" Cassidy, had joined forces with Cortez ranchers Matt Warner and Tom McCarty to race Warner's mare Betty, the fastest in the Four Corners. Now, with their winnings spent on drink and gambling, the men were looking for easy money.

Tom McCarty suggested robbing a bank. Warner, a seasoned outlaw, agreed. It was Cassidy who suggested the gold mining town of Telluride, one of his old haunts. Far from anywhere, the robbery would be easy to pull off. For good measure, he'd pay the marshal to leave town.

On June 24, 1889, Warner, Cassidy, McCarty, and another man later identified as Longabaugh arrived in Telluride and proceeded to steal between $10,000 and $30,000 from the San Miguel Valley Bank. Shortly thereafter, Cassidy and some of the Wild Bunch had their photo taken and mailed to the bank, dressed to the nines. It included Longabaugh, who had been released from Sundance jail in Wyoming a month before the robbery. The legend of Butch Cassidy and the Sundance Kid had been born.

controlled growth doesn't have to mean monoculture. All the hallmarks of a real community are here: a lively downtown of architecturally pleasing, old and new buildings; a variety of businesses; good social services and an interest in healthy living; people of all income levels, skin colors, and nationalities; and a big heart (the community Free Box in downtown is widely used to donate and find good recycled clothing and other items). Beneath the welcome sign at the entrance to town is another sign stating "Citizen Rights Safe Zone." They really mean it.

This open-door policy is most visible in the arts. The year-round program of readings, lectures by scientists and other thinkers, and summer festivals (the most in the country) is more indicative of what you'd find in an arts town like Santa Fe. It's remarkable in a town of 2,319 people. Major festivals include Mountain Film over Memorial Day weekend; Telluride Blues and Brews, held the third weekend in September; and Telluride Film Festival, over Labor Day weekend.

Cheap fun

Although Telluride can be on the pricey side, you don't have to have big bucks to have a good time. Among free activities are the popular day hike 2½ miles (4km) east of town to view 365ft (111-meter) high **Bridal Veil Falls**, the highest in the state; the Friday afternoon **Farmers' Market** on South Oak Street; and the **Telluride Ski Gondola Ride** to **Mountain Village**, part of **Telluride Ski Resort** (565 Mountain Village Boulevard; tel: 970-239-7050; www.tellurideskiresort.com), which offers great views of the town.

Hiking and camping are, of course, the cheapest ways to get to know a place. You can hike for days in the 41,296-acre (16,712-hectare) **Lizard Head Wilderness**, southwest of Telluride, reached via CO 145 over 10,222ft (3,116-meter) high **Lizard Head Pass**. There are several, well-run US Forest Service campgrounds in the vicinity of **Ophir Pass** (the Matterhorn Campground has hot showers). From here, you have good views of the 14,000ft (4,270-meter) high **Wilson Mountains**, where some of *True Grit* was

FACT

Actor and environmentalist Dennis Weaver (1924–2006) built an Earthship home (www.earthship.com) in Ridgway and was known for his local philanthropy. His wife and sons still live in the town, and a memorial park was dedicated to him on August 25, 2007.

Telluride's Mountain Village is a great place for summer fun.

Measuring 365ft (111 meters) high, Bridal Veil Falls outside Telluride is the highest waterfall in Colorado.

shot. In 1891, this area became the first in America to use commercially generated electricity, by Nicola Tesla's alternating current (AC) method, to process ore.

The San Juan Skyway loop continues south on CO 145 to rejoin US 160, following the beautiful Dolores River through its deep canyon to **Cortez** and **Mancos**. The 1879 mining town of **Rico** lived up to its Spanish name, meaning "rich," with one of the richest mines in Colorado history: the Enterprise. But no one got rich until the Rio Grande Southern Railroad blasted a route through the mountains in 1891, reducing by 90 percent the cost of hauling ore from Telluride and Rico to smelters at Durango.

As you head south on CO 145, you follow the route of the railroad through the Dolores River Canyon. The **Rio Grande Southern Railroad** Museum (tel: 970-882-7082; www.gallopinggoose5. com; summer Mon–Sat 9am–5pm, winter Tue and Thu 10am–2pm; free) in **Dolores**, housed in the restored rail depot, has more information on the historic railroad and also displays one of the San Juans' famous "Galloping Goose" train cars (Galloping Goose No. 5), which were created in the 1930s from converted autos.

The central San Juans

There's lots to see and do on the San Juan Skyway loop. Things are much quieter east of Durango, on US 160. The highway leads through Pagosa Springs and over majestic Wolf Creek Pass, then turns north on the 75-mile (121km) **Silver Thread Scenic Byway** through the central San Juan Mountains on US 149. You'll find all the fascinating high country mining history, outdoor activities, and small-town charm of the San Juan Skyway here, but spread out on a much larger canvas.

Roughly halfway between Durango and Pagosa Springs, on US Forest Service–managed lands, is **Chimney Rock National Monument** (Route 151; tel: 970-731-7133, visitor center 970-264-2287; www.chimneyrockco.org; May–Sept 9am–4.30pm, foot access only off season; seasonal guided tours by trained volunteers 9.30 am, 10.30am, 1pm, and 2:30pm; self-guided tours between 10:30am and 2:30pm), one of the country's newest national monuments. Essential for anyone interested in the prehistoric archeology of southwest Colorado, these *pueblo* ruins, located close to the Piedras River, were excavated in the 1930s, then more extensively in the 1970s and 1980s by archeologists from the University of Colorado at Boulder.

Theories about Chimney Rock vary, but two different cultures appear to have occupied the site during the Classic Pueblo period, over a thousand years ago. One group was composed of local people who had gradually worked their way up the river system from the Animas and Pinos rivers to the Chimney Rock site above the Piedras River valley in the 1000s. They seem to have been joined by a group with connections to Chaco Canyon, who built a Chaco outlier next to the twin Chimney Rocks the 11th century. Their main purpose at Chimney Rock seems to have been to cut wood for use in construction at Chaco.

The presence of Chaco kivas and a great house next to a major landmark leads archeologists to believe that the community – probably mostly single men – was conducting ceremonies at the site. There is strong evidence that skywatching priests calculated the lunar standstill by tracking the passage of the moon and planets through the rocks.

Pagosa Springs

Pagosa Springs (pop. 1,719) ❾ has the largest public hot springs in the West in its attractive historic downtown. These pools were important to the Southern Ute people, whose reservation lies nearby, and to early Spanish explorers. The 150°F (67°C) waters are used to heat some of the town's buildings. Developed pools at the attractive resort, next to the river, have been cooled to between 96° and 105°F (36°–41°C) and are open to the public daily. Pagosa Springs has

become a popular resort town, complete with shopping malls, condos, and other signs of sprawl on its newer west side. It is now the hub for a vast outdoor recreational industry, providing access to nearby **Wolf Creek Ski Area** (tel: 970-264-5639; www.wolfcreekski.com). This affordable family ski resort is easily accessible from Durango and sees the heaviest snow in Colorado (465ins/11.8 meters a year on average). The rest of the year, it serves as a jumping-off point for hiking, rafting, snowmobiling, fishing, and hunting trips.

Heart of the San Juans

Head over Wolf Creek Pass and drive north on US 149 to the headwaters of the Rio Grande and the heart of the San Juans. There's an opportunity to gas up and buy supplies at the junction community of **South Fork**, then you will quickly find yourself heading into the great open spaces of the 120-mile (193km) Silver Thread Scenic Byway, which winds across the Continental Divide to the Gunnison River Valley and US 50.

WHERE

Keep an eye out for the strange landmark known as Lizard Head, south of Telluride off CO 145. This remarkable peak is rated in climbing circles as the ultimate challenge: the rock face goes straight up.

Camping, fishing, and hiking are all possible in Uncompahgre National Forest.

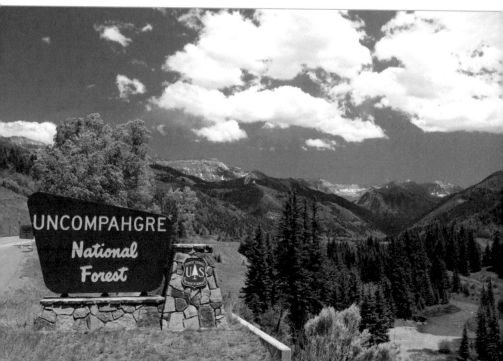

The road parallels the Rio Grande through **Wagon Wheel Gap** . The hot springs here were used by Utes, who also found significance in the eroded volcanic formations in the **Wheeler Geologic Area**, in the La Garita Wilderness a few miles to the east, which at one time was preserved as a national park but has since been downgraded. After the Utes were removed to reservations in the mid-1870s, this area saw an influx of Eastern and European tourists, enticed by descriptions of the Upper Rio Grande Valley in books such as *Ingersoll's Crest of the Continent* and *Crofutt's Gripsack Guide*. The Barlow and Sanderson stagecoaches made daily runs between the towns of San Luis Valley, Lake City, and Wagon Wheel Gap. By 1883, the Denver & Rio Grande Railroad was transporting tourists to the rail depot in town, and people were coming to "take the waters" at hot springs resort hotels. You can still see the historic bathhouse at the 4UR Ranch, south of Creede, one of several historic ranches that profited from tourism (it remains a popular dude ranch known for its fly fishing and horseback riding.)

The mountain lakes near Telluride are perfect for boating.

Creede

In 1890, Nicholas Creede and Georg Smith discovered a high-grade silve vein in Willow Creek, a tributary c the Rio Grande, and a late silver rusl was on. Prospectors from all over Co orado hurried to the mining camp Almost overnight, the new town o **Creede** ⓫ grew to 10,000 resident many of them occupying hastily con structed shacks in a series of settle ments strung along the narrow valle Silver fever was so high that peopl worked day and night, promptin local newspaperman Cy Warman t pen a ditty in 1892 with the refrair "It's day all day in the day time, An there is no night in Creede."

Lawman Bat Masterson, ex-teache Poker Alice Tubbs, conman Soap Smith, and other Wild West charac ters no longer stroll the streets of hard scrabble Creede (pop. 700), but yo half expect to run into them at place like the 1892 **Creede Hotel and Re taurant** (120 N. Main Street; tel: 719 658-2608; www.creedehotel.com), whic still offers food and lodging. The hote is next to **Creede Repertory Theatr** (124 N. Main Street; tel: 719-65 2540; www.creederep.org), recognized one of the best theater companies i Colorado and the town's top attra tion. The **Underground Minin Museum** (407 N. Loma; tel: 719-65 0811; May–Sept daily 9.30am–3pr Oct–Apr Mon–Fri) authentically re reates an underground mine fro the late 1800s (the town's communi center is down here, too). Don't mi the 17-mile (27km) **Bachelor His toric Loop** through Creede's minir district, a rough road that begins i the canyon north of downtown. T get the most from the drive, pick u a self-guided tour brochure from t tourism office before setting off.

An increasing number of hom grown bed-and-breakfasts, art gallerie and other businesses indicate that th funky little mountain town has bee discovered. Its location makes it pe fect as a weekend getaway for hikir fishing, skiing, and exploring the outdoors, but its isolated location has so far protected it. The tiny permanent population includes ex-miners, artists, and writers like Pam Houston, author of *Cowboys Are My Weakness*, who, a few years ago, fell in love with the San Juans and bought a ranch north of town.

Land of lakes and forests

Once you get beyond Creede, you're in big country, where distant ranches and jewel lakes dot high country moors and forested mountains managed by the Gunnison and Rio Grande national forests and the Bureau of Land Management. Many people come to fly-fish the headwaters of the Rio Grande, reached by turning west from the main highway just before **Bristol Head**, a massive eroded headland that dominates the eastern horizon. Just beyond Bristol Head is **North Clear Creek Falls**, tumbling down a series of black, volcanic boulders into a narrow canyon. Archeologists have found evidence of paleo-hunter use from 10,000 years ago here, making it one of the highest-elevation Folsom sites known.

At the northern end of the Silver Thread Scenic Byway is **Lake City** ⑫, named for **Lake San Cristobal**, the second largest natural lake in Colorado, 3 miles (5km) south of town. The lake, a favorite with boaters, was created when the massive **Slumgullion Slide** blocked the Lake Fork of the Gunnison River. Lake City was a prominent Victorian supply town for mines in the Galena and Lake mining districts, growing from a single cabin built by toll road pioneer Enos Hotchkiss in 1874 into a town of 500 in the 1880s. Wagon roads, stagecoach service, and the railroad helped Lake City grow and allowed it to make a quick transition from mining to tourism in the 1900s.

Today, Lake City's pristine setting, nestled in the shadow of 14,309ft (4,361-meter) high **Uncompahgre Peak**, draws thousands of vacationers.

It is one of western Colorado's most scenic yet accessible towns – the only one, in fact, in Hinsdale County, which is 97 percent public lands. The historic downtown retains an authentic Victorian ambience. It's still a good supply spot for travelers, with a gas station, a new locally owned market offering regional produce and home-baked goods, several good restaurants, and a small youth hostel (you can also shower here, for a fee) with an internet café next door.

Stop at the **Hinsdale County Visitor Center** (800 Gunnison Avenue; tel: 970-944-2527; www.lakecity.com; Mon–Fri 9am–5pm, Sat 9am–3pm, Sun noon–3pm), which has maps, walking tour brochures, and information on public lands access, the nearby Alpine Loop Jeep Trail, and the ghost towns of **Carson, Sherman,** and **Burrows Park**.

CO 149 closely follows the lively Gunnison River north to its junction with US 50, where the tour ends along the shores of the dammed Gunnison River, now preserved as **Curecanti National Recreation Area**.

Enjoy the hot springs and the sunset at the same time in Pagosa Springs.

Taking a break next to Indian paintbrush wildflowers on the Alta Lake Trail in Telluride.

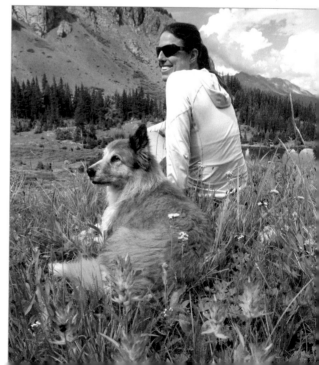

MESA VERDE AND THE SOUTHWEST CORNER

Four states and a collage of ancient and modern cultures come together in a region that is home to one of the nation's great national parks.

The southwestern region of Colorado is quite different in appearance and feeling from elsewhere in the state. Politically, it's an anomaly: the unique conjunction of four states – Colorado, New Mexico, Utah, and Arizona – in an area known as the Four Corners. Geographically, it's the boundary between two geologic provinces: where the Southern Rockies bump up against the 130,000-sq-mile (340,000-sq-meter) Colorado Plateau, a mile-high uplift carved by wind and water into mazelike canyons, crumbling mesas, and ebony-hued volcanic crags. But most of all it's a meeting place of cultures, both ancient and modern, with roots reaching far back into prehistory.

People have hunted, gathered, and farmed on the mountains, river valleys, and mesa tops of southwestern Colorado for thousands of years. Nowhere is this more evident than at Mesa Verde National Park, which, since 1906, has preserved 4,400 archeological sites, including 600 cliff dwellings, built by the ancestors of today's Pueblo people, between AD 550 and 1300, atop a verdant mesa in the Mancos Valley. Thousands more sites lie on the adjoining Ute Mountain Ute Reservation and the surrounding Great Sage Plain. Mesa Verde National Park, Hovenweep National Monument, and Canyons of the Ancients National

Anasazi Heritage Center.

Monument are all part of the longer **Trail of the Ancients**, a scenic byway that winds through the Four Corners, visiting Indian reservations, museums, parks, archeological centers, and miles of extraordinary scenery.

Cortez

The trail begins in the small ranching and farming town of **Cortez ❶**, a convenient base for exploring the area and well supplied with visitor facilities. Your first stop should be the **Cortez Cultural Center** (25 N. Market Street; tel:

Main Attractions
Mesa Verde National Park
Ute Mountain Ute Reservation
Anasazi Heritage Center
Canyons of the Ancients National Monument
Hovenweep National Monument
Unaweep–Tabegauche Scenic Byway

Mesa Verde and the Southwest Corner

0   20 miles
0   20 km

970-565-1151; www.cortezculturalcenter
org; Mon–Sat 10am–5pm, Indian dances
7pm Mon, Wed, Fri), run by the University of Colorado. Housed in a 1909
historic building in the frontier-style
downtown, the center has a museum,
art gallery, and gift shop and is a great
place to get oriented to the area. Newly
expanded, its museum has interpretive exhibits on the Basketmaker and
Ancestral Pueblo people who lived in
the Four Corners for 1,300 years, as well
as some of the area's best interpretation
of the contemporary Navajo and Ute
Mountain Ute tribes, whose reservations lie to the south. Cultural presentations between Memorial Day and Labor
Day include Native American storytelling and lectures, dances, and day tours
to archeological sites.

Ancient dwellings

Foremost among the archeological
sites in the area is, of course, **Mesa
Verde National Park ②** (tel: 970-529-
4465; www.nps.gov/meve; year-round)
Mesa Verde was the first national park
to be set aside to preserve the works of
mankind and remains a favorite with

FAR VIEW LODGE

If you want to splurge on a luxurious
hotel room and a special dinner while
visiting Mesa Verde National Park,
Far View Lodge might just be the
place (tel: 800-449-2288; mid-April–
mid-Oct, reserve well ahead).
Located across the street from the
visitor center, the lodge looks like a
plain motel from the outside, but
don't judge too quickly. Every room
has an extraordinary view of the San
Juan Basin as well as a private balcony where you can enjoy the drama
of the sudden summer thunderstorms that sweep across the desert.
The Metate Dining Room has equally
stunning views. The restaurant
serves New Southwest cuisine featuring elk, bison, trout, and other
local delights – definitely a cut above
standard park fare.

visitors, who regularly vote it America's top national park. Mesa Verde lives up to the hype. In few places in the Southwest do the works of man blend with a natural landscape of such beauty and rich resources. Moreover, it's a large park – some 54,000 acres (22,000 hectares) spread over the fingerlike Chapin and Wetherill mesas – and there's a lot more here than Cliff Palace, which was discovered in 1888 by the Wetherill brothers.

For starters, there are numerous mesa-top pithouses – the semi-subterranean homes of the Basketmakers, the ancestors of the Ancestral Pueblo people who began to congregate in aboveground *pueblos* in the 700s. There are traces of fields, too, where residents once grew large quantities of corn, beans, and squash. Standing in the cliff dwellings, you can just make out the chiseled toeholds in the vertical cliffs, where people once climbed up to their fields and down into the canyons to hunt mule deer, rabbits, and other game. Mesa Verde's success stemmed largely from the people's skill in using all of the resources of their land and in

their adaptation of new technologies, such as agriculture, basketweaving, and pottery, learned through contact with people from the south.

Still, you have to wonder, what would it be like to spend a particularly snowy January here? Despite Mesa Verde's pronounced southward tilt and abundance of moisture, winter nighttime temperatures, even in a south-facing *pueblo*, can't have been comfortable. Visit here in winter, and you'll find out. Although Cliff Palace, Balcony House, and the ruins along the 12-mile (19km) Wetherill Mesa Road are closed, the Ruins Road on Chapin Mesa is kept clear year-round. Chances are you will have many of the ruins all to yourself.

This is when **Spruce Tree House** ⓐ, the park's second largest ruin, located behind **Park Headquarters** and **Chapin Mesa Archeological Museum** ⓑ (daily Apr–Oct 8.30am–6.30pm, Nov–Mar 9am–5pm), comes into its own. Warm and dry under the overhang in winter, you can linger in this lovely side canyon in the park's best-preserved and most accessible ruin, watching rufous-sided towhees

Scientific studies abound at Crow Canyon Archeological Center.

Long House, the second largest cliff dwelling at Mesa Verde, was occupied for about a century by 150–175 people.

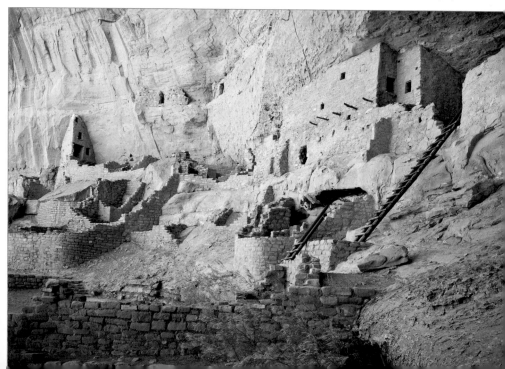

TIP

In summer, try to sign up for the 9am tour of Cliff Palace, the first tour of the day. You will avoid tour bus crowds, and the relative quiet awakens the imagination about life here centuries ago.

scratching in the duff below pinyon pines laden with snow. The spirits of the Ancestral Pueblo people feel close at hand. You can easily imagine them, robed in warm cloaks of hide and feathers plucked from domesticated turkeys, anxiously observing the movements of the sun, moon, and planets for signs of the winter solstice and warmer days ahead. At the time of writing, Spruce Tree House is closed for geological tests due to safety concerns following a rockfall in 2015. An overlook near the museum offers superb views, however. Be sure to check out the museum before leaving. It's a great place to view distinctive black-on-white pottery, bone and wood tools, yucca sandals and clothing, and other Ancestral Puebloan artifacts.

Far View

In summer, stop first at **Mesa Verde Visitor and Research Center** (tel: 970-529-4465; open year round, May–Sept 7:30am–7pm, Oct and Mar, 8am–5pm, Nov–Apr 8:30am–4:30pm), 15 miles (24km) beyond the park entrance, to buy tickets for hour-long,

ranger-led tours of **Cliff Palace** and **Balcony House** ruins on Chapin Mesa and Long House on Wetherill Mesa.

Note that advance planning is essential as this park is remote and very popular. Those hoping to do the Chapin Mesa tours and the 90-minute tour of **Long House** , the park's second largest cliff dwelling, in one day (not recommended) should plan their time carefully. It's a 45-minute drive to less developed Wetherill Mesa from the visitor center, on a winding road with stops at Long House, **Two Raven House, Badger House Community** and **Kodak House** , so named because Gustaf Nordenskiold, the Swedish archeologist who worked with Richard Wetherill, stashed his camera nearby. Visitor facilities at Badger House and Step House were badly burned in the 2000 Pony Fire, which swept across Wetherill Mesa. Recovery will take decades. For those interested in bicycling in the park, bikes are permitted on all public roads *except* Wetherill Mesa Road. However, 5-mile (8km) **Long House Loop**, formerly a tram route, has been redesigned as a bicycle route.

Another early archeologist (and later park superintendent), Jesse Walter Fewkes, named **Far View** (elev. 7,700ft/2,350 meters), one of a number of mesa-top *pueblo* communities that used Mesa Verde between AD 900 and 1300. From here, 100-mile (160km) vistas take in Ship Rock, the Chuska, Lukachukai and Carrizo mountain ranges, and the Monument Valley Upwarp on the Navajo Reservation, south of the San Juan River. Sleeping Ute Mountain marks the Ute Mountain Ute Reservation to the west. To the northwest are the Abajo and La Sal mountains adjoining Arches and Canyonlands national parks in Utah. And to the northeast are the La Plata Mountains, one of several ranges in the San Juan Mountains, near Durango, an alternative base for travelers in this area.

Cliff Palace

Mesa Verde architecture displays little of the elegant construction that characterizes the great houses and kivas at Chaco Canyon, to the south, which was abandoned long before these cliff dwellings were built. But as Chacoans began to move to the northern San Juan area, it seems logical that some of that culture's architectural ingenuity would have influenced Mesa Verdean masons. **Cliff Palace 🄶** is justifiably celebrated for its beauty and harmonious construction, and, as at Chaco, the effort that went into its planning suggests that these were public buildings for use by the whole community.

The minimal number of hearths and burials tells archeologists that Cliff Palace was occupied by a small population. Some were almost certainly priest astronomers who left behind red calendar markings on the smooth plastered interior of one of the tower kivas. These are no mystery to contemporary descendants of pueblos like Santa Ana in New Mexico. Ritual leaders continue to use such markings to monitor the skies and plan annual crop ceremonies around the solstices.

On the other side of the mesa, **Balcony House 🄷**, a rare east-facing structure, has several shallow basins pecked into the floors of its rooms – also thought to be associated with astronomical observation. Like Cliff Palace,

Visitors at Balcony House, Mesa Verde.

SPANISH RUINS

The Anasazi Heritage Center in Dolores is located next to the Dominguez and Escalante ruins, named for the two friars who became the first Spaniards to travel through the region in 1776, while looking for a route between Santa Fe, New Mexico and Monterey, California. These ruins are small but significant. The four-room Dominguez Ruin, built in AD 1123, contained the burial place of a female of high status who was interred with a variety of grave offerings, including 6,900 turquoise, jet, and shell beads and a unique shell-and-turquoise frog pendant.

The larger Escalante Ruin, at the top of the hill, was built in 1129 by Chaco immigrants and is one of the northernmost of Chaco's many outliers. It was reoccupied by Mesa Verdeans in 1150, then again in 1200.

Blue-tailed skink.

Balcony House is divided down the middle by a wall, suggesting a social division of some kind among its 50 estimated residents. A small *pueblo*, a dizzying 600ft (180 meters) above the canyon, Balcony House has an intimacy that will linger in the memory long after you leave Mesa Verde. The children won't forget it, either, as they scale ladders and squeeze through tunnels to enter and exit the *pueblo*.

As many as 5,000 people may have lived at Mesa Verde during the Classic or Pueblo III era (AD 1100–1300). In the Pueblo II era (AD 900–1100), the region was part of a vast trading network bringing items from as far away as Mexico and the Mississippi Valley for redistribution at Chaco Canyon. When Chaco collapsed, the people of Mesa Verde became more insular, perhaps in an effort to protect the attractive resources in their homeland and avoid the same fate as their neighbors to the south.

Defensive measures?

Exploring Cliff House.

Archeologists are unsure why Mesa Verdeans began to build their pueblos in alcoves in the canyon walls in the 1200s. Some think that worsening drought and diminishing firewood and other natural resources forced the people to use creative new ways of survival. Cliff dwellings were well suited to the protected canyons of the Four Corners. They made good use of solar energy, and springlines seeping through the porous sandstone cliffs into the back of the alcoves offered a ready water source. People living there were hidden from view but could still climb to the mesa tops to work fields and travel into the dense pinyon-juniper and oak forests of the canyons to hunt and gather.

It's hard to escape the conclusion that the cliff dwellings were used to defend the population against an external danger, perhaps the burgeoning population on the Great Sage Plain or incoming Utes, Navajos, and Apaches vying for Pueblo lands. No mass deaths have been found at Mesa Verde, but there are signs of ritual violence throughout the Four Corners. As a 24-year drought settled in, and powerful ceremonies failed to bring rain, one can imagine the despair that must have gripped the people of the Four Corners as the land that had always supported them failed. By 1300, Mesa Verde was empty. Today, some 24 pueblos, including the Hopi villages in Arizona, and Zuni, Acoma, and the Rio Grande *pueblos* in New Mexico, trace their ancestors to Mesa Verde.

Exploring the Four Corners

As increasing numbers of people moved to Mesa Verde in the 1100s, space was clearly at a premium. Mesa-top sites at the head of narrow canyons in the northern San Juan region, which offered water, agricultural land and good places to build multistory *pueblos*, quickly began to fill up. Soon, people were spilling out all across the Four Corners in search of suitable places to live. A number of these sites have been restored and are open to the public. Often undeveloped, they offer a chance to escape the crowds at Mesa Verde and earn more about the people who once lived in the Four Corners.

A case in point is **Ute Mountain Ute Tribal Park** ❸ (tel: 970-565-3751, ext.330 for reservations for half-day or full-day group tours; www.utemountain tribalpark.info; open seasonally), which adjoins Mesa Verde on the south. The Weminuche Ute who live on this small reservation are one of seven Ute hunter-gatherer bands that were living in the Four Corners by the 1400s. Forced onto a small reservation in southern Colorado in 1873, Chief Ignacio and 11 other Ute leaders were persuaded to lease Mesa Verde to the government for 10 years to protect it from pothunters. The Utes lost that land permanently in 1906, when President Theodore Roosevelt created Mesa Verde National Park. In 1911, the government took another 14,000 acres (5,700 hectares) from the Utes, including Balcony House. The part of Mesa Verde that remained under Ute control was set aside as a tribal park in the 1960s.

Today, the Ute Nation and the National Park Service work closely together to protect archeological sites, and in summer, for a fee, Ute Mountain Utes offer guided backcountry tours to sites in the tribal park. Easy half-day tours (9am–noon; 1–4pm tours by special arrangement) take in Ancestral Pueblo petroglyphs, scenic lands, Ute pictographic panels, geological land formations, and surface sites. The more demanding full-day tour (9am–4pm) visits four well-preserved canyon cliff dwellings in Lion Canyon, reached by a 3-mile (5km) hike and climbing ladders to the cliffs. To sign up, call or stop at the tribal park visitor center/museum. Check-in time is 8.30am for a 9am departure. Gas up and be prepared to drive your own car across the reservation: 40 miles (64km) for the half-day trip and 80 miles (130km) for the full-day excursion. You should wear a hat, good shoes, and sunscreen, and bring plenty of water and a lunch; these are not available on the tour. Gas, food, and

lodging are available at Towaoc and nearby Cortez.

Archeology center

Several other archeological sites near Cortez make good day trips. Don't miss the attractive **Anasazi Heritage Center** ❹ (27501 Highway 184, Dolores; tel: 970-882-5600; www.blm.gov/co/st/en/fo/ahc.html; daily Mar–Oct 9am–5pm, Nov–Feb until 4pm; charge), 10 miles (16km) north of Cortez, off CO 184. The Anasazi Heritage Center's museum will be a surprise to those accustomed to the dated exhibits often found at national parks. It was built by the Bureau of Reclamation to house 2 million artifacts that were excavated from the nearby Dolores River Canyon before it was lost forever under McPhee Reservoir. More than a million artifacts from excavations in the Four Corners have been deposited here, making it the single best research center in the area.

Operated by the Bureau of Land Management, the center has an impressive museum that will appeal to children and adults alike. Interactive exhibits offer a variety of ways to understand

One of the many cultural sites at Canyons of the Ancients National Monument.

Lowry Pueblo, Canyons of the Ancients National Monument.

Pueblo building, Canyons of the Ancients National Monument.

why archeology is important. Large photographs show step-by-step excavations of nearby sites. Computers allow you to make a virtual tour of an ancient *pueblo*. Smaller artifacts are located in drawers and can be opened and examined. You can even try your hand at grinding corn using a metate (grinding stone) and mano (hand stone). Pueblo women spent hours doing this each day. It's not as easy as it looks.

The Anasazi Heritage Center is the headquarters for 164,000-acre (66,000-hectare) **Canyons of the Ancients National Monument** ❺, located to the west on Cajone Mesa. This BLM-managed national landscape monument contains the highest known density of archeological sites in the nation – 6,000 so far, and some areas have more than 100 cultural sites per square mile – spanning 10,000 years of use. It remains largely unknown and undeveloped, so it's important to stop at the Heritage Center (see page 271) and pick up information on visiting. The monument incorporates one previously excavated and restored site: **Lowry Pueblo National Historic Landmark**,

a 40-room *pueblo*, with eight kivas and rare great kiva that archeologists believe must have served as a ceremonial center. To reach Lowry, turn west onto County Road CC at the south end of Pleasant View and drive 9 miles (14km) to the site on CR 7.25. Booklets for the self-guided wheelchair accessible trail are available at the trailhead.

CO 10 continues south through the monument. It's a lonesome place with views across the Four Corners and south to Monument Valley. You can hike almost anywhere, but this is not a place for the uninitiated. It's easy to get disoriented. If you want to hike, your best bet is 6-mile (10km) **Sand Canyon Trail**, a one-way route from the monument south to Road G in McElmo Canyon. Although it's rugged, this is a popular trail, attracting some 17,000 hikers each year.

Crow Canyon

Research in Sand Canyon has been carried out for a number of years by **Crow Canyon Archaeological Center** ❻ (23390 Road K, Cortez; tel 800-422-8975; www.crowcanyon.org; daily by reservation), a private institution located near **Sand Canyon Pueblo**, a few miles west of Cortez. Ongoing excavations here have established that 420-room Sand Canyon Pueblo, at the northern end of the trail, was one of the largest *pueblos* to be occupied in the final decades of occupation of the Mesa Verde region. It has 100 kivas and 14 towers. Fieldwork at the smaller **Castle Rock Pueblo**, at the southern end of **Sand Canyon Trail**, revealed that the occupation there ended with a battle – one of the best documented examples of warfare from the ancient Southwest.

If you've ever wanted to know what archeology is like on the ground, this is the place to find out. You can make a reservation to participate in the ongoing dig at Sand Canyon or accompany staff to a variety of archeological sites in the area. Longer residential courses include Cultural Exploration programs with leading Pueblo scholars and hands-on activities, such as weaving and ceramics with American Indian artisans.

Primitive camping on monument roads is permitted at Canyons of the Ancients National Monument, but it has no developed camping facilities. However, there is an excellent little campground at nearby **Hovenweep National Monument** ⑦ (tel: 970-562-4282; www.nps.gov/hove; daily), one of those delightful, unexpected parks that remain relatively undiscovered.

Six 12th- and 13th-century Mesa Verde–style buildings, built in unusual round, square, and D-shaped towers, line the rim of **Little Ruins Canyon** at this small national monument, between Blanding, Utah and Cortez, Colorado. Two short rim trails lead from the attractive visitor center and campground to Square Tower Group, Hovenweep Castle, and other structures used by prehistoric farmers.

River of sorrows

Although drought led Ancestral Pueblo people to abandon the Four Corners, the area around Cortez now supports numerous ranches and small farms.

They raise bumper crops of beans, an important staple for ancient Pueblo people. Farming on this scale in the Cortez area is relatively recent. It was made possible by irrigation water brought onto the Great Sage Plain by the damming of the Dolores River, the "river of sorrows," named by early Spanish explorers. Finish your tour by turning right on CO 141, just beyond **Dove Creek**, and following the pretty Dolores River as it winds north into the redrock country of western Colorado. CO 141 eventually reaches **Naturita**, the start of the spectacular **Unaweep–Tabegauche Scenic Byway**, which continues to **Whitewater**, just south of Grand Junction.

There's nothing sorrowful about this pleasant scenic byway, which passes through verdant mountains and soaring redrock canyons carved by the Dolores and San Miguel rivers. In the 1800s, these remote canyons were a favored hideout for cattle rustlers from Utah. One of these places, the evocatively named Sewemup Mesa, is one of the most pristine ecological environments in western Colorado, encircled by 1,000ft-high (300-meter)

Road through Mesa Verde National Park.

Wingate cliffs. The clifftops are home to peregrine falcons and golden and bald eagles, which fish the Dolores River from high ledges.

Uravan

Until it closed, **Uravan** ❽ was a major producer of uranium, radium, and vanadium for the nuclear industry, processing 42 million lbs (19 million kg) of uranium and 220 million lbs (100 million kg) of vanadium between 1936 and 1984. A $70 million Superfund cleanup project is stabilizing the tailings above the old Joe Jr Mill. In 1888, the Montrose Placer Mining Company built a 13-mile (21km) hanging flume in the side of Dolores Canyon to bring water from the San Miguel River for gold processing at Mesa Creek Flats. Abandoned three years later, the disintegrating wooden flume can still be seen high above the river rapids.

CO 141 then turns away from the Dolores River, exiting at Whitewater on the northern end of the verdant Uncompahgre Plateau, a great place for hiking, mountain biking, camping, and four-wheel-drive explorations.

At **Gateway**, the road passes through magnificent Unaweep Valley, with red rocks on the west and high mountains composed of 1.7-billion-year-old rocks on the east. Ranches and farms abound. Watch for the pullout for Unaweep Seep Research Natural Area, an important breeding ground for rare Nokomis fritillary butterflies. For anyone who loves canyons *and* mountains, this pretty spot will seem like heaven on earth. A New York capitalist, Lawrence Driggs, evidently thought so, too. Between 1914 and 1918, he hired local stone masons to construct a hunting lodge on 320 acres (130 hectares) of land near Gateway using water from West Creek. The Driggses moved here in 1918 and stayed just a few weeks. The ruined mansion now sits abandoned in a pasture in the huge new Gateway Canyons development. This Southwest-style, greenbuilt planned community, spearheaded by Discovery Channel founder John Hendricks, is providing infrastructure, jobs, and recreation opportunities for outdoor lovers in this historic area just south of Grand Junction.

Spruce Tree House, Mesa Verde.

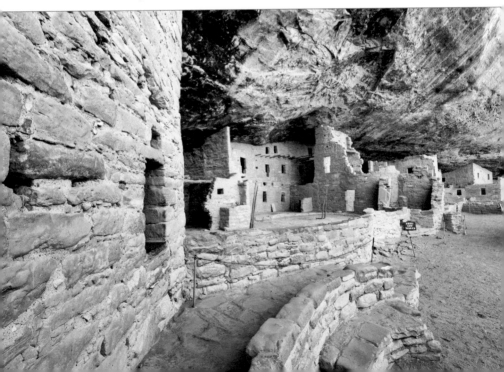

The Utes

Once nomadic, two remaining bands of Ute Indians live on reservations on Colorado's Western Slope: The Ute Mountain Ute, near Cortez and the Southern Utes, near Ignacio.

The Utes, from the Spanish word *yuta*, were named by the first Spaniards to trade with them in Taos, New Mexico, around 1610. They call themselves the Nuche, or The People, and speak the same Uto-Aztecan language as the Aztecs, Hopis, Comanches, Paiutes, and Shoshones. They may have entered northwestern Colorado from the Great Basin – or, as some Utes believe, northern Mexico – between 500 and 800 years ago. Like their Archaic forebears, they were consummate hunter-gatherers. They began farming informally after entering the canyon country of western Colorado, possibly after mingling with Fremont Indians in the area.

By historic times, there were six Ute bands in Colorado. The Mouache band's territory included the eastern Rockies, the San Luis Valley, and northern New Mexico, where they mingled with the Kapote band. The Weminuche lived in the canyon country of the Four Corners. These three bands are known as the Southern Utes. The Kapote and Mouache bands now occupy the Southern Ute Reservation, east of Durango. The Weminuche live on the more traditional Ute Mountain Ute Reservation, south of Cortez.

The largest Ute bands occupied northwestern Colorado and were known as the Northern Utes. Chief Ouray's band – the Tabeguache or Uncompahgre Utes – lived in the Gunnison and Uncompahgre valleys, where they hunted atop 10,000ft-high (3,050-meter) Grand Mesa and wintered near Montrose and Delta. North of the Tabeguache were the Parianuc or Grand Valley Utes, who lived along the Colorado River, and the Yampa band, who lived in the Yampa River Valley.

These two bands were renamed the White River Utes after Nathan Meeker established an Indian agency in Meeker. Tragedy struck when, in an effort to get Utes near Craig to take up farming, Meeker plowed up their horse racetrack, triggering a fist fight; Army involvement; the massacre of soldiers, Meeker, and eight of his men; and the taking of white women as hostages. This crisis led to the White River Utes and Chief Ouray's band being forced to move to the bleak Uintah Basin of east-central Utah in 1880 – a landscape with so few resources it was said even the birds wouldn't fly over it.

The Mouache and Kapote bands, led by chiefs Severo and Buckskin Charley, were forced to become farmers after accepting land allotments on the Southern Ute Reservation in 1863 – an activity scorned as women's work by the skilled hunters. Chief Ignacio and the Weminuche band held fast to a traditional way of life for decades, living in tents on the undeveloped Ute Mountain Ute Reservation until well into the 1930s.

Today, Utes have bowed to the inevitable and taken up Anglo pursuits, such as farming, ranching, construction, tourism, gaming, and motel-keeping. Even so, traditional Ute gatherings still take place. Chipeta Day, for example, is held every September at the Ute Indian Museum, south of Montrose, on Ouray's old farm, where his second wife Chipeta and her stepbrother John McCook are buried. It includes dancing, food, traditional beaded handicrafts, movies, silent auctions, and other activities. All three reservations still perform the Bear Dance every spring, a multiday event that celebrates the end of winter, a transition signified by a bear waking up from hibernation.

Chief Severo and family, c.1885.

COLORADO WINE COUNTRY

Warm, sunny days and cool nights create perfect grape-growing conditions on Colorado's Western Slope, jumpstarting the growth of 140 wineries throughout the state.

Since Stephen Smith founded Grande River Vineyards in 1987, one of the largest grape-growing operations in Colorado, wine production has grown from some 279 liters to 1,335,850 liters in 2015, contributing well over $100 million in economic impact from wine tourism in the state. Colorado has two areas that have been designated American Viticulture Areas (AVAs): the Grand Valley AVA, around Grand Junction, and the West Elks AVA, in the North Fork Valley of the Central Rockies between Paonia and Delta, both of which have the right growing conditions and make wine onsite. Two other regions make wine from grapes grown on the Western Slope: the Four Corners region, around Durango, and the Pikes Peak and Arkansas Valley of the Front Range. Of these, Grand Junction and its eastside suburbs of Palisade and Fruita, along the Colorado River, have by far the greatest number of wineries – 24 at last count. Conditions here favor Bordeaux-type red wines such as Merlot and Cabernet Sauvignon, while the North Fork is known for its whites and Rieslings. Increasingly, however, wine makers are blending grapes grown in both regions, so that these days you may also find excellent Rhones like Syrah and Chardonnays in Grand Junction and Pinot Noir, Pinot Gris, and Cabernet Franc in the North Fork Valley.

The Colorado wine industry suffered a setback when the state went dry in 1916, four years before Prohibition.

Isabella Bird described finding wild grape vines growing on mountain slopes near Estes Park in A Lady's Life in the Rocky Mountains, published in 1879.

The vines at Garfield Estates in Palisade are self-rooted rather than grafted, and the soil is predominantly clay loam, which is rich in mineral content.

The Infinite Monkey Theorem Winery is located in Denver's RiNo (River North Art District) neighborhood.

CREATIVE WINE MAKERS

Wine, like art, is a creative medium, suited to artisans with an iconoclastic streak. Two such Colorado vintners both happen to have British roots and are winning international acclaim for their complex boutique wines. Sutcliffe Vineyards, in the Four Corners, is cultivated by John Sutcliffe, whose eclectic career has included a stint in the British Army, high-end restaurateur, cowboy, and now vintner. Sutcliffe Vineyards' pastoral acreage in Mancos Canyon near Cortez is about as idyllic as it gets, a perfect setting for the owner's gourmet wine dinners, guest stays, and exploring nearby Pueblo ruins. A tasting room is located in nearby Durango. Ex-Londoner Ben Parsons, whose Infinite Monkey Theorem Winery is housed in an old Quonset hut in the arts district of Denver, is equally passionate about the wine experience but the setting couldn't be more different. Parsons learned wine-making in Australia and the Western Slope but decided to strike out on his own to make wine that sings to his particular soul. His deep, fruity wines can be found at top Denver restaurants, where chefs have embraced this winemaker's passion for wines with a strong urban identity.

...neyard beneath the palisades in Mesa County. The town of ...ade is known mostly for its peaches.

...pes are harvested using a combination of traditional ...ual labor and modern harvesting machines.

Ex-Londoner Ben Parsons creates urban wines at his Denver winery, the Infinite Monkey Theorem.

THE NORTHWEST CORNER

Dinosaur fossils, red rock canyons, and raging rivers
are just a few of the attractions in a rugged country
where the intrepid John Wesley Powell unveiled the
wonders of a great Western landscape.

olorado's least developed region, its northwestern corner, has begun to be discovered. This is due, in part, to cyclical oil, gas, uranium, and coal mining booms that have periodically swelled the population and led to the construction of good highways and rail links. But mostly it's because of the presence of Dinosaur National Monument and the growth of recreation in the gorgeous Colorado red rock canyons surrounding **Grand Junction** (pop. 59,778), the main shopping center for the region and a logical base for explorations.

Junction, as locals call it, is located just north of the confluence of the Colorado and Gunnison rivers, in the majestic **Grand Valley**. With its valley setting, the forest-clad Rockies to the east, and the mile-high Colorado Plateau to the west, Junction has one of the loveliest settings of any city in the Southwest. To the north is Interstate 70 closely paralleling the imposing facade of the **Book Cliffs**. To the south is the **Uncompahgre Plateau**, the only place apart from the Continental Divide where two rivers – in this case the Uncompahgre and Dolores – divide and flow east and west, respectively.

On its northern end, the orange sandstone of the Uncompahgre Uplift has been carved by wind, water, and ice into vertical cliffs, monuments, and headlands that offer endless possibilities

Fishing in Grand Mesa National Forest.

for recreation in **Colorado National Monument** and adjoining **McInnis Canyons National Conservation Area**.

Grand Mesa

Recreation is also plentiful on the 500-sq-mile (1,300-sq-km) forested volcanic plateau known as **Grand Mesa**, 35 miles (56km) east of Grand Junction. An outdoor-lover's paradise, 10,000ft-high (3,000-meter) Grand Mesa is the largest flat-topped mountain in the world. Its cool forests, 200 sparkling lakes and numerous backcountry trails

Main Attractions
Grand Mesa
Grand Junction
Colorado National
  Monument
Dinosaur National
  Monument
Museum of Northwestern
  Colorado, Craig
Meeker
Rifle Falls State Park

Northwest Corner

0 ————————— 20 miles
0 ————————— 20 km

N

Wyoming

Baggs
Savery
Slater

Hiawatha

Powder
Wash

Browns
Park
NWR

Gates of
Lodore ★

Great
Divide

Routt
National
Forest

Vermillion Creek

Little Snake

Green

Greystone

Utah

Harpers Corner
Trail ★
★ Echo
Park

Dinosaur
Quarry

Green

Josie Bassett
Morris Homestead ★

Dinosaur
National Monument

Sunbeam

Lay

Museum of
Northwestern
Colorado ★

Yampa
River SP

Maybell

Little Yampa
Canyon BLM Rec. Area

6 Craig

Yampa

Jensen

Canyon
Visitor Centre
5

Dinosaur

Blue
Mountain

Massadona

Elk
Springs

Danforth Hills

Hamilton

Williams Fork

Pagoda

Axial

Kenney
Res.

Rangely

White

White
River
Museum ★
7 Meeker

Routt

National Forest

North Fork

Buford

South Fork

Canyon Pintado
National Historic
District
4

Cathedral Bluffs

Piceance
Basin

Piceance Creek

Rio
Blanco

White River

The Flat Tops
National Forest

East Tavaputs
Plateau

Douglas Pass
8268

Roan
Plateau

Rifle Falls
SP

Rifle Gap
SP

Harvey Gap
SP

New Castle

W. Salt Creek

Roan Cliffs

Roan Creek

Rulison

Antlers

Silt

6

70

Glenwood
Springs

Rifle
8

Book Cliffs

Highline
Lake SP

Grand Valley
BLM Rec. Area

De Beque

Parachute

Colorado

Battlement
Mesa

White River

National Forest

Green River, Utah

6
50

Mack
Loma

Dinosaur
Journey
Fruita

2

Colorado

Gunnison

Colorado River/
Island Acres
SP

70

Cameo

6

Mesa

Plateau

Molina

Collbran

Vega SP

Rabbit Valley
Research Natural
Area ★

McInnis
Canyons National
Conservation Area
3

Colorado
NM
2

Grand
Junction
1

Clifton

Palisade

Skyway

Grand
Mesa

Grand
Mesa
National
Forest

Buck Mesa

Glade Park

Orchard
Mesa
Dominguez Canyon
BLM Rec. Area

Whitewater

50

Grand Mesa

beckon to hikers, campers, and fisher-men all summer, when temperatures in the valley reach 100°F (38°C). In winter, "The Mesa," as it's called, becomes a haven for cross-country and downhill skiing, snowmobiling, and other snow sports at Powderhorn Mountain Resort, and is a popular place for weekend getaways at rustic lodges with views all the way to the farmlands of the Uncompahgre and Grand Valley.

Located on the banks of the Colorado River, Grand Junction itself grew up around the railroad in 1881. It has been known as a commercial center ever since. Early settlers capitalized on the ready irrigation water and planted peach and apple orchards and vineyards, which today still thrive in the pretty suburbs of **Clifton, Palisade,** and **Fruita.** Grand Junction's loveliest bed-and-breakfasts are located in these leafy communities, where you can spend lazy days strolling and bicycling, wine tasting, fruit picking, and admiring the spectacular cliffs surrounding the valley.

Sadly, **Grand Junction ❶** itself, squeezed between I-70 on the north and the Colorado River on the south, seems to be losing the fight with urban sprawl. New housing developments and miles of "big box" superstores, chain hotels, and restaurants on the wide avenues leading from I-70 have given the city a nondescript Anytown-USA appearance. That's a pity because there's lots to see and do in this historic city, once you get your bearings.

Grand Junction

Start in the restored historic downtown, near the railroad station. In 1963, Junction received nationwide acclaim for its **Downtown Shopping Park,** an attractive, five-block Main Street redevelopment that features restored historic brick buildings housing shops, galleries, and the city's best restaurants, breweries, and cafés. One of the highlights of the downtown is its innovative **Art on the Corner** project, which was launched in 1984 and features lifesize sculptures on annual loan to the city

from local artists. A stroll along the tree-lined, curving streets makes for a fun art walk on a warm summer evening.

When Exxon dropped a multimillion-dollar oil-shale extraction project in nearby **Parachute** in 1984, Grand Junction fell on hard times, with nearly 15 percent of its homes vacant by 1989. But the city has worked hard to improve amenities, which has had a positive effect on its cultural institutions. The restored 1923 **Avalon Theatre** (645 Main Street; tel: 970-263-5700; www.avalontheatregj. com) is the linchpin of the Downtown Shopping Park, hosting plays, concerts, and other entertainment throughout the year. **Mesa State College,** founded in 1925 and located halfway between I-70 and downtown, is a four-year liberal arts college. It is home to the stylish **Western Colorado Center for the Arts,** otherwise known as the **ART Center** (1803 N. 7th Street; tel: 970-243-7337; www. gjartcenter.org; Tue–Sat 9am–4pm; charge, Tue free), where you'll find historic and contemporary works by Western artists and special exhibitions all year.

Junction's main cultural institution, the **Museum of Western Colorado,**

Palisade is known for its peaches.

Book Cliffs, near Grand Junction.

Lone cyclist, Colorado National Monument.

Colorado National Monument.

is the largest museum between Denver and Salt Lake City. It has three branches. Downtown's **Museum of the West** (462 Ute Avenue; tel: 970-242-0971; www.museumofwesternco.com; May–Sept Mon–Sat 9am–5pm, Sun noon–4pm, Oct–Apr Mon–Sat 10am–4pm, closed Sun) is an accessible, modern museum featuring a one-room schoolhouse, a uranium mine, Indian pottery, guns, and many other exhibits (look for the one on Alferd Packer, the infamous "Colorado Cannibal").

East of town, in **Clifton**, is the **Cross Orchards Historic Site** (3073 F. Road; tel: 970-434-9814; Apr–Oct most Thu–Sat 9am–4pm). This branch of the museum is living history at its best, recreating traditional farm life in one of Colorado's largest apple orchards. Exhibits include a blacksmith shop, a bunkhouse, a barn and packing house, and the historic orchards, where you can buy fruit in fall. Living history demonstrations take place daily between April and October, and there are numerous special events, including arts and crafts workshops and displays of traditional farming methods.

The most popular branch of the museum for children is **Dinosaur Journey** (550 Jurassic Ct, Fruita; tel: 970-858-7282; May–Sept daily 9am–5pm, Oct–Apr Mon–Sat 10am–4pm, Sun noon–4pm), west of town, in **Fruita**. Dinosaur Journey has a strong novelty feel, with its TV-generation exhibits and half-size robotic Dilophosaurus, Utahraptor, Apatosaurus, and other dinosaurs. But it is also perfectly located to teach kids about real-life paleontology. Just up the street, at the east and west entrances to Colorado National Monument, are **Riggs Hill** and **Dinosaur Hill**, where paleontologists from the museum conduct ongoing fossil digs. **Rabbit Valley Research Natural Area,** 24 miles (39km) west of Grand Junction, is another area rich in dinosaur bones.

Colorado National Monument ❷ (tel: 970-858-3617; www.nps.gov/colm; daily June–Sept 8am–6pm, Mar–May, Oct–Nov 9am–5pm, Dec–Feb 9am–4pm) is the top scenic drive in Grand Junction. From the west entrance at Fruita, 23-mile (37km) long **Rimrock Drive** winds onto 2,000ft (6,000-meter) high red rock cliffs on the south side of Grand Valley and is one of the most popular scenic mountain bike rides in an area famous for its biking. More than a dozen scenic vistas offer views of the Colorado River, Grand Junction, the Book Cliffs, Grand Mesa, and the eroded headlands, monument rocks and odd-shaped hoodoos of the monument. This landscape "felt like the heart of the world" to pioneer John Otto, who lived alone in the wild canyons. Otto built miles of trails through the area and helped get it set aside as a monument in 1911. He served as the park's first caretaker until 1927.

Campers can either spend the night in the park's pleasant 80-site campground near Saddlehorn Visitor Center (be warned: it gets busy), or turn south at East Glade Park Road and drive to a BLM campground within the 123,400-acre (49,938-hectare) **McInnis Canyons National Conservation Area ❸** (2815 H. Road, Grand Junction;

el: 970-244-3000; www.blm.gov/co/st/en/nca/mcnca.html). Designated in 2000, McInnis Canyons (formerly known as Colorado Canyons) is an extraordinary resource for Junction visitors and residents alike. You can hike a variety of trails in 75,500-acre (30,554-hectare) **Black Ridge Canyons Wilderness** (the sandstone arches of Rattlesnake Canyon are particularly memorable); mountain bike to Moab, Utah, on 137-mile (221km) **Kokopelli's Mountain Bike Trail**; and raft the canyons of the Colorado River from Loma Boat Launch through lovely **Ruby** and **Horsethief Canyons** to **Westwater Canyon**, Utah.

Dinosaur National Monument

Take your time making the three-hour drive along the winding scenic highway from Fruita through the **Book Cliffs** and **Piceance Basin** to reach Dinosaur National Monument, one of the best-kept secrets in the National Park System. On your way, look out for wild horses running in the Piceance Basin, part of several herds in the area managed by the Bureau of Land Management. Also of interest is the **Canyon Pintado National Historic District ❹**, which preserves the entrancing rock art left behind by Fremont Indians who lived in this river valley more than a thousand years ago. At **Rangely**, SR 139 joins SR 64 and enters an austere desert landscape of pale crumbly shales weather-blasted by erosion. Oil and gas are the mainstays of this hot, dusty town of see-sawing oil derricks, oversized trucks and cowboy hats, where the only water in sight is the **Kenney Reservoir** on the **White River**, just north of town.

Blink and you may miss tiny **Dinosaur**, 18 miles (29km) north of Rangely, gateway to the Colorado side of Dinosaur National Monument. Your first stop should be the **Colorado Welcome Center at Dinosaur** (101 E. Stegosaurus Avenue; tel: 970-374-2205), at the junction of SR 64 and US 40, where staff will help you use your time wisely and pass on priceless insider tips on good places to take photos, view wildlife, hike little-known trails, and even hang-glide – a popular sport on the cliffs above the serpentine canyons of Dinosaur. **Canyon**

McKee Springs petroglyph, Dinosaur National Monument.

BROWNS PARK

Browns Park is 80 miles (130km) northwest of Craig, via a rough road that crosses a swing bridge over the Green River into Browns Park National Wildlife Refuge. The valley was a rendezvous point in the 1820s and 1830s, where mountain men traded with Comanche, Ute, Cheyenne, Arapaho, and Navajo hunters. Homesteaders arrived in 1873, and by the 1880s, the valley's isolation attracted outlaws like Butch Cassidy and the Wild Bunch (see page 258), who used it as a remote hideout. The 44-mile (71km) section of the river between Little Hole Boat Launch and Little Swallows Canyon has Class I flatwater, several hiking trails, and free campgrounds. Private whitewater river trips through Dinosaur National Monument are by lottery permit only. Annual deadline for applications is February 1.

T. rex welcomes visitors to Fruita, home of Dinosaur Journey and the site of ongoing dinosaur excavation.

Geo-scientists measure cracks and stability in the rock containing the dinosaur bone beds, Dinosaur National Monument.

Visitor Center ❺ (4545 E. US 40, Dinosaur; tel: 970-374-3000; www.nps.gov/dino; May–Oct daily9am–5pm, Apr–May Sat-Sun 9am–5pm, closed in winter) is 2 miles (3km) east of the junction, on US 40, at the entrance to the Canyons section of the monument and has information and an audiovisual program on the park. Note: there are no dinosaur bones on the Colorado side of the park; they are all in the Utah section.

Remote and inaccessible, the Yampa River, which flows west to join the Green River in Echo Park in what is now Dinosaur National Monument, was a mystery to most early Americans. Fremont Indians and Utes had wandered there for centuries. The Spanish Dominguez-Escalante expedition of 1776 had passed to the south, through the fertile Colorado River valley, site of present-day Grand Junction, searching for a cross-country route to California from New Mexico. Fur trapper William Ashley was the first American to run the Green River in 1825, when rapids nearly destroyed his hide-covered bullboats.

But it wasn't until 1869 and 1871, when Major John Wesley Powell ran

the length of the Green and Colorado rivers in the first government survey of the region, that Americans glimpsed the treasures at the heart of Colorado's wild canyonlands. The expedition passed through a lovely red-walled canyon on the Green River that Powell named the Gates of Lodore. Later the men camped at a huge river bend where the Yampa joined the Green River and snaked around an 800ft (240-meter) high sandstone wall shaped like a ship's prow. The distinctive formation (later dubbed Steamboat Rock) magnified the sound of the men's voices. Powell called it Echo Canyon.

Yampa River Canyon

In 1928, A.G. Birch, a reporter for the *Denver Post*, decided to take a trip down the Yampa River. For three weeks, headlines such as "Expedition to Risk Death in Wild Region" and "Post's Expedition is Nearing Perilous Trip Down Canyon" captivated readers following Birch's adventures in the rugged almost unknown Colorado canyon country bordering Utah and Wyoming.

"There is nothing like the Yampa River Canyon that I have ever seen," he told his readers. "Imagine seven or eight Zion canyons strung together end to end; with Yosemite Valley dropped down in the middle of them; with half a dozen 'pockets' as weird and inspiring as Crater Lake; and a score of Devil's Towers plumbed down here and there for good measure – then you will just begin to get some conception of Yampa Canyon."

Birch's message was clear. The canyons of northwestern Colorado merited national park status. The National Park Service took note, sending out surveyors who concurred with Birch that the area was worthy of inclusion in the park system. How to accomplish this during the lean years of the Depression was another matter. Finally, in 1938 President Franklin D. Roosevelt quietly added 200,000 acres (81,000 hectares) of Colorado canyon country to the nearby Dinosaur National Monument.

Eighty-acre (32-hectare) Dinosaur National Monument had been set aside in 1915 to prevent the wholesale removal of an important quarry of dinosaur bones that had been found embedded in the fossil-rich Morrison Formation in 1909. But although the desert rocks surrounding the Colorado River in northeastern Utah held numerous dinosaur fossils, there were none deep in the billion-year-old canyons in northwestern Colorado, where the main features were extraordinary scenery, historic ranches, and abundant wildlife.

Wall of bones

If you have kids, you'll want to visit the **Dinosaur Quarry** on the Utah side of the monument first, then perhaps return to the Colorado side to spend time at the Canyons. The Dinosaur Quarry is a 45-minute drive from Dinosaur, 7 miles/11km north of Jensen, Utah, so plan accordingly.

The Dinosaur Quarry's central exhibit is its Wall of Bones, which contains 1,500 bones of 10 different dinosaur species, including Camarasaurus, Stegosaurus, Diplodocus, and Dryosaurus, first discovered here in 1909 by Carnegie Museum paleontologist Earl Douglass. Since then, excavations have uncovered more than 2,000 bones of dinosaurs embedded in the Morrison Formation. This is probably just a fraction of the number of dinosaurs that were entombed here when a catastrophic river flood wiped them out 150 million years ago. The clay rocks of the Morrison Formation may have yielded dinosaur treasures but they have unfortunately proven very unstable for structures, and in 2006, the Dinosaury Quarry was forced to close for safety reasons. In 2009, the Park Service received $13.1 million in stimulus funds to create the attractive new **Quarry Visitor Center** (tel: 435- 781-7700; daily May–Sept 8am–6pm, Sept–Dec 9am–5pm). The former visitor center now houses the **Quarry Exhibit Hall** (May–Sept 8am–5:30pm; limited access by vehicle caravan from the visitor center rest of the year), which is supported by 70-ft steel micropile columns that extend into the clay formation and keep the Wall of Bones stable. During visitor center hours in summer, regular shuttle bus takes visitors from the visitor center to the exhibit hall, ¼ -mile (0.4km) away.

This part of the monument sits on the Green River, below Split Mountain, a huge tilting, geological anticline with a plated profile that looks oddly like a stegosaurus (it's easy to get dinosaurs on the brain here). Geology is a big part of the story of Dinosaur. The park displays 23 different geological formations, the most complete geological record of any national park. That tops even the Grand Canyon.

The 22-mile (35km) **Tilted Rocks Scenic Drive** offers a closer look at Split Mountain and the Green River, both of which have campgrounds for hikers and river runners. Signs of human occupation can be seen all along this easily accessible road. A prehistoric rock shelter that was used by Paleo-Indians as long ago as 7,000 BC can be viewed at the start of the scenic drive; it has many examples of Fremont

WHERE
Northwestern Colorado and northeastern Utah are part of the huge Dinosaur Diamond Scenic Byway, which includes Riggs Hill, Dinosaur Hill, and Rabbit Valley Research Natural Area in Fruita, and, of course, Dinosaur National Monument.

Pottery at the Museum of Western Colorado.

Indian art. At the end of the road, in Cub Creek, you'll find the fascinating **Josie Bassett Morris Homestead**. Morris was a pioneer who spent her early years in Browns Park, just north of Dinosaur park, and knew Butch Cassidy. She moved to Cub Creek a year before Dinosaur became a national monument and was well known locally. When she died in 1964, her homestead became part of the expanded park.

Canyon country

Morris wasn't the only homesteader drawn to Dinosaur's spectacular river canyon setting. In the early 1900s, Ralph Chew, originally from Blackburn in Lancashire, England, built a ranch on a tributary of the Green River, close to Echo Park, in the Canyons section of the park. The Chew family continues to ranch in Dinosaur, but the historic ranch, including a well-preserved chuck wagon, log cabins, and corrals, is now part of the park and can be seen along the rugged, 13-mile (21km) drive down to Echo Canyon. The Chew Ranch is one of the highlights of the 23-mile (37km) **Harpers**

Hopi Kachina dolls at the Museum of Western Colorado. The dolls are not toys for children, but are effigies that embody the masked spirits of the Hopi tribe.

Corner Scenic Drive to Harper's Corner in the eastern section of the park. It's easy to see what drew the Chews, the Mantles, the Ruples, and other early ranchers: a sense of space, abundant grass, reliable water, and plenty of game, from elk to deer to jackrabbits.

If you're here in summer and you have a four-wheel-drive, high-clearance vehicle, plan on spending at least one night in the popular campground at **Echo Park**, where history and landscape are at their most beguiling. This is one of the most beautiful canyon settings in the Southwest and a perfect place to tune into the ancient rhythms of rock, sky, and river. Gentle breezes on the river brush across your face at night as you sleep, and rangers offer nightly skywatching and campfire talks, and morning hikes through the cottonwoods along the river. Next day, drive the **Yampa Bench Road**, east of Echo Park, which has a number of sights, including historic cabins, river views and the Mantle Ranch, still a private holding here. Before leaving, continue to the end of the Harpers Corner Scenic Drive and hike the 2-mile

THE FIGHT FOR ECHO PARK

Throughout the 1940s, out-of-the-way Dinosaur National Monument remained a well-kept secret, but in the early 1950s the park found itself at the center of a major controversy over government plans to construct huge dams at Echo Park and Split Mountain. The Sierra Club and more than 70 other environmental organizations formed an unprecedented alliance and successfully defeated the irrigation project. Many people still recall that their introduction to Dinosaur came through a flurry of outraged magazine and newspaper articles aimed at saving the park's canyons from immersion under a huge reservoir.

Backed by respected Western writers Bernard de Voto and Wallace Stegner, landscape photographer Philip Hyde and newly named "environmentalists" like the Sierra Club's David Brower, Dinosaur became the poster child for a growing anti-development struggle in America. Nationwide support for saving wild lands in Dinosaur paved the way for the landmark 1964 Wilderness Act. Outdoor lovers came out to run the rivers they had saved and to camp at Echo Park, but the victory at Dinosaur was overshadowed in 1962 by the flooding of Glen Canyon, north of Grand Canyon, "The Place No One Knew," a defeat that cast a long shadow over the environmental movement. Dinosaur returned to obscurity. For another generation, it was just a park of old bones.

(3km) **Harpers Corner Trail** for views of Whirlpool Canyon and the massive Mittens Fault in the Weber Sandstone.

Wild West

Finish your tour by returning to Grand Junction through the eastern portion of the Piceance Basin. You can take the fast route on US 40 to **Craig ❻**, a major coal-mining town. The main attraction in town is the interesting **Museum of Northwestern Colorado** (590 Yampa Avenue; tel: 970-824-6360; www. museumnwco.org; Mon–Fri 9am–5pm, Sat 10am–4pm; free), which displays one of the West's largest collections of cowboy and gunfighter memorabilia.

A more scenic drive crosses the basin's heart on SR 64, following the pretty White River through Rangely to **Meeker ❼**. Meeker (pop. 2,493) is a quiet, historic town surrounded by national forest, making it a popular outdoor-lover's getaway. It was named for a naive but well-intentioned missionary, Nathan Meeker, who came to the White River Ute Indian Agency in the 1870s. Meeker's plan to teach the Utes how to farm was met with stiff resistance from the tribe, whose beliefs taught them to live in harmony with what nature provided and forbade tilling the soil as a desecration of Mother Earth. The cultural clash ended tragically when Meeker plowed up the tribal racetrack, an important social area for this horse-loving people, and he and eight others were murdered, along with several soldiers. Unfortunately, their actions played right into the hands of government officials who, despite the intervention of Chief Ouray, used the massacre to justify removing the Utes from Colorado, thereby opening the way for white settlement.

You can learn more about this sad story at the **White River Museum** (565 Park Street; tel: 970-878-9982; www.meekercolorado.com/museum.htm; daily Apr–Nov 9am–5pm, Dec–Mar 10am–4pm; free) in Meeker, housed in an old log-cabin army barracks in the town center. On the opposite side of the plaza is the Victorian-era **Meeker Hotel & Café** (560 Main Street; tel: 970-878-5255; www.themeekerhotel.com), built in 1896. This hunting lodge–style hotel's illustrious guest list includes Teddy and Franklin Roosevelt, Billy the Kid and, more recently, Dick Cheney, who, like many outdoorsmen, enjoyed hunting and fishing in **White River National Forest**.

SR 13 heads south for 39 miles (63km) to the town of **Rifle ❽**, where you can join I-70 to return to Grand Junction or turn south to pick up the **Grand Mesa Scenic Byway**. Take a short detour to **Rifle Falls State Park** (5775 SR 325; tel: 970-625-1607, 5am–10pm). Exiting from nearby mountains, **East Rifle Creek** has created a lush year-round oasis in a dry land, where water from the creek spills over a limestone cliff, creating three waterfalls. In 1910, the waterfalls were used to power Rifle Hydroelectric Plant, the first in Colorado. A brief stroll takes you to the falls, then a short, steep climb leads to the top. Rifle has a year-round campground that makes the perfect place to cool down before heading back to the sizzling Grand Valley.

Rifle Falls State Park.

Sunset in Sedgwick County, near the Nebraskan border.

TRAVEL TIPS
COLORADO

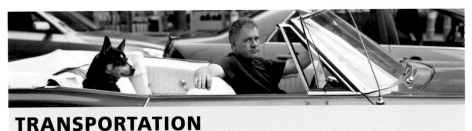

TRANSPORTATION

GETTING THERE AND GETTING AROUND

From the United States

Two major interstates – the north–south I-25 and east–west I-70 – and several major US highways that ring the western and southern Rocky Mountains serve Colorado, but distances between major cities are so great, even within the region, it frequently makes more sense to fly in from elsewhere in the US. For example, Albuquerque, in the adjoining state of New Mexico, is about an eight-hour drive from the Denver Metro Area, even taking I-25 all the way and traveling at 75mph (120kmh), the speed limit.

From more distant states, including California, you will almost certainly want to fly. Both nearby Colorado Springs and Grand Junction in Western Colorado have small commuter airports served by regional airlines, but even so, you are going to find better prices if you fly into Denver and rent a car to get where you are going.

From abroad

All major international airlines serve Denver International Airport, one of the busiest airports in the United States, and this is invariably the airport of choice for international arrivals in Colorado, due to its proximity to the Denver Metro Area and competitive air fares and car rental charges.

By air

Colorado is served by two major airports – Denver and Colorado Springs. The $4.3 billion **Denver**

International Airport (8500 Pena Boulevard; tel: 303-342-2000; www.flydenver.com), also known as DEN, ranked in the Top 10 airports internationally, is the largest airport in the US (twice the size of Manhattan), has a landing rate of 120 planes an hour, and is currently the 18th busiest airport in the world, accommodating more than 54 million passengers in 2015. The 1.4-million sq ft (130,000 sq meter) terminal building is a distinctive architectural landmark. The roof is constructed of a Teflon-coated fabric shaped into 34 peaks, which symbolize the Rocky Mountains or – depending on who you ask – the tepees of Arapaho and Cheyenne Indians who once camped along the South Platte River.

The following carriers serve Denver International Airport:
Aeromexico, tel: 800-237-6639; www.aeromexico.com
Air Canada, tel: 800-247-2262; www.aircanada.com
Alaska Air, tel: 800-ALASKAAIR; www.alaskaair.com
American, tel: 800-433-7300; www.aa.com
Boutique Air, tel: 855-268-8478; www.boutiqueair.com
British Airways, tel: 800-AIRWAYS; www.britishairways.com
Delta, tel: 800-221-1212; www.delta.com
Denver Air Connection, tel: 855-235-9322; www.denverairconnection.com
Frontier Airlines, tel: 801-401-9000; www.frontierairlines.com
Great Lakes Airlines, tel: 800-554-5111; www.greatlakesav.com
Icelandair, tel: 800-223-5500; www.icelandair.com
JetBlue Airways, tel: 800-538-2583; www.jetblue.com

Lufthansa, tel: 800-645-3880; www.lufthansa.com
Southwest Airlines, tel: 800-435-9792; www.southwest.com
Spirit Airlines, tel: 801-401-2222; www.spirit.com
Sun Country Airlines, tel: 800-359-6786
United, tel: 800-864-8331; www.united.com
Virgin America, tel: 877-359-8474; www.virginamerica.com
Volaris, tel: 866-988-3527; www.volaris.mx

Colorado Springs Airport (tel: 719-550-1900; www.springsgov.com/airport/index) is served by Alaska, American, Delta, and United, as well as **Allegiant Air**, tel: 702-505-8888; www.allegiant.com

Travelers wishing to visit western Colorado can make connections to Grand Junction Regional **Airport** (tel: 970-244-9100; www.gjairport.com) in Grand Junction, which is served by Allegiant Air, American/American Eagle, Delta, United, and US Airways.

A note about security: Stricter airport security is expected to continue indefinitely and will impose some constraints on passengers and visitors. Keep these guidelines in mind as you prepare for your flight.

Allow plenty of time for check-in prior to your scheduled departure time. As much as two hours may be required. Anticipate very long lines at airline ticket counters, increased security screening, and other delays. Your airline can advise you in advance of how much extra time to allow.

The Transportation Security Administration (TSA) is responsible for the passenger screening at the security checkpoint. For more information about screening policies, visit www.tsa.gov.

New baggage restrictions allow only one carry-on bag and one personal item such as a purse, briefcase, or laptop computer per passenger (laptops must be removed from their case and placed in a separate tray for screening). Liquids in hand luggage are restricted to one small baggie containing 3oz containers; if you exceed this, you will be required to dispose of the items. Many airlines now charge for checking bags. If you have more items than allowed, you will be asked to go back and check the extra items at the ticket counter. Full-body x-ray scanners and patdowns for those choosing not to – or unable to – go through the scanners were introduced at Denver International Airport by TSA.

By bus

One of the least expensive ways to travel in America is by interstate bus. The largest national bus company is **Greyhound**, tel: 800-231-2222; www.greyhound.com. The company routinely offers discounts such as go-anywhere fares. A Discovery Pass (available online at www.discoverypass.

Green Travel

For a low-impact vacation, take the train to Denver and get around using RTD light rail and bus; taxis in Colorado are often hybrid vehicles such as the Toyota Prius. It's easy to reach small ski towns in the mountains by shuttle, or rent a hybrid vehicle to get there. Sightseeing trams operate in and around historic downtowns like Telluride and Aspen, and old mining towns like Durango and Georgetown have narrow-gauge scenic trains for excursions into the valleys. Ski resorts now compete with one another to operate sustainably by recycling, using longlife CFL bulbs, and reducing water use. Many communities have weekly farmers' markets and eateries serving locally sourced food. You can even stay on a farm and pick your own food, if you like, or help restore habitat on a Nature Conservancy property or mountain trail. Ambitious bikers may want to sign up for the four-day, 238-mile (383km) Colorado Peace Ride (www.thepeaceride.com) along the narrow winding San Juan Skyway, a fundraiser for the Sophia Peace Center and Volunteers of America.

com) offers unlimited travel for 7, 15, 30, or 60 days. Greyhound serves more than 60 locations in Colorado, including Alamosa, Boulder, Cañon City, Colorado Springs, Denver, Durango, Englewood, Fort Collins, Fort Morgan, Frisco, Glenwood Springs, Grand Junction, Greeley, Gunnison, Idaho Springs, Pueblo, Salida, Silverton, Steamboat Springs, Vail, and Winter Park. A rental car or other transportation is necessary to reach remote locations.

By car

Colorado can be reached via three major interstate highways. I-25 heads north from New Mexico and climbs Raton Pass to enter southeast Colorado at Trinidad and continues north, with the Front Range on the left and the Plains on the right, all the way to Denver, then north into Wyoming. In Denver, I-25 is joined by I-70 from Kansas and I-76 from Nebraska. Busy I-70 forms the most traveled east–west route across the Colorado Rockies to Utah, providing access to major ski resorts like Breckenridge, Vail, Aspen, Steamboat Springs, and the towns of Glenwood Springs and Grand Junction in northwestern Colorado. Elsewhere in Colorado, US highways wind around and through the Rockies. From Nebraska, US 50 passes through Lamar and La Junta, crosses I-25 at Pueblo, and continues west to Salida, Poncha Springs, and Gunnison to connect with US 550 at Montrose, the main north–south route on the Western Slope. Between Durango and Montrose, US 550 is known as the San Juan Skyway Scenic Byway. From Montrose it continues north to Grand Junction. US 160 begins from I-25 at Walsenburg and passes through Alamosa and Monte Vista to Pagosa Springs and Durango in southwestern Colorado. US 285 enters southern Colorado south of Antonito and follows the Rio Grande Valley into the heart of the Rockies, passing Salida, Buena Vista, and Fairplay to join I-70 at the main interchange south of Boulder, in Golden.

By train

Amtrak offers more than 500 destinations across the US. The trains are comfortable and reliable, with lounges, dining cars, snack bars and, in some cases, movies and live entertainment. Most routes offer sleeper cars with private cabins in addition to regular seating.
Amtrak's California Zephyr runs from Chicago to San Francisco, with

stops in Colorado at Fort Morgan, Denver, Winter Park, Granby, Glenwood Springs, and Grand Junction. The Southwest Chief runs from Chicago to Los Angeles and stops at Lamar, Trinidad, and La Junta.
Ask about two- or three-stopover discounts, senior citizens' and children's discounts, and Amtrak's package tours. International travelers can buy a USA Railpass, good for 15 to 30 days of unlimited travel on Amtrak throughout the United States. Contact Amtrak (tel: 800-872-7245; www.amtrak.com) for detailed scheduling.

GETTING AROUND

Its nickname says it all: Rocky Mountain State. Two-thirds of Colorado consists of high mountains, with a third of the state, on its east side, made up of the flat Great Plains. The major travel corridors are the paved all-weather highways of I-25, I-70, US 550/50, and US 160, which ring the mountains. **Mountain highways**, such as scenic US 285, make for pleasant driving through historic mining areas but are frequently challenging in winter due to heavy snowfall in the high Rockies.
Denver is the state capital and the main city in Colorado. Many first-time visitors are surprised to find out that Denver is not actually in the Rocky Mountain Front Range but sits on the flat Plains, about 25 miles (40km) east of the Rockies, with the high peaks of Rocky Mountain National Park in view to the west and the dusty plains spooling out to the east.
A modern city of skyscrapers, freeways, and malls, Denver is notable for its historic downtown buildings, museums, and parks and natural areas linked by an extensive trail system. The South Platte River, an urban waterway, passes through Denver. Interstate 25, the main north–south route, passes close to the heart of downtown Denver and landmarks like Invesco Field. Interstate 70 connects northeastern Denver with the Northern Rockies and is the main cross-mountain route for the state.
Because this is a farflung area, transportation is mainly by personal vehicle (highways are very clogged around Denver but quite pleasant, if more remote and mountainous, the farther you get from the state capital). All major car rental companies are located at the airport, where rates are the best.

Distances and driving times

Denver–Boulder: 29 miles/47km (0.5 hr)
Denver–Colorado Springs: 69 miles/111km (1.25 hrs)
Denver–Fort Collins: 65 miles/104km (1.25 hrs)
Denver–Estes Park: 65 miles/104km (1.5 hrs)

Denver–Glenwood Springs: 157 miles/253km (2.5 hrs)
Denver–Steamboat Springs: 166 miles/267km (3.5 hrs)
Denver–Aspen: 159 miles/256km (3.75 hrs)
Denver–Crested Butte: 228 miles/367km (4.75 hrs)

Shuttles run from Denver International Airport to Denver and communities in the Metro Area. Ski resorts also offer private mountain shuttles from the airport to resorts in the mountains. A public bus system is convenient for many commuters within the Denver area, and well-priced if you are on a budget. Some cities, such as Trinidad and Durango, now have free trams linking attractions in their historic downtown core.

Light rail service links outlying communities within the Denver Metro Area with downtown Denver and is a good option if you are staying outside the downtown area.

To and from Denver International Airport

As of April 2016, Denver RTD's newly opened **University of Colorado A Line** offers a much-anticipated direct link between Denver Union Station and Denver International Airport using faster rail cars than light rail. Regularly scheduled service begins at 3:15am from Union Station and continues until 1am, taking 37 minutes from station to station. RTD also runs **Skyride Public Bus Service** between the airport and Denver Tech/Aurora, Boulder, and Northglenn/Thornton. Cost is $9 for either rail or bus. For more information about routes and schedules, tel: 303-299-6000; www.rtd-denver.com/airport.

For door-to-door service, commuter shuttles pick up travelers at their home, office, or hotel throughout the Denver Metro Area and transport them at a reasonable cost via shared minivan to Denver International Airport, 23 miles (14km) northeast of the city, a journey that can take anything from a half-hour to an hour, depending on destination and time of day. **Denver Super Shuttle** (tel: 303-370-1300; www.supershuttle.com/locations/DenverDEN) is one such service. Some hotels also offer shuttles between the airport and Denver. Inquire on booking.
Colorado Mountain Express

(tel: 970-7547433; www.coloradomountainexpress.com) links the airport with the ski towns of Vail, Beaver Creek, Breckenridge, Copper Mountain, Keystone, Aspen, and Snowmass. A number of companies offer **private limousine service** to pick you up or take you to the airport. Taxis run between the airport and the eight counties that make up Denver Metro Area. Note: taxis offer flat-rate service to the airport from throughout the Denver Metro Area. For example, $55.57 from downtown Denver and $88.57 from Boulder.

By bicycle

Bicycle riding verges on an obsession in Colorado for many people. This is the home of commuting long distances by bike on a network of trails throughout the Denver Metro Area, cycle touring on winding highways, and taking part in road races like the Iron Horse Classic from Durango to Silverton and fat tire festivals in mountain towns like Crested Butte, which invented the mountain bike. Bicycle Colorado (1525 Market Street, Suite 100, Denver, CO 80202; tel: 303-417-1544; www.bicyclecolorado.org) is an excellent resource for cyclists.

By bus

As noted above, RTD bus service (www.rtd-denver.com) links Denver, Aurora, and Boulder in concert with Denver's light rail system. Most larger Colorado cities, such as Grand Junction and Pueblo, have local bus services. A number of mining and ski resort communities operate sightseeing trams in their downtown historic districts, including Trinidad, Salida, Vail, Aspen, Telluride, and Estes Park. Most buses in Colorado allow bicycles on the buses.

By car

Driving is the most convenient way to travel in Colorado, especially outside the major cities. Major roads are well maintained, although some backcountry roads may be unpaved. If you plan on driving into remote areas or in heavy snow, mud, or severe weather, it's best to use a four-wheel-drive vehicle with high clearance. Jeeps are very popular for off-road travel in Ouray.

Driving in remote areas

If you plan to drive in uninhabited areas, carry a spare tire and extra water – at least 1 gallon (4 liters) per person per day. A cell phone is a good idea, too, though some areas may be out of range of the nearest communications tower. Gas stations can be few and far between in remote areas. Not every town will have one, and many close early. It's always better to have more fuel than you think you will need.

Maps and information

Your greatest asset as a driver is a good road map. Maps can be obtained from state tourism offices, AAA, gas stations, supermarkets, and convenience stores. Although roads are maintained even in remote areas, it is advisable to monitor road conditions by checking local radio and TV, the website for Colorado Department of Transportation (CDOT.gov), or by asking local officials, especially in winter or if planning to leave paved roads. Mountain passes are often closed by heavy snowfall in winter.

A word of caution: If your car breaks down on a backroad, do not

AAA Membership

Anyone spending a significant amount of time driving US highways is strongly advised to join the Automobile Association of America (Triple A). Benefits include emergency breakdown service, excellent road maps, travel literature, and personalized trip planning, as well as discounts at motels like Best Western and other chains. Premier level offers towing up to 200 miles (320km) from breakdown site – important if you are in the middle of nowhere – and lockout, refueling and jumpstart service. Insurance is also available through the association, which has a reciprocal arrangement with some of the automobile associations in other countries. Tel: 800-874-7532 or visit www.aaa.com. In Denver: AAA, 4100 E. Arkansas Drive, Denver CO 80222; tel: 800-222-4357.

A pedi-cab peddles the Sixteenth Street Mall in downtown Denver.

attempt to strike out on foot, even with water. A car is easier to spot than a person and provides shelter from the elements. If you don't have a cell phone or your phone doesn't work, sit tight and wait to be found.

Vehicle rental

Car rentals

Auto rental agencies are located at all airports, in cities, and many large towns. In most places, you must be at least 21 years old (25 at some locations) to rent a car and you must have a valid driver's license and at least one major credit card. Drivers under 25 may have to pay an extra fee, as will additional drivers. Foreign drivers must have an international driver's license. Be sure that you are properly insured for both collision and personal liability. Insurance won't be included in the base rental fee. Insurance cost varies depending on the car and the type of coverage, but it is usually $15–35 per day. If you are a US resident, you may already be covered by your own auto insurance or credit card company, so check with them first.

Most rentals include unlimited mileage. Rental fees often vary depending on the time of year, location, how far in advance you book your rental and if you travel on weekdays or weekends.

Inquire about discounts or benefits for which you may be eligible, including corporate, credit card, or frequent-flyer programs.

Advantage, tel: 720-324-2260; www.advantage.com
Alamo, tel: 877-222-9075; www.alamo.com
Avis, tel: 303-342-5500; www.avis.com
Budget, tel: 800-527-0700; www.budget.com
Dollar, tel: 303=317-0598; www.dollar.com
E-Z, tel: 800-277-5171; www.e-zrentacar.com
Enterprise, tel: 800-261-7331; www.enterprise.com
Hertz, tel: 800-654-3131; www.hertz.com
National, tel: 877-222-9058; www.nationalcar.com
Payless, tel: 800-PAYLESS; www.payless.com
Thrifty, tel: 800-367-2277; www.thrifty.com

RV rentals

No special license is necessary to operate a motor home (or recreational vehicle – RV for short), but they aren't cheap. When you add up the cost of rental fees, insurance, gas, and campsites, renting a car and staying in motels or camping may be less expensive.

Keep in mind, too, that RVs are large and slow and may be difficult to handle on narrow mountain roads. If parking space is tight, driving an RV may be extremely inconvenient. Still, RVs are very popular, and some travelers swear by them. For additional information about RV rentals, call the Recreational Vehicle Rental Association, tel: 703-591-7130; www.rvra.org.

By light rail

Denver's **RTD Light Rail** (www.rtd-denver.com/lightrail.shtml) serves central, southeast, and southwest Denver. Scheduled trains on seven lines stop at 52 stations between 5:30am and 1:30am. Scenic **narrow-gauge railroads** link small mining towns in the Central and South Rockies, including Durango & Silverton Narrow Gauge Railroad, Cumbres and Toltec Scenic Railroad, Cripple Creek and Victor Narrow Gauge Railroad, Georgetown Loop, and the Royal Gorge diesel train. The Pikes Peak Cog Railroad operates on Pikes Peak near Colorado Springs. Wilderness packers can arrange to ride the Durango & Silverton train and get off and hike back along parts of the 500-mile (805km) Colorado Trail.

By taxi

There are 16 taxi companies in Denver. The largest, **Metro Taxi** (tel: 303-333-3333; www.metrotaxidenver. com), has the city's largest green fleet.

A – Z

A HANDY SUMMARY
OF PRACTICAL INFORMATION

A

Accommodations

Colorado accommodations range from rustic cabins to extravagant resorts. Resorts, spas, and dude ranches are destinations in themselves. Make reservations well ahead of the high season – winter in ski areas and summer in mountain resorts. Budget travelers may find off-season discounts. Self-contained destinations will be the most expensive and, in Colorado, include ski-in and ski village resort condos and hotels, small boutique and restored grande dame hotels in historic downtowns, and national park gateway communities like Estes Park and Durango. Lavish resorts and dude ranches are in a category by themselves. Dude ranches, in particular, operate on a multi-day, all-in American Plan basis, including lodging, food, and all activities. You will find attractive, inexpensive, well-run campgrounds throughout Colorado, as well as some good

hostels in places like Denver. Chain motels may be bland but they are reliable. For accommodations listings, see the free app that comes with your book. Instructions on how to download it feature on page 2 of this book.

Admission charges

Admission is usually charged at both private and public museums and attractions and national and state parks. As a rule, entrance fees are $10 or under per person, although very popular sites, such as Rocky Mountain National Park and special traveling exhibits at nationally known museums, may charge as much as $20. Museums often offer free or reduced entrance fees certain days or evenings.

Consider buying **multisite passes** for attractions in Denver, if available. Local visitor centers and state welcome centers can assist you with planning and many also offer discount coupons, with excellent deals on local attractions, hotels, and dining.

National Park Passes

Most parks charge an entrance fee, usually $10–25, which allows unrestricted vehicle entry for a car and up to four passengers for one week. If you plan on visiting several national parks on your vacation, or to return within a year, you should buy **America the Beautiful Annual Pass** ($80). Passes are available at the entrance gate to national parks that charge admission or may be purchased online or by

phone (www.store.usgs.gov/pass; tel: 888-ask-usgs.) If you wish to support a particular national park, buy your pass at the site, as the park will get to keep at least 80 percent of the fee. The pass offers access to all public lands managed by the National Park Service, US Forest Service, US Fish and Wildlife Service, Bureau of Land Management, and Bureau of Reclamation.

B

Budgeting for your trip

The US remains a good buy for travelers, especially those traveling around by auto, where the main cost will be car rental, gas, lodging, and food, and you can search out bargains en route. You can save considerably if you camp, stay in budget motels, eat in hometown cafés like the locals, and purchase food direct from farm stands and farmers' markets for picnics, easy to do in Colorado, one of the top ranching and agricultural states in the country. Boulder Farmers' Market, for example, has an extraordinary selection of prepared foods, including wine.

Allow $80–100 a day for good-quality motels for two people; really memorable hotels and bed-and-breakfasts tend to run $125–175 per night and offer a good way to connect quickly with the local scene. At the other end of the spectrum, you'll find an array of attractive, well-run campgrounds throughout Colorado for $16–25 a night; hostels are often a great budget choice in Colorado (there are excellent ones in Denver and Salida) and tend to run from $30–50, depending on whether you bunk in a dorm or have a private room. Reliable budget chain motels are in the $60–80 range (look for AAA discounts and online deals at chains like Best Western and La Quinta).

You can probably squeak by with $30 per day per person for food, if you stick to basic diners, cafés, markets, farm stands, food trucks, and inexpensive restaurants, especially ethnic ones, and make breakfast your main meal, eating more lightly

Children play in an old-fashioned sack race in Cañon City.

for lunch and dinner, and avoiding alcohol. However, if the high-elevation Rocky Mountain air doesn't get you high, you can always tour Colorado's many fine microbreweries, wineries, and distilleries to enjoy free and low-cost tastings of Colorado microbrew ales, wines, and even whiskey (Stranahan's Distillery in Denver).

Meals in better restaurants cost a lot more, but if you're determined to visit a famous high-end establishment and don't have the cash, book for lunch instead: you'll find many dinner menu items at much lower prices.

Budget $2.50–$3 per gallon for gas costs for your rental car; most economy vehicles get over 30 miles (48km) per gallon, but if you plump for the four-wheel-drive (a good idea on Colorado's rugged backroads at any time of year, and vital on most roads in winter), you'll likely get only around 20 miles (32km) per gallon. Inexpensive or free trams, light rail, buses, and other public transportation are available in Denver and other cities, such as Trinidad and Grand Junction, as well as ski resort towns.

C

Camping

Most campgrounds in national and state parks and forests are now on a central reservation system (essential during peak summer season), with just a few campsites available on a first-come, first-served basis. Both www.recreation.gov and www.reserveamerica.com offer online campground reservations at public lands managed by 12 federal participating partners, including the USDA Forest Service, Army Corps of Engineers, National Park Service, Bureau of Land Management, Bureau of Reclamation, Boundary Waters Canoe Area Wilderness, U.S.

Fish and Wildlife Service, and National Archives & Records Administration. Colorado State Parks can be reserved by logging on to www.coloradostate parks.reserveamerica.com; tel: 800-678-2267. Fees are charged for developed campsites; free dispersed camping is allowed in national forests. Permits are required for backcountry camping in parks.

Children

Two things about traveling with children: first, be prepared and second, don't expect to cover too much ground – think quality not quantity. Take everything you need, along with a general first-aid kit, and wet wipes, and Ziplock baggies. Away from the Front Range and ski resort towns, Colorado is primarily a state of remote mountain towns, with limited supplies and often no nearby hospital. If you need baby formula, special foods, diapers, or medication, carry them with you.

Colorado's Front Range communities, ski resort towns like Aspen in the Central Rockies, and Western Slope communities like Grand Junction and Durango have museums and activities geared toward families. Away from towns, make sure that mountains, backcountry areas, and parks are suitable for kids. Are there abandoned mine shafts, steep stairways and trails, cliffs, or other hazards? Is a lot of walking necessary? Are food, water, shelter, bathrooms, and other essentials available at the site? Everyone should be careful of dehydration in this high-elevation state by drinking plenty of water before and during outdoor activities and eating high-energy foods. Don't push children beyond their limits. Rest often and allow for extra napping. Good advice for adults on vacation, too.

Climate

What to wear

With few exceptions, Western dress is informal and geared toward practical clothing for enjoying the outdoors. A pair of jeans or slacks, a polo or button-down shirt, and boots or shoes are appropriate at all but the fanciest places and events. Shorts and light shirts are suitable for most situations in the warmer months, though. Year round, be sure everyone wears sunscreen with an SPF of at least 30, polarized eye protection, a broad-brimmed hat protecting the neck, layered clothing with sleeves and legs that can be rolled down as sun protection, and sturdy hiking sandals or boots that secure the foot for walking on rough ground – no flip-flops or flimsy shoes.

If you're hiking, a thin, inner polypropylene sock and a thick, outer sock will help keep your feet dry and comfortable. Blisters or sore spots can develop quickly. Cover them with moleskin or surgical tape, available at most pharmacies or camping supply stores. Bring a warm cover-up and rain shell; even in summer, high country weather can be cool and suddenly rainy.

When to visit

Colorado is a popular four-season state for tourism. It spans a wide range of climate and life zones, but generally has sunny skies, low humidity, and limited precipitation. Climate varies widely with elevation. Climbing 1,000ft (300 meters) is equivalent to traveling 300 miles

Environmental ethics

Remember the old saying: "Take nothing but pictures, leave nothing but footprints." The goal of low-impact/no-impact backpacking is to leave the area in the same condition as you found it, if not better. If you're camping in the backcountry, don't break branches, level the ground, or alter the landscape in any way. Make fires in designated places only. Otherwise, use a portable camping stove. When nature calls, answer with a trowel: dig a hole 6ins (15cm) deep and at least 200ft (60 meters) from water, campsites and trails. Take away all trash, including toilet paper. Ziplock bags and Dr. Bronner's eco-friendly peppermint soap are a camper's best friend.

TRANSPORTATION

A – Z

CLIMATE CHART

Denver

Legend:
- ■ Maximum temperature
- □ Minimum temperature
- — Rainfall

(500km) northward. Conditions atop the highest peaks are akin to those in the Arctic. There are even a few permanent ice fields like St. Mary's Glacier, the southernmost glacier in North America.

Colorado enjoys 295 days of sunshine annually. The climate is semi-arid. Yearly precipitation ranges from 16ins (41cm) on the eastern plains and 14ins (36cm) in the Front Range to less than 10ins (25cm) on the Western Slope. Most rain falls in brief, intense thunderstorms during the summer season, when small streams, dry washes, and narrow canyons are prone to flash floods. Violent electrical storms are common on mountain peaks during summer afternoons. Nights in the mountains can be chilly even in July and August, and winds are often brisk, so bring a sweater or jacket. Snow, hail, and sleet are possible at the highest elevations at any time of year.

The spring thaw usually begins in March, though snow lingers well into July on the highest peaks and passes. Summer weather begins in late June or early July. Fall begins in September,

Photographing wild elk in Rocky Mountain National Park.

a lovely period of sunny days, chilly nights, and spectacular colors on the Rockies' forested slopes. Winter sets in by late November, though ski areas such as Arapahoe Basin and Loveland sometimes open as early as late October (with the aid of snow-making machines) and close in June.

Average high temperatures in summer reach 88°F (31°C) in **Denver** (elev. 5,280ft/1,609 meters), 94°F (34°C) in **Grand Junction** (elev. 4,586ft/1,398 meters), and 80°F (27°C) in **Aspen** (7,773ft/2,369m). Nights are crisp and pleasant, usually ranging from 45°F (7°C) to 65°F (18°C).

Winter is very chilly but often sunny, with average lows of 16°F (-9°C) in Denver and Grand Junction, and 6°F (-14°C) in Aspen. Annual snowfall in Denver is typically 45–65ins (114–65cm), though warm spells between storms reduce large accumulations. Annual snowfall in excess of 300ins (760cm) is common in the ski areas around Aspen. Winter storms roll into Colorado from the Pacific, lose moisture over the desert Southwest, and then dump piles of the light, dry powder for which the Rocky Mountains are famous.

Crime and safety

A few common-sense precautions will help keep you safe while traveling in Colorado. For starters, know where you are and where you're going. Whether traveling on foot or by car, bring a map and plan your route in advance. Don't be shy about asking for directions. Most people are happy to help

Don't carry large sums of cash or wear flashy or expensive jewelry. Lock unattended cars, and keep your belongings in the trunk. If possible, travel with a companion, especially after dark.

Carry a cell phone. Few items are more useful if you are lost, have

had an accident, need to report an emergency, or your car has broken down. However, don't rely on GPS or cell phone service: in the mountains, many places have no signal.

If involved in a traffic accident, remain at the scene. It is illegal to leave. If you have no cell phone, or no signal, find a nearby telephone or ask a passing motorist to call the police, then wait for emergency vehicles to arrive.

Driving under the influence of alcohol carries stiff penalties, including fines and jail. Wearing seat belts is required. Children under four must be in a child's safety seat.

Customs regulations

Everyone entering the United States must go through US Customs, often a time-consuming process. You may now bring in duty-free gifts worth up to $800 (American residents) or $100 (foreign travelers). Visitors over 18 may bring in 200 cigarettes, a reasonable amount of tobacco, 4.4lbs (2 kilos) of smoking tobacco, and 100 cigars; quantities permitted are higher for US residents. Those over 21 may bring in 1 US quart (1 liter) of alcohol. Travelers with more than $10,000 in US or foreign currency, traveler's checks, or money orders must declare these upon entry. Among prohibited goods are meat or meat products, illegal drugs, firearms, seeds, plants, and fruits. For a breakdown of customs allowances, write to US Customs Service, PO Box 407, Washington, DC 20044; tel: 877-227-5511; www.cbp.gov.

D

Disabled travelers

The 1995 Americans with Disabilities Act (ADA) brought sweeping changes to facilities across America. Accommodations with five or more rooms must be useable by persons with disabilities (where possible). Older and smaller inns and lodges are often wheelchair accessible, but always ask. For the sight-impaired, many hotels provide special alarm clocks, captioned TV services, and security measures. To comply with ADA hearing-impaired requirements, many hotels have begun to follow special procedures; local agencies may provide TTY and interpretation services.

Check with the hotel when you make reservations to ascertain the degree to which the hotel complies

Electricity

Standard electricity in North America is 110–115 volts, 60 cycles AC. An adapter is necessary for most appliances from overseas, with the exception of Japan.

with ADA guidelines. Ask specific questions about bathroom facilities, bed height, wheelchair space, and availability of services.

Many major attractions have wheelchairs for loan or rent; most national parks today also offer paved "barrier-free" or "accessible" trails. Some provide special visitor publications for disabled visitors and interpreters and visitor guides. The Society for Accessible Travel and Hospitality (tel: 212-447-7284; www.sath.org) publishes a quarterly magazine on travel for the disabled.

E

Embassies

Australia: 1601 Massachusetts Ave NW, Washington DC 20036, tel: 613-238-1040.
Canada: 501 Pennsylvania Ave NW, Washington, DC 20001, tel: 202-682-1740.
Great Britain: 3100 Massachusetts Ave NW, Washington, DC 20008, tel: 202-588-6500.
Ireland: 2234 Massachusetts Ave NW, Washington, DC 20008, tel: 202-462-3939.
New Zealand: 37 Observatory Circle NW, Washington, DC 20008, tel: 202-328-4800.

Emergencies

Dial 911 (the operator will put you through to the police, ambulance, or fire services). The call is toll free anywhere in the US, including on cell phones. If you can't get through, **dial 0** for an operator. In national parks, it's best to contact a ranger.

Etiquette

When traveling in Colorado, you'll notice a big difference in tone among people who live in the fast-paced, highly developed, modern urban communities strung out along the Front Range, which feels very like California, where many residents are from; and the slower-paced, more tightly knit rural mountain communities and farm and ranch

towns on the Western Slope, whose residents tend to be more conservative and courtly and polite in their manners.

The first rule of travel is to blend in and take your cue from local etiquette. This is particularly true should you happen to visit the Ute Mountain Ute Indian Reservation, just south of Cortez, or the Four Corners Navajo Tribal Monument, where you'll meet Navajo and Ute people. Indian reservations are sovereign lands, with their laws and moral code, and call for unique sensitivity and cultural awareness to avoid giving offense.

Follow all Indian regulations, and do not presume anything while on the reservation. Travel as lightly among people as you would on sensitive lands.

G

Gay and lesbian travelers

GLBT travelers will find few problems traveling in Colorado, even in more far-flung rural areas or conservative Colorado Springs, home to Focus on the Family and other religious groups. This is, after all, a state that prides itself on its international sophistication and embrace of diversity and political correctness. For GLBT resources, check out the Gay and Lesbian Yellow Pages (tel: 800-697-2812; www.glyp.com). In Colorado, contact Gay, Lesbian, Bisexual, and Transgender Services (tel: 303-733-PRIDE (7743); www.glbtcolorado.org). PrideFest takes place in Denver in mid-June.

H

Health and medical care

Insurance

It's vital to have medical insurance when traveling. Although hospitals are obligated to provide emergency

Abandoned Mines

Exercise caution around old buildings and abandoned mines. Structures may be unstable and the ground may be littered with broken glass, nails, and other debris. Mine shafts are particularly dangerous. Never enter a mine shaft or cave unless accompanied by a park ranger or other professional.

treatment to anyone who needs it, regardless of whether they do or don't have insurance, you may have to prove you can pay for treatment of anything less than a life-threatening condition. Know what your policy covers, and have proof of the policy with you at all times, or be prepared to pay at the time service is rendered. Your travel insurance should cover both yourself and your belongings. Your own insurance company or travel agent can advise you on policies, but shop around since rates vary. Make sure you are covered for accidental death, emergency medical care, trip cancellation, and baggage or document loss.

Precautions

Altitude sickness: People traveling from sea level, no matter their fitness level, may feel uncharacteristically breathless at elevations as low as 6,000 or 7,000ft (1,800–2,100 meters). The sensation usually passes after a few days. Elevation sickness symptoms, including nausea, headache, vomiting, extreme fatigue, light-headedness, and shortness of breath, intensify over 10,000ft (3,000 meters). Although the symptoms may be mild at first, they can develop into a serious illness. Move to a lower elevation and try to acclimatize gradually.
Cactus: To avoid being pricked, stay on trails and wear long pants and sturdy boots.
Dehydration: Drink plenty of liquids and, if outdoors, carry liter bottles of water and salty,high-energy snacks to eat, even on a short hike. The rule of thumb in arid conditions is 1 gallon (4 liters) of water per person per day. Don't wait to get thirsty – start drinking as soon as you set out, but avoid drinking too much water on an empty stomach, as this can lead to hyponatremia, an electrolyte imbalance that can be just as dangerous as dehydration. One easy suggestion is to add a little raw sea salt to all your water to keep electrolytes balanced.
Drinking water: All water from natural sources must be purified before drinking. *Giardia* bacteria are found in streams throughout the West, even in crystal-clear water, and can cause severe cramps and diarrhea. The most popular purification methods are tablets or filters (both available from camping supply stores) or by boiling water for at least three minutes. You can also find water bottles with filters that do a good job.
Flash floods: Sudden downpours – even those falling miles away from

your location– can fill canyons and dry river beds with a roaring torrent of water and mud that will sweep away everything in its path. Travelers should be especially careful during the summer "monsoon" season. Avoid hiking or driving in *arroyos* (dry gulches) or narrow slot canyons in canyon country, and never try to wade or drive across a flooded stream. If rain begins to fall, or you see rain clouds in the distance, move to higher ground. It's impossible to outrun or even outdrive a flash flood. Take action before the water level begins to rise.

Frostbite: Symptoms of frostbite, which occurs when living tissue freezes, include numbness, pain, blistering, and whitening of the skin. The most immediate remedy is to put frostbitten skin against warm skin. Simply holding your hands for several minutes over another person's frostbitten cheeks or nose may suffice. Otherwise, immerse frostbitten skin in warm (not hot!) water. Refreezing will cause even more damage, so get the victim into a warm environment as quickly as possible. Check other members of your party. If one person is hypothermic or frostbitten, others may be too.

Hypothermia: This occurs when the core body temperature falls below 95°F (35°C). At altitude, combinations of alcohol, cold, and thin air can produce hypothermia. Watch for drowsiness, disorientation, and sometimes increased urination. If possible get to a hospital; otherwise, blankets and extra clothing should be piled on for warmth. Don't use hot water or electric heaters and don't rub the skin. The elderly should be especially careful in extremely cold weather.

Lightning: In Colorado, lightning is the number one life-threatening weather hazard. In the past 10 years, there have been an average of three deaths and 15 injuries from lightning each year. Stay alert for fast-changing weather conditions. It doesn't have to be raining where you are for lightning to be a threat. If driving, stay in your car. If you're hiking, avoid being the tallest object in the area, and stay away from other tall objects, such as a small group of trees. If hiking in the mountains, go early in the day, before thunderstorms develop. Above tree line, there are few places to take cover. If you are in the mountains when a storm is moving in, descend from high points. If you can't get away from an exposed area, make yourself

as small as possible, crouching down or perching on a small rock with insulation such as a poncho or foam pad under you, your feet touching rock and your hands clasped around your knees or on all fours on the ground. Never seek shelter under a lone tree, in a shallow cave or under a rock overhang.

Sunburn: Even a very short time outdoors can result in sunburn, so protect yourself by applying a high-SPF sunscreen and wear polarized sunglasses. The elderly and the ill, small children, and people with fair skin should be especially careful. Excessive pain, redness, blistering, or numbness mean you need professional medical attention. Minor sunburn can be soothed by a cool bath.

Snakes and insects

Insects: Bees are abundant, which should concern only those allergic to the sting. Those with severe allergies should carry an EpiPen or other form of emergency treatment, especially if hiking in remote areas. The bite of a black widow spider or tarantula and the sting of a scorpion's tail can pack a punch but is rarely a serious health threat to adults. Scorpions are nocturnal, so use flashlights and don't walk barefoot. They often hide in recesses, dark corners, and wood piles and like to crawl into protected places, so shake out clothes or sleeping bags that have been on the ground and check your shoes before putting them on.

Snakes: Of the 25 species of snakes in Colorado, the Western rattlesnake and the massasauga are the only venomous species. The Western rattlesnake appears in most habitats throughout the

An alligator farm in the San Luis Valley.

state. The massasauga is limited to the southeastern grasslands. There are six basic ways to distinguish these two venomous snakes from their non-venomous relatives: 1) rattles at the end of the tail; 2) fangs in addition to their rows of teeth; 3) facial pits between the nostrils and eyes; 4) vertical and elliptical pupils that may look like thin lines in bright light (non-venomous snakes have round pupils); and 5) a broad triangular head and narrow neck. Only about 3 percent of people bitten by a rattlesnake die, and these are mainly small children. Walk in the open when possible, proceed with caution among rocks, sweep grassy areas with a long stick before entering, avoid dark or overgrown places where snakes might lurk, shake out bedding or clothing that has been lying on the ground, and wear sturdy hiking boots. Snakes often lie on roads at night because of the residual heat radiating from the pavement, so use a flashlight if walking on a paved road after dark. Keep your hands and feet where you can see them, and don't let children poke under rocks or logs.

Snakebite kits are good psychological protection, but there is some question as to how effective they really are. The most useful snakebite kit consists of car keys and coins for calling a hospital. If bitten, try to remain calm so as not to increase circulation and spread the venom faster. Remove rings, watches, bracelets, and other articles that may constrict swelling below the bite area, if possible. Wash the wound with soap and water. Immobilize the bite area and keep it below the heart. Get to a hospital immediately – do not wait for the pain to become severe. The use of an approved anti-venom is the most effective treatment. Do not use a tourniquet, make an incision at the bite site, suck out the venom with your mouth, or pack the limb in ice.

Internet

Many public libraries, copy centers, hotels, and airports offer wireless (wi-fi) email and internet access, either on their computers or your laptop. At Starbucks coffee houses, for example, you must first purchase a T-Mobile Hot Spot pass or Boingo Pass (currently about $10 a day), before being able to log on; many other coffee houses and restaurants offer free wi-fi as a customer incentive. The modems of many foreign laptops, handheld computers, and smartphones won't work in the US. You may need to purchase a global modem before leaving home or a local PC-card modem once you arrive in the US. For more information, log on to www.teleadapt.com.

M

Maps

Accurate maps are indispensable in Colorado, especially when leaving primary roads. Road maps can be found at bookstores, convenience stores, and gas stations. Free maps are also available by mail from state or regional tourism bureaus and in person at visitor centers, tourism offices, and state welcome centers. Free city, state, and regional maps as well as up-to-date road conditions and other valuable services are available to members of the **Automobile Association of America** (AAA; see page 292.)

Maps of national parks, forests, and other public lands are usually offered by the managing governmental agency. Good topographical maps of national parks and forests are available from **Trails Illustrated**, 212 Beaverbrook Canyon Road, Evergreen, CO 80439, tel: 303-670-3457 or toll-free 800-962-1643; www.natgeomaps.com/trail-maps/trails-illustrated-maps. These maps are often found in bookstores. Extremely detailed topographical maps are available from the **US Geological Survey**, PO Box 25286, Denver Federal Center, Denver, CO 80225, tel: 303-236-7477; www.usgs.gov/sales.html. Like maps from Trails Illustrated, USGS maps are often available in higher-end bookstores and shops that sell outdoor gear.

Media

Magazines

Several Colorado lifestyle magazines are worth checking out for their regional articles on interesting destinations and local people, as well as restaurant listings and a calendar of events: *5280: Denver's Mile-High Magazine*, *Zone 4: Living in the High Country West*, *Aspen Magazine*, *Colorado Homes and Lifestyles Magazine*, *Mountain Living Magazine*, and *Telluride Magazine*.

Newspapers

In this rapidly expanding era of electronic publishing and free information on the worldwide web, print media has undergone a massive contraction. Yet most communities still publish print editions of newspapers, as well as electronic editions, and the opinions and endorsements of columnists and editorial boards continue to play an important role in community life. Colorado's top newspaper is the Denver Post. Other Colorado newspapers include the *Aspen Daily News*, the *Boulder Daily Camera*, *Colorado Springs Gazette*, the *Colorado Tribune* in Pueblo, *The Daily Sentinel* in Grand Junction, the *Durango Herald*, the *Estes Park Trail Gazette*, the *Telluride Daily Planet*, and *Vail Daily*. *High Country News*, headquartered in Paonia, is an award-winning environmental journal.

Television

All of the main TV broadcast networks have affiliates in Denver and Colorado Springs/Pueblo on the most populous Front Range. On the Western Slope, in Durango and Grand Junction and in Montrose, Steamboat Springs, Glenwood Springs, and Fort Collins, satellite broadcasts from Denver or Albuquerque can be found. In addition, a large selection of cable/satellite channels and pay-per-view stations is available on most TV lineups.

Money

Automatic Teller Machines (ATMs)

ATMs are the most convenient way to access cash and are widely available throughout the state. They are usually found at banks, shopping malls, supermarkets, service stations, convenience stores, and hotels. Debit cards may also be used at grocery stores and gas stations, much as credit cards are. Many stores offer free cashback with a debit card purchase.

Credit Cards

These are very much part of daily life in the US. They can be used to pay for pretty much anything, and it is common for car rental agencies and hotels to take an imprint of your card as a deposit. Rental companies may oblige you to pay a large deposit in cash if you do not have a card.

You can also use your credit card to withdraw cash from ATMs.

Before you leave home, make sure you know your PIN (personal identification number) and find out which ATM system will accept your card (or charge you less, for example for taking out foreign currency if your card was issued at a bank outside the US.) The most widely accepted cards are Visa, MasterCard, American Express, Diners Club, and Discovery.

Money may be sent or received by wire at any **Western Union** office (tel: 800-325-6000), **American Express Money Gram** office (tel: 800-543-4080) and even online through services like Paypal.

Currency

The basic unit of American currency, the dollar ($1), is equal to 100 cents. There are four coins, each worth less than a dollar: a penny or 1 cent (1¢), a nickel or 5 cents (5¢), a dime or 10 cents (10¢), and a quarter or 25 cents (25¢).

There are several denominations of paper money: $1, $5, $10, $20, $50, and $100. Each bill is the same color, size, and shape; be sure to check the dollar amount on the face of the bill.

It is advisable to arrive with at least $100 in cash (in small bills) to pay for ground transportation and other incidentals.

Traveler's checks

Foreign visitors may want to carry US dollar traveler's checks, since exchanging foreign currency – whether as cash or checks – can be problematic. A growing number of banks offer exchange facilities, but this practice is not universal. Most shops, restaurants, and other establishments accept traveler's checks in US dollars and will give change in cash. Alternatively, checks can be converted into cash at the bank. Alternatively, you may want to carry a preloaded debit card in dollar currency, available at UK post offices, for example.

O

Opening hours

Standard hours for business offices are Monday–Friday 9am–5pm. Many banks open a little earlier, usually 8.30am; a few open on Saturday morning. Post offices are usually open Monday–Friday 8am–5pm and Saturday 8am–noon. Most stores and shopping centers are open weekends and evenings.

P

Photography

Although most people are now using digital cameras or smartphones to take photos, film is still widely available throughout the US, should you need it – typically at big box stores like Walmart and Best Buy, which also offer rapid development or conversion of digital to paper prints. Colorado, in particular, is spectacularly photogenic. Some of the most rewarding photography is of mountain vistas and lakes in places like Rocky Mountain National Park, Maroon Bells and the red rock country around Grand Mesa. Seek out wildlife events such as the elk rut in Rocky, sandhill cranes wintering in San Luis Valley or prairie chicken dances in Comanche National Grasslands. Old mining towns in the Central and Southern Rockies make particularly haunting subject matter. Everywhere in Colorado, you'll find unique and colorful festivals and sporting events. Photography workshops are held throughout Colorado. One of the more spectacular locations is Crested Butte, which offers photography

Public Holidays

On public holidays, post offices, banks, most government offices and a large number of shops and restaurants are closed. Public transport usually runs less frequently.
New Year's Day: January 1
Martin Luther King, Jr's Birthday: The third Monday in January
Presidents Day: The third Monday in February
Good Friday: March/April – date varies
Easter Sunday: March/April – date varies
El Cinco de Mayo: May 5
Memorial Day: Last Monday in May
Independence Day: July 4
Labor Day: First Monday in September
Columbus Day: Second Monday in October
Election Day: The Tuesday in the first full week of November during presidential election years
Veterans Day: November 11
Thanksgiving Day: Fourth Thursday in November
Christmas Day: December 25

workshops during its summer Wildflower Festival. Several well-known photographers live in the old town and maintain galleries there.

Postal services

Even the most remote towns are served by the US Postal Service. Smaller post offices tend to be limited to business hours (Mon–Fri 9am–5pm), although central, big-city branches may have extended weekday and weekend hours.

Stamps are sold at all post offices. They are also sold at some convenience stores, filling stations, hotels, and transportation terminals, usually from vending machines, as well as online.

For reasonably quick delivery within the US at a modest price, ask for **Priority Mail**, which usually reaches its destination within two or three days. For overnight deliveries, try **Express Mail** or one of several domestic and international courier services:
FedEx, tel: 800-238-5355
DHL, tel: 800-345-2727
United Parcel Service (UPS), tel: 800-742-5877

Poste Restante

Visitors can receive mail at post offices if it is addressed to them, care of "General Delivery," followed by the city name and (very important) the zip code. You must pick up this mail in person within a week or two of its arrival and will be asked to show a valid driver's license, passport, or some other form of picture identification.

R

Religious services

Colorado is one of the least religious states in the US. In a poll conducted in 2016, only one-third of Coloradans described themselves as religious. Of those who do, most define themselves as Christian, mostly Protestant but with a fair number of Evangelical Christians and Roman Catholics. Far fewer define themselves as Jewish or Muslim, and 15 percent state no religious preference at all. Colorado Springs is home to a number of conservative religious groups, including Focus on the Family, an activist anti-abortion group. Two well-known churches may be visited in the area: the Cadet Chapel on the US Air Force Academy,

known for its interesting modern architecture; and Chapel on the Rock, an historic Roman Catholic church on the grounds of the Saint Malo Retreat Center near Allenspark. An Easter Sunrise service at Red Rocks Amphitheater is a popular annual event, attended by thousands.

Boulder is a center of alternative health and spirituality and home of Naropa University, a well-regarded Tibetan Buddhist educational institution that includes meditation and other spiritual practices in its curriculum. Theravadan and Zen Buddhist meditation centers and retreats in the mountains that are associated with Naropa are very popular. Well-known international teachers of Buddhism and Tibetan lamas are frequently in residence at centers in Boulder and Front Range communities, and also in Crestone in the San Luis Valley.

S

Shopping

Colorado shopping runs the gamut. In the rapidly expanding Denver Metro Area, along I-25, and towns like Grand Junction, off I-70, you'll find the usual big-box stores in rather nondescript malls, of which 16th Street Mall, Cherry Creek Mall, and Larimer Square in Denver are by far the swankiest and most memorable. At high-end resorts in Aspen, Vail, Steamboat, and elsewhere, you'll find exclusive designer boutiques selling knickknacks and fine art for those with deep pockets. Pearl Street Mall, an attractive outdoor pedestrian-only street mall in downtown Boulder, has a mix of quirky shops selling ethical and ethnic gear to suit the city's mainly green residents, along with fun and hip restaurants and street entertainment. A popular farmers' market is nearby. Most enjoyable are the funky boutiques and galleries selling one-of-a-kind arts and crafts in former mining cabins and brick buildings in old mining towns like Salida, Creede, Ouray, Crested Butte, Paonia, Durango, and Telluride in the Central and Southern Rockies, and historic downtown Grand Junction in the Colorado River valley, where you may score an antique, a Western souvenir, a quirky teapot, some silver jewelry, or perhaps a piece of beautiful woven fiber art. For more on shopping, see the free app that comes with your book. Instructions on how to download it feature on page 2 of this book.

Spectator sports

Coloradans enjoy spectator sports – from major league football, basketball, baseball, and hockey to auto racing and horse and dog racing. The National Football League **Denver Broncos** (www.denverbroncos.com) play September to December at Sports Authority Field at Mile High Stadium. The National Baseball League **Colorado Rockies** (www.rockies.mlb.com) play April to October at Coors Field. The National Basketball Association **Denver Nuggets** (www.nba.com/nuggets) play at the Pepsi Center. And the Stanley Cup–winning **Colorado Avalanche** (www.avalanche.nhl.com) ice hockey team play at the Pepsi Center. Auto racing is popular at a number of tracks in Colorado, including **Pikes Peak International Raceway** in the shadow of the famous Pikes Peaks. There are also tracks in Morrison, Erie, Fort Morgan, Pueblo, Denver, Commerce City, and Olathe. Horse and dog racing take place on tracks in Aurora, Colorado Springs, Pueblo, and Commerce City. For sports listings, see the free app that comes with your book. Instructions on how to download it feature on page 2 of this book.

T

Tax

Like most states, Colorado levies a flat sales tax on goods and services. It varies from city to city but is a lot lower than in many states. The combined sales tax rate in Denver is 7.65 percent, 4 percent on food and liquor, and 7.25 percent on auto rentals of less than 30 days and 10.75 percent lodger's tax; in the rest of the state, sales tax is just under 3 percent.

Telephones

In this era of cell phones, you'll find fewer public telephones in hotel lobbies, restaurants, drug stores, garages, roadside kiosks, convenience stores, and other locations. The cost of making a local call from a payphone for three minutes is 25–50 cents; 800 numbers are free. To make a long-distance call from a payphone, use either a prepaid calling card, available in airports, post offices, and a few other outlets, or your credit card, which you can use at any phone: dial 800-CALLATT, key in your credit card

number, and wait to be connected. In many areas, local calls have now changed to a 10-digit calling system, using the area code. The main area codes in Colorado are as follows: Denver Metro Area, including Boulder – 303 and 720; Southeastern Colorado, including Colorado Springs and Pueblo – 719; the rest of the state is 970.

Watch out for in-room connection charges, especially in more upmarket hotels; it's cheaper to use the payphone in the lobby. Ditto: Wi-fi internet connections in your room: wireless is frequently free in many hotel lobbies but there is a charge for it in guest rooms, so inquire ahead.

Dialing abroad

To dial abroad (Canada follows the US system), first dial the international access code 011, then the country code. If using a US phone credit card, dial the company's access number below, then 01, then the country code.
Sprint, tel: 10333
AT&T, tel: 10288.
Country codes:
Australia: 61
Austria: 43
Belgium: 32
Brazil: 55
Denmark: 45
France: 33
Germany: 49
Greece: 30
Hong Kong: 852
Israel: 972
Italy: 39
Japan: 81
Korea: 82
Netherlands: 31
New Zealand: 64
Norway: 47
Singapore: 65
South Africa: 27
Spain 34
Sweden: 46
Switzerland: 41
United Kingdom: 44
Western Union (tel: 800-325-6000) can arrange money transfers. Check online (www.westernunion.com) or a phone directory or call information for numbers of local offices.

Fax machines are available at most hotels and motels. Public libraries, printers, copy shops, stationers, and office-supply shops may also have them, as well as some convenience stores.

Time zones

The continental US is divided into four time zones. From east to west,

later to earlier, they are Eastern Standard Time, Central Standard Time, Mountain Standard Time, and Pacific Standard Time, each separated by one hour. Colorado is on Mountain Standard Time (MST), seven hours behind Greenwich Mean Time. On the first Sunday in April, Coloradans set the clock ahead one hour in observation of daylight savings time. On the last Sunday in October, the clock is moved back one hour to return to standard time.

Tipping

Service workers in US restaurants are paid rock-bottom wages, with the expectation that they will make most of their income from tips, which have to be declared for tax purposes. Tipping is left to your discretion – gratuities are not automatically added to the bill – but unless you receive very poor service you are expected to tip. The standard tip in the US is 15–20 percent before tax for waiters, taxi drivers, bartenders, barbers, and hairdressers. Porters and bellmen usually get $1 per bag; chambermaids in upscale hotels are usually tipped several dollars a day after the first night's stay.

Tourist information

The state tourism office, www.colorado.com, has in-depth online information about visiting Colorado, including sections on arranging travel to Colorado from the UK, Italy, France, Germany, and Japan. The website has feature articles on special-interest tours, from microbreweries and wineries to visiting and staying on farms and ranches, connecting with the art scene, volunteer opportunities for environmental cleanup, and taking part in sports and other special events.

Colorado Welcome Centers are located at the state line. They are staffed by volunteers who can give you maps, brochures, discount coupon books, and general advice on your stay and have restrooms, water, snack vending machines, and often hot coffee. Most communities have visitor centers that offer information and trip planning. When visiting national parks, be sure to stop at the visitor center or ranger station first. Rangers there can help you get the most out of your time in the park. Colorado has 25 spectacular scenic and historic drives designated by the government as scenic byways. Check out www.byways.org to find out more.

Tourist offices

Alamosa Visitor Information Center
Cole Park, Alamosa, CO 81101;
tel: 800-BLU-SKYS; www.alamosa.org
Aspen Chamber Resort Association
425 Rio Grande Place, Aspen,
CO 81611; tel: 970-925-1940;
www.aspenchamber.org
Aurora Chamber of Commerce
14305 E. Alameda, Ste 300, Aurora,
CO 80014; tel: 303-344-1500;
www.aurorachamber.org
Beaver Creek Ski Area
210 Offerson Rd c301, Avon,
CO 81620; tel: (970) 754-4636;
www.beavercreek.com
**Boulder Convention and Visitors
Bureau**
2440 Pearl Street, Boulder,
CO 80302; tel: 303-442-2911;
www.bouldercoloradousa.com
**Breckenridge Chamber of
Commerce**
111 Ski Hill Road, Breckenridge, CO
80424; tel: 888.251. www.gobreck.
com
Buena Vista Chamber of Commerce
343 Highway 24 S, Buena
Vista, CO 81211; tel: 719-
395-6612 or 800-311-0605;
www.buenavistacolorado.org
Buttermilk Ski Area
PO Box 1248, Aspen, CO 81612;
tel: 970-923-1227 or 800-525-6200;
www.aspensnowmass.com/our-
mountains/buttermilk
Cañon City Chamber of Commerce
403 Royal Gorge Boulevard, Cañon
City, CO 81215; tel: 719-275-2331 or
800-876-7922; www.canoncity.com
Castle Rock Chamber of Commerce
420 Jerry Street, Castle Rock,
CO 80104; tel: 303-688-4597 or
866-441-8508; www.castlerock.org
Central City Visitors Center
141 Nevada, Central City, CO 80427;
tel: 303-582-5251; www.colorado.
gov/pacific/centralcity
Colorado Springs Visitors Bureau

104 S. Cascade, Colorado Springs,
CO 80903; tel: 719-635-7506 or
800-368-4748; www.visitcos.com
Colorado Tourism
1672 Pennsylvania Street, Denver,
CO 80203; tel: 303-832-6171 or
800-265-6723; www.colorado.com
Cortez Chamber of Commerce
928 E. Main Street, Cortez,
CO 81321; tel: 970-565-3414;
www.cortezchamber.com
**Craig Chamber of Commerce and
Moffat County Visitor Center**
360 E. Victory Way, Craig, CO 81625;
tel: 970-824-5689 or 800-864-4405;
www.craig-chamber.com
**Creede-Mineral Chamber of
Commerce**
PO Box 580, Creede, CO 81130;
tel: 719-658-2374 or 800-327-2102;
www.creede.com
**Crested Butte Chamber of
Commerce**
PO Box 1288, Crested Butte,
CO 81224; tel: 970-349-6438;
www.cbchamber.com
**Cripple Creek and Victor Chamber
of Commerce**
PO Box 650, Cripple Creek, CO
80813; tel: 719-689-5877;
www.ccvchamber.com
Delta County Visitor Bureau
PO Box 753, Delta, CO
81416; tel: 970-874-9532;
www.deltacountycolorado.com
**Denver Metro Chamber of
Commerce**
1445 Market Street, Denver,
CO 80202; tel: 303-534-8500;
www.denverchamber.org
**Denver Metro Convention and
Visitors Bureau (Visit Denver)**
1555 California Street, Ste 300,
Denver CO 80210; tel: 303-892-1112
or 800-233-6837; www.denver.org
Durango Chamber of Commerce
111 S. Camino del Rio, Durango, CO
81302; tel: 970-247-0312 or 800-
463-8726; www.durango.org

Weights and Measures

Despite efforts to convert to metric,
the US still uses the Imperial
System of weights and measures.

**Estes Park Convention and Visitors
Bureau**
500 Big Thompson Avenue, Estes
Park, CO 80517; tel: 970-577-9900
or 800-44-ESTES; www.visitestespark.
com
Evergreen Chamber of Commerce
30480 Stagecoach Blvd., Evergreen,
CO 80439; tel: 303-674-3412;
www.evergreenchamber.org
Fort Collins Visitors Bureau
19 Old Town Square, Ste 137,
Fort Collins, CO 80524; tel: 970-
232-3840 or 800-274-3678;
www.ftcollins.com
**Glenwood Springs Chamber of
Commerce**
802 Grand Avenue, Glenwood
Springs, CO 81601; tel: 970-945-
6589; www.glenwoodchamber.com
Golden Chamber of Commerce
1010 Washington Avenue, Golden,
CO 80402; tel: 303-279-3113;
www.goldenchamber.org
Grand Lake Chamber of Commerce
14700 US 34, Grand Lake, CO 80447;
tel: 970-627-3402 or 800-531-1019;
www.grandlakechamber.com
Gunnison–Crested Butte Tourism
PO Box 314, Gunnison, CO
81230; tel: 877-213-5357;
www.gunnisoncrestedbutte.com
Lake City Chamber of Commerce
PO Box 430, Lake City, CO 81235; tel:
970-944-2527 or 800-569-1874;
www.lakecity.com
Lakewood Chamber of Commerce
1667 Cole Boulevard, Bldg 19, Ste
400, Lakewood, CO 80401; tel: 303-
233-5555; www.westchamber.org
Leadville Chamber of Commerce
809 Harrison Avenue, Leadville,
CO 80461; tel: 719-486-3900 or
888-532-3845; www.leadvilleusa.com
Loveland Chamber of Commerce
5400 Stonecreek Circle, Loveland,
CO 80538; tel: 970-667-6311;
www.loveland.org
**Manitou Springs Chamber of
Commerce**
354 Manitou Avenue, Manitou
Springs, CO 80829; tel: 719-
685-5089 or 800-642-2567;
www.manitousprings.org
**Mesa Verde Country Visitor
Information Bureau**
928 E. Main Street, , Cortez, CO
81321; tel: 970-565-8227 or 800-
530-2998; www.colorado.com/
official-colorado/mesa-verde-country-
visitor-information-bureau.com

Golfers take advantage of Colorado's natural beauty and good weather.

Kids explore at Dinosaur Journey in western Colorado.

microbreweries. Outfitters offer guided trips of the outdoors. The possibilities in outdoorsy Colorado are virtually limitless, including fishing, hunting, river rafting, horseback riding, skiing, rock climbing, mountain biking, and Jeep touring. Heritage and agricultural tourism are growing in popularity in Colorado, including tours of archeological sites on the Ute Mountain Ute Reservation with native guides, learning ranch and farm skills from cowboys and farmers on the Western Slope, and taking part in paleontological digs near Dinosaur National Monument.

V

Visas and passports

A machine-readable passport, a passport-sized photograph (note: the size required in Britain is different from that in a US passport), a visitor's visa, proof of intent to leave the US after your visit, and (depending upon your country of origin) an international vaccination certificate are required of most foreign nationals for entry into the US.

Visitors from the UK staying less than 90 days no longer need a visa as part of the visa waiver program (VWP); however, it is compulsory for non-US residents from VWP countries to submit information about themselves online to the Department of Homeland Security and register via the website of the Electronic System for Travel Authorization (ESTA) (www.esta.us/travel_authorization.html) to be pre-approved for travel to the US at least three days before they travel.

Vaccination certificate requirements vary, but proof of immunization against smallpox or cholera may be necessary.

US citizens traveling by air between the US and Canada, Mexico, the Caribbean, and Bermuda must present a current passport: a birth certificate and photo ID are no longer valid proof.

Up-to-date details on entry requirements and machine-readable passports may be found on the US State Department's website: www.travel.state.gov/content/visas/en/visit.html.

Any non-US citizen wanting to extend their stay should contact US Immigration and Naturalization Service at 425 I Street, Washington DC 20536; tel: 202-501-4444 or 888-407-4747.

Monte Vista Chamber of Commerce
947 1st Avenue, Monte Vista, CO 81144; tel: 719-852-2731; www.monte-vista.org
Montrose Visitor and Convention Bureau
107 S. Cascade Avenue, Montrose, CO 81401; tel: 970-497-8558 or 855-497-8558; www.visitmontrose.com
Monument Chamber of Commerce
300 Highway 105, Monument, CO 80132; tel: 719-481-3282; www.trilakeschamber.com
Ouray Visitors Bureau
1230 Main Street, Ouray, CO 81427; tel: 970-325-4746 or 800-228-1876; www.ouraycolorado.com
Pagosa Springs Chamber of Commerce
PO Box 787, Pagosa Springs, CO 81147; tel: 970-264-2360 or 800-252-2204; www.pagosachamber.com
Pueblo Chamber of Commerce
302 N. Santa Fe Avenue, Pueblo, CO 81002; tel: 719-542-1704 or 800-233-3446; www.pueblo chamber.org
Silverton Chamber of Commerce
414 Greene Street, Silverton, CO 81433; tel: 970-387-5654 or 800-752-4494; www.silvertoncolorado.com
Snowmass Village Resort Association
130 Kearns Road, Snowmass Village, CO 81615; tel: 970-923-2000 or 866-352-1763; http://gosnowmass.com
South Fork Chamber of Commerce
PO Box 1030, South Fork, CO 81154; tel: 719-873-5512 or 800-571-0881; www.southfork.org
Sterling Chamber of Commerce
PO Box 1683, Sterling, CO 80751; tel: 970-522-5070 or 866-522-5070; www.logancountychamber.com
Summit Chamber of Commerce
PO Box 5450, Frisco, CO 80443; tel: 970-668-2051; www.summit chamber.org

Telluride Visitor Services
PO Box 653, Telluride, CO 81435; tel: 970-728-3041 or 888-605-2578; www.visittelluride.com
Vail Valley Tourism Bureau
101 Fawcett Road, Ste 240, Vail, CO 81657; tel: 970-476-1000; www.visitvailvalley.com
Winter Park Chamber of Commerce
PO Box 3236, Winter Park, CO 80482; tel: 970-726-4221 or 800-903-7275; www.playwinterpark.com

Tour operators and travel agents

Even if you are planning on doing the driving yourself, you may want to hook up with a local tour operator to let someone else show you around for a few days. You can locate a US tour operator by checking listings on the websites of the **US Tour Operator Association** – USTOA (www.ustoa) and the **National Tour Association** (www.ntaonline.com), or by contacting the visitor center at your destination for official listings. In Colorado, contact Tour Colorado (tel: 888-311-TOUR; www.tourcolorado.org).

Top tour operators serving all of the US include **Tauck Tours** (tel: 800-788-7885; www.tauck.com), **Abercrombie and Kent** (tel: 888-611-4711; www.abercrombiekent.com), both of which specialize in luxury tours. The **Smithsonian Institution** (tel: 855-330-1542; www.smithsonianjourneys.org) offers educational tours to sites of archeological, historical, and scientific interest, such as Mesa Verde National Park, guided by authorities in the field.

Specialty tour operators offer guided trips tailored to your interests, from walking tours of historic downtowns and gold mines to balloon trips and visits to the state's numerous wineries and

FURTHER READING

FICTION

Angle of Repose, by Wallace Stegner. A reflective, Pulitzer Prize–winning work by a master of Western literature.
Blinded, by Stephen White. A mystery series set in Boulder, Colorado.
Centennial, by James A. Michener. An intergenerational epic set mostly on the plains of eastern Colorado.
Eventide, by Kent Haruf. The lives, loves, and trials of a small town on the high plains of Colorado by the late Salida author.
Hells Bottom Colorado, by Laura Pritchett. Linked short stories about families and ranch life on Colorado's high plains by an award-winning young author.
On the Road, by Jack Kerouac. Much of Kerouac's Beat Generation classic takes place in Denver.
The Serpents Trail: A Maxie and Stretch Mystery, by Sue Henry. This instalment of the series takes place in and around Grand Junction, Colorado.

NONFICTION

Culture and current events

The Beast in the Garden: A Modern Parable of Man and Nature, by David Baron. A mountain lion attack in Colorado prompts the writer to explore human–wildlife relations.
Culinary Colorado: The Ultimate Food Lover's Guide, by Claire Walter. An encyclopedic tour of Colorado's food culture.
Deep in the Heart of the Rockies, by Ed Quillen. Wit and wisdom from a Denver Post columnist.
No Easy Answers: The Truth Behind Death at Columbine, by Brooks Brown and Rob Merritt. One of the better treatments of the tragic Columbine High School shooting.
The Spiral Notebook: The Aurora Theater Shooter and the Epidemic of Mass Violence Committed by American Youth by Stephen and Joyce Singular. What started out as an exploration of the Aurora theater shooting by true crime writers ends

up examining how bloodthirsty video games, school bullying, prescription drugs, and ineffective courts create an impossible environment for today's youth.
When I Was Cool: My Life at the Jack Kerouac School, by Sam Kashner. A memoir of the author's experiences as a student at Boulder's Naropa University.
Whiteout: Lost in Aspen, by Ted Conover. A memoir of the author's experiences as a low-wage worker in high-rent Aspen. A revealing look at celebrity culture and the transformation of a former mining town.

History

Colorado: A History of the Centennial State, by Carl Abbot, Stephen J. Leonard and David McComb. Modern

Send Us Your Thoughts

We do our best to ensure the information in our books is as accurate and up-to-date as possible. The books are updated on a regular basis using local contacts, who painstakingly add, amend and correct as required. However, some details (such as telephone numbers and opening times) are liable to change, and we are ultimately reliant on our readers to put us in the picture.

We welcome your feedback, especially your experience of using the book "on the road". Maybe we recommended a hotel that you liked (or another that you didn't), or you came across a great bar or new attraction we missed.

We will acknowledge all contributions, and we'll offer an Insight Guide to the best letters received.

Please write to us at:
Insight Guides
PO Box 7910
London SE1 1WE
Or email us at:
hello@insightguides.com

urbanization, multiculturalism, boosterism, and Colorado history.
Denver: From Mining Camp to Metropolis, by Stephen J. Leonard and Thomas J. Noel offers a thorough examination of the Mile High City, then and now.
Eccentric Colorado: A Legacy of the Bizarre and Unusual, by Kenneth Jessen. Weird and wonderful lore about life in the Colorado Rockies.
I Never Knew That About Colorado: A Quaint Volume of Forgotten Lore, by Abbott Fay. Entertaining collection of little-known facts about Colorado.
A Lady's Life in the Rocky Mountains, by Isabella Lucy Bird. Memoir of a 19th-century Englishwoman's life exploring the Colorado Rockies, alone and on horseback.
Money Mountain: The Story of Cripple Creek Gold, by Marshall Sprague. Truth is more fantastic than fiction in this enjoyable look at Cripple Creek history.
The Rockies, by David Lavender. The standard history on the Rockies by the late Colorado historian.
Utes: A Forgotten People, by Wilson Rockwell. The most complete history of the Utes available.

Travel

100 Classic Hikes in Colorado, by Scott S. Warren. A good trail companion.
Colorado Close-Up, text by Conger Beasley, photos by J.C. Leacock. Nature essays and photos by a Colorado writer/photographer team.
Colorado's Fourteeners: From Hikes to Climbs, by Gerry Roach. Ambitious hikes over 14,000ft (4,270 meters).
Colorado Scenic Byways: Taking the Other Road, text by Susan Tweit, photos by Jim Steinberg. Award-winning celebration of Colorado's backroads by a Salida naturalist.
Colorado Wildlife Viewing Guide, by Mary Taylor Young. Watchable wildlife in Colorado.
Complete Guide to Colorado's Wilderness Areas, text by Mark Pearson, photos by John Fielder.
Roadside Geology of Colorado, by Halka Chronic. An excellent series on state geology.

CREDITS

Photo Credits

123RF 25, 99, 208, 211T, 222T, 276/277T, 277BL
Alamy 142B, 181B
Amon Carter Museum 34
Aramark Parks and Destinations 267B, 270T
Auberge Resorts 231T
AWL Images 12/13, 14/15, 124/125, 128/129, 229
Bigstock 64/65, 222B
Carol M. Highsmith 23, 60/61, 62, 101, 106, 126/127, 192/193, 244/245, 257, 288
Colorado Historical Society 35, 37, 46, 54, 55, 107, 117, 183
Colorado Tourism/Andrea Golod 143
Colorado Tourism/Denise Chambers 6BL, 262
Colorado Tourism/Matt Inden 7B, 7MR, 8T, 17T, 27B, 72, 73, 77, 78BL, 79BL, 81, 87, 94, 96, 104, 123, 138, 142T, 144, 146, 147B, 195T, 195B, 204BL, 210T, 219T, 223, 225T, 225B, 237, 263B
Corbis 42, 79BR
Denver Metro Convention & Visitors Bureau 6MR
Denver Public Library, Western History Collection 20, 22, 43, 44,

45, 48, 49, 50, 52, 53, 56, 57, 92, 102, 108, 111, 112, 114/115, 154, 200B, 217, 224B, 242, 256
Dreamstime 6ML, 6MR, 16, 32, 67, 71, 95, 98, 109, 145, 194, 201, 206, 209T, 216, 218, 220B, 224T, 226, 227B, 233, 238, 239, 258, 294
Getty Images 1, 4/5, 10/11, 58, 90, 118, 120, 121, 210B, 228, 274
iStock 7ML, 7TL, 9B, 31, 39, 59, 74, 75, 76, 79TR, 80, 85, 86, 88, 103, 105, 122, 136, 139, 147T, 161BL, 163, 165, 167B, 178T, 204BR, 205BL, 207, 209B, 215, 221B, 231B, 236T, 240T, 251B, 251T, 260, 283, 284B, 304
J.C. Leacock Photography 160BR, 160BL, 161BR, 161 ML, 161TR
Library of Congress 26, 27T, 28, 29, 30, 36, 38, 40, 41, 51, 119, 141B, 234, 240/241B, 275
Monkey Theorem 277BR, 277TR
Naropa University 166T
Nowitz Photography/Apa Publications 7MC, 7TR, 8B, 9T, 17B, 18, 19L, 19R, 24, 33, 63, 66, 68, 69, 70, 78/79T, 78BR, 79ML, 82, 83, 84, 89, 100, 110, 113, 116, 130, 131T, 131B, 134/135, 137T,

137B, 141T, 148, 149, 151B, 151T, 152B, 152T, 153, 155, 156, 157T, 157B, 158T, 158B, 159, 162, 164, 166B, 167T, 168T, 168B, 169, 170T, 170B, 171, 172, 173, 175B, 175T, 176, 177, 178B, 179, 180, 181T, 182, 184, 185, 186, 187, 189T, 190, 191, 196, 197, 199, 200T, 202T, 202B, 203, 204/205T, 205ML, 214, 219B, 220T, 221T, 227T, 235, 236B, 246, 247T, 247B, 248, 249, 252, 253T, 253B, 254, 255T, 255B, 258/259, 261, 264, 265, 267T, 269, 270B, 271, 272T, 272B, 273, 276BR, 276BL, 277ML, 278, 279, 281B, 281T, 282B, 282T, 284T, 285, 286, 287, 290, 293, 295, 296, 298, 302, 303
Press Association Images 160/161T
Public domain 21, 47
Robert Harding 243
Rocky Mountain Field Insitute 205BR, 205TR
Sand Dunes National Park 189B
Spring Resorts 263T
Steamboat Ski & Resort Corporation 211B, 212, 213
Tripp Fay, Copper Mountain 91, 93, 97

Cover Credits

Front cover: Garden of The Gods and Pike's Peak *Shutterstock*
Back cover: Ouray *Carol M. Highsmith*
Front flap: (from top) Aspen Trees at

the base of Mount Sneffels *iStock*; Black bear *iStock*; Durango & Silverton Railroad *Carol M. Highsmith*; Snowboarders at Copper Mountain *Tripp Fay, Copper Mountain*

Back flap: Crystal Mill *Carol M. Highsmith*

Insight Guide Credits

Distribution
UK, Ireland and Europe
Apa Publications (UK) Ltd;
sales@insightguides.com
United States and Canada
Ingram Publisher Services;
ips@ingramcontent.com
Australia and New Zealand
Woodslane; info@woodslane.com.au
Southeast Asia
Apa Publications (SN) Pte;
singaporeoffice@insightguides.com
Hong Kong, Taiwan and China
Apa Publications (HK) Ltd;
hongkongoffice@insightguides.com
Worldwide
Apa Publications (UK) Ltd;
sales@insightguides.com
Special Sales, Content Licensing and CoPublishing
Insight Guides can be purchased in bulk quantities at discounted prices. We can create special editions, personalised jackets and corporate imprints tailored to your needs.
sales@insightguides.com
www.insightguides.biz

Printed in China by CTPS

First Edition 2006
Fifth Edition 2017

www.insightguides.com

Editors: Kate Drynan and Helen Fanthorpe
Author: Nicky Leach
Head of Production: Rebeka Davies
Picture Editor: Tom Smyth
Cartography: original cartography Stephen Ramsay, updated by Carte

Contributors

This updated edition was commissioned and copyedited by **Kate Drynan**. Santa Fe-based writer **Nicky Leach** has worked with Insight Guides for over 20 years, creating and updating guides on Florida and the American West, including *Arizona, New Mexico,* *Utah, US National Parks West,* and *USA on the Road.* This edition builds on the contributions of several experts on Colorado, including **Conger Beasley**, **Richard Harris, Edward A. Jardim**, and **Claire Walter**. The index was compiled by **Penny Phenix**.

About Insight Guides

Insight Guides have more than 45 years' experience of publishing high-quality, visual travel guides. We produce 400 full-colour titles, in both print and digital form, covering more than 200 destinations across the globe, in a variety of formats to meet your different needs.

   Insight Guides are written by local authors who use their on-the-ground experience to provide the very latest information; their local expertise is evident in the extensive historical and cultural background features. All the reviews in **Insight Guides** are independent; we strive to maintain an impartial view. Our reviews are carefully selected to guide you to the best places to eat, go out and shop, so you can be confident that when we say a place is special, we really mean it.

Legend

City maps

	Freeway/Highway/Motorway
	Divided Highway
	Main Roads
	Minor Roads
	Pedestrian Roads
	Steps
	Footpath
	Railway
	Funicular Railway
	Cable Car
	Tunnel
	City Wall
	Important Building
	Built Up Area
	Other Land
	Transport Hub
	Park
	Pedestrian Area
	Bus Station
	Tourist Information
	Main Post Office
	Cathedral/Church
	Mosque
	Synagogue
	Statue/Monument
	Beach
	Airport

Regional maps

	Freeway/Highway/Motorway (with junction)
	Freeway/Highway/Motorway (under construction)
	Divided Highway
	Main Road
	Secondary Road
	Minor Road
	Track
	Footpath
	International Boundary
	State/Province Boundary
	National Park/Reserve
	Marine Park
	Ferry Route
	Marshland/Swamp
	Glacier Salt Lake
	Airport/Airfield
	Ancient Site
	Border Control
	Cable Car
	Castle/Castle Ruins
	Cave
	Chateau/Stately Home
	Church/Church Ruins
	Crater
	Lighthouse
	Mountain Peak
	Place of Interest
	Viewpoint

INDEX